THE
SURCOUF
CONSPIRACY

The facts of history, like the letters of the alphabet, can be arranged to mean anything

Aboard the elegant luxury liner SS FRANCE, Cristobal, Canal Zone, January 1967. From left to right: Robert S. Kerr, Press Officer, Panama Canal Company, Captain Joseph F. Ropars, Master, SS FRANCE, and the author, Captain (then Commander), Julius Grigore, Jr., USN, Retired

Bob Kerr and author were luncheon guests aboard the FRANCE, and during conversational banter, the author, asked Captain Ropars: "Whatever happened to that huge French submarine, the one which carried a seaplane?" The Captain replied, "Oh, you mean *Surcouf*! Why she disappeared under very mysterious circumstances during the war."

So, began the author's long quest to determine the truth about *Surcouf's* disappearance.

Credit: The Wren Grigore *Surcouf* Memorabilia Collection, 2003.

THE
SURCOUF
CONSPIRACY
A Penetrating Analysis of the Worst Submarine Disaster in History

One of the Most Pathological, Philosophical, Psychological, Psychoanalytical and Strangest Stories Never Told about the World's Worst Submarine Disaster!!!

Perhaps the Greatest Untold Submarine Story of World War II!

The Greatest Mystery of the Sea to Emerge From World War II!

The Most Controversial Submarine in the World of Underseas Warfare!

How the Imperial Japanese Navy Intended to Use SURCOUF-type Seaplane Carriers to Destroy the Panama Canal!!!

The Weird and Forceful Role Women Played in SURCOUF's Life and Death!!!

Why SURCOUF was Destined to Die in the World's Worst Submarine Disaster!!!

Why President Roosevelt Threatened to Deploy the Battleship USS ARKANSAS Against SURCOUF; an Allied Submarine!

A $1,000,000 in Gold if it can be Officially Proved that SURCOUF was a Traitor Submarine!!!

or

$1,000,000 in Gold if it can be Officially Proved that SURCOUF was not Sunk by the SS THOMPSON LYKES

CAPT. JULIUS GRIGORE JR.,
US NAVY, RETIRED

iUniverse, Inc.
Bloomington

THE SURCOUF CONSPIRACY
A PENETRATING ANALYSIS OF THE WORST SUBMARINE DISASTER IN HISTORY

iUniverse books may be ordered through booksellers or by contacting:

iUniverse
1663 Liberty Drive
Bloomington, IN 47403
www.iuniverse.com
1-800-Authors (1-800-288-4677)

ISBN: 978-1-4620-3147-4 (sc)
ISBN: 978-1-4620-4869-4 (hc)
ISBN: 978-1-4620-3148-1 (ebk)

Library of Congress Control Number: 2011915941

Printed in the United States of America

iUniverse rev. date: 09/27/2011

Contents

Dedication vii

Foreword xi

Epigraph xiii

Introduction xv

Part I: Prelude to SURCOUF's Death 1

Part II: The SURCOUF and Muselier Affair 125

Part III: Blaison's Last Letter to Therese Analyzed 156

Part IV: SURCOUF's Rendezvous with Death 167

Part V: SURCOUF After Death 365

Afterword 373

Annotated Bibliography 377

Acknowledgements 387

Appendix "A" 397

    The Allegorical Interpretation of Symbols on the
Front and Back Covers 397

Appendix "B" 409

    The Evolution of SURCOUF 409

Notes 423

Index 435

By the Same Author 443

About the Author 447

Capitan de Frigate Louis Georges Blaison, Free French Navy,
the last Commanding Officer of *Surcouf*, whose idols were the
Cross of Lorraine and Joan d' Arc. He was a graduate of France's
Naval Academy, Ecole Navale, Class of 1929.

In 1961 and 1994, The Government of St. Pierre and Miquelon did
not forget Blaison's and Surcouf's contribution to liberating the islands
from the grip of Vichy France on December 25, 1941.

Credit: With the permission of the Service Historique de la Marine, Vincennes,
and St. Pierre and Miquelon Islands Philatelic Bureau.

Dedication

**To Therese and Francine Blaison, the wife and daughter
of Capitaine de Frégate Louis Georges Nicolas Blaison,
Commanding Officer of the Free French Submarine SURCOUF,
and to those who were lost with her**

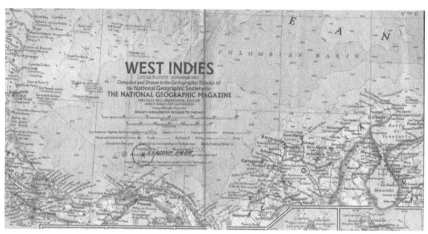

"X" indicates the area where the *SS Thompson Lykes-Surcouf Collision* occurred, which was plotted as being at Longitude 10° 28.5' North, Latitude 79° 21' West, at a depth of about 8,000 feet, and not in the Gulf of Mexico as Vice Admiral Russell R. Waesche, Commandant, U. S. Coast Guard, forcefully insisted.

Credit: The Wren Grigore, Surcouf Memorabilia Collection,
Venice, Florida, 1985.

The following Foreword for *SURCOUF and the Bermuda Triangle* was authorized by the Blaison women-folk, Madame Therese Blaison and her daughter, Mlle Francine Blaison on July 4, 1982. *The SURCOUF Conspiracy* is an abridged version of *SURCOUF and the Bermuda Triangle.*

As expressed in the Introduction to *The SURCOUF Conspiracy*, the author, for reasons far too complicated to relate here, curtailed further involvement in matters concerning SURCOUF until 2010 when he decided to revive what had remained unnecessarily dormant since about 1984.

Essentially, The Blaison women folk, were they present today, would have no qualms about the content of *The Surcouf Conspiracy* as nothing was included therein by the author that they had not agreed upon if *SURCOUF and the Bermuda Triangle* were published.

Captain Henry Johnson, the ancient mariner and Master of the *SS Thompson Lykes,* whose ship collided with and sank the powerful Free French submarine *Surcouf.*

However, some French, especially Blaison's women folk, firmly believe THOMPSON LYKES was guided into SURCOUF by something out there seen or heard by Captain Johnson that most of us would have been unable to sense without an aid??? Like a message written on the wind. Or, that she was sunk by limpet mines attached to her hull while she lay at dockside, HMS Ireland Dockyard, Bermuda.

The loss of *Surcouf* with 130 souls continues to be listed in the *Guinness Book of Records* as the world's worst submarine disaster.

Credit: *Panama Canal Review*, a U. S. Government publication, 1967, and *Kings Pointer Magazine*, U. S. Merchant Marine Academy, Summer, 1981.

Foreword

SURCOUF AND THE BERMUDA TRIANGLE, as written by Captain Julius Grigore, Jr., USN, of Venice, Florida, is accurate and true as concerns our dearly departed Capitaine de Frégaté Georges Louis Blaison, Free French Navy, and my daughter Francine and me.

Contrary to what some high placed French naval officials believe, and based upon the evidence presented by Captain Grigore, it seems that many mysteries were associated with SURCOUF's death which had their origins in the Bermuda Triangle before she left on her fatal voyage from Bermuda to Tahiti. But, even if SURCOUF and her officers and men were not affected by strange forces within, or along the perimeter of, the Bermuda Triangle, this should not have overridden the responsibility of the American and Royal Navies to assure that SURCOUF, or any Allied submarine, would not be overrun by ships operating along the heavily trafficked Caribbean Sea approach to the Panama Canal Zone on the night of 18 February 1942.

Captain Grigore makes it obvious that there were serious decisions made by the British Admiralty, which vitally concerned and affected SURCOUF and Capitaine de Frégaté Blaison, and his gallant officers and men, while they were in Bermuda in February 1942, and sad mistakes made by the American Navy in the Canal Zone, while SURCOUF traversed the Caribbean, in February 1942; which contributed to and caused their deaths.

Not until late 1976, when we began to assist Captain Grigore in researching for *SURCOUF and THE BERMUDA TRIANGLE*, which book he proposes to be followed by *SURCOUF and THE ROYAL NAVY*, did we realize that the SURCOUF Disaster was the worst in submarine history and that it remains so to this day.

Captain Grigore's book because of its dire implications concerning past and future Allied cooperations and interrelationships, civil, diplomatic, political, and military and naval-wise, should be required reading by every officer and enlisted man of the French Navy, by all members of the other armed forces of France and by those concerned with planning and carrying out her defense. His book should also be used as a case study in national schools for developing French line and staff officers destined for higher command. The Allied armies, air forces and navies should also held this admonishment for protecting the future welfare of our Free World. Much of what has been told here must never be allowed to happen again if we wish to remain free and unified Allies.

We are grateful to Captain Grigore for applying his tencity, intellect and imaginative insight, with undiminished force and without subordinating truth, to make his monumental work possible about the future of French and Allied Navies and about the loss of our beloved Capitaine de Frégaté Georges Louis Blaison, Free French Navy; his fateful submarine SURCOUF, which he cherished immensely, and about his devoted officers and men who rest with him and SURCOUF at the bottom of the Caribbean.

But no one has said the final word about SURCOUF and it is doubtful if it will be possible within our time.

Madame Therese Zelie Francine Blaison Franchelli
Mademoiselle Francine Claire Marie-Magdeleine
Paris, France, July 4, 1982.

Epigraph

I have a rendezvous with Death
At some disputed barricade.
And to my pledged word am true.
I shall not fail that rendezvous.
                    Alan Seeger

Charles Quarles Peters on the left, John Mann is with the beard. The donkey is Mike, and the two San Blas Indians, to the right and left of Mike are: Onlokoss (Freddy) and Ricardo Tejada (Ricky) from Carti Tupile Island, along the San Blas archipelago.

Charlie, formerly a radio operator for Pan American Airways, was adamant that, after the SS THOMPSON LYKES_SURCOUF Collision, *Surcouf's* hulk was observed afloat off San Blas Point, where there was a radar station operated by the U.S. Army and a cemetery for the bodies of sailors who periodically drifted ashore.

Charlie was also adamant that *Surcouf's* hulk was finally sunk by U. S. Army Air Corps bombers to keep it from drifting into a minefield that was protecting the Caribbean entrance to the Panama Canal.

Credit: With the permission of the John Mann Trust, 1988.

Introduction

Each of us live and die for a purpose. This is the reason why Captain Julius Grigore, Jr., USN, was the man who was born to write the history of SURCOUF.

Rear Admiral Robert Le Nistour,
Medical Corps, French Navy

History would be far different were it not for the incredible coincidences that shape our destinies.

Alan Vaughan, *Incredible Coincidences*

SURCOUF—130 dead—in the world's worst submarine disaster that occurred on the night of February 18, 1942

Entered into the *Guinness Book of World Records*
by the Author of *The SURCOUF Conspiracy.*

As you read *The SURCOUF Conspiracy* place yourself in each scene to better involve your senses and emotions. Focus the characters in your mind's eye to assist you to grasp the profound significance of the story line.

There appears much on the Internet and in literature about SURCOUF, which during her lifetime was the largest and most powerful submarine in the world, but none so completely different in context, depth, scope, and engrossing thought as appears in *The SURCOUF Conspiracy.*

Here is where it seems appropriate to set the scene for SURCOUF's entry into World War II, just before France's pathetic surrender to Hitler's Germany June 25, 1940. For this purpose, the following is quoted from *France and Germany, The Legacy of Charlemagne,* by Rene Lauret:

> Two weeks before the World War II began, on September 1, 1939, Minister of Defense Georges Bonnet asked Juliusz Lukasiewicz if his country had any fortified positions facing Germany; the Polish Ambassador replied that this was not necessary: "The Polish Army will invade Germany in the first days of the war." There was less optimism in Paris. With the situation reversed by the defection of Russia, some wondered if the Franco-Polish Alliance might not be reconsidered. It was for this purpose that a war council was convoked as soon as the German-Soviet Pact was known.
>
> The question was whether France was capable of making war with only Poland's support. The British Army would not be ready for several months. Finding the answer was more the responsibility of military men than of the politicians. So they were asked. The following is based upon the minutes of this meeting written by General Jordon Decamps"
>
> To the question, "are the army, the navy, and the air force capable of honoring our commitments to Poland?" General Maurice Gambien and Admiral Jean Louis Darlan answered "yes," without reservations. Guy Chambre, Minister of Aviation, declared less categorically. In reality, he said, France was building two hundred planes a month, but the Germans were building a thousand.

Literature confirms that Poland fell to the Germans almost immediately, and that the French Government capitulated to Germany on June 22, 1940, with an Armistice signed between France and Germany effective on June 25th.

For Germany, its invasion and defeat of France, and the rout of the British Expeditionary Force along the English Channel shore of Dunkirk, France, was a spectacular victory unrivalled in war annals.

The Vichy government was the regime set up in France by Marshal Henri-Philippe Pétain in July, 1940, subsequent to the Franco-German Armistice of June 22. Petain was then 83 years old. He had been in retirement since before World War I. In three weeks, England will have her neck wrung like a chicken, Marshal Petain remarked.

The terms of the Armistice divided France into occupied and unoccupied zones, with a rigid demarcation line between the two. The Germans would directly control three-fifths of the country, an area that included northern and western France and its entire Atlantic coast. The remaining section of the country would be legally administered by the French government at Vichy under Marshal Petain, but under strict German presence. Vichy's tenuous control also included its colonies, mainly in North Africa, Dakar, Africa, French Indo-China, Syria, the Caribbean island of Martinique, and the St. Pierre and Miquelon Islands in the Gulf of St Lawrence, off Newfoundland.

The Vichy government, which was never recognized by the Allies, became a German tool in the hands of such men as the Supreme Commander of the French Navy and Vice Premier of Vichy France, Fleet Admiral Jean François Darlan. When the American and British troops and naval forces invaded North Africa in November 1942, Hitler annulled the Armistice of 1940 and occupied all France. But, the Vichy government continued a shadowy existence, eventually fleeing before the Allied advance to Sigmaringen, Germany, where it collapsed when Germany surrendered in 1945.

In the interim of France's extreme military disaster and political upheaval, on June 17, 1940 Brigadier General Charles De Gaulle broadcast an appeal over BBC radio, London, for French men and women to join him and the British in the fight against Nazi Germany, and on June 18th, Specifically, the dishonorable extent of Vichy's collaboration with Hitler's Nazi Germany, much to the detriment of the Allied cause and affecting the Free French submarine SURCOUF and the souls aboard her, is revealed on the Internet link: http://seacoast. sunderland.ac.uk/~os0tmc/occupied/collab.htm.

SURCOUF, while undergoing repairs and with only one engine operable and with a jammed rudder, escaped from German troops approaching her moorings at the French Naval Base, Brest; arriving at the Royal Navy's Devonport Dockyard, Plymouth, England, on the 19th.

So, after providing the above scenario, SURCOUF's wartime service with the Royal Navy began as an unholy alliance, and this is where the two threads of her life begins.

Two versions of SURCOUF's death are addressed: the occult and the real. They were in search of one another as both were integral to her loss as the world's worst submarine disaster. So many supernatural incidents preceded SURCOUF's death that they ultimately fused with actuality. Even if you do not believe, SURCOUF's story as told here can be an intriguing revelation.

Most people are mainly concerned with what is going on right now and are less concerned with what happened yesterday, last week or last year and why. The further in the past an event or development the less we seem to be concerned about it, and the less becomes our appreciation of its cause.

This appears to be our nature and results in an inability to fathom strange occurrences still beyond our capability to understand. What follows is an exposé about several happenings and how they afflicted the Free French submarine SURCOUF and caused the world's worst submarine disaster.

Every legend has an untold story. This one about the dishonor and forces of evil, which relentlessly plagued SURCOUF, the deadliest submarine of her time, is revealed. Evil comes in a linked chain. It was like a serial sequence of occurrences with one evil link leading to another in SURCOUF's shadow life. Nowhere in World War II literature of the sea, or in naval histories, has much of what you are about to read been published. In the reading, you shall gain enormous insight into the machinations and operations of the sanctimonious British Admiralty, Whitehall; the inner sanctum of the the White House and Departments of Navy, State and Treasury, Washington; No. 10 Downing street and the Foreign Office, London; the Forces Françaises Libres (FFL), government in exile, at 4 Carlton Gardens, London; and the French Vichy government, Vichy, France; Flag Officer, Submarines, Northways, London; HMNB Devonsport Dockyard, Plymouth, England; Halifax, Canada; the St. Pierre and Miquelon Islands; the Caribbean Island of Martinique; U. S. Naval Shipyard, Portsmouth, New Hampshire; Office of Intrepid, British Security Corporation, New York City; HMNB Ireland Dockyard, Hamilton, Bermuda; the Bermuda Triangle; the Fifteenth Naval District, Panama Canal Zone; Tangiers, Spanish Morocco; and Casablanca, North Africa—such as few contemporary naval historians about World War II have penetrated

What is a conspiracy? Legally, it is a combination of two or more persons to accomplish an unlawful act by unlawful means. Justice Oliver Wendell Holmes wrote "a conspiracy is a partnership for criminal purposes." A conspiracy can be planned or committed without any formal meeting or written agreements. Only a tacit understanding among the conspirators to achieve an unlawful act is necessary.

Conspiracies are coupled with a motive, or reason, why a treacherous act is committed. And, it is essential to acknowledge that a conspiracy can also involve casting an evil omen, telling a falsehood or spreading a foul rumor, or maliciously influencing another by mind control or mental assassination, as frequently occurs in *The SURCOUF Conspiracy*. Each can be as deadly as an act of physical violence.

You shall also read of the shattering force of events which affected SURCOUF in Bermuda that had no connection with the deadly phenomena of the Bermuda Triangle, but which was as deadly, if not more so, than anything emanating from that devilish area. It was from man himself, the most terrible monster of them all, capable of the most inhuman atrocities, including circulation of venomous rumors about SURCOUF and a campaign of extinction sanctioned by war. It was as Ernest K. Gann wrote in *Hostage to Fortune*, "Wars are all encompassing and capable of destroying people and things unrelated to the conflict."

Even more is yet to come, however it will be not all be of SURCOUF'S making. Rather it will be of a kind contrived by those in high places while Commandante de Frégaté Louis Georges Blaison, Free French Navy, and SURCOUF, the submarine he commanded, were in the Bermuda Triangle, and which was beyond their capability to dispel.

In American fiction, *The Greatest Man in the World*, by James Thurber, there seems to be a close, almost humorous, eerie parallel to what you are about to read about SURCOUF. The gist of Thurber's short story, as could relate to the death of SURCOUF, the greatest, most despised submarine in the world, is:

> The American "Thirties" had a new hero: Jack "Pal" Smurch, who somehow managed to pilot his rickety, one-engined, excuse for an airplane on the first solo flight, non-stop around the world, leaping the Atlantic and Pacific as if they were millponds.
>
> "Pal" has an adoring public, but to really know him, because of his unsavory exploits, is to loathe him. He is an illiterate, incorrigible, lout, without an ounce of ethics.
>
> His former high school principle recalls being knifed by him, "Pal's" mother would not have been sorry to see him make an unscheduled landing in the Atlantic and his hometown, in Westfield Iowa, regards him as a nuisance and menace to their society. As he was successfully completing his epic exploit, it was determined that the story of his life should not be printed, especially for children.
>
> Smurch's crude manner and grimy appearance are not the stuff of national heroes. Consequently, a prominent newspaper editor and the American Secretary of State, felt that they had better leave unrevealed Smurch's true life style to millions of his fans. They prayed that "an understanding Providence might" somehow bring disaster to Smurch.

The disposition of "Pal" Smurch, who was headed for a greater glory than any man of his time had ever known, is told by Thurber substantially as follows:

> Smurch was received at Roosevelt Field with such elaborate and pretentious ceremonies as rocked the world. Fortunately, the worn, spent hero had to be removed from his plane, and, in the act was promptly spirited without his having opened his mouth once. Thus, he did not jeopardize the dignity of his first reception, which was illuminated by the presence of the Secretaries of War and Navy, the Mayor of New York, the Premier of Canada, a gathering of Governors, and a brilliant array of European dignitaries.
>
> On the day that Smurch was allowed to talk, he did not wait for questions. "You'se guys," he said—and the *Times* man winched—you'se guys can tell the cockeyed world dat I put it over on Lindbergh, see? Yeh—an' made an ass of them two frogs." The "two frogs" being a pair of gallant French fliers who, attempting a flight of only half around the world, two weeks before, unhappily were lost at sea.
>
> Smurch walked over to an open window and stared down to the street, nine floors below. In the tense little knot of men standing behind him, a quick and mad impulse flared up. An unspoken word of appeal, of command, seemed to ring through the room. Yet, it was deathly silent. The President of the United States, pale, grim, nodded. Brand, a tall, powerfully built man, once a tackle at Rutgers, seized the greatest man in the world by the seat of the pants and shoved him out the window.
>
> "My God, he's fallen out of the window!" cried a quick witted editor.
>
> "Get me out of here!" cried the President of the United States.
>
> The editor of the Associated Press took charge, being used to such things. Crisply, he ordered some to leave, others to stay; just as quickly he outlined a story which all the newspapers

were to agree on. In a word, he skillfully set the stage for the gigantic task of breaking to a grief-stricken world the sad story of the untimely, accidental death of its most illustrious and spectacular hero.

Smurch's funeral was the most elaborate, the finest, the solemnest, and saddest ever held in the United States of America. At a given hour, there was two minutes of silence throughout the Nation. In Westfield, Mrs. Emma Smurch bowed her head over two hamburgers sizzling on her grill-bowed her head and turned away so that the Secret Serviced man could not see that twisted, strange leer on her lips as if she were implying good riddance to the greatest man in the world.

Throughout this story, every reader has the opportunity to play detective or to assume the role of a judge or juror, to determine if sufficient clues and facts exist, or if the evidence presented is strong enough, to conclude that there was a conspiracy to eliminate SURCOUF from the face of the sea.

Nothing should preclude a reader from acting independently to investigate a lead, to act upon a hunch, or to communicate with the author, in an attempt to solve some mystery or to contribute some tidbit about the history of SURCOUF. It was in this manner, through a meeting of minds, that the author was able to determine that SURCOUF, and not USS THRESHER, was the world's worst submarine disaster.

What appears here is a vastly expanded version of my talk presented before the Anglo-Panamanian Society, August 30, 1988, at the British Embassy Residence, Panama, Republic of Panama, under the title: *The SURCOUF Conspiracy.*

It was an extract from my works *SURCOUF and the Royal Navy; SURCOUF in the Bermuda Triangle; SURCOUF and the London Naval Conference of 1930; The SURCOUF Affray of July 3, 1940; The SURCOUF Dossier of Rumors; and SURCOUF and the Alien Mind.* (However, for personal reasons not necessary to mention here, these fascinating and well documented accounts about SURCOUF have remained dormant since 1988.)

Under these scenarios, secrets of the Free French super-submarine SURCOUF, which was born for controversy and sacrifice, unfolded. Why SURCOUF's story has remained one of the great-mysteries of World War II and why it is one of the weirdest and most occult sagas of misadventure and revenge at sea never told, is not within the realm of the author to understand—except to say that he was born to write it just as Vice Admiral Robert Le Nistour, Medical Corps, French Navy, foretold. Even if written as science fiction *SURCOUF and the Alien Mind,* for example, could be too strong for fantasy.

In the interim of his investigations and writing, the author had three articles published about SURCOUF in *The Kings Pointer Magazine,* a publication of the U. S. Merchant Marine Academy Alumni Association; and in *Shipmate Magazine,* a publication of the United States Naval Academy Alumni Association, both were entitled *SURCOUF Not USS THRESHER is the Worst Submarine Disaster;* and the third was *Needed: Lethal Big Gun Submarines,* which also appeared in *Shipmate.* A fourth article, also about submarines, appeared in the *U. S. Naval Proceedings Magazine* under the title of *The Submarine O-5 is Down.* Then my more elaborate monograph about SURCOUF entitled, *Free French Sub SURCOUF and St Exupery of the Sea,* is regularly offered on Ebay. Also, my several other books and numerous articles about various subjects; appear on Ebay. Each are listed under *By the Same Author.*

But, nothing more was written by me about SURCOUF for a multitude of reasons. Perhaps I merely wanted to let the subject season while I evaluated after thoughts about what still has never been told, My manuscripts about *SURCOUF* are the result of a long evolution of investigation and thought, over a span of many years, with the compilation of *SURCOUF and the Royal Navy* being the chronological repository pertaining to SURCOUF's interface with the American, Canadian, Free French, and Royal Navies. It serves as my reservoir for a numerous array of articles and books I have written about, or planned for, SURCOUF.

Another purpose of this repository is to collect tidbits of hard information that can be pieced together into a meaningful finding, as enabled the author to confirm that SURCOUF and not USS THRESHER was the worst submarine disaster in history and then having the result published in the *Guinness Book of Records*. God rewards an honest quest for truth.

Besides *The SURCOUF Conspiracy,* three others are in the stages of near completion. They are: *SURCOUF and the London Naval Conference of 1930, SURCOUF in the Bermuda Triangle, and The SURCOUF Dossier of Rumors*—each being excerpted from *SURCOUF and the Royal Navy.* (Most of SURCOUF's World War II career was served with the Royal Navy and within the confines of the Bermuda Triangle, where she died along its Caribbean fringes.)

Recently it was decided to revive SURCOUF's tumultuous wartime history as it is my privilege to do whatever suits my fancy during declining years so long as it is morally right. Besides, from 1988 until now, no one has remotely rivaled what was revealed about SURCOUF in my works, and much that did appear elsewhere was mainly a reiteration of untruths, inconsistencies of time-frame, imitations, repetitions, or variations of what others wrote, and inaccuracies. Or, they were the same stories in such stodgy verbiage that they sounded indisputable. Very little of this chaff did I endeavor to correct so not to depreciate my findings, even incrementally. Besides, much of my significant content, like that of an iceberg, the substantial part of which lies hidden beneath the surface, was derived from personal interviews with, and correspondence with, many who are no longer alive Therefore, their verbal and written revelations, which few may duplicate, have survived with me. *(It seemed good to me also, having had perfect understanding of all things from the very first, to write unto thee in order that thou mightiest know the certainty of those things, wherein thou hast been instructed. Luke 1:3-4. KJV)*

That I elected to authoritatively interweave metaphysical and supernatural content into my version of the SS THOMPSON LYKES-SURCOUF Collision, and elsewhere, was a justified prerogative of mine. Why merely write with blandness and lack of imagination or settle for unrealistic generalities??? This is why *The SURCOUF Conspiracy* falls into that rare category of fact being more fantastic than fiction and probably making it one of the more fascinating and strangest World War II stories of the sea never told. *(Incline thine ear unto wisdom, and apply thy voice for understanding. Seekest her as silver, and searchest her as for hid treasures. Proverbs 1: 2-3 KJV)*

Though SURCOUF's story transfigures time and death and integrates history with the occult, the boundaries of fact and fiction have not been crossed. Nor has accuracy or truth been looked at obliquely, time played with, history distorted, or events or things exaggerated or invented to overly dramatize or to deliberately force the plot of *The SURCOUF Conspiracy*.

Where appropriate, in the portions devoted to the SS THOMPSON LYKES-SURCOUF Collision, the author empathized his version with inputs from Samuel Taylor Coleridge's *The Rhyme of the Ancient Mariner*. My inspiration was derived from written dialogue with the Captain of the SS THOMPSON LYKES, Henry Johnson, which lasted for several years. During our discourse, he often referred to himself as an Ancient Mariner, like the one who figures conspicuously in Coleridge's weird narrative of the sea.

> **He held him with his glittering eye;**
> **So he could not choose but hear;**
> **And thus spoke on that ancient man,**
> **The bright-eyed Mariner.**

And, Commandante Louis Georges Blaison and SURCOUF, as told, were no less involved with Coleridge's psychological burden that was likened to a wrathful curse upon both—that albatross.

Also, to lend correlative interpretation and reality, support and viability to various entries within *The SURCOUF Conspiracy*, snippets about Ninjas were inserted from *Ninjutsu, The Art of Invisibility and Japan's Feudal Age Espionage Methods,* by Donn Draeger, which was published by Lotus Press Limited, Tokyo, Japan, 1977. The insert of edifying and supportive scriptural passages from the *King James Version of the Bible* were also appropriately and liberally included to support the theme of, and provide justification and reasons for statements made, throughout *The SURCOUF Conspiracy. (The Lord is nigh unto all them that call upon him in truth. Psalms 145:18 KJV)*

My far-reaching investigations about the evolution, life, and death of SURCOUF included an extensive study about naval history, especially about World War II and events preceding it, like the Washington Naval Conference of 1922 and the London Naval Conference of 1930; interviewing and corresponding with numerous persons knowledgeable about SURCOUF, who lived in Bermuda, Canada, England, France, Germany, Ireland, Italy, Japan, Monte Carlo, New Zealand, Norway, Panama, Switzerland, and throughout the United States; and also prolonged contact with the following government facilities:

National Archives, Washington, and the Public Record Offices of Bermuda, Canada, England, and France,

Library of Congress and Smithsonian Institution, Washington, Central Intelligence Agency, Defense Intelligence Agency, and Federal Bureau of Investigation, Washington, United States Army and Navy Investigative Services, Scotland Yard, London, United States Maritime Commission, Washington, Canal Zone Government, Balboa Heights, Canal Zone, Naval and Maritime Archives and Museums of Canada, England, France, Germany, Italy, Norway, Japan, and the United States, and Captain Jacques Y. Cousteau's Office of Oceanography, Monaco.

This in-depth and expansive research project also involved extensive travel, a concerted international advertising campaign, the hire of translators, and archive searchers in England, France, and Japan.

AMBASSADE DE FRANCE
AUX ETATS-UNIS

Le Contre-Amiral
Attaché Naval

Washington, 22 October 1979

Dear Mr. Meyer:

As I promised you last week in Savannah, I forward
to you the name and address of the gentleman, which, I
think is the best historian about the "SURCOUF":

Mr. Julius GRIGORE, Jr.
425 Harbor Drive
South Venice, Florida 33595

Phone: (813) 485.6019
(813) 488.3744

I hope his outstanding knowledge about the French
submarine can help you in your research.

Sincerely yours,

Ambassade De France
aux États-Unis

Rear Admiral Pierre MENETTRIER

Rear Admiral Pierre Menettrier, the Senior Naval Attaché of
the French Embassy, Washington, in his 22 October 1979 letter,
established the author, Captain Julius Grigore, Jr., USN, Retired, as
being the preeminent authority about the Free French submarine
Surcouf.

Moreover, another French rear admiral, Robert Le Nistour,
Medical Corps, French Navy, philosophically reiterated, that: "Each
of us live and die for a purpose. This is the reason why Captain
Julius Grigore, Jr., USN, was the man who was born to write the
history of SURCOUF."

Really, in furtherance of both French admiral's remarks, the
author's status can never be diminished, as will become evident
throughout *The SURCOUF Conspiracy*, because he possesses too
many first-hand accounts obtained through official and personal

correspondence, including personal interviews, about Surcouf that cannot be replicated.

The total consequence of these investigations resulted in an accumulation of records and photographs about SURCOUF, much of it from private sources, that is probably more varied than the combined public records of the archives of the American, British, French, and Canadian governments or on the Internet.

From my review of the *Annotated Biography* and the *Acknowledgements and List of Contributors* what still stands out significantly in my mind, aside from the SURCOUF-SS THOMPSON LYKES Collision, is the influential role womenfolk have played in SURCOUF's prior life, her peacetime and World War II existences, and after her death.

Not since Lady Hamilton, Lord Nelson's mistress, have women appeared as forceful and vengeful in naval history, in the forefront and behind the scenes, as throughout SURCOUF's embroiled life and following her frightful loss.

The most determined women of all were Madame Theresa Blaison (nee Franchcelli) and her daughter Francine, formerly of Paris and both deceased, as they devoted their waking hours and dreams to seeking nothing but the truth about how and why their beloved Capitaine de Frégaté Louis Georges Blaison and SURCOUF died when and as they did. Since both are now in their heavenly resting place, where they are side-by-side with Capitaine de Frégaté Blaison, he has told them.

My extensive correspondence with them, they in Paris and me in Venice, Florida, included their sharing Blaison's wartime letters with me. Moreover, my association with the Blaison woman-folk was such that we often visited; myself to Paris and their residing in Venice for almost a year.

Aside from Francine and I visiting with Charles Berlitz, the author of *Without a Trace,* to interest him in my book *SURCOUF and the Bermuda Triangle,* which was an exercise in futility, she and the author also scoured much of France interviewing persons who could tell us more about SURCOUF than what the French Ministry of Marine, Sea Lords of the Royal Navy, Canadian Ministry of Defense, or the

American National or Office of Naval History archives could or would reveal. Our findings were appropriately inserted into the above manuscripts.

In the intervening years, the author mistakenly took several sources into his confidence, and was quickly betrayed, even to the extent of one author altering a retrieved J. Edgar Hoover (former Director of the Federal Bureau of Investigation) March 3,1942 document that I trustingly shared with him. What the culprit did was unethically alter a portion about SURCOUF's after life in the Hoover letter to make it appear that it was not the copy I had shown him so as to suit his publishing purposes.

Another false hope occurred when a reporter from the *London Daily Sunday Times* visited my home to gather details about SURCOUF with the promise of giving me considerable credit. The outcome was his broken word.

Then a prominent British author and contributor to the BBC published some of my findings about SURCOUF's last hour to support his theory that her hulk was bombed into oblivion by the U. S. Army Air Corps based in the Panama Canal Zone. For him or anyone who believes that SURCOUF died in ways other than by collision with the SS THOMPSON LYKES, the author has offered a $1,000,000 reward (payable in gold) if it is proven OFFICIALLY that SURCOUF died otherwise.

Concerted research and correlation of documents led the author to determine that there was a 130th sailor aboard SURCOUF as contrasted to the 129 names carved in stone on the Cherbourg Memorial to SURCUF's War Dead, including three of the Royal Navy. This led the author to suggest to the *Editors, Guinness Book of Records* that SURCOUF replace the USS THRESHER as the world's worst submarine disaster since THRESHER was lost with only 129. Verification from the American, British, Canadian, and French Navies involved a two year back and forth effort before my claim was accepted by *Guinness* in 1980. To this day, SURCOUF's loss with 130 souls unenviably remains the worst.

The author considered that he had an even greater responsibility to the 130th man. For nearly 40 years his parents in France had not learned what happened to him. They finally learned. My contribution did not end with them as, at my request, the French Ministry of Marine graciously added the 130th name to War Memorial to SURCOUF's dead.

My research about SURCOUF involved tens of thousands of dollars, but this expenditure of effort, monies, time, and travel included two threats to my life while inquiring about SURCOUF.

SURCOUF, although she was a creature not of God's Law, had a life of her own—an inner spirit, a menacing sea instinct, a proud heritage, and defiant soul derived from myths and glories of the past. It was as if she had ancestral genes and memory embedded within her. And, she did!!!

SURCOUF, the submarine, was named after Baron Robert Surcouf, in anticipation that she, as if she were a clone of the Baron, but as a powerful cruiser submarine with twin 8-inch guns, would seek out and kill enemy shipping as viciously as did her namesake. Thus, the Royal Navy, and many English, had every reason for remembering, even detesting, the name Surcouf—a revered name throughout France—even up to the beginning of World War II; when the French and Royal Navies united to eventually defeat Hitler's forces at sea.

Baron Surcouf had fiercely defied anything English, especially ships of British East India Company and France's traditional enemy, the Royal Navy, whose battle flag, the White Ensign, the submarine SURCOUF, through a twist of fate which only wars can conceive, would one day sail and fight under its colors.

During Napoleon's war with England, between 1803-1814, Robert Surcouf had incurred fame, fortune, and title while viciously pirating British East Indiamen in the Indian Ocean. At that time the British East India Company, established during the reign of Elizabeth I, was the greatest and wealthiest monopoly in the history—producing more revenue for the Crown than its homeland. So, pirating the Company's ships was likened to directly attacking the Crown of England and belittling the Royal Navy.

During Surcouf's legendary career, he captured 47 ships and became renowned for his fearless gallantry and chivalry, earning the nickname of *Roi des Corsaires* ("King of Corsairs"). He believed in leading by example and charged into every engagement brandishing a pair of custom-made pistols. Recall Baron Surcouf's two-gun peculiarity when reading about SURCOUF with her twin 8-inch guns and during *The SURCOUF Affray of July 3, 1940. (**The Ninja encompasses a variety of specialized fighting skills whch make him a relentless and ruthless warrior.**)*

The savage cruelty of Surcouf's men during the seizure of KENT, the pride of British East India Company, while she was plying the Indian Ocean trade routes, remains almost unparalleled among famous sea fights. This particular Surcouf conquest was colorfully recollected by *Time-Life Books* in *The Seafarers: The East Indiamen,* to commemorate the history of maritime adventure, which documents that Baron Robert Surcouf was not evolved from French mythology.

Surcouf's victory over KENT, but mainly because of his bitter cruelty, caused the British Government to offer a £250,000 reward for his capture—preferably dead!!! It was this long and bitter heritage, as if SURCOUF had inherited the genes of Baron Surcouf that festered an intense anti-English hatred that was branded, as if by a hot iron, upon SURCOUF—the submarine. This indelible marking plagued her throughout her existence, some of which, ironically, was during World War II service with the Royal Navy.

This passionate hatred of the British towards the name Surcouf, flared more brightly when, during June 1940, Admiral of the Fleet Jean Louis Xavier François Darlan, a fierce Anglophobic, unfurled his true colors by refusing to allow the French Navy to save England from an invasion attempt by Hitler's amphibious panzer forces.

It occurred more explicitly during *The SURCOUF Affray of July 3, 1940,* when Royal Navy and French Navy officers and men killed each other along her decks during Operation GRASP. GRASP had been initiated by the Winston Churchill Government to prevent French ships in English ports from returning to German occupied France to fight against her. It was the first time bad blood had been spilled between the two navies since Lord Nelson defeated the French during the Battle of Trafalgar in 1805. Regardless, Operation GRASP, and its counter-part Operation CATAPULT, which occurred in Alexandria, Egypt and the French North African port of Mers-el-Kébir, sent an effective and realistic message to the world, especially to the United States, that a determined England had no intention of being defeated and occupied by Nazi Germany. http://www.dailymail.co.uk/news/article-1248615/Mass-murder-stroke-genius-saved-Britain-As-closer-ties-France-planned-betrayal-forgive.html#ixzz1M0q3drmz

Some readers inquire: "Why revive SURCOUF's sensitive story? It is merely history now. In realiy, it is as Michael Korda, in *Worldly Goods*, said: "What can be more sensitive than history?" The history of history reveals that it is highly sensitive to being changed. Because of the inquiring mind, and through casual revelations, new truths about history are continually discovered. (Sometimes the truth is a lie that hasn't been found out. Besides, imagination is the only key that can unlock the truth about the past.) Moreover, the best way for history to repeat itself is for us to ignore it, or not to tell it accurately and completely. *("You cannot speak of the past. Of course you can," wrote F. G. Fitzgerald.)*

Besides, truth about some of the greatest stories never told still lie in musty archives, but here the author's version of SURCOUF's story surfaces for the determination of general readers and for students and historians of submarine warfare and naval history to appreciate, study, and further unravel. All secrets of World War II have never been told, and some believe, especially many French, that SURCOUF's is far and above among them. It is as Sherlock Holmes remarked, "When you follow two separate chains of thought, you will find some point of intersection which approximates the truth."

With the probability that one of the next confrontations could be catastrophic, it is absolutely essential for us to learn of the presence of those who could be subversively responsible for devastating our lives just as a many unethical persons did to us during World War II and wars thereafter. It is better than suffering annihilation from the hands of those we allow to secrete and to plot among themselves the shape of what is left of our freedom. If we refuse to diligently and truthfully unearth history we must expect to suffer the consequences.

Besides, France needs the soul-stirring SURCOUF legend, and that of her last commanding officer, Capitaine de Frégaté Louis Georges Blaison, as a public vehicle of identity, inspiration, and truth which seems to have broken down throughout her postwar era. France's old legends and myths seem no longer effective, and new ones seem not to have arisen to revitalize France's psychological energy and to symbolize her submission to a power higher than materialism

Just as a Japanese bonsai tree ages with enthralling beauty, so can the SURCOUF and Blaison legend evolve for France as an enshrinement and symbol of everything good and great about France and French men, women, and children.

From the sources cited in the *Annotated Bibliography* so much new history about SURCOUF was uncovered that her past history had to be rewritten and preserved. We cannot read history books unless they are written. So, in a great sense, the author's several monographs about SURCOUF have become a repository for future reference.

For those who have any further doubts about why SURCOUF's history should be rewritten, please refer to Dr. Lucy Maynard Salmon's utterly fascinating, but intellectually enlightening, book, *Why is History Rewritten*, wherein she wrote:

> History must always be rewritten because we can only approximate to absolute truth, never hoping to attain it; history must be rewritten because the story of the past is the protoplasm that keeps alive the past and shows its unity of development; the pursuit of truth must be its goal because truth must be the objective point of all knowledge,

SURCOUF died an abnormal death that still remains surrounded by too many unnatural circumstances and conspiracy lies and rumors. There is barely mention of SURCOUF, relative to her technological contribution to the advancement of the state of the art and about her diplomatic and political impact of her introduction upon foreign navies, mainly the American Navy, French Navy, Imperial Japanese Navy, and Royal Navy, before, during, and after World War II.

Others inquire: "What is so utterly absorbing and fascinating about one submarine, such as to justify spending considerable monies and thousands of man-hours researching and writing about her?" One can reply: "Read on for your are as likely to contract that incurable disease *Surcoufitis* as I did in 1967."

Really there were many valid reasons for my having investigated and unraveled SURCOUF's story, and for piecing it together from literature and first-hand personal accounts, including mine, as one were creating a fine mosaic. The succeeding paragraphs will reveal why my interest has remained so intense and why I was so determined to seek the Truth and tell it about SURCOUF's life and death.

When reading the foul rumors spread about SURCOUF, even to this day, coupled with commentary about an alien mind from another world that afflicted SURCOUF, and supposedly Captain Henry Johnson, Master of the SS THOMPSON LYKES, of a kind that we are not able to discern its source other than its being of an evil intent, consider their influence a CONSPIRACY to diminish her capability or to kill her.

Conversely, when reading of the extrasensory perceptions appearing in *The SURCOUF Conspiracy*, especially as concerned Blaison's women-folk, again phenomena of a kind beyond our comprehension to discern and benefit from, consider them as having been DIVINELY inspired. Really, have we an alternative, otherwise???

Therefore:

©Open Your Mind
That your eyes may see
The vast channels of reality.
Project your components
So the reaches inscribed
Let not the darkness
Cause you to hide.
For to fear the unknown

> **Or what you might find**
> **Is to fear the truth**
> **In our fabrics design.**
> **Through each of us channel**
> **Ourselves in some way**
> **All the elements still have their say**

It is now for the reader to decide if *une mystique de l'historire* surrounded SURCOUF's existence and unexpected death and to assist the author in probing further into the circumstances of, before and after, her crushing loss by collision.

As for me, one gulf of mystery resides in why the circumstances preceding SURCOUF's death remained as if dead for so long??? Also, why I, an American retired naval officer, rather than a Frenchman, was destined to separate most of the truth from rumor and falsity about SURCOUF remains a further mystery???

Similarly, you shall be introduced to Hector C. Bywater, a former secret agent for the British Admiralty and a prominent naval journalist, who anticipated the French Navy's creation of SURCOUF and her death by collision with foreign merchantman, years before each event, and who was allegedly murdered because his intuitive writings foretold the American-Japanese War of the Pacific—also years before it occurred. Perhaps the answer to this perplexing question lies in what Adela Rogers wrote in *Some are Born Great*: "Nobody in the world can stop an inquisitive writer, not even himself."

On the scale of normal to strange, *The SURCOUF Conspiracy* greatly exceeds the bounds of human imagination while remaining within the realm of truth, but not exceeding the core of fiction.

Enough said, so on with *The SURCOUF Conspiracy* to see if you or anyone else can earn that golden million dollars. Really, if further truth were to become known about SURCOUF her story would drastically alter naval history and be worth countless tens of millions of dollars. So, the odds of this offer, which is in a perpetual trust fund that carries out my wishes even after death, are strongly in favor of the author and or his heirs for re-writing the naval history of World War II.

WARNING: From your exposure to things SURCOUF, blame the author if you become afflicted with that rare disease: "Surcoufitis".

Julius Grigore, Jr.
Captain, USN, Retired
scadta@comcast.net

Part I

Prelude to SURCOUF's Death

The occult and superstition can play a significant roles in naval history. That either subject should be associated with a naval event does not cancel or reduce the importance of that event. It can enrich and add a new value to an object or an act. For example, acceptance of mysticism, numerology, occult, superstition, and symbolism in our lives can open the door to the immediate reality for us that everything or every occurrence may be linked to a law of assimilation and correspondence.

Numbers and Symbols in Naval History
Captain Julius Grigore, Jr., USN, Retired.

It may be a crackpot idea but the notion that there's an alien species out there, which is more-advanced then we are, is a good idea.

Professor John Condry, Psychologist,
College of Human Ecology, Cornell University.

The Vulcans were capable of great feats of physical and mental prowess, and they had unique powers of telepathy: the Vulcan mind-meld allowed a Vulcan to enter into another being's thoughts.

The Star Trek Wars by Gene Ronheberry

There are no magical forces operating in the Universe which control human destinies. Therefore, any system of ideas or set of practices which depends upon influencing such forces cannot possibly be true. This is not to say that all natural forces are fully understood. There is much that remains to be learned. But there is no accepted evidence to support the existence of forces beyond or outside of natural laws, and a great deal of opposing scientific thinking that such forces do not exist.
                    Psychology for You, by Sol Gordon, Professor of Child and
                              Family Studies, Syracuse University, New York.

The predicted event was filled in a maze of coincidences, as if my inner 'blueprints' interconnected with those of many others. It was a pattern I had seen again and again; a series of coincidences involving the fulfillment of a predicted event.
                              Patterns of Prophesy by Alan Vaughan

Aboard a submarine greatness is obscure, and servitude is total. It is a lesson in soul and unity.
                    Capitaine de Frégaté Louis Georges Blaison,
              Free French Navy, Commanding Officer of SURCOUF.

As *The SURCOUF Conspiracy* unfolds, it should become very evident that the Free French Navy and SURCOUF were involved in three triangles: One was between the Free French Navy, the Royal Canadian Navy, and the Royal Navy. Another was between the Free French Navy, the Royal Navy and the American Navy. Their third and final engagement involved the latter three navies in the Bermuda Triangle.

None of these triangles were *triads d'amour* for poor SURCOUF or for the Free French Navy, and each *pris entre deux feux* should be viewed as ultimately contributing to *un affaire fatal* for her. That much of these "affaires" occurred within the arena and along the fringes of the sinister Bermuda Triangle, where SURCOUF extensively patrolled, home-ported, and departed from on her fatal voyage, lends an evil connotation to *The SURCOUF Conspiracy*; unlike anything ever to emerge as documented naval history.

In 1921, following the end of World War I, the Royal Navy began work on the X Class submarine, which was armed with two 5.25" guns in separate turrets. X-1 was launched in 1925, however the it was a dreadful failure and spent most of her time in the shipyard for modification and repairs. England too little avail, as future events proved, highly broadcast its painful abortion for concern that Japan, rapidly becoming a naval rival in the Far East, might copycat and improve the concept of big gun submarines.

But, the French believed in the concept of massive, more powerful, and versatile submarines. Therefore, in 1922, the French Admiralty drafted plans for a fleet of six submarine cruisers intended for commerce raiding. It took much political wrangling until its proposal was authorized in 1927 when design and construction finally began at Cherbourg on a monstrous submarine. Before launching, in late 1929, the hull was christened SURCOUF, in recognition of the epic exploits of Baron Robert Surcouf, the ruthless French corsair and fervent opponent of the Royal Navy during the Napoleonic Wars between 1803-08.

That the French Navy submarine SURCOUF was an engineering marvel far in advance of her time was apparent from her neat appearance, configuration, size, firepower, and seaplane carrier capability.

It was as if a futuristic genetic scientist had contrived her from various parts. Recall that Mary Shelley's souless monster, created by Dr. Victor Frankenstein, was assembled from various human parts Well, when SURCOUF was launched she surprised the naval world because she was a hybrid: part submarine; part heavy surface cruiser, with her twin 8-inch guns; and part aircraft carrier.

Because of this commingling of entities, it was necessary to make SURCOUF larger than conventional submarines, therefore, she became the world's largest submarine and because of her immense firepower and aircraft carrying capability she was also the most powerful and technically advanced submersible in the world.

However, in sharp contrast to Frankenstein's frightful creature, SURCOUF was a beautiful representation of man's ability to incorporate into her the most attractive and finest features of naval architecture and ship construction while outfitting her with the indispensible requisites for locating and destroying her enemy at sea.

SURCOUF's design and construction, which was fundamentally different in three ways yet complimentary in total, proved that the French were different not only in their culture, customs, and language, but also in their technological philosophy—as they never built anything like the rest of the world. The Eiffel Tower was an outstanding example.

SURCOUF was a sleek, yet grotesquely monstrous, weapon that integrated the treasures of France's past with the technology of the present; serving as a symbol of the French Navy's crusade to excel its historic rival, the Royal Navy. She was a predatory sea creature with a uniqueness alien to the navies of her day, as if she were a deliberate transgression of their conventionality or a mutant. Her introduction to do battle on the sea as a ruthless killer could be likened to the powerful Nephilim giants who arose on Earth. (*Genesis 6-34 KJV*)

While there was nothing else like SURCOUF in the world, because of a global war, she eventually became the forerunner of the larger, even more powerful submarines like the monstrous I-400 class seaplane carriers of the Imperial Japanese Navy—which Navy had copied and improved upon the seaplane feature of SURCOUF long before she died, even though the Japanese voted to kill more of her class at the London Naval Conference of 1930.

If the Imperial Japanese Navy had incorporated SURCOUF's twin 8-inch gun feature on about 20 of its submarines, which size weapon they were fanatic about for their surface cruisers, it is probable that the history of the American-Japanese War of the Pacific, 1941-1945, would not be as it is written today.

SURCOUF—a hyper-intelligent weapons package—was the elite submarine of the French Navy and the eventual flagship of the Free French Navy. She was the most beguiling, most expensive to construct, the most streamlined, the largest, and the most powerful submarine in the world and a threat to the supremacy and rivalry of the American, British, and Italian Navies.

By evolving SURCOUF, the French Navy sinned against the conventionality of other navies, and the wages of that sin was eventual death for her. The appearance of French Navy's SURCOUF in 1929, upset the Royal Navy considerably as both navies—historically were like steel and flint flashing against each other—striking sparks and starting an occasional war or bitterly clashing with one another at naval limitation conferences.

Although England had the largest, most powerful navy in the world and ruled the waves, her concern about France building more SURCOUF submersible cruisers was that her Royal Navy was not large enough to protect her vast merchant fleet that plied the oceans between her colonies and England itself. (So as to not encumber or detract from the continuity of *The SURCOUF Conspiracy* the specifics concerning SURCOUF's development and construction, and about the principal personages concerned with her birth, continues as **Appendix "B", The Evolution of SURCOUF**.)

Just as SURCOUF's namesake, Baron Robert Surcouf had single-handedly threatened England's trade route to India in the early 1800s, it did not take much imagination to set the scenario of how a fleet of SURCOUF's, coupled with the German Navy being at her back door, could isolate England, as an island nation, from her world empire, which her inhabitants depended upon to sustain even minimal economic and industrial survival.

With justification and concern, SURCOUF was the topic of conversation behind the closed doors of admiralties and naval operations, foreign offices, secret services, especially within the White House and No. 10 Downing Street. Regardless, the Free French submarine SURCOUF, during her involvement in World War II, was considered too expensive and too large for the likes of the Royal Navy. Her superior capabilities and threatening existence on the high seas, therefore, became her Achilles Heel. (*That which increaseth knowledge increaseth sorrow. Ecclesiastes 1:18 KJV*)

SURCOUF's tempestuous involvements with her Allies, in the diplomatic, intelligence, naval, political, and wartime arenas, especially during the London Naval Conference of 1930; the deadly affray between French and Royal Navy officers in her wardroom during Operation GRASP on July 3, 1940; *The SURCOUF and the Muselier Affair*; the *SURCOUF and The St Pierre and Miquelon Affair*; and the fatal *SURCOUF-SS THOMPSON LYKES-Collision* is the right stuff for armed forces war college case studies. **(See Part II for *The SURCOUF and the Muselier Affair.*)**

Why more has not been written about the immortal SURCOUF remains an enigma to the author. But what continually seems to be prevalent about her story is the sameness of information and mis-information told of a kind that continues to be passed on by one author to another. Nowhere is this more apparent than in a current edition of *Wikipedia* and throughout the Internet, both of which are replete with serious lies, half-truths, untruths, and misconceptions about SURCOUF. These devilments about her, that previously appeared in literature and coordinated media since World War II, and with now with sameness on the Internet, have influenced others to blindly repeat them in a copycat manner, or as a herd mentality, or as Pied Piper followers.

To make corrections for the benefit of *Wikipedia,* for an example, would undermine *The SURCOUF Conspiracy* in advance of its publication and make my exhaustive research efforts, and the expense incurred to acquire the facts, valueless. Half-truths, untruths, misconceptions, and false myths will not be prevalent throughout *The SURCOUF Conspiracy.* Only the naked, self-evident truth, based upon my meticulous investigations and analysis, is revealed here, coupled with what has remained untold until now from direct correspondence and personal interviews. Thus, a two-edge sword of determined effort was wielded in every direction to find and divulge only the truth about SURCOUF and those who served her. *(And ye shall know the truth, and the truth shall make you free. John 8:32 KJV)*

In one of the most dramatic and ironic episodes in naval history, as will be told, SURCOUF, as did the monster created by Frankenstein, turned with vengeance against her maker. In the case of SURCOUF, she transferred her loyalty from the Nazi Germany dominated Vichy French Navy to that of the Free French Navy. This occurred when SURCOUF was captured by the Royal Navy during a violent affray when English and French blood was regrettably spilled along her decks. Thereafter, she served under the aegis of her former nemesis, the Royal Navy, as a Free French submarine. *(Behold how good and how pleasant it is for brethren to dwell together in unity. Psalms 133:1 KJV)*

However, the fact that England and France were allied in a war against a common enemy did not appreciably endear SURCOUF to the hearts of Englishmen in light of the deaths of three of the Royal Navy killed along her decks by French Navy officers. That one of the French Navy also died in the affray was of no consequence as it was a savage revenge for the days when Robert Surcouf had plundered British East India merchantmen and avoided capture by the Royal Navy during the Napoleonic Wars.

Though SURCOUF's story transfigures time and death and unites history with the occult, as if she were a part of two worlds, the boundaries of fact and fiction have not been crossed. Nor has accuracy or truth been looked obliquely, time played with, history distorted, or events or things exaggerated or invented to overly dramatize or to deliberately force the plot of *The SURCOUF Conspiracy.*

It is as Gene Ronheberry wrote in *The Star Trek Wars*: "The Vulcans [Nihilisms] were capable of great feats of physical and mental prowess, and their power of telepathy gave them ingress into another being's thoughts."

There is also another world in which SURCOUF was continually involved. It was that secret world of intelligence—throughout which she became the victim of competing clandestine teams of many foreign nations—including her Allies. *(**The Ninja, who is a master of deception, gathers intelligence to sow the seeds of dissension, create false rumors, nuture subversion, and create confusion to demoralize the enemy.**)*

The earliest sources of intelligence began, and still exist, in the age of belief in supernatural intervention—involving prophets, seers, oracles, mythomaniacs, soothsayers, and astrologists. Interwoven with the main theme of SURCOUF's magnanimous, mind-boggling story, without affecting validity, is a vast wealth of naval history incredibly laden with bizarre happenings—involving malign legends, mystery, foul rumors and lies, pathology, psychology, psychoanalysis, secrecy, superstition, and symbolism—coupled with biocommunications, biorhythmic effect, generic memory, idea transference, and mental intercession (the super-weapon of the future) some events, caused by others and auguring badly for SURCOUF, occurred years before her creation as a submarine. *(Thou shalt not go up and down as a talebearer among thy people: neither shalt thou stand against the blood of thy neighbor: I am the Lord. Leviticus 19-16 KJV)*

There have been so many lies and false rumors about SURCOUF that barely anyone knows the truth about her. The Big Lie is a strategy for spreading rumors so audaciously false that they push away the memory of what is true. About poor SURCOUF there was no truth revealed, only death.

How adversity tragically entangled SURCOUF, a thing of steel, torpedoes, and artillery—a thing of fatal beauty with Death's hand upon her—and of how she commingled with the lives of those who influenced her and of whom she devastated, with seeming perfect continuity and logic, forms an extraordinary fascinating yarn of the sea.

It seems that the beauty SURCOUF depended upon to save her really condemned her as she was always on trial for her life—as if she were haunted by ancient ghosts and living in the shadow of death. SURCOUF was all alone in the world and the innocent victim of her own life. Never was there such a submarine. You shall learn that prescience, while a highly lauded virtue and a gift few possess, is another two-edged sword. *(For the word of God is quick, and powerful, and sharper than a two-edge sword . . . . and is a discerner of the thoughts and intents of the heart. Hebrews 4:12 KJV)* Here the sword's keenness is used to cut down the false diabolical ideas and lies about SURCOUF; Capitaine de Frégaté Georges Louis Nicolas Blaison, her commanding officer; and the SS THOMPSON LYKES (Captain Henry Johnson)—the fatal trinity—whose destinies intertwine on a lonely Caribbean night off the approaches to the Panama Canal. Triangles are triangles, but those involving humans have a special geometry of their own.

Truly, it was as if force from a distant world—alien to our own—was conspiring to make SURCOUF fall from grace within the American and Royal Navies, and make her become the world's worst submarine disaster. Both happened!!!

We are still at a stage of our evolution, emotionally and intellectually, whereby we cannot afford the luxury of discounting the unexplained simply because we do not understand it. No fortress is more impregnable than a closed mind. To know is to predict. But, in our attempt to see the light of reality, we continue to endure and suffer only total darkness.

There are many other facets of SURCOUF's story, which amazed me as they unfolded. One, which relentlessly came to my attention, was the unusual and dominant role that women—the enchantresses of history—have played in SURCOUF's wartime saga on and beneath a souless sea.

Although woman is a refined version of man, his admiration for womankind, a power that conquers him, never falters. In the mariner's lore it is told that of all the spellbinders in human form, none is as dreaded as the legendary *fem fatales* or brewers of hell-broth as they conjure contrary winds and wreck ships to abduct sailor's souls.

Not since Lady Hamilton, Lord Nelson's mistress, have women appeared as beguiling and forceful in naval history, in the forefront and behind the scenes, as they did throughout SURCOUF's embroiled life and after her frightful death.

Some femmes were alluring, compassionate, and devotedly loved their man, whereas others—even great distance was not enough to keep SURCOUF and her Commanding Officer, Blaison, safe from their deadly ways and wiles. The role of several will be told. *(Thine eyes shall behold strange women, and thine heart shall utter perverse things. Proverbs 23:33 KJV)*

About women and war, it is as Rear Admiral Ben Bryant, Royal Navy, Retired, wrote in his book *Submarine Commander*: "Women do not get much fun out of war." Thus, whether through love, fear, or hate, women's encounter with SURCOUF caused their lives to be horribly marred.

The politically confused, deluded souls aboard SURCOUF gave their lives for the Free French cause, but when death cut them short their broken-hearted women were left to mourn, to fight abuse, and to be consoled by heroic speeches. Thus, the pathetic burden of women, as a cost of war, is always their violation beyond endurance. No other concept of humankind has destroyed the happiness of women as that of the hellish occupation of men defending their honor and seeking glory.

Blaison's womenfolk, wife and daughter, with a fierceness and tenacity born of love and devoted loyalty to him and to the Free French cause, persistently challenged indifferent bureaucracies, even within France, to ferret the raw truth about SURCOUF's disappearance, but to little avail. Until they met the author, all they could learn was that SURCOUF was lost with all souls aboard her by collision with the SS THOMPSON LYKES, that seeming robot killer ship.

Each dutiful and high-minded woman seemed to have a wisdom about things SURCOUF that approached clairvoyance. To them, SURCOUF had a kinship with the Deity, and was an eternal symbol that represented an imperishable state of mind and heart—second only to Joan de Arc.

Women of their determination and perspicuity had a second sense as they firmly believed, as do many Frenchmen, that there was far more to SURCOUF's loss than the information revealed—even by this work. They were adamantly convinced that they were being deceived and blindsided by the American, British, Canadian, and French Governments—at the highest levels. It seemed to them that the more officials knew about SURCOUF, the less they wanted to tell.

Supporting the courage of their unshaken convictions is that efforts have never been made to locate SURCOUF—to confirm that she was, indeed, sunk in the Caribbean. Should SURCOUF actually be found there, with evidence that she was actually rammed by the American merchant ship, SS THOMPSON LYKES, then, and only then, can some of the story concerning her death be put to rest.

The fatal indignity against SURCOUF occurs when the SS THOMPSON LYKES, whose master, Captain Henry Johnson, had a subconscious desire to kill a submarine, disembodies the helpless SURCOUF—as she stood alone and surfaced in utter darkness on the night of February 18, 1942. Then that predator ruthlessly drove SURCOUF with 130 souls of the Free French and Royal Navies into the eternal depths of the Caribbean Sea.

For this cruel injustice, SURCOUF became the world's worst submarine disaster; but that unenviable award was instead bestowed upon the USS THRESHER when she was lost on April 10, 1963 with only 129 on board. It seems that because SURCOUF was so unwanted by the American and Royal Navies, even during wartime, that they cared not to render her the distinction of being the world's worst submarine disaster. In continuance of this indignity, and contrary to the finest traditions of the sea, no Christian memorial service has ever been conducted over her ocean gravesite to respectfully honor her and those war dead souls who gave their lives to free occupied France from the grips of Nazi Germany.

Connecting the occult and the prophetic with history, as appears here, does not cancel or otherwise depreciate the event. Rather it adds a new dimension and greater interest to reading and learning. Here, throughout *The SURCOUF Conspiracy*, so many dire predictions are revealed that you anxiously await their unfoldment into reality.

In reality, everything and every occurrence can be linked to laws of assimilation and correspondences. After all, according to Eduard de Beaumont, in *The Sword and Womankind*, history should be judged not only by its sense of proportion, but also by its perspective and imaginative interpretation of events and facts.

Even Admiral Viscount Horatio Nelson (1758-1805), hero of the coup de Trafalgar and the foremost admiral the Royal Navy ever produced, embodied mysticism, symbolism, and even the power of numbers. According to Oliver Warner, in his work *Nelson*, the admiral spoke of "a radiant orb which seemed to beckon him to renown." If we, like Nelson, believe a thing is real and act in accordance with that belief, the consequence of our actions could become real.

While beauty has its advantages, there is the increased liability of becoming the focus of attention, being the victim of ridicule, and of being reduced to the level of the ridiculer. SURCOUF's beauty and the aura of mystery surrounding her coupled with her power and size were a fatal attraction that seems to have ultimately caused her death.

Regardless, SURCOUF's story should rank as one of the most bizarre and occult to emerge from World War II or any war, and it should strain the curiosity of readers to want to determine more of her tumultuous life and death.

Contrary to what Professor Sol Gordon stated in his authoritative work, *Psychology for You*, the author is more inclined to accept Professor John Condry's theory that "there's an alien species out there which is more advanced than we are." If not, how can we explain away those inexplicable occurrences in our lives that are still beyond the mysteries and whirlpools of our mind (capability) to unravel (understand)???

Concomitantly, how can we explain the supernatural phenomena implicating SURCOUF and the Blaison's that will be revealed??? For examples: the "Albatross Connection", as you shall read about, involving Commandant Blaison, Captain Johnson, and SURCOUF, while in her death throes; or the dreaded psychic connection between Madame Blaison and the sinking of the British submarine HMS L-24 in 1924; the traumas suffered by Blaison's daughter, Francine, following the loss of the French submarine PHENIX; or when her malicious cousin, Alain, conjured at a garden pool demanding that her father must die with SURCOUF; or of the English naval correspondent, author, spy, and Japanophile, Hector Charles Bywater, who, in 1924, anticipated the creation of, and subsequent loss, of a SURCOUF-type submarine by ramming during the American-Japanese War of the Pacific, 1941-45, a war he also foretold.

Then you shall read of Captain Johnson's three incredible course and speed changes which placed SS THOMPSON LYKES on a collision course, in the dead of night, with SURCOUF, as if someone or something with "unique powers of telepathy" had controlled Johnson's mind to cause him to deliberately guide his ship into SURCOUF and destroy her.

If the reader can explain these strange connections, other than by interpreting them to be rare coincidences, then the author could be led to believe Sol Gordon's theory. But no, these hints of controlled evil, are beyond explanation, let alone understandable, because they were based on "ideas and practices" beyond our present concept of natural laws; beyond academic reasoning.

Professor Gordon was quick to qualify his first positive assertion that not "all natural laws are fully understood" and "that there remains much to be learned" by mankind. The fact that there is "no accepted evidence" does not preclude the probability that "magical forces" do exist. Then, only an alien mind, a twisted intelligence, could have deliberately started and perpetuated those weird and vicious rumors disseminated to destroy SURCOUF.

The existence and workings of an "alien mind" about us should not be overlooked as a reality when reading *The SURCOUF Conspiracy.* Alien minds who, in their outer world, view the inner substance of human life to learn what is going on in the world of humans and who can knit together and dominate the skein of man's events while man lives in the illusion that he actually controls the cross-current of events concerning his error, folly, disgrace and death. Regardless, it will become obvious that there were alien minds of a human kind that were working-in-force to eradicate SURCOUF.

Sometimes beautiful and admired, sometimes devilish and despised, an alien mind, a phantom intelligence of an evil kind, seemed determined to destroy SURCOUF; long before humans who finally performed that repugnant task. Being aboard SURCOUF, the most powerful submarine in the world was no safe haven from evil. It was as if the Fates were playing sinister games with SURCOUF and those about her.

When considering the probability of that frightening alien mind, or power of evil, superstitions should not be ignored as they are extensions of our fear; maybe fear of that alien mind. Nothing should be brushed aside because it is not immediately understood. What may be far-out to one reader may well be near-in to another in this or in an alien world.

Here in *The SURCOUF Conspiracy*, we shall delve upon those superstitions that can affect sailors and the sea. Of all people, sailors must deal first hand and helplessly with the unknowable and uncontrollable material and natural attacks by the sea, and it is only instinctive that their folk-lore should be, in part, landlubber stories fitted with sea meanings, and, in part, blind explanations of the sea's phenomena. Superstition is, therefore, a potent force with sailors, particularly during wartime, and as much a part of every ship as the water she floats upon. Superstition, a human instinct, is also a kind of prayer to enable us to fear naught, from anyone or anything, unless it is God. "What is one person's superstition may be another's belief or religion," remarked Clarence Maloney in *The Evil Eye*.

It would be easy as a wink to shrug off the coincidences, connections, and correspondences which follow as being mistaken for causes and that evidence needed a link or two with fact to separate it from fantasy. Yet, a fact is not always the truth, and one should never dismiss a coincidence that cannot be explained.

The curious fact is that SURCOUF did sail into the realm of disaster and did die as was foretold by more than just a person or two. It is like Professor Inayat Khan, the great prophet and mystic of Sufism and father of Noor (*Light of Womanhood,* a *Light that Forever Shines,* with *nom de guerre* of Madeleine) Inayat Khan, and who was once theatrically involved with Mata Hari the World War I voluptuous spy, said: "When something exists in the imagination you can be sure there is a plane upon which it has real existence." Actually, prophetic implications similar to the SURCOUF Disaster, in one form or another, occur all over earth, too numerous to record as figments of our imagination or of our interpreting them to suit the event.

If you believe what follows then no further explanation is necessary. If you do not believe, then no further explanation is possible. But where does that explanation lay, it lies between the thin veil of what we believe and disbelieve, between what we accept as fact or as fantasy. Yet sometimes fact can read as fantasy, and what frequently seems fantasy is often fact.

Regardless, the reader is presented with many different psychic events which should enable him or her to draw objective conclusions about how and why the SURCOUF-SS THOMPSON LYKES Collision occurred; which, when viewed psychically, is one of the most unusual disasters in naval history.

There is virtually no chance of proving or disproving what appears in *The SURCOUF Conspiracy* through present day scientific knowledge. But readers should appreciate, when retro analyzing the SURCOUF Disaster, that we are not dealing with that disaster alone, but with what seems to be a series of haunting forebodings and ill omens which may have contributed to making that disaster occur; long before the event. Alan Vaughan said it best in *Incredible Coincidences*: "Everyday coincidences show the artfulness of our unconscious minds in creating our lives. The least we can do is to give that creative expression our full support." In other words, coincidences can be accidents or events waiting to happen.

The SURCOUF Conspiracy also seems to be a contest between coincidence and precognition, even though both are rare events. Here precognition seems to occur so often that the possibility of a long series of connecting coincidences peculiar to SURCOUF's death must be seriously considered.

For but a glimpse into the occult machinations of an alien mind there follows several examples, as if they emerged from an apocalypse unsealed, centered around the Blaison's, Captain Johnson, and SURCOUF.

Now, the author will begin to unravel how Samuel Taylor Coleridge's "Albatross" and that alien mind" seemed inexorably tied in a complicated sailor's knot, such as to have you believe that the corpse of an "Albatross" was really draped around the necks of Blaison and Johnson; and that of SURCOUF, just as it was around that of the Ancient Mariner in Coleridge's disquieting and masterful ode *The Rhyme of the Ancient Mariner*. (No one can dispute that *The Rhyme of the Ancient Mariner is* one of the most original poems in the English language, or deny that its passages have the extraordinary vividness of a dream.)

15

Bill Wisner wrote in *Vanished*: "Mariner's superstitions should be included among mysteries of the sea if for no other reason than their origins are mostly unknown. Besides they form colorful threads in the tapestry of maritime history." Then Wisner when on to speak about Coleridge's "Albatross," with its connotations of ill omen, which enters SURCOUF's story insidiously:

> Of all the kinds of sea birds that figure in seafarers' superstitions, historically the most prominent is the albatross, immortalized by Samuel Taylor Coleridge's epic poem *The Rhyme of the Ancient Mariner.*
>
> Somewhere, way back, there was born a strong superstition that to harm or, worse yet, kill an albatross brought a sure-fire ticket to perdition. The Ancient Mariner finds this out—**"With my cross-bow I shot the Albatross,"** he confesses. **And thereafter his vessel's luck is all the worst kind.**

That the Caribbean Sea, just off the edge of the Bermuda Triangle, served as the hellish cauldron for Blaison and Johnson to consign poor SURCOUF to the "perdition" of a watery grave makes for reading extraordinaire about one of the most dreadful and penetrating epics of the sea ever told. Beyond being "colorful."

Regardless, many years later, after piecing together the intriguing puzzle of SURCOUF's death, it was clear that she was doomed to die on the night of February 18, 1942. Looking back, one might believe that a curse from the archives of evil had been cast upon poor SURCOUF by avenging East India Company merchantmen who had been ruthlessly ravaged by Baron Robert Surcouf's corsairs during the Napoleon's War with England between 1803-1814.

> **The pang, the curse, with which they died**
> **Had never passed away.**

This quotation from Coleridge's supernatural ballad, *The Rhyme of the Ancient Mariner*, completed in 1798, and those which follow, are included because of the weird correspondence between Coleridge's sea bird, "the albatross" with Blaison and Captain Henry Johnson (the unwitting soul who administered that death blow to SURCOUF).

It was Captain Johnson, who referred to himself as "The Ancient Mariner" in a September 1, 1967 letter to the author. This was an alert to the possibility of an unnatural, "mysterious", connection between Blaison and SURCOUF's death, and that, perhaps, Captain Johnson had a hidden story to tell; one far beyond that which he told before the U.S. Coast Guard's Board of Inquiry convened on March 11, 1942, to investigate the circumstances of SURCOUF's loss. And, it seems certain that the author was "the man" destined to "hear" Captain Johnson's "ghastly tale", as seemed to be the case with others who have appeared in *The SURCOUF Conspiracy.*

> **Forth with this frame of mind was wretched**
> **With woeful agony**
> **Which forced me to begin my tale**
> **And then it set me free**
> **Dear Lord in Heaven!**
> **I know the man thathear me,—**
> **To him my tale I teach**
> **And until my ghastly tale is told,**
> **This heart within me burns**
> **There was a ship," quoth he.**

By some strange curiosity, could these lines have been applicable to SURCOUF and her men??? If not, why did Blaison and Johnson, whose blacked out ships met nearly bow-on that foul and fateful night, have experiences with an albatross, Coleridge's unlucky bird, years before their tragic encounter in the Caribbean??? It seems as if Coleridge, in his uninhibited release of creative imagination, subconsciously had written his terrorizing poem, founded on a dream as a blueprint for these two strangers to meet in the night so as to kill SURCOUF on cue. "Literature always anticipates life," Oscar Wilde wrote, "It does not copy it, but molds it to its purpose."

How Coleridge's immortal poem is locked with SURCOUF's disaster will be evident. That the stage for this nightmarish epic of the sea began in the Bermuda Triangle and ended along its Caribbean Sea fringes adds to the bizarreness of *The SURCOUF Conspiracy*, one which is almost beyond belief. About the collision between their two ships the reader will be made well aware of in **Part IV, SURCOUF'S Rendezvous with Death,** where their "albatross" affinity collides.

But what about that strange force that fused Capitaine de Frigate Georges Louis Blaison and Captain Henry Johnson together on that fateful night of February 18, 1942??? Whatever it was, it was as if it were a deliberate mystical conjunction of their two lives; a synchronistic, paranormal phenomena. Of course we may never learn the answer to such a perplexing question, at least not in our time, but should that riddle be solved it is likely that an albatross, like a symbol portending a future event, may have been the focal point of this mystery.

Captain Johnson was an avid reader of 19th century literature and enjoyed Conrad, Poe, Stevenson and the Harvard Classics. One could, therefore, assume that his affinity with *The Rhyme of the Ancient Mariner,* one of Coleridge's three great mystery poems, had been self-induced by first reading that weird epic of the sea. Strange to tell, however, it happened with a more horrible, chilling reality. This is how he related that grizzly episode, in his January 2, 1976 letter, following the slaying of an albatross aboard the sailing ship GLEWARD:

> The belief that killing an albatross brings bad luck to a ship came up on a voyage aboard the Finnish full rigged ship GLEWARD, 3,000 tons, on which I sailed as an Able Bodied Seaman in 1911. She was bound to Melbourne from Sweden with a load of lumber.
>
> On that voyage the carpenter caught and killed an albatross. Not wantonly, but to make a cane for the Captain. The topic of killing the albatross was argued for some length amongst the crew, and it was on that voyage that I heard for the first time:

Water, water, everywhere
Nor any drop to drink.

Not until Captain Henry Johnson read *The Rhyme of the Ancient Mariner* in 1928, did he know from where these lines were derived. Since then he have read the poem from time to time, before and after his encounter with Blaison and SURCOUF.

Captain Johnson's yarn vividly provides hard evidence that *The Rhyme of the Ancient Mariner*, a fable of crime and punishment, was inevitably tied tight as a sailor's knot into his life, and at an early age. But more occurred on that long voyage than the slaying of that poor albatross. "Indelibly etched on my mind and memory" is how the ship owner tried to dissuade his determined son from going aloft with on icy rigging "that tempestuous night"!!!

And now there came both mist and snow,
And it grew wonderous cold:
And ice, mast-high floating by,
As green as emerald.
The ice was all between
The ice was here and the ice was there,
The ice was all around:
An Albatross did follow

At the time of this writing, 1985, the Blaison womenfolk and Captain Johnson had an earthly conjunction as Blaison's widow and daughter lived in Paris and Captain Henry Johnson lived in New Orleans on a street named Paris.

It would be that same inevitability that would bring Blaison and Captain Harry Johnson, of the American merchant marine, together on that fateful night in the Caribbean Sea—seemingly through Coleridge's albatross, to cause the worst submarine disaster in history.

Commandante Blaison's connection with Coleridge's albatross will be told appropriately, but for now permit a brief digression.

No history of the Royal Navy can be complete without accurate and adequate mention of the interface between SURCOUF and the Royal Navy, which began at the Washington Naval Conference of 1921-22, and continues to be played out to this day. Yet, many histories about SURCOUF persist portraying her as a traitor submarine. WHY, why, why???

The Royal Navy's wartime position regarding SURCOUF cannot be attributed to appalling ignorance or error in judgment. Rather the downplay of SURCOUF is attributed to an intense, hidden desire to suppress a competitor, and to avenge defeats handed by the ruthless Baron Robert Surcouf (1773-1827) to the Royal Navy and British East India merchantmen plying the Indian Ocean during the Napoleonic Wars.

Likely, some within the British Admiralty (Whitehall), like the Irish, had the longest memories of anybody. Only revelation coupled with truth can remove that stigma of the SURCOUF albatross from the conscience of the Royal Navy. And the American and Canadian Navies, coupled with the American Coast Guard Service, as will become evident, must share the "heavy weight" of that albatross burden.

To bring *The SURCOUF Conspiracy* into a closer chronological prospective, now is introduced how Mademoiselle Theresa Franchcelli, Blaison's future wife, suffered a severe trauma over the loss of the Royal Navy's submarine HMS L-24 as a young woman, and of how she and Blaison first met in St. Malo, the home of the privateer Baron Robert Surcouf.

It is absolute to now mention that the Royal Navy mine laying submarine HMS L-24 (Lieutenant Commander Paul Leatherly Eddis, Royal Navy), on January 10, 1924, while operating off Portland Bill, England, during a mock attack on the Home Fleet battleships HMS RESOLUTION and HMS Revenge, broke surface under the bow of RESOLUTION and was instantly sunk with 43 officers and men. It was the third worst submarine disaster in history.

(The hulk of L-24 is at a depth of 52 meters. Her hydroplanes remain set to hard dive, indicating that she was trying to take evasive action. A hatch is open and there is obvious damage where *Resolution* sliced into her hull. A memorial to L-24 is located in St Ann's Church in HMNB Portsmouth, and her site is designated as a *protected place* under the Protection of Military Remains Act 1986.)

L-24's loss was preceded, on August 21, 1923, by that of the Imperial Japanese Navy's submarine RO-31 (ex-No. 70), with 88 on board. Later, on October 28, 1923, the American submarine USS O-5 collided with the United Fruit Company banana boat SS ABANGAREZ (Captain W. A. Card) in Cristobal Harbor, Panama Canal Zone. O-5 sank immediately, but with the loss of only 3.

Of the three, L-24, RO-31, and O-5, the RO-31, with 88 lost, became the worst submarine disaster in history. (Strangely, O-5 went down about 90 miles from where the hulk of SURCOUF now lays at the site of the world's worst submarine disaster.)

RO-31 remained the world's worst submarine disaster until the sinking of HMS THETIS on June 1, 1939, followed immediately by the losses of USS SQUALUS and the French Navy's PHENIX. At that time, THETIS became the worst submarine disaster with 99 lost.

The losses of L-24, SQUALUS, and PHENIX have great relevance with Blaison and his bride to be, the *tres chic* Parisian, Mademoiselle Therese Franchcelli.

By some mysterious fate, bordering upon precognition and the supernatural, the L-24 disaster had a severe psychological effect upon Therese—in a manner that, beyond doubt, had a direct connection with Blaison's and SURCOUF's tragic deaths. Here is how she confided that dreadful experience, a psychological wound, in a January 5, 1978 letter to the author:

> I was a very young girl at the time and particularly impressed by stories of the sea and about Baron Robert Surcouf, my ideal French hero after whom SURCOUF was named. When I learned of the catastrophe to the British submarine L-24 and its poor sailors, who were beating on her hull and pleading for help during their five days of entombment, I became hysterical with fear and pity for them and had nightmares for months.

For almost a year my mother tried to console me about the disaster until finally one day, knowing how much I loved the sea and sailors, she seriously admonished me by saying: **"My poor girl, you must never marry a naval officer, and, above all, one who is a submariner, If you do, your life will become one of nothing but anguish and tragedy."** (Bold emphasis added by the author.)

Another twist in this story occurs when an officer of the Royal Navy introduced Therese and Blaison during August of 1930 at the casino at St. Malo, the birthplace of Baron Robert Surcouf. Then, Blaison was an Ensign First Class Blaison and executive officer aboard the French Navy supply ship REMIREMONT with no thought of ever serving in a submarine.

Here is how Madame Blaison told of her first meeting with Blaison, through an apparent "Surcouf connection, such as to provide a continuity between her psychic shock connection with the L-24 and the submarine SURCOUF—a mysterious inevitability—like a past time event stepping far into the future:

> Besides my mind's agony because of the loss of HMS L-24, there was another strange predilection that I have often thought about since the loss of SURCOUF with Louis.
>
> I spent most of my childhood vacations by the sea. I adored the sea. There is nothing in the world more beautiful, more attractive, more impressive and lively than the sea. I admired also with all my soul the French corsair, Baron Robert Surcouf, a sailor naturally.
>
> I had read all the books about him and it was in that small, community of St. Malo that I was to meet for the first time that man who was to become my husband, a sailor with a proud soul like the Baron's.
>
> The previous year, at St. Malo, I had made an acquaintance with Royal Navy officers of the HMS QUENTIN ROOSEVELT. Then I met them again the following year while

at St. Malo. Since they were leaving the next day, one of them offered to introduce me to his friend lieutenant de vaisseau Louis Blaison, who was serving as the executive officer aboard the REMIREMONT. After some hesitation, I accepted and it was on REMIREMONT that I met Louis.

During the evenings of his five day stay we youth got together at the casino to dance. All that time Louis and I did not leave each other, going swimming, organizing excursions, and attending cocktail parties given by Commandante Paul Rey aboard the REMIREMONT. I still keep in memory the starlit skies and walks we had along the ramparts of St. Malo while Louis spoke of his life and ambitions as a French naval officer, and told the names of many stars that shone in the sky.

Mine was a very exciting vacation and the start of a lasting friendship with Louis, but too soon, Louis returned to Brest with REMIREMONT. A few days later, I returned to Paris to continue my law studies at the University of Paris, but a strong correspondence started between us for the next eight months.

Strange that, during the summer of 1930, Blaison would be introduced to Therese by a Royal Navy officer. It was as if that officer had been ordained to effect the union of their two souls. That Blaison, later in his naval career, would have an extensive relationship with the Royal Navy; that his earthly marriage with Therese would end in his death with a liaison officer of the Royal Navy aboard SURCOUF; that his and SURCOUF's last voyage would be ordered by a senior officer of the Royal Navy; and that a Royal Navy officer would be present at SURCOUF's inquest, provides an engrossing and subtle interplay with the events of this story—like events contrived to foretell the occurrence of a menacing tragedy. Alan Vaughan, in *Incredible Coincidences*, cites that the events may seem trivial, but they often have an unusual emotional impact, spanning space and time that eventually turns coincidence into the realm of destiny; fantasy occurring before fact.

It seemed as if Louis and Therese were fated to met at St. Malo, then birthplace of the ruthless Baron Surcouf; whose descendents were patrons of the submarine SURCOUF when she was launched at Cherbourg on October 18, 1929.

However, this was not a mere chance encounter for their game of love had been arranged, but a sophisticated computerized dating service could not have planned their introduction better. Seemingly, an ominous omen was casting a shadow of future events before them. Someone or something alien had conspired to bring the two lovers together, a *pas de deux*, at St. Malo, for a purpose. It was as if the world's worst submarine disaster, in the form of SURCOUF, was brought steps closer to reality by their rendezvous.

About their meeting, Vaughan would probably remark that maybe we are linked on a psychic level, in some subtle and complex manner, and in ways which we still do not comprehend. Regardless, what occurred at St. Malo between the two lovers, who were without a care in the world, was far beyond their control.

At that time, Blaison was disinterested in becoming a submariner, and that subject never entered their conversations until the winter of 1930-31. But, unbeknownst to Blaison, at one time Therese intended to break her engagement with him for his having become a submariner. Did she do this to be consciously be rid of him for that reason??? Or was she attempting to protect the man she adored from dire consequences from which he could not escape; the nature of which she may have sensed, but could not explain???

Now for the Blaison Connection with the albatross, not any albatross; only Coleridge's "Albatross", through coincidences which only destiny or an alien mind could have prearranged. There are only a few moments when humans can face the powers that control their destiny and not be annihilated immediately.

On March 18, 1931, a very prophetic letter was written by Blaison to his fiancée, Therese, in which he chastised her for her seeming silence and indifference to him for not writing for two weeks. At the time, Blaison was in his second month of training at the French Navy Submarine School, Toulon.

That portion of Blaison's letter, giving a hint of his connection (a sense of continuity) with Coleridge's "albatross" and of his commonality with that "ancient mariner," Captain Henry Johnson, follows:

> It is almost two weeks since I received your last missive and I have looked at it in vain, not the least long envelope, blue, green, or yellow comes anymore. A joyous note to be read during my café at the hotel or at school. What have I done to deserve such punishment. This is silent without my expecting it.
>
> We weigh anchor tomorrow morning for two days and I would gladly let you take the watch in the bathtub of our submarine, to remain in the corner of my heart, because from the time when there is even a little sea the watch on a submarine is a session of hydro-therapeutics of the first order and not enjoyable to endure. This prospect I foresee as I keep an enormous towel around my neck to seal my body from the drench of the sea.
>
> After four hours at this trade, I am able to withdraw only to a cupboard cabin rendered hellish by the noise, smell, and vibration of the diesels. I find the feet of another officer who also lives in my small box. The room is so tiny that we have hardly room for our length.
>
> Only the commander has a right to his own cabin, while others are compelled to greet the feet of his neighbor when he wants to stretch out. It is very much less poetic than the story of the old mariner grasping, in the torment of dying, at a great sea bird, but it must surely be true, as I once told you, that true stories of sailors are not good to tell.

Did Blaison, exposing all that is mortal and unsure, give truth to that supernatural manifestation of unqualified madness, *The Rhyme of the Ancient Mariner*, an incursion of evil into human life, when he wrote "it surely must be true, as I once told you, that true stories of sailors are not good to tell???"

It seems so, as Hemingway, that cult figure for the young and restless, once said, "all true stories end in death." In an extraordinary revelation, with undertones of anticipation, death and menace, Blaison had identified himself as having a profound understanding of Coleridge's bizarre ballad, when he undeniably associated himself to Coleridge's "Albatross" by reference to an object around his neck (the towel) and to "the old mariner grasping, in the torment of his dying, at a great sea bird." Through an ultimate fiasco, Blaison would receive the highest honor the Free French Navy could bestow upon him—the gift of death brought about by collision of SURCOUF with the SS THOMPSON LYKES piloted by "an ancient mariner", Captain Henry Johnson.

Blaison's encounter with Captain Johnson and his disaster with SURCOUF, on that fateful night of February 18, 1942, seems to substantiate the validity of his prophetic words to Therese: "true stories of sailors are not good to tell."

Maybe it was Blaison, as an ancient submariner, one of the oldest and most experienced in the French submarine service, who was among those "grasping" for life while "in the torment of dying" with SURCOUF before the eyes of the startled Captain Johnson, who was helpless to rescue them from sinking to death into the bottomless pit of the Caribbean Sea. Indeed, the true story of SURCOUF's death, as you shall read in **Part IV, SURCOUF's Rendezvous with Death,** is not "good to hear."

But Commandant Blaison, as was learned from his daughter, Mademoiselle Francine "MacTavish" Blaison, had an even stronger connection, a double exposure, with the "albatross", than the author realized. Francine, during her August-September 1979 visit with the author to collaborate about *SURCOUF and the Royal Navy*, revealed that among her father's favorite poets was the Frenchman Charles Baudelaire, who wrote *The Albatross*. She added that during his midshipman days at the l'Ecole Navale, Blaison faithfully and frequently read Baudelaire's poetry, being especially "impersonated" by Baudelaire's *Albatross*:

> Sometimes to entertain themselves, the crew Lure upon deck an unlucky albatross, one of those vast Birds of the Sea

that follow unwearied the voyage through, Flying in slow and elegant circles above the mast.

No sooner have they disentangled him from their nets Than this aerial colossus, shorn of his pride, Goes hobbling pitiably across the planks and lets His great wings hang like heavy, useless oars at his side.

How droll is the poor floundering creature, how limp and weak—He, but a moment past so lordly, flying in state! They tease him: One of them tries to stick a pipe in his beak; Another mimics with laughter his odd lurching gait.

This sea bird is like that wild inheritor of the cloud, A rider of storms above the range of arrows and slings, Exiled on earth, at bay amid the jeering crowd, He cannot walk for his unmanageable wings.

There are words of Baudelaire's immortally beautiful poem, about the "unlucky albatross" which closely relates to SURCOUF; as if he wrote it especially for her. Wasn't SURCOUF, in her slowness to dive beneath the waves, a "poor floundering creature???"

Didn't SURCOUF's seaplane represent some kind of "aerial colossus"??? Blaison, himself, referred to SURCOUF as that "clumsy fellow." Throughout the 1930's, and until she died on the night of February 18, 1942, was that "moment past so lordly" for SURCOUF; the largest, most powerful and most unique submarine in all the world. And you shall read of how poor SURCOUF was "teased" by her allies and enemies and referred to as "SOURCOUF" and as a "White Elephant" by submariners. And you shall read of how some within the Royal Navy wanted to be rid of SURCOUF, as if they intended her to be "Exiled" off the face of the Atlantic. Not even death could take "poor" SURCOUF "above the range of slings and arrows" cast by a "jeering crowd" of antagonists; even to this day.

Here is how Doctor Hardin Goodman, Associate Professor of English, Florida State University, explained the concept of the "albatross around one's neck", and from his interpretation we are able to derive how that "albatross" came to be figuratively placed around the neck of the Royal Navy as concerns the life and death of SURCOUF:

> Sailors regard the albatross as a symbol of evil that brought them bad luck and shot it. Coleridge lets his readers imagine that the albatross had a soul (birds have been used as symbols of souls in poetry for centuries). It was Coleridge's thesis in his poem that the selfish destruction of anything in Nature, the failure to value everything in God's creation, was a sin that would destroy the soul and place the perpetrator in a metamorphic hell throughout his life—thus a heavy, intolerable weight of sin that is inexplicable.
>
> The Biblical phrase referring to a millstone around one's neck refers to an insufferably heavy weight or burden; the albatross about the neck is indicative of utter damnation, specifically for the cardinal sin of murder. In the Coleridge poem, the mariner shot the albatross after accepting it intuitively as a "Christian Soul," or in other words a creature of God in God's organic universe. The shooting of the albatross was murder, the spiritual murder of a "Christian" and therefore, since the poem is set in the middle ages, the practice of chaining the victim to the murder's neck was appropriate justice in the absence of legal authority for the crime. The albatross, then, has come to mean more than just a burden; it signifies a most grievous burden of inexpiable sin and conscience.

We know that the Royal Navy considered SURCOUF as an "evil" thing because of her threat to England's eminence as a great sea power: "Britannia Rules the Waves." We also know that during the London Naval Conference of 1930 the Royal Navy strived to deliberately kill SURCOUF at the conference table; being only successful in eliminating the SURCOUF-class of submarine. We also know that during World War II the Royal Navy committed the "cardinal sin" of failing to value SURCOUF for what she was, a powerful, big gun submarine, and that during that war some within the Royal Navy tried to have SURCOUF beached and dismantled for use as a gun emplacement, or relegated to the "Malta Death Run" for submarines in the Mediterranean Sea, or to be decommissioned and sent to the ship breaker's yard.

Finally, as you shall read, the Royal Navy with the cooperation of the American Navy, seemingly eradicated SURCOUF for the surface of the sea in an episode which Francine Blaison, to this day, refers to as "they murdered SURCOUF and my father." For these reasons, along with the affray that occurred on July 3, 1940, and whether the Royal Navy would care to admit it or not, SURCOUF, may for the centuries to come, remain as an "albatross around the neck" of the Royal Navy.

Now back to the main stream of our narrative:

Love that mystery of Life, had its way for Blaison and Therese. People must do what they are fated to do, even at cost to themselves and to others. Because of her profound love for Blaison, deeper than the deep blue sea, Therese ignored her mother's prophetic warning and, following his graduation from submarine school, she became engaged to submariner Blaison on April 18, 1931. *(The measure of love is what you are willing to give up for it. Albert Lewin's lush, 1951, technicolour fantasy Pandora and the Flying Dutchman.)*

On October 15, 1931, in the Holy Trinity Cathedral, Paris, Therese and Lieutenant de Vaisseau Georges Louis Nicolas Blaison entered into and accepted the covenant of marriage. *(Who can find a virtuous woman? For her price is far above rubies. Proverbs 31:10 KJV)*

That Madame Franchcelli was unable to suppress her bitter resentment towards Blaison for eventually becoming a submariner, and because Therese had entered into what she (the mother) determined was an unholy matrimony re-surfaces shortly—in a macabre way—when the episode about the loss of the French submarine PHENIX is related to the author by Therese, and her Child of the Sea, Francine,.

But another strange twist occurred in the lives of Blaison and Therese shortly after their marriage. It was as if a contorted alien mind, one not of this world, was continuing its conspiracy against them. For Therese it was another strange conjunction with HMS L-24 and the Royal Navy, and for Blaison it was one that was to incur a fatal consequence for him and SURCOUF while they served, together, with the Royal Navy.

It happened when, at the very beginnings of Blaison's career as a submarine officer, he and Therese attended a reception aboard the HMS RESOLUTION, flagship of the Mediterranean Fleet, during its show of the flag at the French Naval Base at Toulon in the spring of 1933. Commanding HMS RESOLUTION was its firebrand Captain (later Vice Admiral) Max Kennedy "K" Horton, Royal Navy, a highly decorated hero of World War I submarine warfare.

By a twist of circumstances which only wars can provide the reason of how and why, Blaison and SURCOUF were destined to serve under the aegis of Vice Admiral Horton, while he was Flag Officer Submarines, Northways, London, during World War II.

It was as if Fate had decreed that Blaison should come into Horton's presence to receive his blessing as a newly appointed submarine officer, for it would be Vice Admiral Horton who would be that despoiler who, without mercy, would give that ultimate order for Blaison and SURCOUF to depart Bermuda on an extra specially hazardous voyage so that they could receive the *coup de grâce* from the bow of the SS THOMPSON LYKES on the night of February 18, 1942.

What hideous entity could have conjured such an ominous beginning and such a disastrous end for Blaison and SURCOUF??? It was as if Someone or Something had been deliberately preying upon them as ONE being!!! Why???

To this perplexing question, referral is made to Vaughan: "Often we create coincidences through our subconscious ESP, whereby we attract the people or circumstances we wish to or will encounter without realizing it. Or, in cases of psychic-choreography, in which a number of people we meet, including the strangers, contribute with precise timing to an eventual encounter."

This we can say with certainty, from the Blaison's union emerged their "Child of the Sea," Francine Claire Marie Magdeleine, also referred to as "Cicine" and "MacTavish", after the Scot fighter, by her grandfather and father respectively. She was tabbed MacTavish because of her liking to play football and fight with boys along the Cours de A'got seaside, Cherbourg, rather than with girls and dolls.

Blaison, wherever he may be, would have been lovingly proud of his Francine, beyond pricelessness, because of her determined crusade throughout France and across the Free World to keep alive his untarnished his name and that too of SURCOUF's, and because of her obsession to learn the true circumstances of their loss. *(The Ninja avowed to revenge the death of his father to re-establish family honor and traditions.)*

It was as if she were relentlessly praying for her father to rise from the depths of the Caribbean to unlock the truth about how he and SURCOUF died. *(Withal praying also for us, that God would open unto us a door of utterance, to speak the mystery of Christ, for which I am also in bonds. Colossians 4:3 KJV)*

However, she was on her own because for her France's naval archives were likened to a "Black Hole" from where no such information could escape. Or, was it a conspiracy of silence to promote or protect selfish interests? *(Ever learning and never able to come to the knowledge of the truth. II Timothy 3:7)*

Francine, as the author knew her, was an accomplished, distinguished woman—a rare beauty, a chic Parisian, a gifted actress, a blue ribbon horse woman, an extraordinary Italian linguist, a connoisseur of classical literature, music and of the fine arts, a lover of animals, especially cats and dogs, as sensitive to superstition as a sailor, and that she was a woman of the sea with a insatiable tdesire for being nearby.

Beyond all that, Francine was Blaison's sense of eternity, with a passionate desire to singlehandedly learn everything about the death of her father, SURCOUF, and the Free French Navy, and to the extent that she was an Associate of the Charles de Gaulle Institute, Paris. She despised anything and everything about those Vichyists who collaborated with the Nazis during the war.

Theirs would have been an extraordinary affection that seems to exists between fathers and daughters. With awe, Blaison would have recognized an aura of nobility about her, a quality of divine fearlessness, such as a modern day Joan of Arc would possess in the face of bureaucratic force or against any undue criticism of her father and SURCOUF. You can tell a lot about a virtuous woman by the enemies she has made. With Francine, it was like one of Frances' greatest poets, Pierre Corneille, wrote in *The Wolf's Death*, "To he who seeks to revenge his father's death nothing is impossible."

If a woman is right, if only one woman, she has the strength of ten men. With lone gallantry, Francine had an irrepressible spirit in the face of danger. She was a woman rebel. At one time, in France, it was permissible for women to challenge men to a duel if they were insulted. If dueling were in vogue, it is likely Francine would have helped rid France of Vichyism long ago. (When need be, the female can be as deadly as the male.)

Because of her tenacious and fiery spirit, Francine, daughter of a legend, was known throughout France as *"La Panthere."* And, the *Paris Revue Match*, in its June 10, 1953 edition, referred to Francine as *"le orphan de Surcouf"*.

Blaison would have been saddened to learn that the irresistible Francine had not found a man to marry who could compare with him. It was not that she was unattainable or never had that opportunity, but revenge can also become one's life work for this woman of the sea.

Now again, back to the main stream of *The SURCOUF Conspiracy:*

That Madame Franchcelli was unable to suppress her resentment towards Blaison, her son-in-law, for becoming a submariner, and because Therese had entered into what she (the mother) determined was an unholy matrimony re-surfaces shortly—in a macabre way—when the episode about the loss of the French submarine PHENIX unfolds.

A perplexing question to ask is whether there was some irresistible alien force, other than love, which drew Therese and Louis together??? This inquiry is particularly pertinent because Mlle Therese Franchcelle's mother had admonished her never to marry a submariner. Disregarding that dire warning, Therese did marry Blaison and subsequently five of the six submarines he served on during his career were lost or scuttled, and Blaison was destined to be lost in the worst submarine disaster in history.

Death seems not only to have stalked SURCOUF, but also the illusive Blaison. Except for "lucky" MARSQUIN, which ended her life under a scrapper's hammer, and AGOSTA and REQUIN, which were scuttled by the Vichy Navy during World War II, all the other submarines to which Blaison was assigned, since 1931, were lost with all hands. They were PHENIX and LA SIBYLLE. This is remarkable, and unenviable record, for few submariners in naval history survived to make this claim. One who did, Captain R. G. S. Garwood, Royal Navy, appeared at SURCOUF's inconclusive inquest during March 1942.

In furtherance of these submarine disasters, you shall read of how the tragic losses of USS SQUALUS, HMS THETIS and PHENIX, in one, two, three succession, traumatically touched the Blaison's. Here is how Madame Blaison wrote of it in January 1977, and in her telling we gain enormous insight into the prewar French Navy submarine service, the woes of a submariner's wife, about Blaison, and a sensing into their possible connection with disasters; but above all it seems that what occurred was a warning for Madame Blaison to expect a disastrous calamity:

> In June 1938, there was much talk about the distribution of submarine commands. There was a negative side of Louis against which I fought and reacted the best I could. It occurred rarely, but still it was a source of annoyance to me. At the time, he was pessimistic about his future in the French Navy. That he saw everything from the dark side was, I believe, inherited from his mother, who had that fault in a manner more evident and lasting.
>
> One day in Toulon, Louis, in a depressed state, told me that his Commanding Officer aboard PHENIX (Capitaine de Corvette Robert Bouchacourt), was a good friend but, erroneously, Louis believed that Bouchacourt carried no weight on his behalf regarding promotion and his receiving a command of his own.

Up to this time, Louis had served as Executive Officer on MARSQUIN, AGOSTA and, now, PHENIX. That Louis had no strong family connections within the French Navy also made him view his career opportunities as dismal. He believed he would only obtain a command by pure happenstance, and if he did it would surely be some twisted hulk that could barely put to sea.

I reacted harshly toward poor Louis; how I wish now that I had not. I reminded him that only women had the right to be pessimistic, and that he tried my nerves with his complaining without cause. This approach always calmed him immediately.

Two days, later, I saw a radiant Bouchacourt arrive at our home to announce that Louis had just been made Commandante of LA SIBYLLE. She was, of all the French submarines, among the newest, and best. Louis was jubilant compared to his recent fit of blackness. He was adamant to remain aboard PHENIX, but just as adamantly his superiors insisted that he assume command of LA SIBYLLE as a career move.

PHENIX was due to leave for Cam Ranh Bay, Indochina and Louis regretted her leaving without him, as he had contributed so much to her seaworthiness and upkeep. The crew regretted his leaving also, and it was at the Bouchacourt's home that a very emotional delegation gave us a beautiful pair of bronze bookends, which I cherish to this day.

In the interim of the long voyage of PHENIX to Saigon, LA SIBYLLE and Louis had been ordered to Oran for three months, where I joined him; Francine remaining in Cherbourg with my mother.

Enroute to Marseilles by car, to embark for Algiers on the liner SS VILLE d' ORAN, I had the horrifying grief to learn about the loss of the American Navy submarine USS SQUALUS. This tragedy was, in a few days, followed by the shocking loss of the Royal Navy submarine HMS THETIS.

This double disaster stunned me as if someone had struck me with two blows to my head. I felt the same numbed terror of my youth, when the loss of L-24 nearly caused my insanity. Now, it was increased tenfold because of how that same kind of disaster could involve the one man who was the dearest in the world to me. Only the thought that I was going, two days later, to find Louis in Algiers and relive those delightful moments of supreme happiness, which always followed our reunions, helped to erase from my mind the recollections of SQUALUS and THETIS and all of their unfortunate crews.

I will always remember the arrival of SS VILLE d' ORAN at the roadstead of Algiers. With binoculars I saw my dear husband on the dock, nervously pacing, lighting cigarette after cigarette which he would throw, away after a couple of puffs. I could tell that the loss of SQUALUS and THETIS had been miserably preying on his mind.

We were together in Oran about ten days when one morning, I received from our devoted Kerandreu, the maitre d' LA SIBYLLE, that third paralyzing shock; one that struck closer to our home. It was the unfortunate loss of PHENIX in Cam Ranh Bay. (PHENIX's loss, incidentally, occurred 15 days after the British submarine HMS THETIS sank in the English Channel, with 99 aboard, in the world's worst submarine disaster, and within a month after the loss of the American submarine USS SQUALUS off Portsmouth, New Hampshire on May 24, 1939.)

Knowing how much Louis had remained attached to Bouchacourt, and to those of his former submarine, I immediately went to LA SIBYLLE to bring Louis the comfort of my presence. I found him pale with drawn features. He told me there was nothing to hope for and that the rescue of those aboard PHENIX was a lure.

For days, he remained silent and pensive. He seemed almost shattered. I would only hear him violently reproach himself to have abandoned Commandante Bouchacourt at a time when he was needed most, and to have neglected to have told him about his lack of confidence in his new Executive Officer, mostly because he had known him as a classmate, and to not have advised Bouchacourt that he should have refused to leave Cherbourg with a battery in the deteriorated condition that it was. I never realized, until then, the endearment of an officer for his men and of the united family that resulted from a well-organized, commanded submarine.

So ends Madame Blaison's petrifying account of how Blaison escaped death with PHENIX. Her loss, with all 71 of her complement, was the third worst submarine disaster in history; exceeded only by HMS THETIS with 99 men on June 1, 1939, and Imperial Japanese Navy's RO-31 (ex-No.71) with 88 on August 21, 1923.

Later, you shall read of how SURCOUF, with Blaison, was the third in a sequence of three submarine disasters; with hers becoming the worst in the history. From what we know today, it seems that some alien mind, out of sympathy for Madame Blaison being a woman and a mother, had been gradually and seductively programming her to expect the worst—the worst submarine disaster in history.

Mentioned was Madame Blaison's trauma over the loss of L-24, now let me tell you of Francine's extrasensory account about her pitiful plight resulting from the PHENIX Disaster; a story of how evil, through humans, attempts to prey on and control another's mind, even a child's. (*Many shall be purified, and made white, and tried; but the wicked shall do wickedly; and none of the wicked shall understand; but the wise shall understand. Daniel 12:10 KJV*)

It was as if that alien, diabolic power, acting through her vindictive grandmother, had tried to force Francine into accepting that her father had been aboard PHENIX when she sank with all hands in Cam Ranh Bay that June day; before the start of World War II. Here is how she privately related it to me:

When PHENIX was lost, my parents were in North Africa with LA SIBYLLE. I was alone with my grandmother, on my mother's side, at the Hotel de Nord, in Cherbourg. This was a hotel for officers of the French Navy. I say alone because I was never on very good terms with her.

That day, while looking at the newspaper, she shrieked: "Vi! PHENIX has sunk. Your father's submarine!" Defiantly, I retorted, "No!' LA SIBYLLE is my father's submarine!" Adamantly, in convincing terms, she replied: "I know better than you, poor seven year old girl! Your father's commanding PHENIX!"

Anxiously, almost believing her in spite of my assurance, I ran from the hotel as she roared for me to stop. When I reached the main gate of the Cherbourg Dockyard, near where the entrance to the Centre Commandant Blaison is today, I stopped the first man to come out. Without telling him my name, I asked: "Please, can you tell me the name of PHENIX's commanding officer?" He was a Petty Officer. He looked at me a little surprised, I believe he recognized me, and answered: "Oh, yes, he was Commandant Bouchacourt."

I thanked him with relief. It was as if a weight had fallen from my shoulders. I returned happily to the hotel where my grandmother punished me for disobeying her. Despising her as much as I did, I never told her why I ran away from her and she never spoke to me again about her strange misconception about PHENIX and my father.

What was extraordinary about Francine's harrowing experience during her grandmother assault was that, at that time, some guardian angel told her to authoritatively resist, and reverse, the old Siren's, aggressive mental suggestion that Blaison had died with PHENIX. *(Now the works of the flesh are manifest . . . . idolatry, witchcraft, hatred of which I told you in times past, that they that do such things shall not inherit the kingdom of God. Galatians 5:19-21 KJV)*

During her next demonical encounter, Francine would be utterly helpless to destroy a cousin's evil, mesmeric suggestion that her father and SURCOUF were destined to die.

There would have been nothing unusual about Francine grandmother's "strange misconception" except to reiterate that it was she who had admonished Francine's mother never to marry a submariner. Her siren's song that Blaison was commanding PHENIX was probably her subconscious wish that she had been undisputedly right.

But, her irresponsible timing was off. That sibylic gloom of doom would have to wait for the beginning of another sequence of three submarines to die tragically; of which Blaison's submarine would be the worst, before her prophecy could be fulfilled. Three years later, that event did occur, for Blaison died with SURCOUF, in the last of a sequence of three submarine disasters, and the event, had she known, would have been beyond her greatest expectations, for it was the world's worst!!!

John Klein and Adam Spears biblical scholars, in their book *Devils and Demons and the Return of the Nephilim*, would cite Francine's grandmother as possessing the following diabolical characteristics:

> The unholy legions of detestable demons seek to reside in someone, and deceive and rule over their victim or they can take on human form for extended periods. They want to feed upon our fear, our hate, our pain, our lust, or any other human emotion. Using their black magic, demons want to control their victim to create intense sensation—painful or pleasurable, it does not matter. *(For such are false prophets, deceitful workers, transforming themselves into apostles of Christ, and no marvel; for Satan himself is transformed into an angel of light. II Corinthians 11:13, 14 KJV)*
>
> Demons are false prophets and deceitful workers, often disguised as of angels of light, who want to feed on sensory stimulation and use alluring bribes, fear and intimidation to try to convince us otherwise, but we need not be fooled if we know how to spiritually refute their evil power. *Yet Michael the archangel, when contending with the devil he disputed about the body of Moses, durst not bring against him a railing accusation, but said, The Lord rebuke thee. Jude 1:9 KJV)*

There may have been nothing more extraordinary about the grandmother's dreadful misconception that Blaison had died with PHENIX, or about Francine's vehement denial of her grandmother's death wish, were it not for a newspaper article that announced the pathetic loss of PHENIX.

A strong supernatural twist was given to the grandmother's and Francine's diametrically opposed views as to who was really lost with PHENIX when directly connected with the newspaper article in *Le Figuro*—as it unknowingly foretold that SURCOUF was doomed to die!!! This is how it happened: As if forecasting a future event, on June 23, 1939, in the early morning edition of the Paris newspaper *Le Figuro—the photograph supporting the article announcing the tragic loss of PHENIX was of SURCOUF, not of PHENIX!!! Le Figuro's* horrendous error was quickly corrected in a later edition.

Thus, the commonality with the grandmother's and *Le Figaro's* misconceptions was not only with PHENIX, but also with Blaison—since he had a direct connection with PHENIX and was to have a fatal one with SURCOUF. But, can we say that sub-consciously the grandmother was almost right in her protestation that Blaison was dead, or can we say that the eventual death of both Blaison and SURCOUF was being orchestrated in another world—one which is still alien to our society? Until we can affirmatively, and intellectually, respond to such perplexing questions of our time—with certainty—who's to say that our inquiry is wrong??? Only through intense and profound research and discovery into realms still unknown to us may we eventually evolve the correct answer.

Strange to say, however, that Francine was unaware of the *Le Figaro* article until 39 years later, when the author revealed it to her. Her reaction was stunning bewilderment and profound shock. For the next few days, her mother and I were humanly concerned because Francine was in a state of confused turmoil, bitter remorse, and vehemently critical of her grandmother; even though she died long ago.

Ordinarily such an oversight by *Le Figaro* could be accepted as human error, but when that error is connected with Francine's near-simultaneous trauma over the loss of PHENIX and that *Le Figuro* article, one could consider these combined occurrences as an excellent example of unconscious foreknowledge or precognition because of the eventual involvement of SURCOUF and Blaison in the world's worst submarine disaster.

However, there was an even stronger episode of occult that occurred years before the deaths of HMS L-24, PHENIX, and before that of SURCOUF's.

For readers who may be inclined to disbelieve or who would not care to give credibility to Madame Blaison's prophetic trauma, followed by that of Francine's, then perhaps they would accept the premonition of a naval expert. From widely acclaimed literature, it is possible to draw a strong, but strange analogy or correlation with SURCOUF's death on February 18, 1942.

Shortly before Blaison entered the l'Ecole Navale, Brest, on October 1, 1925, as a midshipman, the journalist for the *London Daily Telegraph*, Hector C. Bywater, who was born on Trafalgar Day, on October 21, 1884, and who during child and adulthood made a concerted study of naval theory and practice, published his book *The Great Pacific War, A History of the American-Japanese Campaign of 1931-32.*

With an uncanny genius and vision for anticipating in fiction, coupled with historical truth, what has not yet occurred in fact, Bywater, the naval journalist who conceived the American-Japanese War of the Pacific and who knew and wrote more about the navies of the world than a room full of admirals; influenced American military and naval strategists to alter War Plan Orange, which was America's strategic plan in event of war in the Pacific against Japan, vividly perceived the:

> American-Japanese War of the Pacific; the Imperial Japanese Navy's treacherous and deceitful surprise attack on Pearl Harbor, Hawaii to annihilate the American battle fleet; capture of the Philippines and Guam; the Japanese tactical raid upon Alaska; capture of most of our Pacific island possessions (the Philippines, Guam, and Wake Islands); successful employment of amphibious warfare by the Japanese; and that the superiority of Japanese cruisers and submarines would wreak havoc with

American warships; Japanese would bomb the United States Pacific coast with its aircraft carrying submarines; and that Japan would attack upon the Panama Canal with monster aircraft carrying submarines.

(But for me, this is not revealed to me for any wisdom that I have more than any living, but for their sakes that shall make known the interpretation to the king, and that thou mightiest know the thoughts in my heart Daniel 2:30 KLV.)

In *Visions of Infamy, The Untold story of How Journalist Hector C Bywater Devised the Plans that Led to Pearl Harbor,* by William h. H. Honan, it was ironically remarked that, in the 1920s, Bywater and Franklin Delano Roosevelt, then Assistant Secreary of the Navy,during their long-running debates took diametrically opposed views on the inevitability of a Pacific war between Japan and the United States.

Honan continued by stating that Bywater's writing of *The Great Pacific War* was deliberately prompted to refute the man who would be at the helm of the United States, President Franklin D. Roosevelt, when Japan put Bywater's ideas into practice at Pearl Harbor on December 7, 1941.

Bywater's alarmingly prophetic masterpiece, *The Great Pacific War*, was authoritative and beyond guesswork because of his unique ability to think Japanese, but it was written with great personal risk to his reputation and life.

One of his remarkable inputs was his imaginary commentary about the 7,000-ton Japanese HAKODATE class cruiser submarine, the largest and most powerful submersible in the world. By some strange coincidence, Bywater's evolutionary conception of HAKODATE—its characteristics, configuration and tactical deployment—duplicated those embodied into SURCOUF by her planners and designers—nearly hand-in-glove. For example, HAKODATE had twin 8-inch guns enclosed in a watertight turret and carried a seaplane.

Pertinent also is that Bywater prophetically wove into his fictionalized narrative the destruction of the mythical monster submarine HAKODATE. Strangely, SURCOUF's death by collision,

41

in 1942, was a near carbon copy of how HAKODATE died, as told in Bywater's fascinating book published in 1925:

The HAKODATE second of series of six, made one cruise to the South Seas without accomplishing anything of note, and was then attached to the battle fleet.

Suffering constantly from machinery troubles, which materially reduced her cruising speed of seventeen knots, she became more of a hindrance than a help, finally ending her career by surfacing a few yards ahead of the battleship YAMASHIRO, whose bow crushed her like an egg-shell.

As with HADOKATE, SURCOUF was a brute submarine, was the first of what the French Navy intended to be six of a class; SURCOUF achieved no victories at sea; she sailed in convoy with HMS RAMILLIES of the Royal Navy's Third Battle Fleet (Pear Admiral S.S Bonham-Carter, Royal Navy); she suffered constantly from machinery and other troubles; she was a drain on Allied repair facilities and was enroute to the South Seas when she was crushed and sunk by the bow of the veritable death ship SS THOMPSON LYKES, which was safely concealed within a cloak of darkness.

You may consider Bywater's eerie account of a psychic connection with SURCOUF's death as pure fantasy, something too incredible to be true. If so, how can you explain the uncanny fact that in 1898 Morgan Robertson's *Wreck of the Titan* fictionalized with similar accuracy a maritime disaster which was to parallel the death of the unsinkable SS TITANIC in 1912?

TITANIC's sinking resulted in the greatest loss of life in the history of the sea—1,494 souls—fourteen years after Robertson's prediction! Allan Vaughan in *Incredible Coincidence*, cities the Robertson-TITAN-TITANIC Connection as "one of the most celebrated fictional cases of thought by parapsychologists to demonstrate unconscious foreknowledge." But the Robertson-TITAN-TITANIC's case is a meager pittance compared to Bywater's HADOKATE-SURCOUF connection, which was the outcome of his long years of intense study of past aand present naval tactics and strategy, geography, and international diplomacy and politics—mainly devoted to his foretelling of an unavoidable armed conflict between Japan and the United States which he was born to write about.

Bywater also foresaw how a submarine of SURCOUF's configuration and power should be employed in combat—by placing NAGOYA, a HAKODATE-class submarine, in a wartime scenario devastating elements of the American Navy at Truk, a powerful naval base in the Southwest Pacific. Ironically, as events turned, Truk was a powerful Japanese naval base during World War II, from which elements of that navy devastated the American fleet around Guadalcanal, and SURCOUF, in 1942, was enroute to the Battle of the Pacific when she collided with the SS THOMPSON LYKES in the Caribbean. Citing from Bywater again:

> NAGOYA appeared at Truk a fore night after American occupation. On the morning of July 12th, in Eten Harbor, the American cruisers COLUMBUS (Captain Louis Batemen) and HARTFORD, eight destroyers, the aircraft carrier ALASKA, and a number of transports and auxiliaries were at anchor.
>
> Six miles offshore the destroyers MELVIN, CLEMSON, REID, and THORNTON were patrolling, the first pair to the eastward, the other two more to the north. Nevertheless, the enemy was able, in spite of this vigilant watch, to spring a surprise. A look-out in CLEMSON was the first to sight the huge submarine as she surfaced midway between the destroyer and shore. Her turrets swung around, and two tongues of flame spurted from her twin 8-inch guns and exploded with deadly effect. CLEMSON was brought to a standstill and promptly holed at the waterline by two more shells.
>
> Having disposed of CLEMSON in less than a minute, the monster fired on MELVIN, whose commander, realizing the futility of attacking with only 4-inch guns, maneuvered to use torpedoes. One torpedo was fired wide of the mark.
>
> MELVIN was about to fire another torpedo when shells from NAGOYA burst on a rack of torpedoes causing MELVIN to disappear instantly in a sheet of flame and smoke.

NAGOYA now directed her fire against REID and THORNTON with such deadly accuracy that they were compelled to throw up a smoke screen to escape, but not before REID was holed.

This was the kind of action which the French Navy expected from a fleet of SURCOUF class submarines, which would have been greatly feared by the American and Royal Navies if they were ever at war with France. This was not an impossibility following World I and especially during World War II when there was an undeclared war between England and Vichy France while the latter was under the control of Nazi Germany.

How much the French Navy in 1926 was prompted by Bywater's book to build a more "incomparably superior submarine than any other navy" is conjectural. That SURCOUF's design and construction started soon after Bywater's book appeared, incorporating eight-inch guns and a seaplane, places the choice of the French Navy well outside the realm of coincidence.

Aside from other influences, there must be considered the strong rub-off from two French naval officers, Darlan and Muselier, who successively held key positions in the Ministry of Marine when SURCOUF was in the throes of creation.

Captaine de Frégaté (later Vice Admiral of the Free French Navy) Emile Henri Desire Muselier, who, with his predominate black mustache and piercing eyes, gave the hint of being a ruthless pirate, appeared on the scene on April 14, 1925 as Assistant Chief of Military Cabinet, Ministry of Marine, Paris. He was relieved by Captaine de Vaisseau (later Admiral of the Fleet) Jean Louis Xavier Francois "The Little Fellow" Darlan, the son of a former Minister of Justice, on December 11, 1925. The untouchable and politically favored Darlan would continue in the Ministry, as Chief of the Military cabinet, until August 30, 1927.

That these two personages, who were destined to become admirals, were mortal enemies, dating back to their midshipman days at L'Ecole

Navale, would have an enormous influence upon SURCOUF, from her inception and until her death during World War II.

Just how much Muselier contributed to SURCOUF's inception is not known, but being the kind of naval officer he demonstrated himself to be during World War II, it is extremely likely that he, described in a *Pamphlet on Admiral Muselier and the Free French Navy*, by Commander G. K. Collet, Royal Navy, "as being a man with a heart of gold", would have promoted any submarine project which would have given France a deadly weapon for future naval warfare, even though he was not a submariner.

Darlan, as did his distant cousin, Baron Robert Surcouf, fiercely detested the Royal Navy. Regardless, during the London Naval Conference of 1930, Darlan, sided with the Imperial Japanese Navy delegation to disallow the construction of six more SURCOUF class submarines for the French Navy.

The London Naval Conference of 1930 was an Allied den of dunces or dupes who, because of deliberateness for diplomatic, economic, and political purposes, stupid negligence and conformity, and very poor naval intelligence, concurred with the Imperial Japanese Navy delegation that France's program to build more SURCOUF-class submarines should be scrapped. Had the powerful SURCOUF-class survived they could have served as a deterrent to the start of World War II by Germany and Japan.

Darlan's decision, on behalf of France and the French Navy, was based upon an informal, non-aggression pact between France and Japan, having to do with France's Indochina (today's Cambodia, and Laos, and Vietnam) possession. Therefore, more SURCOUF's were no longer required by France to protect its distant territory in the Indian Ocean. Besides, France was severely beset by an economy sword.

However, not known to Darlan of France and to the other Allied delegates from England, Italy, and the United States, was that the Imperial Japanese Navy was secretly building aircraft carrying submarines. Japan's Technical Delegate to the Conference was none other than Captain (later Vice Admiral) Isoroku Yamamoto, the master planner for his navy's attack upon Pearl Harbor on December 7, 1941, who was well aware of Japan's duplicity.

Japan paid no heed to the London Naval Treaty of 1930 and forged ahead, deceptively, far surpassing the Allies in art of submarine development and to the point where its navy ultimately emerged with the I-14 and I-400 classes of aircraft carrying submarines, which were larger, more advanced, and more powerful than SURCOUF.

Darlan, of who you shall read about extensively, in an act of vengeance against England and the Royal Navy, withheld elements of the French Fleet from all fleeing to British or American ports after the Fall of France in June 1940. SURCOUF was an exception, and you shall read about her involvement in the SURCOUF Affray of July 3, 1940, when three of the Royal Navy were murdered by French naval officers in SURCOUF's wardroom during Operations CATAPULT and GRASP. As a consequence, Darlan, who was to serve as Minister of Marine and Vice Premier of Vichy France, became the man Churchill came to hate and against whom he was pledged to eradicate.

Both Darlan and Muselier resurface conspicuously in *The SURCOUF CONSPIRACY.*

Now you shall learn about an even weirder anticipation of Blaison's and SURCOUF's death. Again, Francine related it to me privately during another of our many tête ê têtes in 1979. Here is how Francine was unable to deny the frightening aggressive mental attack by a cousin—one that foretold the death of her father and SURCOUF—because her resistance seemed drastically reduced while living in an orphanage sympathetic to the Vichy French cause—despite Therese's hopeless protests and for reasons far beyond the scope of this story to unravel.

It was an ominous event—one beyond explanation or of being just a subtle influence—such as to again herald the advent of an inescapable death for Blaison and SURCOUF. It occurred during August 1941, six months before they died in the Caribbean. Then, Francine was confronted by a horrifying psychic, mind-bending episode—one which proved to be a ill omen for her father and SURCOUF—through the pitiless machinations of her cousin Alain (not his true name) which she could not blot from her memory.

It seemed as if Alain, with an abominable evil soul and a hellish imagination, had been guided by a sinister alien intelligence, something not human—seething with savage hatred, madness, and cruel disregard of life—to willfully torment and imprint within young Francine's mind, like a memory-implant, the illusion—before the actuality of the event—that Blaison and SURCOUF would be irretrievably caught in a catastrophic death trap and that she would never see her father alive again!!!

Alain, as if he were a nephal, an evil offspring of a bewitching siren not created by God and possessed with monstrous powers with which young Francine was entirely unfamiliar—a god of destruction—else wise she could have taken precautions to have on her person an anti-demon remedy to fence off any hypno-sensorium effect while in his presence. *(Woe to the inhabitants of the earth and of the sea! for the devil is come down to you, having great wrath because he knoweth that he hath but a short time. Revelations 12:12 KJV)*

This is how Francine, on October 21, 1979, recalled Alain's malignant ceremony and dead serious pronouncements—which would have doomed the bravest sailor and the stoutest submarine which, coupled with her trauma over the loss of PHENIX, has remained a maelstrom of violent dreams and soul-shattering torture for her—often threatening her sanity—even in adulthood:

> My father was Alain's godfather and for Alain's birthday, in 1939, he had given him a box of toy soldiers. This was just before the war had started and well before May 31, 1940, the last day that I ever saw my dearest father alive.
>
> It was a regiment, in dress uniform, the commander of which was holding a sword with the blade pointing upward as an officer leading a parade. My cousin always said that the commanding officer, the soldier with the sword, was his godfather. Thus, that officer was precious to me because it

represented my father, who was fighting in the war against Germany and Vichyists.

My cousin was an unintelligent boy, never reading, interested in nothing, a born liar. He disliked me intensely for reason that, I assume, he abhorred being told by his grandparents that he should follow my example to be more athletic and a better student in school.

Soon after my mother and I arrived in Grenoble [not the exact location in Vichy France] in July 1940, to live in my uncle's home, Alain, in a viciousness which never relented, told me: "You shall never see your father alive again." Naturally, his cruel words cut me deeply, and I often ran away crying to hide from his ugly thought. The more he saw me cry the more he tormented me with his hate.

One day, while I was sitting by the garden pool, Alain found me and in spell-binding voice said: "Today, I shall put all my soldiers in a wood ship, put the ship and the soldiers in the pool, and then make a violent storm." Recalling what he had once said about my father, I implored him, begging on my knees, not to do this. Even to this moment, I vividly recall my anxiety and how difficult it was to restrain my fear and tears. The more I pleaded, the more hateful he became and the harder he stirred the water.

As he was drowning the soldiers he said, "I will drown all the soldiers, but not my godfather." After he drowned the last soldier he looked at me with his soulless eyes and, laughingly but defiantly, said: "Now, I will put my godfather in the ship, if he survives my storm your father will live. If not, you shall never see your father again." I knew that I should have ignored him and leave him at that moment, but, I could not for I was transfixed with a mixture of curiosity and dread.

He put the lone commander in the ship and stirred the pool into a frenzy, as if he deliberately never wanted me to see my father again. The little ship sank and with it her commander. It was a moment of horror for me. Then Alain, as if he were the devil incarnated, said: "Now, you know what is the difference between life and death!" All the while he had an evil, insane grin on his face. *(Often the Ninja wore a hideously carved mask of himself or of some well-known demon or evil spirit.)*

A few days later, the old gardener emptied the pool to clean it. I sifted through the mud and dead debris to find the commanding officer. The gardener, who had compassion for me, helped. We found all the soldiers and the boat, but we never found her commanding officer.

For weeks I was in anguish, I had nightmares and could not forget the blunt horror of Alain's cruelty towards me and his godfather, who loved him as if he were his own son.

Francine was wrong about Alain in one respect. He was intelligent, but his was that of a hideous intelligence of a unseen creature, with enhanced multisensory powers, living in a world alien to our own. *(There shall not be found among you any one that maketh his son or his daughter to pass through the fire, or that useth divination, or an observer of time, or an enchanter, or a witch, or a charmer, or a consulter with familiar spirits, or a wizard, or a necromancer. Deuteronomy 18-10-11. KJV)*

Without knowing it, Alain had used one of the most effective comprehension techniques ever developed, called Visualization/ Verbalization, as referred to by Lindamood-Bell Learning Processes of San Luis Obispo, California. *(The Ninja with absolute confidence in himself always offered mumbling incantations to evil gods and made use of signs to effect mental control over his victim.)*

Had the youthful Francine been a devotee of Clement of Alexandria, who wrote in his *Exhoration to the Heathen*: "Let not strange sea-folk, with rapturous song, cheat you of your senses, sail past their luring chant; it works death; exert your will and you have overcome ruin," she may have nullified Alain's hostile incitement during his enactment of that dreadful garden pool scene??? But the truth was that Alain played upon the pathetic fear reflected in Francine's troubled face.

It was as if Francine's mind—her receptivity and state of attention—had been fixed by some psychic-magnetic force—much like those who watch a horrific docudrama on TV or in movie theater. She appeared transfixed and powerless—to turn her eyes away from Alain's hypnotic charade—yet she was too stimulated and determined to observe everything evil that he envisioned would happen to Blaison and SURCOUF.

Probably a portion of Francine's fascination was that Alain's seductive incantations—his death wish fulfillment—bordered on what she perceived to be credible. What was happening was real to Alain, but Francine—who was the focal point to his vile plan—was fighting against believing what could be reality for her.

It is not too far-fetched to believe that Francine had empathy and sensitivity with Alain's benign and willful signals because she—through ancestral memory—had subconsciously experienced similar psychic events—like her mother's near mental collapse when HMS L-24 was lost and her own trauma when PHENIX was lost—through genes inherited from her grandmother and her mother.

We are all products of ancestral or genetic memory and are thus haunted to some degree with memories and experiences locked in our genes—or in the hidden recesses of our mind—of what went on before us from generation-to-generation. Those who are invested with this innateness have a greater susceptibility to an alternate existence, one teeming with unsuspected information—like past apparitions—and they are therefore more prone to stimulate their sub-consciousness to act upon acute perceptions.

Admittedly, there is often bad blood and competition between cousins, but it is unheard of that a civilized boy, unless he was the Devil's advocate on earth, should want the death of his godfather without some justifiable pretext or to psychologically hurt a young relative. Why was Alain—with his seeming capability to look into the future and into another's mind—so determined to inhumanly conjure the death of the two souls—Blaison's and SURCOUF's??? Blaison would have been gravely ashamed of his having been a witness to his godson's baptism.

Who had given Alain, a seeming purveyor of grotesque and philosophies of phenomenal psychic powers and strong, positive life and death force commingled into one force—enabling him to transcend space and time to machinate Blaison's and SURCOUF's misfortune??? Had Alain tapped into some kind of psychic energy—like a magic to kill by indirection—not yet understood by present scientific knowledge??? These are the kind of questions which should be answerable within this century since our thought levels are the highest they have ever been during the civilization of humankind, and with increasing frequency.

Alain's was a power of perceiving sense—the likes of which occurs rarely throughout the civilization of mankind—like that of the notorious Rasputin—that grisly unholy man of Russia—seer and seeker of enlightenment—who many vehemently claim could predict the future. Did Alain have the power, above that of human physical laws, which was strong enough to upset the war plans of the American, Royal, and Free French Navies by having Blaison and SURCOUF eliminated from the surface of the seas???

Toys are important to children, yet it mattered not to Alain that he had sacrificed his toy ship and soldiers to display his prowess over poor Francine. Nor did he care to seek their recovery.

Was Alain more than human???—a purveyor of demonomancy —which, according to Zolar in *The Encyclopedia of Forbidden Knowledge,* is divination through the use of demons???

Was he one of those rare psychics who—through ancestral memory or through some complex mutation of genes—a historical-biological mutant—that required hundreds of generations of breeding to create??? Could Alain look into another's mind to confuse or twist their thought??? Was he a sinister mind-scanner???

That Blaison and SURCOUF died, as Alain had conspired and, as if he had inspired knowledge that this future event would be fulfilled—could lead one to believe that their loss was inevitable. What Alain did, as if he had received mind-control transmissions from a mermaid-Siren, was to perform an act of lecanomancy—involving divination and unholy canting of irresistible songs over a basin of water. (The garden pool was that basin)

Through crossing centuries, continents, and cultures, a parallel to Alain's cunning act of witchcraft, dating back to Nectanebo, a King of Egypt who reigned about 358 B.C., appears in *The Mysteries and Secrets of Magic*, by C. J. S. Thompson:

> Nectanebo ruled by his magical powers. For example, he placed models of the ships and men of his navy and of his enemies in a pool of water and taking an ebony wand and pronouncing words of power he invoked the gods [alien mind] to come to his aid. He contrived that the models representing his enemy would sink to the bottom of the pool, as did his real ships sink his enemy's ships on the sea.

It was as if Alain was playing out the role as one of the three witches observed to be stirring their black caldron that famous scene from Shakespeare's *Macbeth*.

To reveal that Thompson's entry is not an idle mixing of history, and that Blaison and SURCOUF did not have a forlorn hope of survival, another similarity to Alain's sinister conjurations appears in *The Black Art, A Black Magic Book of Terror,* by Rollo Ahmed:

> Witches were believed to cause storms and shipwreck by placing a dish in a pail of water. Then they said incantations and spells over the pail to agitate the water, whereby a storm sprang up at sea. When the dish filled and sank, a certain ship would be wrecked.

Alain's depraved conduct was not the result of an overwrought imagination. His was a cruel act of animal magnetism and witchery, as if he intentionally desired to affect the death of Blaison and SURCOUF. His meaningful implications defy our ability to comprehend, except to say that the despicable thoughts Alain contrived in his mind became a reality through the death of Blaison and SURCOUF and of her officers and men. Also painfully obvious, is our current failure to distinguish between reality and unreality when the choice can mean the decision between life or death.

Francine concluded her occult account, which must rank among the most amazing revelations of witchcraft to emerge from World War II, or any war, by saying: "Now you know why I never saw my poor father alive again. Alain, that mesmeric spell-worker, had placed a monstrous curse upon him as surely as if he had been directed by someone experienced in the black art of soul-killing witchcraft."

Francine should have blatantly ignored by flight or effectively counteracted Alain's evil witchcraft by denying it metaphysically, "Resist the devil and he will flee from you" [James 4:7 KJV], but as a small child how was she to know how to cope with and unmask his aggressive mental suggestion??? The scales are tipped in favor of the evil eye when an individual falls prey to its fascination as Francine did. Society can never be purged from the evil eye, and it will remain as a latent and evil force until we learn how to deny its heinous influence.

Francine was right, for through his deviant behavior, hateful envy, and uniquely developed powers of imagination, Alain did commit an unnatural act of witchcraft by agitating the elements, the air and water in-and-around that garden pool, into a frenzy; he did concoct an evil stratagem; he did foretell, through the power of man-mind, maliciously super induce into Francine's innocent mind—and into the profoundest depths of her soul—the destruction of SURCOUF and the death of Blaison!!!

Imagination is another name for super-intelligence, but more likely Robert Tralins, author of *Clairvoyant Strangers*, would identify Alain's extrasensory perceptive ability as a case of psychokinesis, a term used to describe the power of mind over matter, like projecting one's consciousness through space, or shape-shifting powers of thought through space, or collapsing of time, or making things happen through auto-suggestion or hypnosis. Tralins wrote:

> The clairvoyant or the person with extrasensory perceptive
> ability foretells or predicts what is about to happen or what is

happening elsewhere according to vibrations or impressions he receives from the mind of another.

One could surmise, in light of the remarks by Tralins and from what was told by Francine, along with what has been unfolding throughout this writing, that Alain could have been receiving vibrations from some alien mind to make him deliberately conjure the destruction of Blaison and SURCOUF. If this were true, then Blaison and SURCOUF did not stand a ghost of a chance of surviving its collision with the SS THOMPSON LYKES that Fate, often acting as the goddess of destruction, had arranged for them.

It is extremely important at this point, repeat extremely important, for the reader to mentally recall Tralins' remarks about psychokinesis when reading about Captain Johnson's night orders—his predilection for killing a submarine the night SURCOUF died—as he executed his three course and speed changes such as to place SS THOMPSON LYKES on a direct kill heading for poor SURCOUF.

Can the reader begin to appreciate why the author, since 1967, has been continually astounded and fascinated by SURCOUF's captivating story??? Because of revelations such as proffered by the Blaison womenfolk, as well by other contributors, is why *SURCOUF and the Alien Mind and The SURCOUF Conspiracy has* evolved into one of the most bizarre, provocative, and uniquely different naval histories, let alone submarine stories, never told. There are even more disturbing and startling occurrences to follow, just as they were revealed to the author.

As an aside, as if to divert from the occult, but one having an extremely strong connection with Blaison's and SURCOUF's loss, John Bentley, in *The Thresher Disaster*, made much to do about a single premonition that the genial Second Class Machinist's Mate George J. Kiesecker, 38, had concerning USS THRESHER's impending death. It was mentioned at least four times by Bentley. *(And it shall come to pass that every soul which will not hear the prophets shall be destroyed from among the people. Acts 3:34)* Here is what he wrote about Kiesecker's premonition:

Kiesecker, a genial, open-faced man and quick to flash a smile, was certainly not a morbid or introspective individual. Quite the contrary. He was an avid reader, excellent dancer and played the piano and organ well. Nor could his courage be questioned. He was a veteran World War II submariner who served with distinction on the diesel boats SEA DRAGON, SALMON and DIODON, and had earned a combat insignia for taking part in many war patrols.

Yet, for days before THRESHER sailed on her last trip, George, who was one of her nuclear reactor operators, made no bones about his uneasiness. "THRESHER's a coffin," he reportedly told his wife Lily. "I don't want to go on it. I'm scared to death." As Kiesecker saw it, the work on THRESHER had been hurried so much that he didn't think her ready for sea. "There was so much trouble from the beginning, he maintained. "I know what I am talking about. I've been working twelve hours a day, seven days a week, helping to get her in shape." So strong was Kiesecker's foreboding that he added wistfully, "I have a feeling this will be our last trip, honey. Before this week is over you'll be a wealthy widow"

Kiesecker stands out as the crewman with the nightmare premonition about USS THRESHER'S loss, which proved to be entirely correct and which cost him his life. To the best of my knowledge, this unfortunate man was the only crewmember with such forebodings. That he proved right was all the more tragic.

However, according to Joseph William Stierman, Jr., in his study, *Public Relations Aspects of a Major Disaster: A Case Study of the Loss of USS THRESHER (SSN-593),* Kiesecker had confided similar doubts about the seaworthiness of THRESHER to his sister-in-law, Miss Jacqueline Clover, and to his daughter, Mrs. Andrea Keele of Torrance, California.

He had told them that THRESHER was different; referring to her as a coffin. He had tried to transfer off her several times. Kiesecker's premonition was extraordinary, but his, contrary to Bentley's investigations, was not an isolated case. *The Long Beach Press Telegram* reported the fears of another crewman:

> You might as well get yourself another man, Engineman Bill M. Klier told his wife, Mary, before boarding the ill-fated THRESHER.
> I don't think this tub is going to make it.

Then, according to *The Boston Herald*, Mrs. Laurence Whitten of Northwood, New Hampshire, wife of a civilian electronics engineer aboard, admitted she had no faith in the sub "because they had dragged it into dry dock so many times." She had a premonition of horror. "I told him not to go, but he told me it was his job."

Regrettable, because nuclear powered submarines are highly classified subject, is that Kiesecker, Klier, and the others had no one but family to confide in, i.e., no one else in the civilian world or officially within the United States Navy. There are numerous jokes between military and naval personnel about going to one's Chaplain with a problem, and really, as trite as it may sound, that is who Kiesecker and Klier should have also turned to. But would they have been believed or would they have been condemned as cowards or as mentally unstable once the word got out??? And who in the American Navy hierarchy would have had the courage to act upon the Chaplain's solemn advice???

Adela Rogers St Johns in her stunning book, *My Hollywood Story*, wrote about persons like Kiesecker, Klier, and Mrs. Whitten:

> There are people who are like big brass gongs. To get a sound out of them you must hit them hard with a sledge hammer. Others, are like wind chimes, lovely little panels of glass—a summer breeze, a ripple of bird song, the cry of a child and they make music, ring sweetly, gaily, sadly. The brass gong are what most people have. The wind chimes—so sensitive—that is an artistic temperament few of us possess.

Sensitive, often to feel things others do not feel, see things others do not see. This can be good, it can lead to great art—and sometimes to strange experiences.

There is no doubt about it, Kiesecker and Klier enhanced by with some greater perspicuity than their shipmates, especially Kiesecker with his wartime experiences and artistic inclinations, were sensitives and that they bravely and unashamedly confided their apprehensions to Lily and Mary. Moreover, others aboard THRESHER also had that a strange sensation that something terrible would happen to THRESHER. *(The Ninja, to be a successful professional warrior, must possess a supersensitive warning system, one that foretells something is wrong But what is it? Yes, that's it! The frogs, they've stopped their croaking. But now, there is something else . . . something very wrong The crickets . . . that's it . . . the crickets have stopped chirping their merry melodies.)*

What if they had asked for an audience with their Commanding Officer, Lieutenant Commander John Wesley Harvey, USN, to convey their foreboding that THRESHER was destined for disaster??? In that event, Harvey would probably have considered them cranks. Or, if Harvey had believed Kiesecker or Klier what could he have done without tangible evidence to justify requesting permission from higher authority to abort the sea trials of THRESHER. It was hunch against fact, feeling against proof. The fact is no one would have believed Kiesecker or Klier, and as for Harvey, in our time, to have admitted to believing either of them could have meant his being relieved from his command of THRESHER.

Although Kiesecker nor Klier could not positively avow that their extrasensory thoughts would come true, they wereinalienby right. Both realized one single instant of terrifying truth in their lives, ending in brutal finality. Now they would sleep forever. Had they contacted and been believed by officialdom their lives, along with 127 others and THRESHER's, would have been saved to sail another day. *(It would be foolish to alert all hands, for the brave Ninja warrior must deal with the situation alone. You would be the target of great ridicule and dishonor should this incident be nothing at all so you must not give the alarm, you must do your duty in honor. This is your decision and you know that it is the only one you can make and keep your warrior's self respect.)*

If we could harness our extrasensory feelings, which often intervene and govern our minds, then the power of we human beings would impinge upon the Infinite. We would each be all knowing. But, could we long survive in such a confusing and conflicting world of supreme intellect???

Shortly, you shall read of four other sensitives, Boyer, Burney, Gough and Warner of the British Naval Liaison Officer staff, who, while also at the U.S. Naval Shipyard, Portsmouth, New Hampshire, accurately predicted they would die with SURCOUF, even though she was still undergoing overhaul, as was THRESHER in 1963, when Kiesecker and Klier experienced their premonition while at that same naval shipyard!!!

One of the above four was Lieutenant Francis "Frank" Boyer, Royal Navy, who expressed his dilemma to Vice Admiral Wilfred Franklin "Pooh" French, Royal Navy, KCB, CMG.

At that time, Vice Admiral French was serving as Flag Officer, British Admiralty Repair (BAR), Washington, D. C. His responsibility was to coordinate between the American and British Governments to arrange for the conduct of overhauls (in American shipyards) for ships in the service of the Royal Navy; of which SURCOUF, after patrolling over 22,000 miles at sea, was in that category.

Instead of requesting a board of inquiry about Boyer's agonizing concern, Admiral French accused Boyer of cowardice and had him unceremoniously detached from SURCOUF.

Boyer's replacement was Sub Lieutenant Roger John Gilbert "Rog" Burney, Royal Navy Volunteer Reserve. Three months later Burney and his two Royal Navy ratings, Leading Signalman Harold Frank "Plum" Warner, Royal Navy Fleet Reserve, and Telegraphist Bernard "Bernie" Warner, Royal Navy Fleet Reserve, died with SURCOUF in what was the world's worst submarine disaster.

Where is that fine line of acceptance to be grasped between what is a believable or an unbelievable premonition??? We do not know. Because of this, unharnessed psychic power throughout the world is affecting our society because we have not created conditions whereby it can be abated or made useful. Artificial intelligence, through the use of high-tech, powerful computers, is closely approaching the possibility of corralling psychic power, but not yet.

Even though we are living in the Twenty First Century; a century of more understanding and of more scientific accomplishment than has ever been achieved since the dawn of humankind, the answer remains illusively beyond our mental grasp. We still cannot make a positive connection with that other mind which oft times warns us of future events, but which exasperatingly eludes us as a will-o'-the-wisp. We know it is there, but we can do nothing about even proving the truth of our sixth or other senses because of some ulterior control precluding such an eventuality.

It seems as if a pseudo-intellectual alien being does not wish us to know, but we must and should. Regrettably, it may not be until the Twenty-Fifth Century, during that Buck Rogers Era, that we come to learn what that objectionable alien mind is concealing within the dark recesses of our mind. *(For, behold, I create new heavens and a new earth: and the former shall not be remembered, nor come into mind. Isaiah 65:17.)*

Yet, *The SURCOUF CONSPIRACY,* because of what it unmistakably reveals, could provide clues that enable scientists to bring about an earlier understanding and acceptance of premonitions within our century; if only by identifying those who are sensitive to forthcoming disasters. *(. . . Art thou only a stranger in Jerusalem, and hast not known the things which are come to pass there in these days? St. Luke 24:18.)*

Author's Note: The American Defense Intelligence Agency document, *Controlled Offensive Behavior—USSR*, stated:

> The discovery of the energy underlying telepathic communication will be equivalent to the discovery of atomic

energy. The powers of the sub-conscious mind are vastly superior to those of the normal consciousness.

The only way we can learn about these little known processes is through intensive study and experimentation."

That document further stated that based on ". . . today's knowledge of the human brain it is possible that in the next decade some artificial means will be found to influence the intellectual capabilities of man."

There were many facets of SURCOUF's story which amazed me as they unfolded. One which relentlessly came to my attention was the unusually dominant role that women, the enchantresses of history, played in the nemesis of SURCOUF. Women, such as Blaison's womenfolk, have been the casualties of war since time immemorial. It is not illogical to expect, therefore, that women, with a warlike infatuation and with and invincible spirit should play distinctive and forceful roles throughout SURCOUF's earthly life and after life.

Some femmes were alluring, compassionate, and devotedly loved their man, whereas for others even great distance was not enough to keep SURCOUF and her Commanding Officer, Blaison, safe from their deadly ways and wiles.

Indeed SURCOUF herself did not go unscathed, for witchlike women of an alien mind seemed to have a strange, ethereal and sometimes ruthless effect upon her. By contrast, however, we have already observed the strong influence that Joan de Arc, the patron saint of SURCOUF, had upon Blaison.

And, if you believe in Greek mythology, there was Pandora who was sent into the world by Zeus, punisher of guilt, with a box enclosing all human ills that escaped when she lifted its lid. SURCOUF's story could easily have been entitled *SURCOUF and Pandora's Box* as we certainly know that through Burney's liaison reports to Vice Admiral Max Kennedy Horton, Royal Navy and Flag Officer, Submarines, Northways; from Blaison's personal letters to his wife, Theresa, and from his patrol reports; and the remarks of Mrs. "Jo" Vairinen to the author, that SURCOUF and her crew were plagued by all sorts of "human ills" and discontent, the nature of which are now surfacing publicly.

Then, if you accept the correlation of the theme of Coleridge's *The Rhyme of the Ancient Mariner* with SURCOUF's death you may accept that it was Beauty, the *une femme fatal*, that killed the beast. (. . . *that [SURCOUF's] soul shall live because of thee. Genesis 12:3.*)

That woman
Death, that woman's mate.

How else could Captain Henry Johnson have been enticed to order three incremental changes in course to head his ship directly into SURCOUF, unless **That woman**, a temptress in the guise of a **Nightmare Life-in Death**, had not been preying upon him subconsciously???

They were women of reverence and fury, women of intelligence and intuition, women of death and of history, evil women, women of hope and beauty, women of their time and of today and beyond, and there appears a feminine mystique and psyche which borders upon being a supernatural manifestation even to the point of how, through Mrs. Eunice Richards, a writer for the *Panama Canal Review*, published by the Panama Canal Company, the author became inescapably involved in his tempestuous affair with SURCOUF; that began in 1967.

Here is that story: One day, during January 1967, the author was a luncheon guest of the Master of the elegant luxury liner SS FRANCE (Captain Joseph Ropars). During the course of conversational banter, the author, out of the clear blue, asked Captain Ropars: "Whatever happened to that huge French submarine, the one which carried a seaplane?" The Captain replied, "Oh, you mean SURCOUF! Why she disappeared under very mysterious circumstances during the war."

It was very ironic, probably a psychic event—like a message itself from someone aboard SURCOUF—since that the luxury liner happened to be French and that the author happened to ask that question in Cristobal Harbor, Panama Canal Zone, 80 nautical miles from where the hulk of the Free French submarine SURCOUF, once the largest, most powerful submarine in the world, was, unknown to him, lying in over 8,000 feet of water.

My question was especially puzzling as the author had not recalled SURCOUF since 1934 or so, when as a boy he had seen her photograph in either the *Popular Mechanics* or the *Popular Science* magazines. It was as if he had been beckoned by some mind-after-death force, lurking within the depths of the nearby Caribbean, to connect the burden of her past with the hidden truth about her loss.

It remains a further mystery why the author, the day after his boarding the SS FRANCE, was compelled to reply to Eunice Richards, when she asked how he enjoyed luncheon aboard the FRANCE: "It was great Eunice, but her Captain didn't know a damn thing about SURCOUF, that huge French submarine, with a seaplane, except to say that she was lost mysteriously during the war!"

Eunice, in continuance of an apparent extra-sensory perception (ESP) train of corresponding thought, surprisingly replied, "He must be very uninformed as SURCOUF sank in Canal Zone waters, on the Caribbean-side, in February 1942. I remember the event well because my husband, who was in British intelligence, was called suddenly from a supper party on the night of her loss. Why don't you write your next article for the *Review* about SURCOUF?

So challenged, the author's first article about *SURCOUF, World War II Sea Tragedy That Made No Headlines,* appeared in the August 1967 issue of *The Panama Canal Review*. It was mentioned worldwide via Associated Press releases. The Panama Canal Information Office was swamped with requests for further information about SURCOUF. From that time onward, the subject of SURCOUF became an *idea fixe* with the author as he continued to research her history. This is how he became infected that rare disease "Surcoufitis." And, my affliction with this incurable infirmity must have occurred just as Rear Admiral Robert "Bobbie" Le Nistour, Medical Corps, French Navy, diagnosed: "*Each of us live and die for a purpose. This is the reason why Captain Julius Grigore, Jr., USN, was the man who was born to write the history of SURCOUF.*"

Then there appears in this story like a recurring theme of the Siren Lure—a woman of a particular kind—the sea hag—a sorceress and scepter of power femme fatale—who through her seemingly beguiling ways sought to destroy Blaison and SURCOUF and to insidiously stifle discovery and disclosure of truth about their deaths.

Now back to the main stream of *The SURCOUF Conspiracy*: Some women, like the forthright Mrs. Rosemary Sprague, vehemently detested SURCOUF, as if it were 'a loathsome beast", while others, like the charitable Madame Leonie Richard, and the determined Blaison women-folk, along with an infinite number of French women, cherished SURCOUF as if she were an exalted deity.

"The Frank soldiers", an Arabian scholar wrote during the Crusades, "will not go into battle of deprived of their women." That Capitaine de Frégaté Georges Louis Blaison, Free French Navy and commanding officer of the SURCOUF entered the Battle of the Atlantic with Madame Theresa Blaison and their daughter Mlle Francine Claire Marie Magdeleine (Child of the Sea) forever entwined in his heart, mind and soul, until death and beyond, will become vividly evident.

A common misconception among some Bermudians is the SURCOUF was destroyed by an American bomber while she was attacking a British merchant ship. For the record, SURCOUF did not die in that dreaded area, even though her departure for Tahiti via the Panama Canal was from the Royal Navy Dockyard, Ireland Island, Bermuda. Instead, she went down, with all hands, along the Caribbean fringe of the Bermuda Triangle, that killing zone also referred to as the "Devil's Triangle", the "Devil Sea", "Death Alley", or the "Triangle of Death."

Something is very strange about baffling zone of our inner space as it has earned a most disturbing and almost unbelievable reputation in the world's catalog of the unexplainable occurr3ences. There, since about 1600, hundreds of aircraft and ships have disappeared, and thousands of lives lost, without a clue. But how some strange intelligence, human or otherwise, affected SURCOUF in the sinister Bermuda Triangle will be revealed.

According to author Charles Berlitz, in his enthralling book, *The Bermuda Triangle,* the legendary Bermuda Triangle forms a zone of death and disaster extending from Bermuda, in the northeast, to Southern Florida, then east to a point through the Bahamas past Puerto Rico and the islands of the Spanish Main, to about 40° west latitude then back to Bermuda. As pointed out in *They Dared the Devil's Triangle,* by Adi-Kent Thomas Jeffery, wherein she devotes nearly four pages of commentary to the "vortex" effect created by the presence of ocean trenches, the Bermuda or Devil's Triangle covers the deepest trenches that exist at the bottom of the Atlantic Ocean.

The United States Coast Guard, however, defines the Bermuda Triangle as follows:

> The "Bermuda Triangle" or "Devil's Triangle" is a mythical geographic area located off the southeastern coast of the United States. It is noted for its apparent high incidence of unexplained losses of ships, small boats, and aircraft.
>
> Although the area is usually described as a triangle extending from Miami to the island of Puerto Rico, along the sweep of the Bahamas Banks, thence to Bermuda, search and rescue activity is probably better conscribed by a semi-circle extending from the area previously described to Cape Sable, Nova Scotia and coast Miami.

The U. S. Coast Guard extension of Berlitz's version of the Bermuda Triangle is eastward and northward, to include the entire eastern, northeastern and southeastern coastline of the United States, plus Sable Island, and is feared by mariners of the world. They refer to that treacherous area as the "Graveyard of the Atlantic." This corresponds with the area in which SURCOUF operated from February to March 1941 and from June 1941 to February 1942.

SURCOUF spent a considerable portion of her wartime patrols within the Bermuda Triangle, but while enroute to the Panama Canal she passed through that dreaded graveyard and died along its Caribbean fringes.

It was not an immediate revelation to the author that the greatest submarine disaster ever, a stark, utter destruction-of-genius, had its beginnings in the heart of the Bermuda Triangle. In addition, that, in the making, her tragedy involved a triangle of uselessness about her by the American, Royal, and Free French Navies and the cruelty and ignorance of mortals, which caused the wanton death of 130 souls aboard her. For SURCOUF, her plight was likened to a "dogs breakfast" or a situation conducive to error. So, one could easily conclude that SURCOUF, "the submarine no navy wanted" was a tormented soul and that she wanted to die.

Permit me to introduce the inner self about SURCOUF—that is—did she have a soul??? Yes, SURCOUF did have a soul, as if she were a living thing??? Even though philosophically and theologically refutable, the author believes, as most sailors do, that each ship has an inner soul; an ego and personality of its own. Everything man has created has power. SURCOUF, like every other ship, was a triumph of mind over matter, reflecting the genius, the love and spirit of man—the flames of life itself.

She reflected those Frenchmen—those almighty gods with hearts, minds and souls—whose ingenuity breathed the essence of life into her—those staff officers and officials, naval architects and craftsmen who during the process of her conception, development, and construction evolved her into an aesthetic, fighting entity beyond being merely nuts and bolts, steel plate, weldments and intricate equipment and machinery as well as did those sailors who embarked upon and lived in her.

The French Navy, by introducing SURCOUF, had to consider the ultimate good for France and her colonial empire in defiance of the English and the Royal Navy. With more submarine cruisers such as SURCOUF, Britannica would no longer rule the waves.

SURCOUF was alive with a nervous system alert to the sensations of the sea, to the pulse of the souls on board her, and to her power and reflex to destroy. And, SURCOUF, also, represented the symbolic soul of Free France—the spirit of French resistance against Hitler and Nazism—for only the soul possesses true freedom. By resisting tyranny, through her blood covenant with the Royal Navy and de Gaulle's Free French movement, she would die to save *La Belle France*.

SURCOUF, endowed with a personality, did react temperamentally as an enfant terrible and as if she had a life, mind, and will of her own. The Japanese go so far as to believe that the soul of a ship survives her death as with human beings living on after death. Even after her death, there are mumblings and rumors about SURCOUF, even as these lines are written, as if she were alive.

Captaine de Vaisseau Maurice Guierre, French Navy, Retired (l'Ecole Navale, Brest, Class of 1924), in his memorable book, *L'Epopee de Surcouf et le Commandant Louis Blaison*, expressed it best, as only a Frenchman can:

> Not every sailor believes his ship has a soul, however superstitious. Yet, it is one widely held among cultured sailors. For those who have seen a ship grow piece-by-piece, who have taken the whole to sea in storm, and with their ship have faced the perils of war, struggled and gathered laurels with it, for them there comes from deep within her a low resonance, which are reverberations of her soul. From such a belief, sailors derive a profound attachment to their ship, like a woman.
>
> Yes, Capitaine de Frigate Blaison's SURCOUF had a soul, and what a soul! He knew it well. He knew that there is soul only in Unity, and he and SURCOUF, and her officers and crew, were completely at one with each other.

This is how Vice Admiral Paul Ange Pierre "O" Ortoli, French Navy, Retired (l'Ecole Navale, Brest, Class of 1919), and the first Free French Commanding Officer of SURCOUF, nobly alluded to SURCOUF's soul, and to his comrades who died with her, during an address at the SURCOUF War Memorial, Cherbourg, France:

> SURCOUF was in the broadest sense an intelligent power animated by the devotion and solidarity of her officers and crew.

Blaison devotedly knew that SURCOUF had a soul. SURCOUF was his submarine and his destiny depended upon her. To him, she was like a lovely woman, a living thing—rare and special. This is how he prophetically expressed himself about it in his last letter to his beloved Theresa:

> Be without anxiety for me. I will be with SURCOUF on the high seas. SURCOUF has a soul, she can do nothing more than she has done. If we die less than honorably our souls will never find peace.

Weird isn't it about Blaison remarks? It seems as if Blaison knew his moment of destiny—his rendezvous with Death—was close at hand—as if it were something that had been preordained long ago through a mystical conjunction of his life with SURCOUF's. He and SURCOUF would never be separated and that he would remain "on the high seas" with her forever!!! And, that is the way it happened!!! Both died honorably so that they could rest in peace and be deserving of God's Will. Yes, SURCOUF had a soul!!!

Therefore, as you continue to read SURCOUF's story think of her as a monstrous serpent of the sea exuding Death—a beauty, a single eternity, with a soul for which her human complement was merely on board to guide and to fight her. To mention SURCOUF is synonymous with mentioning Blaison, as if they had a human connection, for since time immemorial the commander and his warship have been considered as ONE.

Like it or not, SURCOUF is an intricate part of the history of the Royal Navy, the oldest navy in the world, which can never be erased—just as Joan of Arc is forever woven into England's colorful past. If the powerful choose to forget something in the past, or change it, they can. However, you can't argue with evidence. History is like faith; it is dependent upon what you believe. However, unlike faith, the body of evidence positively supports the thesis that Baron Robert Surcouf and the submarine SURCOUF are indelibly embedded in the history of England and the Royal Navy.

Outstanding examples of how officialdom desired to forget about SURCOUF, because of her amazing affinity for alienating her allies, will be appreciated when a Canadian defense official, fifteen years after SURCOUF's pathetic loss, remarked: "There still maybe a distinct reluctance to talk about SURCOUF." And why a Royal Navy admiral remarked to an American Navy admiral: "I trust this is the last we shall hear of SURCOUF."

The monthly patrol reports of SURCOUF's wartime activities and whereabouts supported by the Royal Navy's arrival and departure reports and sailing orders concerning SURCOUF; the reports of the British Naval Liaison Officer (BNLO) aboard SURCOUF, to his superior, Flag Officer, Submarines, Northway's, England; and reports about SURCOUF by Commander-in-Chief, America and West Indies and to the British Admiralty, provided the most conclusive information about SURCOUF during the war.

These documents about SURCOUF were not available from the archives of Bermuda, Canada, England, and France, or even United States, until about 1975 for reason of maintaining confidentiality of some World War II events for at least 25 to 30 years after the occurrence. Some World War II records were cloistered for as long as 90 years by France and some may never surface even during following generations.

This official block on information about SURCOUF could have forestalled my making many new findings about SURCOUF, but not so. World-wide advertising in diplomatic, military and naval oriented publications by the author brought many interesting and extraordinary responses about SURCOUF from private individuals, some being first-hand accounts.

From these numerous and varied reports, it was possible to set adrift many misconceptions about SURCOUF; to dispel the many foul rumors about her wartime activities; to conclusively and technologically prove that SURCOUF was indeed sunk by collision with the SS THOMPSON LYKES; and to establish SURCOUF's loss in the *Guinness Book of World Records* as the worst submarine disaster in history.

A culmination of my expensive and exhaustive research, and lengthy devotion of effort and time, resulted in the production of seven manuscripts about SURCOUF. They are:

SURCOUF AND THE ROYAL NAVY
SURCOUF IN THE BERMUDA TRIANGLE
SURCOUF AND THE ALIEN MIND
SURCOUF AND THE LONDON NAVAL
    CONFERENCE OF 1930
THE SURCOUF DOSSIER OF RUMORS
THE SURCOUF AFFRAY OF JULY 3, 1940
THE SURCOUF CONSPIRACY

At least 14 other such scenarios about SURCOUF's epic-making, but tumultuous life could be written. What is revealed throughout THE SURCOUF CONSPIRACY is a composite extract from each of the above works.

As an aside: On August 26, 2010, there appeared on one of television's history channels a documentary about the ten foremost submarines in their history. I was anxiously awaiting to see the commentary about SURCOUF—BUT SHE WAS NOT INCLUDED. This was puzzling, but the reason why appeared in the credits of the documentary as it was produced in England!!! Obviously, it seems, that, even today, the less told about SURCOUF, especially by the English, even truth, the better!!!

Regardless, SURCOUF had more than earned her niche in the annals of pre-war and World War II naval history, but she still has been little recognized and appreciated for significant involvements in her life—especially during World War II—and for her unique differences from other submarines. For examples:

The misconception that SURCOUF sank with her seaplane is wrong.

Her observation seaplane, a Besson (MB 411-AFN-Mureaux), damaged during the German fire bombings upon Plymouth, England, between April 21-27, 1941, was left at Vice Admiral Lord Louis

Mountbatten's Command Base, Devonport Dockyard, for repairs when SURCOUF sailed to Bermuda without it on May 14, 1941.

SURCOUF's seaplane was eventually repaired, but was lost while on board the auxiliary cruiser HMS FIDELITY, which was enroute to Singapore as a part of Convoy ONS 154. During the convoy, FIDELITY was viciously torpedoed and sunk by U-435 on the night of Dec 30-31, 1942.

Another misconception was that SURCOUF had on board the gold of the Bank of France, valued at $2,883,000,000, when she was sunk.

If there was any evidence to support this claim, SURCOUF's gold would have been salvaged long, long ago.

Moreover, according to Clarence Mahoney in *Evil Eye*, gold has the ability to deflect the beams of the powerful evil eye. If SURCOUF, indeed, had that gold aboard she may have avoided disaster from the influence of a third eye.

Immediately upon France's surrender to Germany, on June 29, 1940, the Caribbean island of Martinique and the St. Pierre and Miquelon Islands in the North Atlantic, fell under the dictatorial rule of Vichy France, as did France's colonies along the coast of North Africa. *(France, France what have you done? Nöel Coward in his play Private Lives.)*

Various historical references confirm that before the Fall of France between 250 to 400 tons of gold, previously held by the Bank of France, was transported to Martinique by the French cruiser EMILE BERTIN for safekeeping at Fort Desaix.

That gold became a lure for seizure by the Churchill and Roosevelt governments, and especially before it could be secured by General Charles André Joseph Marie de Gaulle, the symbol of French Resistance to Hitler's existence, and his Free French naval force—using the presence of the powerful SURCOUF.

From what we learn from by H. Montgomery Hyde's work, *Room 3603, The Story of the British Intelligence Center in New York during World War II,* de Gaulle would have had good reason to seize Martinique and that gold as it would have given him enormous economic and political power over the Churchill government, which was financially weak and was only able to survive the war through the grace of God and the American Lend Lease Act of March 1941. Moreover, with that gold, de Gaulle and the Free French cause would have gained imperishable prestige throughout the Allied world. *Every door can be opened with a key of gold!*

In the author's opinion, it would well within the realm of probability that if SURCOUF made a run for Martinique she would be destroyed!!! Even if she was suspected of doing so!!!

According to many references concerning World War II, like *The Last Hero, The Biography and Political Experience of Major General William J. Donovan, founder of the OSS and "father" of the CIA,* by Anthony Cave Brown, while Churchill and Roosevelt had a binding and lasting friendship, neither admired or trusted de Gaulle, whom Roosevelt regarded him as a deluded leader who fancied himself as woven in the same fabric as Napoleon and Joan of Arc. Moreover, both conspired to preclude de Gaulle from learning the utmost inner secrets about how to win the war in Europe because his Free French movement was riddled with Communists and Nazi infiltrators. Particularly, according to David Irving, in *The War between the Generals,* Roosevelt considered de Gaulle as a grim and relentless power seeker.

Nor, did any of the Allied governments want Vichy France to continue to control that gold. Churchill became so concerned about the gold on Martinique that on May 16, 1941, he made the following inquiry about Martinique to General Hastings *Pug* Ismay, his Chief of Staff and Minister of Defense:

> What is the situation at Martinique? Are the 50 million pounds [English currency] still there? What French forces are there? I have it in mind that the United States might take over Martinique to safeguard it from being used as a base for U-boats in view of Vichy occupation of the island.

Seizure of Martinique by the Americans, British, or Free French, would have further infuriated the leaders of Vichy France, as they were not pacified after General de Gaulle and Vice Admiral Muselier, using the intimidating presence of SURCOUF, had unilaterally liberated the St Pierre and Miquelon Islands from Vichy, on December 24, 1941, in violation of the Havana Convention of 1940 and the Monroe Doctrine.

Further antagonizing of certain diplomatic, military, naval, and political leaders within the Vichy Government who were partially sympathetic with the Allies, but not with de Gaulle, particularly those based in Vichy North Africa, could have caused them to withdraw their support during Operation TORCH, the proposed Anglo-American invasion of Vichy North Africa, on November 8, 1942.

Without a firm hold on North Africa, the Allies would have found it extremely difficult to defeat Rommel's Afrika Corps in that region and to use it as a platform to invade Sicily, southern France, and Italy. Thus, the course of the European theater of war, at that moment, seemed hinged on the availability of General de Gaulle's super powerful submarine, SURCOUF.

Therefore, the mutual concern of Churchill and Roosevelt regarding Martinique was to keep de Gaulle from liberating the Martinique from Vichy control, which de Gaulle could easily accomplish, as he did the St Pierre and Miquelon Islands, in the name of Free France, using SURCOUF, which became familiar to the Martinique populace during her port call in 1939.

So long as de Gaulle and SURCOUF were alive, as ONE, the populace of Martinique and that gold could have been liberated from Vichy control. However, without SURCOUF and the threat of her twin 8-inch guns, de Gaulle was powerless to seize Martinique.

Thus, the profound concern by either the Churchill or Roosevelt governments that de Gaulle would use SURCOUF to liberate Martinique and seize its gold would have provided justification for eliminating SURCOUF. Alternatively, serving the greater GOOD by sacrificing a friend to kill to save the lives of thousands.

Churchill and Roosevelt, world leaders determined to win World War II, could have made a decision to sacrifice every soul aboard SURCOUF to save tens of thousands fighting to liberate Europe from the grip of Nazi Germany. According to *Roosevelt's Secret War, FDR and*

World War II Espionage, Churchill and Roosevelt made such a decision to protect ULTRA which decrypting method broke the output of Germany's Enigma coding machines. Churchill and Roosevelt so "zealously guarded the secret that they concealed an American blunder that cost hundreds of American lives rather than reveal that the tragedy was discovered through a decoded German message."

Previously, Churchill had made another such decision when he launched Operation GRASP to seize SURCOUF from serving defeatist Frenchmen who had surrendered France to Nazi Germany. The outcome was the deaths of three of the Royal Navy. In addition, Churchill's same decision concurrently launched Operation CATAPULT during which the Royal Navy attacked Mers el Kébir, North Africa, and destroyed much of the French fleet, killing 1,297; when England and France were not at war. According to Lynne Olsen's *Troublesome Young Men,* Churchill's determination to destroy parts of the French fleet before it fell into the hands of the Germans, was ". . . one of his most traumatic decisions of the entire war."

(As an aside, according to *A Man Called Intrepid, The Authentic Account of the Most Significant Secret Diplomacy and Decisive Intelligence Operations of World War II,* by William Stevenson, the event that led up to launching Operations CATAPULT and GRASP occurred immediately after Churchill pleaded fruitlessly with Marshal Henri Philippe Pétain, the prospective leader of France's future wartime Vichy government, while under Nazi control, regarding the disposition of France's powerful naval fleet. It happened, in essence, as follows:

> Intrepid [William S. Stephenson] was present when he heard Churchill imploring Marshal Pétain not to hand over the French fleet to the Germans. It was the most violent conversation Churchill ever conducted.
>
> Subsequently, Churchill remarked to Intrepid, "We are faced with total French collapse. The total collapse of our civilization as we know it is inevitable unless we put up a successful defense of our islands, and the Vichy French can destroy us all by encouraging the peace advocates.")

Thus, it is reasonable that some French, who were partial to the Free French cause, emphatically insist that the British, through Intrepid, had SURCOUF "murdered" to keep her mere presence rally the Vichy dominated populace of Martinique to de Gaulle's Free French Movement as occurred when SURCOUF was used to the liberate the St. Pierre and Miquelon Islands in the North Atlantic. A further reading of *A Man Called Intrepid*, in conjunction with what more follows, provided the further creditability to their accusation, especially by Blaison's women-folk:

> Sir William S. Stephenson [Intrepid], with the help of his agents on Martinique, had devised plans to seize the island and that gold, some of which he could use to finance anti-Nazi resistance forces across Europe.
>
> Moreover, it was highly suspected that German U-boats were lurking offshore of Martinique as within one month twenty British merchant ships had been sunk in its vicinity. If Germans took over Martinique completely, the gold awaiting them could finance Nazi operations and purchase strategic war materials from South America.

Since the liberation of Martinique and that gold by de Gaulle, using SURCOUF, provided a strong incentive for eliminating her, recall the above commentary while reading about rumors about American and Royal Navy warships shadowing SURCOUF upon her departure from Bermuda and while she is in the Caribbean Sea during February 1942.

As another aside, but one having an extremely close connection with a probable conspiracy to eliminate poor SURCOUF, there was told in *The War Between the Generals, The Behind the Scenes Battle between the Allied Generals who were Supposed to be Fighting the Germans*, by Irving, there was a conspiracy to eliminate de Gaulle:

In May 1943, when American official censors eavesdropped on Churchill's secret conversations with Anthony Eden, his Foreign Minister, about the latest intolerable deeds of Brigadier General de Gaulle. who was Muselier's junior by two stars and who Churchill contemptuously referred to as the cross [likened to an albatross] that he had to bear, it reassured the U. S. State Department eavesdroppers to hear the British Prime Minister exclaim in angry, upset tones, "He owes everything to us," and to urge Eden, "You must strike now. We cannot allow our affairs to be compromised." This is how David Irving reported that attempt:

> General de Gaulle was to fly from London to Glasgow to decorate sailors of the Free French Navy. His personal aircraft was a Wellington Mark 1A bomber placed at his disposal and maintained by the Royal Air Force.
>
> In taking off from Hendon Airfield, the pilot Flight Lieutenant Peter Loat, DFC, Royal Air Force, was required to abort the flight. Upon inspection the elevator control rod was found to have been cut through with acid.
>
> De Gaulle, did not have confidence in the "German sabotage" explanation and he never flew by airplane in England again.

Thereafter, de Gaulle was distrustful of the British, as according to Rolf Hochhuth, in *Soldiers,* "de Gaulle wouldn't go anywhere without French pilots." In November 1943, perhaps fearful of further attempts on his life by the British, de Gaulle transferred his Free French headquarters from London to Algiers, North Africa.

SURCOUF was the only Allied submarine on which it was not choice duty for the British Naval Liaison Officer and his staff.

Two BNLO's, Lieutenant Patrick Maule Kerr Griffiths, Royal Navy, and Sub-Lieutenant Roger John Gilbert "Rog" Volunteer, Royal Navy Reserve, died along her decks. Another Lieutenant Paul Fisher (not his real name), Royal Navy Volunteer Reserve, was threatened to be shot by Captaine de Frégaté Paul Ange Pierre "O" Ortoli, Free French Navy, if he again boarded SURCOUF.

And, Lieutenant Frank Louis Boyer, Royal Navy Reserve, was detached from SURCOUF because he expressed doubts that he and the two Royal Navy ratings on his staff, Leading Telegraphist Bernard

"Tattoo" Gough, Royal Fleet Reserve, and Leading Signalman Harold Frank "Plum" Warner, Royal Fleet Reserve, would die if they remained aboard SURCOUF.

Boyer who remarked that aboard SURCOUF he slept with a pistol near-by and confided his dilemma to Vice Admiral Wilfred Franklin "Pooh" French, Royal Navy and Flag Officer, British Admiralty Repair Mission, Washington. However, French reportedly chastised Boyer and had him unceremoniously detached from SURCOUF. Boyer survived the war, and remembered SURCOUF "with honor" but was "troubled with nightmares about her that were almost impossible to live with." (War converts ordinary men into something completely foreign to their natures.)

Boyer's relief was Sub-Lieutenant Roger John Gilbert "Rog" Burney, RNVR. Here is Boyer's extraordinary account of his discordant meetings with Burney, in late October and early November 1941, upon occasion of Boyer being relieved by Burney aboard SURCOUF at the U.S. Naval Shipyard, Portsmouth, New Hampshire. And, in the Boyer's telling we learn something about Burney, to compare with further remarks to be told about him, and we included an expression of regret by Boyer, even though his meeting with Burney took place over forty years ago, because he and Burney were obviously not on the same wavelength personality-wise:

> I was personally advised about my relief by signal from flag Officer, Submarines, Northways. This, I recall, was sent thru Washington, but my return passage was arranged by Northways.
>
> I wish I had known Burney better. For the few days that we met I tried to get through to him, without reducing him to a pulp of terror, as regards the situation he faced, and, indeed trying to be fair to all. Worse luck, we did like each other, and I had no feeling for him, except pity. He seemed little inclined to listen to me and was merely biding his time until the customary procedures of turnover were completed between

us. He appeared to view my remarks with skepticism, verging on contempt, both for me personally and for my remarks.

When he relieved me on SURCOUF he was very enthusiastic and expressed a great affection for France as a nation and for the French individually. But, he seemed hostile towards them and very unwilling to accept any of the opinions and facts which I tried to pass to him. This reduced his receptivity to me more than I would have liked under the circumstances. However, he was made well aware of my basic thoughts about the reliability of SURCOUF and also, of course, of all the information which I had reported to Sir Max Horton, and to Admiral French.

At any rate, from what you have told me (he was referring to the author), it is apparent that Burney converted to my views very quickly in the game.

Obviously, Boyer and Burney were not in harmony with each other, but as you shall read, Burney would quickly change his tune, learning that it was no "game" of cricket aboard SURCOUF. Too soon Burney would become the "pulp of terror".

Boyer continued his remarks, giving us a further brief background sketch about Burney and of his intention to retain Gough and Warner aboard SURCOUF:

Burney, I think was younger than me. He was not so experienced, but perhaps more worldly wise. At the time, I was not too enthralled with his idea to recall to certain death my two men, Gough and Warner, as I was fond of them and had arranged for them to have a chance for life, regardless of myself. This I think is the sin of pride. I have no idea of where Burney came from or his family, we just didn't seem to have time or want to talk about that.

This I can tell you more about Burney: He arrived in the States from HMS AMBROSE, Dundee, where he served with the Ninth Submarine Flotilla. This base was used by new

British submarines doing their first combat patrols usually off the Dutch and Norwegian coasts.

I cannot recall if he had been to Submarine School, but have the idea that he was a product of the Reserve Officer Training Establishment, HMS KING ALFRED, Brighton.

I left SURCOUF, bag and baggage, at Portsmouth just after she sailed from there for the U.S. Naval Submarine Base, New London, Connecticut. Of course, I boarded her again in New London, but Burney seemed indifferent to my presence so I left him be.

Regrettably, nothing was found to exist in the correspondence of Gough or Warner about their impressions of Burney. Regardless, for his indifference and sad innocence, Burney would pay the price of death. But, Boyer received appreciation for his services aboard SURCOUF from an unexpected quarter before departing; from the Free Frenchman Blaison. Here is what Blaison wrote in a letter to Boyer on November 3, 1941:

S/Marin Surcouf
le 3 Nov 1941

Le lieutenant F.L. Boyer a ete embarque, a titre d'officer de liaison, abord du Sousmarin "Surcouf" du 18 Avril au 3 Noviembre.

Pendant son sejour a bord, cet officier, devoue, actif et coutois, ayant des connaissances approfondies de la langue Francasise, nous a rendu les plus grands services.

Je n'ai pas eu l'occasion de l' apprecier comme officier de quart, mais dans les quelques heures difficiles que nous avons connu, il a toujours montre le plus grand calme.

/s/Le Capitaine de Fregate L. Blaison

So unlike Burney, Griffiths and Sprague, Boyer left SURCOUF without having passed into Death's domain. But, at the time, career-wise Boyer was as good as dead.

A February 13, 1980 letter from the Office of the Commander-in-Chief, naval Home Command, Portsmouth, England, signed by Commander R.R.C. Rawlinson-Cadogan, Royal Navy, gave this tidbit of biographical information about Burney, which proved sufficient for Stan Warner to track-down, in another great, but eerie, piece of detective work peculiar *The SURCOUF Conspiracy*, Burney's place of residence in England:

> Further to my letter of 4 February, I am writing to inform you that we have now received Sub Lieutenant Burney's documents from our archive section.
>
> His full name was Roger John Gilbert Burney and he was born 25 March 1919. He appears to have joined the RNVR as a rating (the date is not recorded), and he was promoted Temporary Sub lieutenant on 7 August 1941. After courses at HMS KING ALFRED (a shore barracks near Brighton, near Sussex) and HMS ELFIN (the submarine depot, Blyth, Northumberland) he joined the SURCOUF on 10 September 1941.
>
> We know he was educated at Wellington College in Berkshire, and also at Peterhouse College, Cambridge. We do not know where he lived prior to the war, but his records show his next of kin as his mother, a Mrs. W.E. Young. We have no address for her other than "Oakfield, Hay on Wye, Herefordshire."

Provided with this sparse information, Stan and Mavis Warner were able to find, in strange ways, the whereabouts of Burney's family home in a quiet English village, where only roses grow, to learn that he had not been completely forgotten by his townspeople. Here is what the Warner's had to say in their August 7, 1980 letter:

Coincidentally, my daughter lives only a few miles from Herefordshire, near Wye village. We thoroughly explored the area looking for Oakfield. We found several similar names, but not the one we were seeking. We also scoured the telephone directories, and found one Burney, but not connected. Finally, we came upon a town Hay-on-Wye, and that is where we concentrated our effort. We had decided to rent a house in July to be near our daughter, and whilst there to go around again seeking Burney. You can imagine how spine tingling it was to us, while looking for a rental, when we found a war memorial in Hay-on-Wye and the first name on the Roll of Honor was Sub Lieutenant Roger John Gilbert Burney, Royal Navy Volunteer Reserve.

We found an elderly local to try to gain more information, but she referred us to a home for the aged, a little way from Wye. We proceeded, finding a Mr. Stokoe, who had been a one-time local news reporter. He was over 80 years of age, and at first he could not recollect the name or any history. Then he said, yes, he did recall a family living nearby. Then coincidence again, he pointed to a large country house, about 800 feet away, standing in its own large parkland (estate), it was Oakfield where Burney had lived as a boy.

What would the reaction of Burney's friends and townspeople have been had they known that he had died in the world's worst submarine disaster with SURCOUF; a submarine which he believed to be a traitorous??? Or, had they known that he was the only Royal Navy submarine officer, and a volunteer reservist at that, to have had his name on two "Rolls of Honor" on two memorials to World War II dead in two different lands; England and France??? Or that a war requiem had been dedicated to him, along with three other wars dead???

Or, had they known that Burney had been the second British Naval Liaison Officer, along with two Royal navy ratings, to be lost, in addition to a boarding officer (Commander Sprague) and a rating (Webb) being mortally wounded and a rating (Heath) maimed for life, as a result of serving his Majesty's Service aboard the Free French Navy submarine SURCOUF??? Or, had they known that Burney was suspected, by some Americans and Canadians, of having written a letter to America Navy authorities inviting death upon himself and those aboard SURCOUF???

Or, had they known that Burney was the younger brother of Major Christopher Burney, British Army, who during the war had earned a reputation throughout the British Secret Service and amongst the Germans occupying France, for being "the King of saboteurs", and who had spent nearly three years in a Nazi prison in Paris and at Buchenwald after being betrayed to the German Gestapo by a communist member of the French Resistance.!!!

With this in-depth presentation about "Rog" Burney, made possible through his sister "Jo", coupled with Boyer's remarks and those by Mrs. Doris Le Blanc and Mr. Paul G. Rowlings, which are about to follow, we are privileged to have gained a penetrating, profound insight into Roger John Gilbert Burney's fortunate life style: who he knew; how they may have influenced his life; his sense of free thinking, the broadness and depth of his intellectual literary and musical interests; his sense of values and the dynamics of his mind and quality of his inner—most thoughts.

We learn also that his material and spiritual needs were for more knowledge, books, more music, more poetry, more poetry, to seemingly help him to better appreciate and understand the core of human behavior. We have come to "really" know, therefore, with more than reasonable assurance, about that sensitive young man who possessed an uncanny ability to see though to the heart of the matter, a problem, a person, a talent; a knowledge far beyond that of his educated contemporaries.

In this light, then, we can better appreciate how the boyish Burney, with persistent, almost feminine intuition, came to write his devastating, but true British naval Officer liaison reports, which seemed far beyond liaison, unlocking mysterious doors previously closed to everyday inquiry about SURCOUF and Blaison, to the "ferocious" Max Horton; those reports which told of strange betrayals and acts aboard SURCOUF, which caused the "Great Max" to retract his words about the vulnerability of SURCOUF to impending disaster and which caused the British Admiralty and Foreign Office to cover-up about her loss.

Burney's reports, revealing his horrible responsibilities, proved not to be overwrought with imagination, even though his mind seemed to have been twisted by fear and by an intense desire for survival. Yet, fear, according to "Jo" was something that was alien to Rog's rather unflappable character. At stake was Burney's integrity and the honor of the Royal Navy; the greatest fighting navy in the world. But, because of Burney's junior rank and inexperience's his remarks were at first disbelieved. This coupled with the slowness of response to his reports to Horton, and with the latter's wartime problems and preoccupations of the day; disaster was allowed to overtake poor SURCOUF.

Burney, within 60 days after his joining SURCOUF, expressed his farewell, at dockside Halifax, to a Royal Canadian Navy officer with these fatalistic words: **"You are shaking the hand of a dead man, if I sail with SURCOUF."** Burney soon died with SURCOUF, as he expected, along with Gough and Warner, during her fatal encounter with the SS THOMPSON LYKES.

Here follows documentation of this weird tete e tete:

December 31, 1980

Dear Captain Grigore,

In reply to you inquiry, I am writing to tell you that I had a friend on SURCOUF. He was the British Naval Liaison Officer aboard SURCOUF, 'Rog" Burney.

I went down to SURCOUF with him prior to SURCOUF's departure from Halifax. And, it was rather weird—he always appeared to be a light hearted, happy-go-lucky person. But, on the jetty, when Roger was saying goodbye, he broke down and said he had been trying to get off SURCOUF for some time, and **that I was shaking hands with a dead man!**

He gave me the address of his mother in England, and when I heard the rumors, which was one of the best secrets of the war, I wrote to her but never received a reply.

Sincerely yours,
Paul G. Rowlings,
Lieutenant, RCN, Retired

It seems as if Burney had a forewarning, from whatever source, that he was destined to die with SURCOUF. What did Burney know, that Blaison did not know???

From an April 21, 1980 letter from another "woman of the war", Mrs. Doris Le Blanc, then of Joggins, Nova Scotia, the author received conclusive evidence that young Burney, after spending approximately seventy days aboard SURCOUF, from November 1, 1941 to January 15, 1942 and while at Halifax, following her involvement in the St. Pierre and Miquelon Affair, "feared for his life."!!! And, that it was his impression that SURCOUF would made a dash for Martinique—the latter of which he would communicate to senior officials in Canada and England, via his liaison reports to Commander, Submarines, Northways, London. Here is what Mrs. Le Blanc told me:

> I was secretary in the Office of staff Intelligence (Royal Canadian Navy) in Halifax during World War II, and met the British Naval Liaison Officer who served on SURCOUF. His name was Roger. I cannot recall his surname. He sat beside me and dictated a report the Admiralty. No carbon copy was made.
>
> Since I was pledged to secrecy under the Official Secrets Act, I am not able to divulge anything I typed in that report. To be truthful, I really cannot remember the details. However, I will say that this young man feared for his life on that submarine. **He slept with a revolver under his pillow at night.** In his report, he requested transfer off SURCOUF when it reached

Bermuda for supplies on its way (he thought) to Martinique. So far as I could ascertain, his request was not granted and he perished with SURCOUF.

So there you have it!!! Where did Burney get the idea that SURCOUF might make a run for Martinique? When he communicated such a thought to his seniors, was Burney then told, that if SURCOUF made a dash for Martinique and that gold she would be killed, and that he, Gough, and Warner, would have to be scarified if that eventuality occurred??? Is this why he told Mrs. Le Blanc that he **"feared for his life"** or when he told Rowlings that he was **"shaking hands with a dead man."**???

Years later, the author, in response to his advertisement in the *Canadian Legion Magazine,* received confirmation of Mrs. Le Blanc's remarks about Burney in the strangest way. Here is what Walter Kingston, who had served in the Royal Canadian Navy during World War II, wrote me:

I first heard of the sinking of the SURCOUF while in the Royal Canadian Navy, which I joined in 1941. The men who related her sinking to me were certain that it occurred near the St. Pierre and Miquelon Islands.

During the Christmas season of 1986, while on a flight from St. John, New Brunswick to Toronto, Canada, I met a lady from Halifax on the plane. She stated to me that she had been the private secretary to the officer commanding the naval base at Halifax. She claimed that she had taken a signal to this officer telling of the loss of SURCOUF in the Halifax area. She also told me that three British naval personnel were aboard and that they had feared for their lives, and had made a strong request to be detached from SURCOUF. Because of the difficulty of getting experienced men in Halifax this could not be done, and the sub sailed with them aboard.

/s/ Walter Kingston, Chief, Canadian Navy, 1941-45.

In the author's opinion. if Burney, Gough, or Warner had been detached from Halifax or Bermuda, it could have foretold Vichyists that the British knew that SURCOUF might make a dash for Martinique, thus its super-secret security network could have been breached.

Burney, Gough, and Warner, therefore, were to be made expendable pawns to preclude revealing that the British Admiralty and Churchill's Foreign Office were privy to very secret information about General de Gaulle and his intentions. In other words, Burney, Gough, and Warner were ransomed for the price they would have had to pay with their lives, to preclude leaking that the Free French and Vichy French codes were probably broken and that SURCOUF may be ordered to liberate Martinique from Vichy control and to also seize the French gold for de Gaulle using the threat of her powerful twin 8" guns and presence to intimidate and subdue resistance on the island. *(Because there is great wrath, beware lest he take thee away with his stroke: then a great ransom cannot deliver thee. Job 36:18 KJV)*

If true, it was a case of doing what they were told, i.e., die because that is what we are telling you to do to keep our secret. The secret service world, often indulgent of its own, can be vicious and deadly to those they use. If true, there are few situations in naval history rivaling Burney's, Gough's, and Warner's agonizing and hopeless dilemma—at least none known by the author. During the cruel reality of war, the rules of cricket and innocence don't apply. Some lives must be deliberately expended to save those of a greater number.

Burney, Gough, and Warner were high enough to have that knowledge, but not high enough to avoid being sacrificed.

Knowing what they did, what holy terror Burney, Gough, and Warner must have suffered, alone on the friendless SURCOUF???

Intrepid, once he learned of Burney's report that SURCOUF might make a dash for Martinique, would have been justified suggesting to Churchill that they be rid of SURCOUF forever.

It is certain that SURCOUF would have been "done-in" by the guns of either the American or Royal Navy to physically preclude her from reaching Martinique waters. As will be told, warships of both Navy's were rumored to have shadowed SURCOUF following her departure from Bermuda, and one, the HMS DIOMEDE, was rumored to have actually killed her.

(As an applicable aside: *A Man Called Intrepid* reveals how Intrepid, using the resources of an alluring *femme fatale* with the *nom de guerre* of Cynthia, obtained the Vichy naval codes by an *affaire d'amour* with a French Navy capitaine who was the naval attaché and press officer assigned to the Vichy embassy in Washington. More about their romantic interlude appears subsequently.)

SURCOUF was the first submarine to cross the Atlantic from West to East during World War II.

In fact, SURCOUF crossed the Atlantic four times during her brief 29-month wartime career: Sep-Oct 1939, Jan 1941, Feb-Mar 1941, and May 1941. She made more crossings of the Atlantic than any other Allied or Axis submarine during World War II.

SURCOUF, at the start of World War II, was the deepest diving submarine of any navy.

According to *Our Navy*, Mid-December 1931 issue, the American Navy submarine USS NAUTILUS (V-5), had set the world's record for deep diving at 336 feet, 4 feet deeper than her sister submarine USS ARGONAUT (V-6). In reality, when commissioned in 1930, SURCOUF had already established a deep diving record of 420 feet; a feat unknown by the Allied navies.

The naval world also thought that SURCOUF only mounted two 5.5-inch guns, whereas she was secretly designed and built to accommodate twin 8-inch guns.

SURCOUF's actual firepower was revealed during the London Naval Conference of 1930 by the Italian delegate, Signor Dino Grandi.

SURCOUF was the largest, most powerful submarine to serve during World War II until the introduction of the super-colossal twin-hulled, long range, I-400 class submarine of the Imperial Japanese Navy, during March 1945. The I-400 carried 3 torpedo bombers and was meant to attack the Panama Canal, New York City, and Washington, D. C., lay mines off harbor mouths, and wreak havoc with Allied shipping:

According to *I-Boat Captain, How Japan's Submarines Almost Defeated the American Navy in the Pacific,* by Captain Zenji Orita and Joseph D. Harrington, I-400 and 401, under the over-all command of Captain Tatsunoke Ariizumi, IJN, were enroute to attempt to destroy the Miraflores Locks of the Panama Canal with aerial torpedoes. The locks were to be attacked by the "Aichi M-6A1 *Serian* seaplane bombers catapulted off I-400 and I-401. The special "Kamikaze" mission was aborted when the military and naval forces of the Japanese Empire surrendered to the Allies on August 16, 1945.

SURCOUF was not the only submarine to carry a seaplane during World War II.

The Japanese applied the concept of the submarine aircraft carriers extensively during World War II. Altogether, 42 of its submarine fleet were built with the capability to carry floatplanes. Of the 35 Japanese submarines which formed a steel ring around Pearl Harbor on Dec 7, 1941, the day of Japan's shattering surprise attack upon that naval base, 11 were seaplane carriers. Similar attacks on the United States and Canada were later made by three other Japanese submarine seaplane carriers:

I-26 torpedoed a Canadian lumber ship off Cape Flattery on June 18, 1942, and then shelled the Naval Wireless and Navigation Station on Estevan Point, Vancouver Island, on the 20th.

I-25 fired twenty shells at the naval facility at Astoria, Oregon on Aug 28-29, 1942; three days earlier she had shelled Port Stevens, Oregon; and then her Yokosuka E-14Y1 *Glen* seaplane fire bombed Oregon's forest belt, nearby Brookings, Oregon, by dropping four 167 (76 kg) incendiaries into that area.

The *Glen* seaplane aboard I-25 was piloted by Warrant Officer Nobuo Fujita, Imperial Japanese Navy. Up to September 30, 1997, he remained the only person to have bombed the continental United States.

As an aside: According to *Wikipedia,* Fujita was invited to Brookings in 1962, after the Japanese government was assured he would not be tried as a war criminal. He gave the City of Brookings his family's 400-year-old samurai sword in friendship. Ashamed of his actions during the war, Fujita had intended to use the sword to commit seppuku if he was given a hostile reception. However the town treated him with respect and affection, although his visit raised some controversy.

Impressed by his welcome in the United States, Fujita invited three female students from Brookings to Japan in 1985. During their visit Fujita received a dedicatory letter from an aide of President Ronald Reagan "with admiration for your kindness and generosity."

On July 21, 1942, I-7 sank the U.S. Army Transport ARCATA by gunfire in Unimak Pass.

On Sep 16, 1942, I-25 sank SS COMMERCIAL TRADER, 2,600 tons, about forty miles off British Colombia.

On Sep 29, the seaplane from I-25 again bombed the Oregon forest belt and escaped.

On Oct 5, 1942, I-25 sank the 7,000 ton tanker SS LARRY DOHEMY between Seattle and San Francisco, and the next day damaged the tanker SS CAMDEN, 6,000 tons.

As a further aside, it was I-26 that, on Aug 31, 1942, torpedoed and seriously disabled the American aircraft carrier USS SARATOGA following the Battle of the Eastern Solomon's. And it was I-26 which sank the American heavy cruiser JUNEAU during the Battle of Guadalcanal on Nov 13, 1942.

Yet, a senior American naval submarine officer, who had commanded submarine forces during the latter phase of the Japanese-American War of the Pacific, considered Japanese Navy submarine seaplane carriers to be "ineffectual." But evidence is very strong, according to Captain Zenji Orita, JMSDF, and Joseph D. Harrington, in *I-Boat Captain,* that Japanese submarine seaplane carriers were quite effective against the Allied navies before the introduction of radar.

During August 1976, my research in Japan, which included an interview with Rear Admiral Orita, revealed that the Imperial Japanese Navy began to secretly build its first submarine aircraft carrier, the I-5, on January 15, 1930, within two years after the launching of SURCOUF, and one month before the appearance of then Captain (Later Grand Admiral and Commander-in-Chief of the Japanese Navy)

Isoruku Yamamoto, as the Senior Naval Delegate to the London Naval Conference of 1930.

It was the Japanese, British, Italian, and American veto at this naval disarmament conference that cast the death knell to France's intention to build six more SURCOUF-class submarines.

SURCOUF was the first Allied submarine to escort a convoy during World War II, and was also the first Allied submarine to see enemy action during World War II.

The SURCOUF escorted slow convoy KJ-2, from Kingston, Jamaica to the approaches of the United Kingdom, during Sep-Oct 1939. The convoy was under the control of the Royal Navy, consisting of 27 merchant and naval ships.

During the convoy, 5 British and French merchantmen were sunk by German U-boats 37, 45, and 48, among them being the 30,600 ton, 350 foot long, SS EMILE MIGUET (Captain Richard Andrade) that was sent to the bottom by U-48 (Lieutenant Herbert "Vaddie" Schutze, German Navy). EMILE MIGUET, at the time, was the largest tanker in the world, and claimed to be unsinkable.

SURCOUF was built by the French Navy in defiance of the Washington Naval Conference of 1922 as France did not want to fight the next war with weapons of the past.

With her twin 8-inch guns, SURCOUF had greater firepower than each of the Royal Navy cruisers, HMS GLASCOW and ORION, with which she served with during Convoy KJ-2. They had only 6-inch guns in accordance with American, British, Italian, and Japanese agreements made during the London Naval Conference of 1930.

SURCOUF, which had no friends at sea, was the only submarine of any war to carry twin 8-inch guns. The French Navy intended that super submarines of her class should be used primarily as commerce raiders, but her firepower was sufficient to blast a World War II type destroyer from the water with one salvo.

Had the Imperial Japanese Navy, which was fanatic about 8-inch guns, placed them on about 20 of its submarines it is possible that the American-Japanese War of the Pacific would have soon ended in their favor, or that Japanese submarines so outfitted would have been a deterrent to its beginning.

History records that the Imperial Japanese Navy, with its 8-inch heavy cruisers, severely mauled the American and Australian Navies during the First Battle Solomon Islands, off Guadalcanal, on August 9, 1942. It was the worst defeat for the American Navy since Pearl Harbor. One or two of the five Japanese heavy cruisers, employed during that devastating battle, were of the Mogami-class, which, in accordance with the terms of the London Naval Conference of 1930, were first outfitted with 6-inch guns, and then before 1941 secretly outfitted with five sets of twin 8-inch guns—as was originally intended.

SURCOUF was the only Allied submarine to regularly carry a doctor and SURCOUF's doctor was the only medical submariner to be commemorated on a plaque in North America.

It is significant to mention that the memory of SURCOUF's doctor, Lieutenant de Vaissau Rene Le Bas, Medecin de Iere Classe de la Marine, was commemorated by a plaque erected on the hospital of St Pierre in the St Pierre and Miquelon Islands following SURCOUF's role in the liberation of those islands on December 25, 1941.

For reasons that will become apparent, it would have done well for SURCOUF's officers and crew to also have had a naval chaplain aboard to conduct worship services and Scriptural studies, to console them, to hear their confessions, to dispel evil gestations and foul rumors about her, and to pray for the resurrection of their souls as she plummeted into the eternal depths of the Caribbean Sea. (*Do not be amazed as the hour is coming in which all who are in the tombs will hear his voice and will come out, those who have done good deeds to the resurrection of life, but those who have done wicked deeds to condemnation. John 5:28-29*)

SURCOUF had a greater wine tank capacity than any submarine afloat.

Unlike the American Navy, which had been dry since the abolition of wine mess in 1914, the Royal and French navies had for centuries regarded alcohol as a part of daily life.

SURCOUF was the first submarine of the war hit by air-to-surface rockets.

This attack occurred in the Irish Channel, on April 12, 1941, while SURCOUF was returning from escort duty with slow Convoy HX-118—from Halifax to the United Kingdom. It was made by a coastal patrol bomber of the Royal Air Force, which mistook SURCOUF for an intruder submarine. They were the first anti-submarine rockets fired by the Allies during the war.

SURCOUF never served in the Mediterranean Sea. Nor was she ever deployed to serve in the Battle of Greece during the German invasion of that nation.

Both claims were erroneously made in 1943 by author Raoul Agilon in his book *The Fighting French*.

SURCOUF was the only Allied submarine ordered to be dismantled and beached for use as a harbor defense gun emplacement, in a British harbor, during the war because of her having fine twin 8-inch armament.

Can you comprehend why anyone would not want a submarine cruiser as powerful as SURCOUF, with her "fine armament" of twin 8-inch guns, for deployment at sea against enemy shipping or against enemy coastal installations???

The Royal Navy's determination to dismantle SURCOUF occurred when there was extreme concern that Nazi Germany would invade England during its proposed Operation SEA LION.

Vice Admiral Henri Muselier, Minister of Marine for the Free French Navy, vigorously resisted the idea to dismantle SURCOUF, and won. And, SURCOUF would gratefully serve his turn during the St. Pierre and Miquelon Affair as you shall learn.

SURCOUF was the only Allied submarine to become politically embroiled in a serious diplomatic and political controversy at the highest levels of the British and Free French Governments involving Vice Admiral Émile Henri Muselier, Commander-in-Chief, Free French Naval Force and Merchant Marine and SURCOUF was falsely accused that she and Vice Admiral Émile Henri Muselier, Commander-in-Chief, Free French Naval Force and Merchant Marine, would to flee to Vichy controlled Dakar, Africa.

Following the surrender of France to Germany on June 25, 1940, Vice Admiral Émile-Henri Désiré Muselier arrived in London by flying boat from Gibraltar on June 30, 1940. Muselier was the only one of fifty flag officers in the French Admiralty to answer General de Gaulle's call for resistance to Axis forces during the second world war.

Thereupon, Muselier was formally designated to create and command the Free French Naval Forces (Les Forces Navales Françaises Libres) on October 27, 1940. Upon assuming command, Muselier adopted Joan d'Arc's Cross of Lorraine as the logo for the flags of the Free French Navy to distinguish ships under his command from those of Vichy French Navy.

The historical significance the Cross of Lorraine reflected the intentions of the Free French Navy to the liberate France from Nazi Germany and to eradicate Vichyism from the soil of France.

In the interim, during July 1940, Pétain's Vichy regime stripped Muselier of his rank, confiscated his possessions, forfeited his French citizenship, and sentenced him to death *in absentia.*

Relations between the Free French and the British were plagued by two successive *affaires Muselier.* First, Vice-Admiral Muselier, the commander of the Free French naval forces, was arrested by the British on January 2, 1941 on false charges of conspiring with the Vichy government. On de Gaulle's intervention he was quickly released, but the incident left its mark, demonstrating the dependence of the Free French on what amounted to little more than the whims of the British.

Free French headquarters in London seethed with turmoil between right wingers and Communists supporters of the leftist Popular Front. Each accused the other of spying for Vichy. During September 1940 and while de Gaulle's was absent from London to command the ill-fated Dakar Expedition (Operation MENACE), the rightists gained control of the Free French security system and forced Andre La Barthe, former Socialist deputy, out of the movement. The General refused to honor Muselier's request to restore La Barthe but eventually sacked the head of security, a man known as, "Howard".

Howard retaliated by having General Maurice Rozoy, Air Attaché at the French Embassy in London, and since repatriated, write a letter to the British Foreign Office stating that Muselier had tipped off Vichy to the embarkation of de Gaulle's ill-fated Dakar Expedition, and a promised that he would return the SURCOUF to a Vichy controlled port. (A reading of *Room 3603, The Center of British Intelligence in the Western Hemisphere,* by H. Montgomery Hyde, however, revealed that the leak about Operation MENACE originated in the Vichy Embassy in Washington.) **Read Part II,** *The SURCOUF and Muselier Affair,* **for the rest of this intriguing story.**

SURCOUF was the first Free French submarine to undergo a Lend-Lease overhaul in the United States.

This was between July 28-Nov 2, 1941 at the U.S. Naval Shipyard (Captain John J. Brow, USN, Annapolis, Class of 1912), Portsmouth, New Hampshire.

Unfortunately, due to the newness of the invention and to the higher priority needs of the American, British, and Canadian Navies, SURCOUF was not equipped with RADAR during her American overhaul. Had SURCOUF been so equipped the SS THOMPSON LYKES-SURCOUF collision may not have occurred.

SURCOUF was the first French submarine to train with American Navy submarines.

This was during November 3-27, 1941 at the U.S. Naval Submarine Base, New London, Connecticut.

SURCOUF was the only Allied submarine to fly the flags of three navies, and to do service with 6 navies.

Between Sep 1939 to Feb 1942 she flew three different flags:

French Navy:	Sep 39 to Jul 40
Royal Navy White Ensign:	Jul 40 to Sep 40
Free French Navy:	Sep 40 to Feb 42

Between Sep 1939 to Feb 1942 she served with the French Navy, Royal Navy, Free French Navy, Royal Canadian Navy, Royal Crown

Colony of Bermuda Navy, and died in waters controlled by the American Navy.

SURCOUF was the only known Allied submarine to have one of its crew members imprisoned at the U.S. Naval Prison, Portsmouth, during the war.

The event causing the imprisonment of the crew member was for his publically expressed anti-de Gaulle and anti-British remarks before the Belgian Club, Woonsocket, Rhode Island. For his unauthorized remarks, and for being over-leave, the crew member was confined for 60 days at Portsmouth, and subsequently detached from SURCOUF.

SURCOUF was the only Allied submarine upon which French and Royal Navy officers and enlisted men were deliberately killed aboard her during a Wardroom shoot-out.

The SURCOUF Affray of July 3, 1940 occurred during the Royal Navy's Operation GRASP, which was the seizure of French warships and merchantmen, seeking sanctuary in British ports, to keep them from capture by the German Occupation Control Commission if they returned to what had become Vichy France following Marshall Henri Philippe Petain's surrender of France to Hitler's Germany on June 22, 1940.

England had faced no greater threat to her shores since King Phillip II of Spain, in 1588, had sent the Spanish Armada, led by the Duke of Medina Sedona, to invade her during the Reign of Queen Elizabeth I.

Operation GRASP, which was the British Isles segment of the grand scale Operation CATAPULT involving the French Fleet at Alexandria, Egypt and at Mers El Kébir, North Africa, was perpetrated by Prime Minister Winston Churchill's wartime government to prevent Vichy French merchantmen and naval ships from falling into the hands of Nazi Germany to support Hitler's ruthless attempt for world domination. Had the powerful French Fleet, under the command of Admiral of the Fleet Jean Louis Xavier François Darlan and newly appointed Minister of Marine for Petain's Vichy Government, been available to Hitler then Germany could have won the Battle of the Atlantic and, indeed, the entire war.

Darlan, early during World War II, had sought revenge against the British Admiralty for the many alleged humiliating defeats and deceptions the French Navy had suffered from the hand of the Royal Navy throughout their long and turbulent history. The satisfaction of an ancient grudge could have been one of Darlan's justifications for deliberately depriving England, in June 1940, the benefit of his now Vichy French Fleet.

By contrast, England, through Prime Minister Winston Churchill's wartime government, pursued the lesser of two evils: Either let the Vichy French Fleet fall into the hands of Nazi Germany and probably lose the war before the United States was prepared to enter, or lose the immediate friendship of France. Churchill gallantly made the right choice for England, although bitterness against poor SURCOUF, for her involvement in that bloody affray, lingered for the duration of her wartime career.

With her overhaul only partially completed, SURCOUF had fled Brest, France, during the night of June 18 and before Petain's surrender, to seek haven at the Royal Navy Base, Devonport Dockyard, and Plymouth, England. Even though SURCOUF avoided capture by German panzer division closing on Brest, the French Navy officers and men were not about to willingly surrender SURCOUF to the Royal Navy.

On July 3, 1940, when Operation GRASP was executed, SURCOUF was alongside the battleship HMS REVENGE at Devonport Dockyard, Plymouth, England, after her fleeing from German troops about to seize the French Naval Shipyard, Brest, France.

While seizure or destruction of the French Fleet could spell survival for an England, which was facing invasion and defeat, for SURCOUF's officers and men lowering the French flag and surrendering their warship to England, even though she was an ally and without explicit orders from their superior, Admiral of the Fleet Darlan, even though he supported Marshall Henri Philippe Pétain's surrender of France to Hitler, was still an act of dishonor—against the heart and soul of proud traditions of the French Navy.

Besides, the honor of the namesake of SURCOUF, Baron Robert Surcouf of St. Malo, France, the daring corsair who fiercely despised the English, who ruthlessly assaulted British East India merchantmen, and the who skillfully avoided capture by the Royal Navy in the Indian Ocean during the Napoleonic Wars, also had to be upheld. Therefore, surrender by the French aboard SURCOUF was unquestionably a matter of death before dishonor. And deaths occurred.

(A Ninja's entry into the castle was perhaps the most dangerous and most challenging, of all the missions because it was teeming with dead-end avenues and watchful sentries meant to trap unwary infiltrators.)

Operation GRASP resulted in a ruthless, point-black shoot-out in the confined wardroom of SURCOUF between the Royal Navy boarding party of thirty and its French officers. The close exchange of gun fire could be likened to those bar room shoot-outs seen in Western movies. It was led by Commander Denis Vaughan 'Lofty" Sprague, Royal Navy, Commander of the submarine HMS THAMES, his Executive Officer was Lieutenant Patrick Maule Kerr Griffiths, who had been assigned as the Royal Navy's Liaison Officer aboard SURCOUF. At that moment, SURCOUF's Commanding Officer, Capitaine de Frégaté Paul Marie Hippolyte Martin, French Navy, was visiting aboard the battleship PARIS, which was moored alongside SURCOUF. *(Tonight you must guard your lord's castle against the Ninja. As you stand your watch, you must be fully confident that you will master any emergency which may arise. It is you first duty to acquit yourself in such a way as to ensure the safety of your lord's castle.)*

The French fired the first shots of the bloody affray. Sprague and Griffiths were taken by surprise and were mortally wounded by shots fired Lieutenant de Vaisseau Pierre Bouillant, the Gunnery Officer, and one Royal Navy rating off HMS REVENGE, Leading Seaman Albert Webb, was killed outright by bullets first fired by Lieutenant de Vaissaeau (later Rear Admiral) Robert "Bobbie" Le Nistour, SURCOUF's doctor. (Medical personnel during wars are considered and respected as non-combatant participants, but Le Nistour over-rode that traditional rule of war.) Another REVENGE rating, Able Seaman William H. Heath, was incapacitated for life, with seven bullets in his arms, face and neck, from the murderous French attack. *(You must bring credit to the lord of the castle for the warrior's code requires such loyalty and devotion of you. If necessary, you must die to preserve his honor.)*

The cost of preserving French honor was the sudden death of Chief Warrant Officer Jacques Jean Marie Daniel, SURCOUF's Third Engineer, by two bullets in his heart. Lieutenant de Vaisseau Bouillant was wounded in his right arm and chest by Sprague's return fire. During the SURCOUF Affray of July 3, 1940, the retaliation by Bouillant, Daniel, and Le Nistour could be likened to the *Three Musketeers,* a novel about honor, courage, and loyalty by Alexander Dumas, whose father served during the Napoleonic War with England.

It was the first blood-letting melee between the two navies since the Battle of Trafalgar in 1805. But actually, *the SURCOUF Affray of July 3, 1940* was a bloody sequel to the numerous engagements between the English and the French since the days of Joan de Arc, the Middle Ages, the Battle of Trafalgar, and their bitter diplomatic compromises and political rivalry across the tables of various naval arms limitation conferences.

(Actually, GRASP was a segment of Operation CATAPULT which the Royal Navy launched against the major portion of the French Fleet at Mers el Kébir, North Africa, also on 3 July, 1940. During that attack 1,300 men of the French Navy were killed, who only days before had been allies.)

On the other hand, perhaps subconsciously; the Royal Navy was seeking the destruction of SURCOUF because she represented a superior kind of submarine that England, for a number of diplomatic, naval, and political reasons, had failed to provide for the Royal Navy. Or, did England consider the SURCOUF class submarines to be a threat to her lines of commerce and communications with her far-flung empire and to her reputation as Sovereign of the Seas?

Strangely, Lieutenant de Vaisseau (later Rear Admiral) Le Nistour, whom the author and Francine Blaison interviewed in February 1978, triggered the affray. Early during our interview Admiral Le Nistour aimed at us the pistol he used to kill Leading Seaman Webb. When asked about this frightful setting he replied that he thought my visit was to execute revenge. Assured that this was not my intent, he quickly enjoyed the presence of lovely Francine, and all ended cordially.

As we bid Admiral Le Nistour adieu, he made this unsolicited remark about SURCOUF:

> Our dear and unlucky SURCOUF, who should have served her life as a brave corsair with a fighting spirit, had her life cut short with too many mysteries in that affair. Will anyone learn them???
>
> Hers was a glorious history, with a cruel destiny; the SURCOUF that jewel of the French submarine fleet, who from birth, until her death, was surrounded by too much controversy.

Our subsequent visit was with Vice Admiral Bouillant, who retired near the huge naval base at Toulon, France. His wife and he were extremely cordial, and our luncheon was enjoyable, with our conversation mainly centered on Francine, her father, and French Navy recollections. During our interview, Admiral Bouillant proudly showed us where the bullet entered his right arm during the SURCOUF Affray.

As for Commander Sprague, he was destined to die as a few days before the SURCOUF Affray, he had expressed a premonition of death to his wife Rosemary. Had he not died aboard SURCOUF, he would have been lost with HMS THAMES as it never returned from her next patrol. She was sunk by a German mine following the affray aboard SURCOUF on July 3, 1940.

A possible hidden truth about SURCOUF is that she may have been diverted from engaging in the Royal Navy's running sea battle with the powerful 42,000-ton German pocket battleship BISMARCK, one of the fastest and largest capital ships deployed

during the Battle of the Atlantic, or with the 10,000-ton heavy cruiser PRINZ EUGEN, with 8-inch guns.

This opinion is expressed after studying SURCOUF's position, radio traffic, and patrol reports for May 20-27, 1941.

At the time, SURCOUF, based in Bermuda, was patrolling the Atlantic Gap, "The Black Pit," somewhere between Bermuda and the Azores for hunter-killer U-boats.

BISMARCK would have eluded the Royal Navy had it not been for two sightings of her by the American weather ship, USCG MODOC, in the Bay of Biscay, and later by a Catalina patrol flying boat, PBY, loaned to the British and piloted by Ensign Leonard Smith, USN. The role played by the Americans in the destruction of BISMARCK was not made public for more than 30 years, mainly because they had been secretly equipped with MAD (a Mark I, Magnetic Airborne Detection device).

Imagine the naval consternation and change in the history of the Battle of the Atlantic, and even that of World War II, if SURCOUF would have attacked or sighted BISMARCK, which had just mutilated and sunk the 42,100-ton battle cruiser HMS HOOD! Imagine, also, the enormous political clout and popularity de Gaulle and his Free French Movement would have enjoyed, during and after the war, had SURCOUF become involved with BISMARCK or PRINZ EUGEN, if only for the chase.

For this reason, many French are firmly convinced that the Royal Navy, the British Admiralty, and the Churchill Government would have gone to extreme lengths to prevent SURCOUF from penetrating the same waters as BISMARCK.

SURCOUF was the first and only Allied submarine to participate in the liberation of territory in North America during the war, and she was the first submarine to use a portion of her crew for that purpose and SURCOUF was involved in the first invasion of North American since the War of 1812.

This occurred on Christmas Eve of Dec 24-25, 1941, during the liberation of the Vichy controlled St. Pierre and Miquelon Islands, in the Gulf of St. Lawrence—just south of Newfoundland. The islands, at the time, were in the naval domain of Commodore Commanding, New Foundland Force, Rear Admiral L.W Murray, Royal Canadian Navy. It was suggested that during the Battle of the Atlantic that the Vichy French controlled St Pierre and Miquelon Islands were being used as a base to transmit radio communications to Nazi Germany about weather conditions and Allied convoys destined for England and Russia.

The operation, which Secretary of State Cordell Hull referred to as "a tempest in a tea pot," was under the command of Vice Admiral Emile Muselier, Commandant, Free French Navy and Minister of Marine, who was acting under the orders of General Charles de Gaulle, leader of the Free French Movement based in London. De Gaulle had ordered Muselier to occupy the St. Pierre and Miquelon Islands despite his avowed promise to Churchill not to do so for reasons beyond the scope of this story to elaborate upon. Thereafter, according to *No Laurels for de Gaulle*, by Robert Mengin, General de Gaulle and his Free French could no longer be depended upon by Churchill and Roosevelt to play a decisive role in winning the war against Germany.

SURCOUF was the only Allied submarine to draw the ire of President Roosevelt, Secretary of State Cordell Hull, and Prime Minster Churchill.

This was for her involvement in the St. Pierre and Miquelon Affair. But Ira Wolfert, author of *An Act of Love, American Guerrilla in the Philippines, One Man Air Force, Battle for the Solomon's,* and *An Epic of Genius,* and former American war correspondent for the North American Newspaper Alliance, who covered a part of the war in Halifax, was the sole correspondent to cover the operation. He had been invited by Muselier to board SURCOUF to observe the Free French occupation of the St. Pierre and Miquelon Islands. Wolfert wrote:

> The liberation of the St. Pierre and Miquelon Islands was the best Christmas present that could be given to peoples desiring to be free. It was what the war all about, and it was one of the first occasions during which people were liberated from the political oppression of Vichy France.

Yet, for her operational role in the St. Pierre and Miquelon Affair, which some diplomats and politicians considered to be an unpardonable sin, and for her continued presence there, President Franklin Delano Roosevelt threatened to deploy the battleship USS ARKANSAS, with twelve 12-inch guns, to forcibly remove SURCOUF, and the three accompanying Free French corvettes ACONIT, ALYSEE, and MINOSA, from the North Atlantic. And Hull had charged that Muselier's was "an act of unauthorized piracy—one which violated the terms of the recently negotiated Havana Convention of 1940, which espoused the Monroe Doctrine.

The American, British, and Canadian Allies of the Free French Government were infuriated by what they considered to be an underhanded, unilateral maneuver by General Charles de Gaulle, leader of Free French movement, to keep France's Empire, especially its Atlantic possessions, intact. De Gaulle, with three corvettes and a submarine cruise, according, to Milton Viorst in his documentary *Hostile Allies*, had defied the most powerful alliance in wartime history, Churchill and Roosevelt, and emerged victorious. However, de Gaulle was to learn that it was dangerous to play games with those two more powerful leaders.

Actually, de Gaulle's unilateral seizure of the St. Pierre and Miquelon Islands contributed to the Allied victory over Germany during the Battle of the Atlantic as the island's Western Union radio transmitting facilities, which, according to *Divided Island*, by William A. Christian, jr., was infested with Vichyists, could no longer be used to report convoy activity to England and Murmansk, Russia and weather reports to the German U-boats.

That there existed deep and prior concern, at least within the British Government, about the role of Western Union wireless transmitters on St Pierre and Miquelon Islands, vis à vis the enemy, before the Free French occupation, is evident from the following SECRET memorandum from John Taylor, the British Consulate, Baltimore, Maryland, to Captain E. S. Brand, Royal Navy, Director of Naval Intelligence:

BRITISH CONSULATE
Baltimore, Maryland
SECRET

By Safe Hand.   1714   10th Sept.1941

No. 1037-5-14

Dear Brand,

The enclosed cuttings contain admissions of negotiations between Western Union and. Vichy representatives for the erection and operation by Western Union of a powerful wireless station on the Island of St. Pierre. Western Union brought over their European Manager, Maurice Cartoux, at the end of the last year, and sent him to St. Pierre; and a tentative agreement was reached for the formation of a company in which the French and Western Union were to be the sole stockholders, and share the revenue.

Whether the initiative came from the French Ambassador M. Henry-Haye, as the American press suggests, or from Western Union as the Ambassador asserts, the fact that such negotiations with the enemy (which is what it amounts to) took place at all at this time is a significant indication of the attitude of those responsible with the policy of Western Union.

Mr. Yuill, Chief Telegraph Censor at Ottawa, will also have heard of another scheme, involving Western Union and the French cable from St. Pierre to Brest, about which nothing has appeared in the press.

Best regards, Yours ever,

John Taylor

Captain E. S. Brand, R.N.
Director of Naval Intelligence

It is significant to mention, and as a matter of interest since SURCOUF was intimately involved in the St Pierre and Miquelon Affair, that, according to *Roosevelt's Secret War, FDR and World War II Espionage,* by Joseph E. Persico and *Room 3603,* by H. Montgomery Hyde, William Vincent Astor, the influential New York City socialite was on the board of directors of the Western Union Telegraph Company. Moreover, as a naval reserve captain, Astor the fabulously wealthy and well-connected New Yorker, not only had the President Franklin Delano Roosevelt's ear, but also the close attention of British Security Coordination.

In fact, William Stephenson (aka Intrepid), who had come from London to New York in June 1940 to run British intelligence, took up residence at the St. Regis Hotel at the invitation of Astor, its owner.

The one thing President Roosevelt always wanted and needed, and one of his favorite methods for gathering clandestine information, was employment of confidential agents who reported to him personally and privately. The world of secret agents, intelligence and espionage thrilled Roosevelt. Roosevelt, had plans for Astor's interest in undercover affairs, and placed him as coordinator of all intelligence functions undertaken by the Military Intelligence Division of the U.S. Army, the Office of Naval Intelligence, the Justice and State Departments and liaison with other information-gathering agencies in the Greater New York City area. This operation, which also included Bermuda, was revealed during the post-war period as the *Roosevelt-Astor Espionage Ring.*

Likely, that William Vincent Astor, as a director on the board of Western Union, knew of Western Union's political inclinations towards Vichy France on the St. Pierre and Miquelon Islands because in some large corporations higher ups do not ask what is going on, and lower downs do not tell them. Or, maybe, as a master intelligence chief for the *Roosevelt-Astor Espionage Ring* he didn't want to know. (http://cryptome.info/fdr-astor.htm)

However, from a reading of *Room 3603,* which is about Intrepid's secret war to combat German and Vichy espionage and fifth column activity in the Western Hemisphere, and Taylor's input about Western Union's attempt to erect a more powerful radio and wireless network, on the St Pierre and Miquelon Islands in cooperation with the Vichy government, it would appear that the board members must of known about the Western Union-Vichy connection long before it was publically revealed.

SURCOUF's role in the occupation of the St. Pierre and Miquelon Islands was the second time during the war that Churchill focused his attention upon her. The first was for her role in *The SURCOUF Affray of July 3, 1940*. There was a more compassionate third time, when SURCOUF and her Free French Navy and Royal Navy officers and men were lost in the Caribbean.

Because of her stormy involvement in the SURCOUF Affray of July 3, 1940 and the St. Pierre and Miquelon Affair, any further rocking of the proverbial boat by SURCOUF would justify ridding her from the surface of the Atlantic Ocean.

Some French adamantly believe that the price that de Gaulle paid for undermining his Allies during St. Pierre and Miquelon Affair was the loss of SURCOUF—allegedly caused by the "big powers."

SURCOUF is the only submarine of any war to be honored by a commemorative postage stamp.

The St. Pierre and Miquelon Affair had such a memorable impact upon the government and people of those islands that in 1961, twenty years after the event involving SURCOUF, a 500 franc air post stamp was issued by that tiny, but grateful possession of France to commemorate the twentieth anniversary of St. Pierre and Miquelon Islands being liberated by the Free French.

The concept of the stamp, ironically, was drawn by Leading Signalman Harold Warner, Royal Fleet Reserve, war illustrator of the sea, at the request of the ardent Free Frenchman; Vice Admiral Henri Emile Muselier—while SURCOUF was engaged in the liberation of the St. Pierre and Miquelon Islands between Dec 26, 1941 and Jan 12, 1942.

Commandante de Frégaté Louis Georges Blaison, the commanding officer of SURCOUF, is the only submarine officer of any war to be honored by a commemorative postage stamp.

In 1994, the appreciative St Pierre and Miquelon Government issued a stamp portraying both Commandante de Frégaté Blaison and SURCOUF on a 2.80-franc stamp, with SURCOUF being so honored a second time. Previously, in 1992, Vice Admiral Henri Muselier, the leader of the expedition which liberated the islands, was also commemorated on a 2.500 Franc St. Pierre and Miquelon Island stamp. His recognition was long overdue until the author suggested that the Administrator of the islands also render the Admiral the appreciation he deserved.

When Charles de Gaulle died on June 15, 1970, St. Pierre and Miquelon Islands issued a 100 franc air post stamp to his memory.

Please know that Muselier, a man with a heart of gold and one of the fathers of SURCOUF, was the only admiral of the French Navy to take it upon himself to escape from France to fight on the side of England against Germany and Italy. It was Muselier's idea to form the Free French Navy, and it was he who conceived the Free French flag, which had the Cross of Lorraine on its banner. It was the symbol which Joan of Arc carried into battle in her quest to rid the British from the soil of France during the fifteenth century.

Yet, Muselier, who was a bitter enemy of Fleet Admiral Darlan, even though they had been classmates at the l'Ecole Navale, because of an unfounded rumor that he intended to flee to Vichy France with SURCOUF, was the only Allied officer to be imprisoned and ordered to be hanged for treason by Churchill. This incident occurred in London in January 1941, but Muselier eventually received the personal apology of King George VI for someone's deliberate and insidious diplomatic, intelligence, and political maneuver to embarrass the Free French movement. **(See Appendix "A", The SURCOUF-Muselier Affair.)**

SURCOUF's doctor, Lieutenant de Vaisseau Rene Le Bas, Medecin de lere Classe de la Marine, was the only submarine doctor ever recognized by the dedication of a hospital to his memory.

This recognition was by the St. Pierre and Miquelon Islands, and was accorded to Dr. Le Bas for the humanitarian services he rendered to the populace during SURCOUF's presence there between December 24, 1941-January 10, 1942. SURCOUF was also mentioned on the dedication plaque. No other submarine has ever been accorded such an honor.

SURCOUF was the only Allied submarine to become politically embroiled in a serious diplomatic and political controversy at the highest levels of the British and Free French Governments involving Vice Admiral Émile Henri Muselier, Commander-in-Chief, Free French Naval Forces and Merchant Marine and SURCOUF was falsely accused that she and Vice Admiral Émile Henri Muselier, Commander-in-Chief, Free French Naval Forces and Merchant Marine, would to flee to Vichy controlled Dakar, Africa.

SURCOUF and her dead were mentioned in the dedication of Alastair Mars book, *British Submarine at War, 1939-45.*

A prominent Canadian woman enters SURCOUF's story.

On November 20, 1980, Madame Leonie Richard, who was specifically mentioned by Capitaine de Vasseau Blaison in SURCOUF's *War Diary* for January 1942, was presented a medal of "honor and gratitude" by His Excellency Pierre Maillard, French Ambassador to Canada, for services she rendered to SURCOUF and her Free French officers and men during World War II.

The house on Vernon Street, Halifax, which quartered Madame Richard's Free French Committee of Hospitality, and which was used to shelter and entertain Free French sailors, was named "La Maison SURCOUF" in honor of SURCOUF the submarine. The house still exists and is owned by the French Government.

How many other women have ever been mentioned in the war diary of a submarine? Also, it is unlikely that many other World War II submarines were accorded the honor of having a club house named after them.

Here is how SURCOUF's last British Naval Liaison Officer was internationally recognized during the postwar period.

It is noteworthy to mention that the memory of Sub-Lieutenant Roger "Rog" Burney, aged 22, who firmly believed he would die with SURCOUF, was commemorated in three ways:

His name appears on the Cherbourg Memorial dedicated to SURCOUF and those souls who died with her;

It is on the memorial to commemorate the war dead of Hay-on-the Wye, England; and by *A War Requiem*, which musically and poetically expresses an eloquent and powerful plea for world peace by denouncing man's inhumanity to man because of wars.

A War Requiem was composed by England's foremost composer, conductor, and pianist, Sir Benjamin Britten. His masterpiece was dedicated to Burney and three other of Britten's Cambridge University friends who died during World War II.

Burney, alleged to have been a homosexual, as was Britten, is the only submarine officer of any war known to be honored by the two different countries, and by the composition of internationally acclaimed music.

(As an aside: Burney's father served with distinction in the Indian Political Intelligence Bureau, New Delhi, India, during the pre-World War II regime of the British Empire, and his brother Christopher was a Commando officer imprisoned at Buchenwald for thirty-five months, until freed by American troops. According to his sister, Joan Adams (nee Burney), the treatment Christopher received from his Nazi captors was so brutal that he severely suffered mentally and physically for the remainder of his life.)

However, what about Gough and Warner, who had been recalled to active service after their retirement from His Majesty's submarine service before the war. How did they react to their duty aboard SURCOUF?

For this extraordinary insight we turn to Boyer's former American wife, Josephine "Jo" Hopkins Boyer Vairinen, later of Corpus Christi, Texas, for a straight forward account of her meeting with them in September 1941. This was while SURCOUF was undergoing an overhaul at the U. S. Naval Shipyard, Portsmouth, New Hampshire.

Obviously, "Jo" had a sympathetic ear for listening to the woes of not only Boyer, but also of "Tattoo" Gough, and "Plum" Warner. Here, in her March 4, 1979 letter, is how she wrote of Gough and Warner's anticipation of death with SURCOUF:

> I remember them vividly. They were the finest type of young married men. Gough was dark and Warner rather good looking. Both were in their late thirties, past being boyish.
>
> We talked of general things, their impressions of the United States, their families, their likes and dislikes. It was not quite the same sort of superficial banter as is often between officers and hosts. Somehow, for this reason, I remember Gough and Warner better than all the rest.
>
> When Frank (Lieutenant Francis Boyer, Royal Navy, and the BNLO aboard SURCOUF) went to the kitchen to mix fresh drinks, both Gough and Warner asked me with pleading voices to request the Lieutenant to do everything he could to get them off SURCOUF. They knew they were doomed men if they weren't relieved soon.

"Jo", in a September 30, 1979 letter admitted that she was not a psychic, but what she revealed about Gough and Warner is one of the strangest forewarnings of death to emerge from World War II—not told by one man, but by two—simultaneously!!!

Surely, Gough and Warner must have tried to quell their fears before their tête ê tête with the ex-Mrs. Boyer. Through her words we can envision them confiding in her as if drawing upon her strength as a woman—two lost souls seeking peace of mind and security through the comfort and presence of a guardian angel. "Men tell women things they would not dream of confiding to another man," wrote John Epingham, in *Man vs Women.* (Listening is a wonderful thing about women.)

Regardless, Gough's and Warner's deadly premonition about themselves and SURCOUF proved fatally and violently true—for they, as well as did "Rog" Burney, predicted that they would die with Blaison and SURCOUF!!! And they did!!!

If there is any doubt about "Jo's" stunning revelation, permit the author to also cite the remarks of Mrs. Ruthie Baker, of Bunker House,

Paget East, Bermuda, in a letter she had written to Mrs. Warner, in the spring of 1942—following her learning of the death of Warner:

> What can I say to you about great loss? My husband and I send you our deepest sympathy. It is a great shock to us.
>
> I feared something was wrong when they left. **It was the first time they ever left without a smile.** We were so happy to have "Plum" as we affectionately called him with us. I always counted the days for his return. It was a privilege to do anything for so gallant a man.
>
> Many people along the road send you their sympathy as there was always a smile for them along that road from "Plum."

Note Mrs. Baker's sad foreboding: "This is the first time that they left without a smile". Not one "left without smile", but both "left without smile." And we sense from Mrs. Baker's chilling remarks that "Plum" often smiled. How many of us could smile serenely in the face of death, except laconically and through gritted teeth, if we knew that we were to die—especially in a submarine? But Gough and Warner—as did Burney—knew they would die with SURCOUF. Yet, each, with determination and courage, did not shunt their duty to their King and Country or from their known rendezvous with Death. Where did Royal Navy find such brave and devoted men???

SURCOUF was the only submarine, which caused Prime Minister Winston. S. Churchill to rewrite an entry in his book *Their Finest Hour*, at the request of a very irate English lady, the resolute Mrs. Rosemary Sprague and more about her.

In continuation of the above Royal Navy commentary, and since the French Navy submarine LA SIBYLLE was introduced, which in the English language is spelled "sybyl", meaning a prophetess or a fortune teller, permit the author to introduce how during World War I a prophetess, *un femme fatale*, accosted Miss Rosemary Corderoy Northcraft, before she became the wife of a submarine officer of the Royal Navy and long before SURCOUF was the cause of her husband's death at an English navy yard during *The SURCOUF Affray of July 3, 1940*. Strangely, her letter arrived as the author was editing *SURCOUF and the Alien Mind*.

On August 8, 1981, Mrs. Rosemary Sprague, nee Northcraft, who has steadfastly claimed she was not superstitious, recounted the following wartime incident about herself, and in the telling made a startling discovery about her life, relative to SURCOUF, through the influence of two women; one, at that time, being a future Queen of England:

> We viewed the Royal Wedding on television, you can see so much more that way, you know. Diana Spencer looked stunning in her grown. In addition, Prince Charles was as handsome as he ever could be. But, I expect you are not in the least interested in "the Wedding", as it has nothing to do with SURCOUF!!! But at least the bride's name began with an "S"!!!, which reminds me of when I was at a ball at the Hotel Savoy, London. It was my first formal affair and my first encounter with a fortuneteller. She was the famous Melta Morgana. As she wandered around, wearing an eye masque, she stopped couples whilst they were dancing. She would hold their hand and in a few seconds tell something about their future.
>
> This was during the first World War, when I was only eighteen. She told me, three things, all in about two or three seconds: that I was going to lose a parent, and six months later my father died; that I was going to lose a brother; my middle brother was killed one year after my father's death; and that "S's" would run through my life.
>
> I was so frightened by her prophecy, and what really occurred thereafter, that it was years and years and years before I would go near a fortuneteller again. When I married Denis Vaughan Sprague, a submariner, there's two "S's" already for you, I remembered and would laugh. But it was only just now, as I was writing to you about Spencer and Surcouf, that it came to me that it was also "S" for Surcouf, that beastly submarine

which caused my life to be deprived of the person I loved most!!!

Isn't it odd, rather strange, that I hadn't made this connection between Denis and Surcouf before?

(It was Commander Denis Vaughan Sprague, Royal Navy, Commanding Officer of HMS THAMES, the fastest submarine in the world and the best and largest in the inventory of the Royal Navy at that time, who was mortally wounded by Lieutenant de Vaisseau (now Vice Admiral, Retired) Pierre Bouillaut, French Navy, and SURCOUF's Gunnery Officer, when the Sprague led a boarding party to seize SURCOUF, at the Royal Navy Dockyard, Devonport, England, on July 3, 1940.)

Notice how Mrs. Sprague's life involved three "S's": Sprague, "for complete happiness", submarines, and Surcouf, "for complete detestation and misery". Also, notice how she so effectively used three exclamation points, and the term "years and years and years", to empathize her point. Yet, she often remarked to the author she was not superstitious.

"Isn't it odd, rather strange," that after sixty three years of concealment within the recesses of her mind, the Royal Wedding should have triggered Mrs. Sprague's recollection of that long past encounter with a gifted seer, and that Lady Diana Spencer's husband, Prince Charles, would also be a Commander in the Royal Navy, as was Denis Vaughan Sprague, Mrs. Sprague's letter could be classified in two categories: a *Close Encounter of the Third Kind,* involving *Thought Transmission Through a Timely Letter* and a *Correspondence to Future Events.*

In the latter case, the striking correspondence of the 1918 predictions into later events are so exact that common sense is stunned. How could that sibyl's prophecy of major events in Mrs. Sprague's life be so incredibly accurate, and involve SURCOUF as early as 1918??? Alan Vaughan would say: "Since the predictions were recorded, this case does constitute scientific evidence that blueprints of life—involving most of the world's future population—extend many, many years into the future."

And here is how Mrs. Sprague told of Commander Sprague's anticipation of death, and of how she took me to task for confusing his expectation with a premonition. First, she had a denial, then an acceptance of that premonition. Her July 31, 1979 letter applies:

> It rather offended me that you openly doubted me; when you said that I thought Denis had a premonition of death. Actually, I didn't think I said that. I think what I said was, as I was told, that "he walked into almost certain death with his eyes wide open", which is quite a difference.
>
> Denis was not the sort of person to have had premonitions, but I think he must have known that he was in for a pretty tricky exercise; the outcome of which was up in the air, and that he faced up to it, which, again, quite different. That is the kind of person he was, accepting things as they are, and doing the best he knew how to cope with the situation.
>
> It is easy to look at things with hindsight, but I knew him so well that I should have known, then, that something was wrong; but we had a happy laughing evening, and I wasn't thinking as I should have. But the letter which was given me after his death, written on the very day I had dinner with him, made me realize that he did have a premonition, and that he knew that it was in the cards that he might not come out alive.

So it was clear: One way or another, whether aboard SURCOUF or aboard HMS THAMES, Commander Denis Vaughan Sprague, Royal Navy, did have a premonition that he was destined to die!!! And it was fulfilled!!! After reading about the many premonitions cited above, and more that will surface in Part IV, how can anyone deny that they could ring true. So, if you have one—TAKE HEED!!! Follow your instincts.

Since the superstitious number three has and will appear so significantly throughout *The SURCOUF Conspiracy*, this number requires analysis. *(In some cases the Ninja played upon the superstitious mind of his enemy.)* While the testifying of two witnesses to the same matters establishes sufficient proof for legal action, three makes the testimony even stronger. The number three, therefore, is used at times to represent intensity, emphasis, or added strength. "A threefold cannot be quickly be torn in two." *(Ecclesiastes 4:12 and Matthew 26: 75, "Immediately a rooster crowed. Then Peter remembered the word Jesus had spoken: "Before the rooster crows, you will disown me three times.")*

Besides SURCOUF had encountered three deaths during her existence: Once when her class of submarine was killed at the London Naval Conference of 1930; again during the SURCOUF Affray of 1940; and finally when she was sunk by collision with the SS THOMPSON LYKES.

Also, for those of a superstitious inclination, and the author is one of them, *The Encyclopedia of Superstitions,* by E. and M.A. Radford, cites this about the superstition of the number THREE:

> It is a point to be remembered that among the ancients for practically every superstition in which some ritual had to be performed the ritual was in threes, or multiples of threes.

If you believe that this superstition has no significance among seafarers, why would the formidable Vice Admiral Philip Vian, Royal Navy, who Churchill distinguished as one of the most resolute and brilliant admirals of World War II, have remarked to Rear Admiral G.W.G. Simpson, Royal Navy, then Captain and Commander, TENTH Flotilla of Submarines, Malta: "Troubles usually come in threes, you should be clear of them now", if he did not sincerely believe in the superstition of triple trouble associated with the number THREE???

And, a point to have remembered about Francine Blaison was not to have three lights on in the same room, or to do anything in a sequence of threes such as could arouse her superstitious nature.

Mentioned was the extremely strong psychic events which had a strong root connection with Blaison's mother-in-law, now permit me to introduce one concerning his mother, but involving a non-alien, profound Christian blessing.

When Blaison last saw his mother, at her home in St. Genes, France—just before the Fall of France in June 1940—as she kissed him goodbye she said: "God save you my son!" But, to tell the truth and despite his mother's Divine blessing, no force on earth could have saved Blaison from his mother-in-law's over-powering determination that he would die in a submarine.

Like Captain Whalley in Joseph Conrad's *The End of the Tether*, Blaison seemed to be the pathetic victim of a shattering force of circumstances that he had not created and over which he had no control! Both he and SURCOUF died "without help, human or divine."

But this strange sequence of occult and mysticism does not end here—it is only a portion of a series of psychic events associated with the Blaison's and SURCOUF's eventual loss.

An analysis of these events—which seemed to be somewhat beyond coincidence—led me to analyze Blaison's submarine career before he relieved Capitaine de Frégaté Paul Ortoli to assume command of SURCOUF, on September 19, 1941, at Portsmouth Navy Yard, New Hampshire.

It was determined that Blaison had a strong affinity for his association with submarine accidents before and after he joined them. Since his graduation from submarine school in 1930, and until he died in 1942, Blaison had served aboard 6 submarines. Of these: MARSQUIN suffered a collision with a Greek freighter immediately before he joined her; PHENIX was lost during an uncontrollable dive after he left her; and three, AGOSTA, REQUIN, and LA SIBYLLE, were lost as a consequence of war, the latter disappearing mysteriously. (From the Internet this was learned about the disappearance of LA SIBYLLE (Capitaine de Vaisseau A. J. R. Raybaud): She departed from Casablanca Harbor on November 8, 1942 and was reported missing thereafter. It is possible that she was bombed and sunk by an American aircraft, but there was also a report of a submarine that sank in an Allied defensive minefield off Casablanca during the night of November 16-17, 1942.

But for a stroke of good luck, Lieutenant de Vaisseau Georges Louis Blaison, at the time 30 years of age, would have been lost with PHENIX as her Executive Officer.

And we know what happened to Blaison and SURCOUF. Only "Lucky" MARSQUIN survived to be routinely demolished by a scrapper's hammer. In each case, however, it seems that the Blaison's or SURCOUF, or both, were directly or indirectly involved with those submarine disasters through a psychic or physical connection.

The submarine losses with which Blaison was associated involved the deaths of about 350 of his shipmates. Was there some strange connection between the losses of each of these submarines with his eventually serving as SURCOUF's commander—when she took her last dive with 130 officers and crew, including three of the Royal Navy, on February 18, 1942??? The question that might also be asked is: Was Blaison unknowingly imbued with malevolence against the submarines on which he served???

Blaison seemed preordained to receive the ultimate fate which only the gods could give him as a submariner—his quest for eternity. As events turned for him, he obtained perpetual command of SURCOUF, the ultimate among the world's submarines, and he was fated to become part of what remains classified as the worst submarine disaster of its kind in history—on their voyage to be to the bottom of the Caribbean Sea, which was their final resting place. Except for the loss of USS THRESHER (Lieutenant Commander John Wesley "Wes" Harvey, USN, Annapolis Class of 1950), with 129 persons, no other submarine commander has come close to breaking that record for almost seventy years.

Was Blaison cursed by some ancient death wish??? How else can we account for Blaison's affinity with submarine disasters??? How could he have avoided four encounters with death and finally be lost with SURCOUF??? **Is it intended that what we don't know now mean that we should never know???**

Who or what was the albatross around Blaison's neck??? Was it SURCOUF??? Was he cursed by some ancient death connection??? How else can we account for Blaison's affinity for association with submarine disasters??? How could he have avoided four encounters with death aboard a submarine and finally have been lost with SURCOUF???

Why did Therese and Francine, as children, have suffered strong mental traumas associated with submarine disasters before Blaison was lost with SURCOUF??? And why was Therese's mother involved with each of their encounters??? Were these three involuntarily involved in an unholy plot against one: Capitaine de Frégate Georges Louis Blaison???!!!

There are many things humankind is not meant to know, but these are haunting and intriguing questions are of a kind that demands inquiry to seek solutions because they are so much a part of our everyday life.

But what about premonitions of SURCOUF's death??? Because of them, one could discern that there really was no way out for poor SURCOUF but to die as she did.

There are many things we are not meant to know, but they linger as haunting and intriguing questions—of a kind which demand more concerted investigation, extending far beyond into the public domain, outside the closed doors of paranormal and parapsychological research institutions, to find solutions since they are so much a part of our everyday existence.

Interestingly, Blaison's tempestuous submarine career and death with SURCOUF was not an isolated case as it had an incredible parallel with the close encounters and death of Lieutenant Lewis L. Hancock, USN, of Austin, Texas (Annapolis Class of 1910) and Commanding Officer of the submarine USS AL-4 (ex-USS L-4) during World War I.

For distinguished service in AL-4, Hancock received the coveted Navy Cross, and later a World War II destroyer, USS LEWIS L. HANCOCK (DD-675), was named in his honor.

Of the thousands of references reviewed by the author, while researching for *SURCOUF and the Royal Navy*, no one was found to equal Blaison's record of unbelievable escapes from death in submarines other than Hancock. And each naval officer, strangely, lost his life in the worst naval disaster of its kind.

The record associated with Hancock's death, as will be told, was shattered with the crash of the world's greatest airship HINDENBURG, the ship of the future, at Lakehurst, New Jersey, while Blaison's world record with SURCOUF, a futuristic submarine, has yet to be broken. While Hancock's death was not submarine connected it is obvious that Death had stalked him just as relentlessly as it had Blaison—this was their other commonality.

Here is how Edward K. Chatterton, in *Danger Zone, The Story of the Queenstown Command,* told of Hancock's confrontations with death while commanding the submarine AL-4 during World War I:

AL-4, along with AL-1, 2, 3, 9, 10 and 11, had just arrived at Queenstown, Ireland, on January 27, 1918, after an unpleasant crossing of the North Atlantic, the first crossings by American submarines in history.

They were based at Bantry Bay where eventually, after training under Captain Dunbar-Nasmith, they relieved Royal Navy submarines on eastern Atlantic patrol.

AL-4, on March 20, 1918, was patrolling off the south coast of Ireland when, at about 4 pm, she sighted the periscope a U-boat. AL-4 proceeded to intercept the enemy and ram. The U-boat apparently had the same idea and struck AL-4 as she was swinging to her new course and a jolt was felt throughout her length. There was no doubt that the two submarines had collided underwater. AL-4 suffered no damage and the U-boat escaped.

(Strangely, Hancock and AL-4 had another commonality with SURCOUF through Captain Martin E. Dunbar-Nasmith, Victoria Cross, Royal Navy, for as Senior Officer and Commander-in-Chief, Home Station, Plymouth, Dunbar-Nasmith flew his flag aboard the Devonport Dockyard, Plymouth, early during World War II, when SURCOUF was seized there by Royal Navy forces under his command during Operation GRASP.)

During the morning of April 12 AL-4 again had another contact with a U-boat, while darkness still prevailed. AL-4 was on station with two torpedoes ready to fire. Lewis fired one from 1,000 yards, but it missed barely ahead. The German sighted AL-4 and both commanders decided to attempt to ram the other. AL-4 barely missed ramming the U-boat, which submerged so near that bubbles from its ballast tanks could be seen boiling all over the American.

On April 26, about midnight, AL-4 sighted a vessel which in the path of the moon was unquestionably German. AL-4 worked its way into an excellent firing position and discharged two torpedoes at an estimated range of 1,000 to 1,200 yards. They were seen to leave the tubes in a normal manner, settle down to good straight runs, but great was the consternation, a few seconds later, when a torpedo was sighted heading for AL-4, and too close for anyone aboard to do anything about it.

The torpedo hit AL-4 forward on the port side, but failed to explode, being thrown off its course by the impact; yet it must have had a truly remarkable steering gear, for the gyro brought the torpedo right back to its course and again struck AL-4! The persistent torpedo repeated the procedure, without detonating, until finally it cleared the stern and was lost to view.

AL-4 must be the only submarine in history to have been hit three times by the same torpedo which was not its own!!!

For some time, Hancock thought his boat had been hit by one of his own torpedoes running erratically; but reports eventually indicated that the torpedo had been fired by a British "P"-boat, which, on account of the striking similarity of its silhouette to those of German U-boats, had mistaken AL-4 as an enemy.

On May 18, AL-4 had an experience which again almost caused the loss of the boat and all hands. At 8:00 a.m., the boat was running off Berehaven, at a depth of twenty-five feet and at two knots, when she became bow heavy. The Officer-of-the-Watch gave the order to "blow" the adjusting tank.

Unfortunately, the man at the valves operated the levers of the flood valve belonging to a different and much larger tank. As a result, no water was expelled from the adjusting tank, and a large amount of water was admitted to the other tank to aggravate the already too-heavy condition of the boat. The error was soon discovered, but not until the boat was out of control and going down fast; in spite of the motors doing full-back and the diving rudders set at hard-rise.

Lieutenant Hancock reached the Control room as the boat became firmly stuck in the mud bottom at 294 feet—ninety-four feet beyond the test depth of the boat! Had she been operating in deeper water, undoubtedly she would have continued her dive to a depth at which her hull would have imploded.

The hull began to leak, due to the extreme pressure, causing the water level in the engine room to raise at an accelerated rate close to the main motors. If the motors were flooded, they could not be used for any purpose. Every pound of leakage meant that the boat would be just that much more difficult to raise.

Hancock calmly surveyed their situation and prospects, then decided that the boat could only be brought to the surface by one desperate measure. There was the possibility that by skidding the boat along the bottom she could be worked up to give the diving rudders lifting power to break the mud suction. During this time water could be expelled from the trim tank by high pressure. Lieutenant Hancock accepted the risk that the trim tank bulkhead might rupture. Should this occur the boat would be lost with all hands.

In the process, the boat began to assume an upward bow angle until she reached a bow angle of six degrees and suddenly broke free. AL-4 had been on the bottom for one hour and ten minutes, and the water was only three inches from the main motors when she was freed. Drydock examination showed that the strains of her deep dive had changed the contour of her bottom from a concave to convex shape and she was no longer fit for service!

Such narrow escapes are the lot of all submariners, irrespective of nationality, just as some brave souls, in their desperate gamble with death, seems to go from one peril to another.

"One might have imagined," Chatterton wrote, "that Lieutenant Lewis Hancock, after his horrendous experiences with AL-4, would have been content in his future peace-time existence to carry on a quieter routine. Alas! This gallant gentleman, instead of continuing to go down below the sea, elected to soar aloft in the dirigible USS

SHENANDOAH, as her Executive Officer, and when she found disaster on September 3, 1925—Lieutenant Commander Hancock lost his life." At the time, the loss of USS SHENANDOAH was the worst aviation disaster in history!!!

When the links of each of these ominous events are connected, what becomes evident is that Death seems to not only have been stalking Blaison and SURCOUF, but also that they were destined to be involved in the worst submarine disaster of its kind. Together!!!

No other submarine family or submariner in the history of submarining has encountered such frightening psychic experiences as the Blaison's—all of which seemed to converge upon Blaison becoming involved in a death disaster with SURCOUF. When it occurred, the event must have given Francine's grandmother a great deal of inner satisfaction—beyond her greatest expectations—for it was the worst of its kind.

It was like Vaughan wrote in *Incredible Coincidences:* "When our consciousness observes something, we can make the future happen." When Madame Blaison's mother admonished her not to marry a submariner, which she did—her mother was determined that she would make the "future happen." And she did—in the worst way.

When you read of the SURCOUF-SS THOMPSON LYKES Collision in **Part IV, SURCOUF's Rendezvous with Death,** you could easily be led to believe that SS THOMPSON LYKES had been guided—as if by some alien mind with a third eye—into deliberately ramming SURCOUF. *(Woe to the inhabiters of the earth and of the sea! for the devil is come down unto you, having great wrath, because he knoweth that he hath but a short time. Rev. 12:12.)*

We need only rely on Tralins for support of this belief by analysis of his theory of psychokinetics relative to Blaison, Alain, Francine, and SURCOUF. But, in supplement of Tralins discourse, the author is privileged to have one of the few existent copies of an unpublished document—a goldmine of empirically deduced studies of psychokinetics (PSI)—by Robert J. Cassidy, EE, PE, deceased, entitled: *The Psychokinetic Laws of Images and Some Significant Postulates, 1966.*

Cassidy's intriguing study about the science of psychokinetics involved the manipulation of conceptual images across separations of time and space. Here is what Cassidy wrote, which could be applied to Francine's extraordinary encounter with Alain:

> There are known to exist certain sensitive relationships between mind and tangible objects.
>
> A calm, sustained, and positive attitude of mind is essential to an all-reliable control of psychokinetic effects.
>
> Whenever the mind makes contact in any manner with another mind, entity, or objects so as to form an impression or image of it, a permanent tie-line or connection is subconsciously established between that thing and its image in the mind.
>
> Eye-beams may very well be mind-beams, but are naturally coupled with ocular activity having to do with the focusing of critical attention by the mind upon an object or image of the object.

Had Alain, during his seductive manipulation of Francine through death symbolism, been in telepathic contact with an alien mind within SURCOUF—one which could have, by some subliminal means, distorted the minds of some aboard her??? This you shall read about!

This conjecture is not too far-fetched to accept, especially after further reading the Defense Intelligence Agency (DIA) report, *Controlled Offensive USSR (U), Behavior.*

In this astounding document, there appeared extraordinary input concerning ship-to-shore telepathy aboard an American atomic submarine, USS NAUTILUS (SSN-571).

It was a story which, after first appearing in French newspapers, apparently distressed scientists in the Soviet Union enough to motivate them into re-igniting and hurriedly accelerating their scientific efforts in biocommunications:

Soviet parapsychology research was actually stimulated by the 1960 French story concerning the American atomic submarine USS NAUTILUS. The French journalists splashed the rather now infamous

NAUTILUS story in the headlines "U.S. Navy uses ESP on Atomic Sub!" Ship to shore telepathy according to the French, blipped along nicely even when the NAUTILUS was far under water.

The speculating French sensationalized: "Is telepathy a new secret weapon? Will ESP be a deciding factor in future warfare? Has the American military learned the secret of mind power?"

In Leningrad, the NAUTILUS reports went off like a depth charge in the mind of L. L Vasiliev. In April of 1960, Doctor Vasiliev, while addressing a group of top Soviet scientists, stated:

> We carried out extensive and until now completely unreported investigations under the Stalin regime. Today the American Navy is testing telepathy on their atomic submarines. Soviet scientists conducted a great many successful telepathy tests over a quarter of a century ago. It's urgent that we throw off our prejudices. We must plunge again into the exploration of this vital field.

Although the U.S. Navy denied the reports of the telepathic testing aboard its atomic submarines, the Soviet hierarchy heeded Vasilev's advice and gave support, both moral and financial, to his dynamic view that: "The discovery of the energy underlying telepathic communication would be equivalent to the discovery of atomic energy.

Since 1962, Doctor Vasilev has headed a special laboratory for biocommunications research at the University of Leningrad. Major aspects of the work of this laboratory are to conduct research and to develop machines capable of monitoring, testing, and studying telepathic communication.

Soviet research into biocommunications phenomena does not appear to be earth-bound and limited to inner space, but apparently extends to outer space as well. The so-called Father of Soviet Rocketry, K.E Tsiolkovsky, started that:

> In the coming era of space flights, telepathic abilities are necessary. While the space rocket will bring men toward the

ledge of the grand secrets of the universe, the study of psychic phenomena can lead us toward the knowledge of the mysteries of the human mind. It is precisely the solution of this secret that promises the greatest achievements.

After reading the above excerpts from the DIA report, which also emphasizes that the power of the sub-conscious mind is vastly superior to normal consciousness, it is plausible that Alain could have had bio-communications with SURCOUF—before and after his manipulations alongside the garden pool.

Just as strange is that the revelations about bio-communications between USS NAUTILUS and shore were by French journalists. Alain was French, and his manipulations, between July and August 1941, were about a French submarine in American waters. Strange isn't it?

The scale of power is tipped in favor of evil when the attacked falls prey to its fascination, as did Francine. Francine should have countered Alain's evil act by denying and metaphysically reversing his suggestion of death for Blaison and SURCOUF. Mary Baker Eddy, in *Science and Health, with Key to Scriptures,* states: "Resist evil—error of every sort—and it shall flee from you. Error is opposed to Life." But, as an innocent child, how was Francine to know how to disrupt the brain waves on which Alain was transmitting his aggressive mental suggestion???

Society may never be purged of an evil eye, so long as we give continued power to let it affect us. It will remain as a latent and inevitable part of our lives until we learn how to apply the countermeasures necessary to destroy evil. Yet if Francine had applied a metaphysical sanction to deny Alain's devilish act of evil, through his imposition of negative mind control, could we say for certain that Blaison and SURCOUF would have survived???

This perplexing question can only be answered, and the adversity alleviated, after we have contacted and eliminated that underlying intelligence in another world which continues to play mischievous tricks on us.

The author observed a strange thing about Francine. She reminded him of the exquisite Fleurette Petrie, in *The Trail of Fu Manchu* by Sax Rohmer. In that **fiendish story**, Fleurette is **helplessly** transformed into *The Sleeping Venus* by the diabolical mind manipulations of Fu.

Since Fleurette was in a subtle state of amnesia, she could not reveal her real thoughts by writing, only by the spoken word. As for Francine, that traumatic psychic experience at the garden pool, involving her father and SURCOUF, caused her too much mental anguish to write about them. Yet, she **hesitatingly** related them to the author **verbally**.

From what you have read about Blaison's woman-folk, particularly about his **deluding** mother-in-law, you would could be led to believe that they each **were** unnaturally sensitive to psychic events—**that they seemed to be supernaturally** able to see, hear, and experience situations **that were far beyond what others encountered normally**. When the author was once asked if he believed, he replied: "Yes, I believe because I want to believe."

Part II

The SURCOUF and Muselier Affair

General, if you were to tell me that Admiral Muselier had tried to lead the Prime Minister's wife astray, I would say, 'Maybe.' But treason! Preposterous!

> Remarks of Captaine de Vaisseau
> Moullec to de Gaulle made in *No Laurels fro de Gaulle*
> by Robert Mengin, translated from French by Jay Allen.

Vice Admiral Muselier was a sailor of the Orient, an Ulysses, who gambled with troubles and amused himself with danger. He loved to maneuver and finesse, but patriotism, uprightness, and truth were his dominant characteristics.

> Capitaine de Vaisseau Louis de Villefosse,
> *Les Iles de la Liberete*

It is mad. Tomorrow I can die at the hands of the Gestapo fighting for England or even at the hands of the British Secret Service fighting for Poland—like Sikorski.

It is the same—all the same.

> Rolf Hochhuth, *Soldiers.*

If you were to substitute the words Muselier or SURCOUF into Hochhuth's remarks, you would have an almost identical story as that which could be told about the unfortunate General Wladyslaw Sikorski (1881—1943), Premier and Commander-in-Chief, Polish Free Forces, during World War II. (The story of Sikorski's plight will be briefly mentioned later).

The term assassination can be broadened to have three interpretations. One can refer to the insidious, defamation of another's character by lies, slander, smear, and spreading of vicious rumors, the second to the annihilation of an idea or ideal, and the third to the secret, treacherous elimination (killing) of a person or destruction of a thing, in this case SURCOUF. But, how can you kill something that is not alive! You do it by killing the idea for which it stands—the Free French Movement. Here, in *The SURCOUF Conspiracy*, the term assassination is liberally applied to each of these odious methods. Not only meaning the physical elimination of SURCOUF, but also the destruction of her reputation and downgrading her capability as a weapon of undersea warfare.

What follows is not about a rumor, but a fact of naval and political history based upon falsehood and a conspiracy. To better appreciate how and why the many rumors about SURCOUF originated, it is also important to reveal how and why Vice Admiral Emile-Henri Desire Muselier, Commander-in-Chief, French National Forces of Liberation (the Free French), was wrongly accused of treason by the British Government, and ordered to be hanged by a wrathful Churchill, over *l'affairs d' espionage*, which involved SURCOUF and nearly brought down the entire Free French movement. One can destroy the chain by destroying a link.

While Muselier, the only French admiral to flee France and rally to the Free French Movement, was cleared of charges against him and personally apologized to by King George VI of England, Prime Minister Winston Churchill, and his Foreign Secretary, Anthony Eden, SURCOUF, on the other hand, would remain unfairly condemned and would eventually die under circumstances which, to some, remain highly suspicious.

As evidenced throughout *The SURCOUF Conspiracy*, slander would be hurled at SURCOUF wherever she sailed, spreading from England to Canada, Bermuda, the United States, and North Africa. *The SURCOUF and Muselier Affair* reveals, especially, how Darlanists of the French Vichy Government of Marshal Henri Petain, based in London, and possibly Communists within the British Secret Service, conspired to double cross Muselier in an attempt to blacken his name, that of the Free French Movement, and of SURCOUF[1].

While the revered "Roquebert" was the design creator of SURCOUF, producing a concept far beyond what was expected of him, a living exercise in science fiction—it is important to know that the credit for fathering SURCOUF, from what the author has determined, must be also handed to Vice Admiral Muselier, while he served as a Capitaine de Vaisseu on the staff of Chef Adjoint du Cabinet Militaire du Ministre des Armes (April-December 1925). **(See Appendix "B", The Evolution of SURCOUF)**

Prior to this appointment, Muselier had served as a Capitaine de Fregate on the Delegation Navale Francois aupres de la Commission de Controle en Allemagne (August 1918-March 1925), and earlier in the Ministre des Inventions, Section Marine, from 1916-18. During Muselier's former appointment, it is probable that he had learned much about the secrets of the once-powerful German Navy's U-boat design and forward planning program, which included designs for more monstrous and powerful submarines still on the drawing boards.

This is how Vice Admiral Paul Ortoli, in his July 21, 1976 letter, told the author of Admiral Muselier's role in the conception of SURCOUF: "Admiral Muselier was a creative and imaginative personality. He was the father of SURCOUF; the idea for her existence belongs to him."

By sharp contrast, however, Vice Admiral Paul Gabriel Auphan, Vichy French Navy, co-author, with Jacques Mordal, of *The French Navy in World War II;* Chief of Staff to Darlan; and Vichy Minister of Marine following Darlan's death on December 25, 1042, in Algiers, told the author, in May 1976, that Darlan fathered SURCOUF during his tenure as Chief of Staff, Ministry of Marine, 1926-27. However, the author's close study of the careers of both admirals, Darlan and

Muselier, leads him to believe that Ortoli was right, that Muselier was more the father of the SURCOUF idea than Darlan.

By what has to rank with some of the strangest and tangential twists of fate in naval history as it was also Vice Admiral Muselier, the outcast of the French Navy, who was sentenced to death in absentia by Darlan, who gave birth to the Free French Navy, who designed the proud flag of Free France (the Cross of Lorraine superimposed on the tricolor of France), who fostered the resurrection of SURCOUF in England, and who saved her from being dismantled, in April 1941, by the Royal Navy for use as a cargo submarine on the deadly Malta run.

Muselier, who had been deliberately promoted then immediately placed on the retired list by Admiral of the Fleet Darlan after the start of World War II, was a graduate of L'Ecole Navale, class of 1899, and a classmate of Darlan's. Both were arch-enemies and bitter competitors—locked in an uncrossable chasm of fierce rivalry—for leadership and control of the French Navy.

Dorothy White, in *Seeds of Discord*, described Muselier as: "A man with the intelligent wind burned face, with black hair and eye, a mere shadow of a moustache, and a dark Mediterranean look of a pirate about him, and simple and human in his approach to people." He was an adventurous corsair, and even men enjoyed working under him. Because of his appearance, Muselier was nicknamed "The Pirate." Because of his often weird actions, he was also referred to as "The Madman."

Commander G. K. Collett, Royal Navy, who was on the Naval Staff of the Spears Mission to the Free French Movement, London, and who was Muselier's escort officer, in his *Pamphlet on Admiral Muselier and the Free French Navy, 31 January 1941,* referred to Muselier as "having a strong character and a heart of gold."

Darlan, it is mentioned in close circles throughout France, was able to advance faster and further than Muselier, who had humbler beginnings, because, it was alleged, his father had once been Minister of Justice, which office held the power of surveillance and control over the lives of every Frenchman. As a consequence, the source of Darlan's power was derived from the dossiers that contained dark secrets about many influential people who then had to comply with his slightest wish or whim to avoid public exposure to a scandal in their lives.

From a gleaning of *The Diaries of Sir Alexander Cadogan*, one of the classics of World War II, by Sir Alexander George Montagu Cadogan OM GCMG KCB, Permanent Undersecretary for Foreign Affairs and Executive Chief of the British Foreign Office, during World War II, one learns how and why *SURCOUF and the Muselier Affair* surfaced on January 1, 1941 and of the repercussions that followed and of the consequences remaining:[2]

> Got further evidence against Muselier. Talked to Anthony Eden [Foreign Secretary] about Muselier. Churchill of course wants to hang Muselier at once. I pointed out the possible adverse effect on the de Gaulle Movement and suggested we must consult de Gaulle first, who is away in the country. Eden agreed.

Muselier was arrested for treason against the British Crown by two Inspectors of Scotland Yard, Special Branch, and in the presence of a counterintelligence officer from MI-5 (Director General, Sir David Petrie, KCM, Kt CIE, CVO, CBE). There also was an intelligence officer of the Royal Navy present to witness the event and to assure that Muselier received proper treatment from Scotland Yard and while he was imprisoned in a cell for commoners at Pentonville.

Since the full official Scotland Yard, MI-5 (British Imperial Security Intelligence Service), and Admiralty versions of Muselier's arrest may not be available to the public, we must mainly rely on Cadogan's and Muselier's inputs.[3] The Muselier version was extracted from his extremely rare book, *Marine et Resistance*, which was allegedly suppressed throughout postwar France during the de Gaulle's regime as President of the Fifth Republic:

> On January 1st at 0200, my evening ended at Old House Hotel in Windsor with "God Save the King" and "Marseillaise", following a benefit for the British Red Cross

and British Women's War Workers. I did not of course dance. Mme Delysia, having had the amiable indiscretion to give my name, I was applauded.

Then a day of rest. I dine at the hotel, go to bed early and then on Thursday the 2nd, I am back home in London, at 49 Hallam Street [Knightsbridge]. I find there awaiting me Commander Stevens sent there by Rear Admiral John Godfrey, Royal Navy, Deputy for Naval Intelligence, and two inspectors, who invite me to follow them to Scotland Yard. I obey, thinking it a mistake.

Meanwhile, some twenty other inspectors were beginning to appear outside my door.

Stevens accompanied me with the greatest correctness. He appears much astonished himself and is altogether friendly with me. Before leaving my apartment, I was allowed to change into civilian clothes, for I do not wish a uniformed Free French admiral to be seen between two police officers, both for my own sake and for the honor of England and France. The Police do not allow me to take any personal effects with me.

(Commander Stevens, Royal Navy, first name unknown, was British Admiralty Liaison Officer for Intelligence to Muselier's Free French Naval Staff.)

What a twist of fate: Yesterday Rear Admiral Sir Charles C. Dickens, Royal Navy, Principal Liaison Officer to the Allied Navies, had telephoned me at Windsor to convey to me a New Year's greeting from the First Sea Lord, Admiral of the Fleet Sir Dudley *The Whale* Pound, Royal Navy, adding to them his own that he would have brought to me in person in London, if I had been there.[4]

Now I am herded under arrest like a common criminal on charges that I do not even know. Even today, 2nd January, I am to lunch with the Minister of Defense by invitation of the

British Government. The Admiralty surely is not involved in this affair, which I admit I cannot understand myself.

At about 1100, at the request of an inspector, Steven leaves. I had asked him to convey to my Chief of Staff the formal order to continue the struggle no matter what happens to me, and to presently conceal my arrest from the crews to avoid any agitation hostile to England and any relaxation of the war effort by the Free French Navy.

Stevens shakes my hand before leaving, and I ask him to call the First Sea Lord, A. V. Alexander, that I give him my word of honor as a sailor that I have done nothing to blame myself for. I remain in a room a Scotland Yard in the company of inspectors who are changed hourly.

They bring me lunch, then, after having me turn over everything that was in my wallet, and upon my asking the reason for my arrest, they inform me of a decree of ejection from British territory and a decree of imprisonment for the rest of the war by order of Prime Minister Churchill; all without giving me any reason for my arrest. About 1530 they transfer me by auto, escorted by two inspectors, to the prison at Pentonville.

There I undergo all the horrors of the treatment of common prisoners: search, measurement, medical exam and cell, or rather a cold dungeon, dark in the daytime, complete blackness from 1900 to 0700. I nevertheless obtain extra blankets after a visit to the doctor. I tell the doctor who pushes me around and thumps me in the side with his fists, "Do you know that I am a French admiral and a disabled war veteran?" He answers me, "If you were an admiral, you wouldn't be here."[5]

Complete access plus search. They removed my empty wallet and pocket book, including a lock of hair from a dead woman found in the lining.

I feel the extremity of misery, but I am ready to suffer even more, my confidence is at peace, as I pray for the liberation of France.

131

The usual fare of the common prisoners; two exercise periods, for about one-half hour each morning and evening, even in the snow. I try, by counting the steps to make five kilometers a day; for clothing: a blue civilian suit, my old black hat that served me as a pillow, and a blue overcoat without insignia of rank during my escape from Paris.

On January 2, Foreign Secretary Anthony Eden personally informed General de Gaulle that Vice Admiral Muselier, whom de Gaulle considered as a rival for power, had been arrested by the British Government for espionage and treason.

De Gaulle, Cadogan wrote, "affects to be skeptical about Muselier." Neither the memoirs of Muselier or of de Gaulle delve as deeply as either one should into this extraordinary affair, except that Muselier, in his second book, *De Gaulle Contre le Gaullisime*, states the entire incident was staged by persons within de Gaulle's Free French Secret Service (Bureau Central de Renseignements et d'Action).[6] Charges had been filed against Muselier based on what was proven to be forged pro-Vichy letters. As you shall read, throughout *The SURCOUF Conspiracy,* similar tactics would be employed to condemn SURCOUF before and after her death.

The charges alleged that the defeat sustained by the Anglo-French attack upon Dakar (Operation MENACE), in late September 1940, had resulted from indiscreet remarks by Muselier, whose disapproval of the operation was an open secret, and that he planned to hand over SURCOUF, the pride of the Free French Navy, to Darlan, whom he despised, for £2,000.

Whatever the reason or source, the repercussions of Muselier's arrest shook the Free French Navy to its lowest echelons. And, it did nothing to relieve the strain and distrust existing at the lowest echelons' between the Free French Navy and the Royal Navy since the SURCOUF Affray of July 3, 1940.

According to Dorothy Shipley White, in *Seeds of Discord,* "The story [of Muselier's plight] went far beyond London—even across the Atlantic. It was known long before the incident at St. Pierre was to occur, and was certainly not anything to increase confidence in the Free French when they came under fire of the diplomatic offices."

One, did not have to know Muselier intimately to know that Darlan, to him, was a scourge upon the honor of France and the French Navy, and that Darlan would have been the last Frenchman that Muselier would ever have spoken to in civil terms, except to invite him to a duel until death.

To provide background for understanding the essence of this chapter and as to why Muselier had a loathing for Darlan (his classmate at Ecole Navale), we must quote from an unpublished document submitted to the Foreign Office on, July 20, 1940—less than a month after the surrender of France to Germany and Italy—by James A. W. Marjoribanks, who was British Vice Consul, Marseilles, when Muselier was Prefecture of Marine there:

> I had dinner last night [in London] with Vice Admiral Muselier, who commands, under General de Gaulle, The French Naval and Air Forces in this country. Perhaps these notes on what I know of Admiral Muselier's character and antecedents may be useful.
>
> During his command of the Marine Nationale, Marseilles, which ended in his forced retirement in November 1939, I was in constant touch with Admiral Muselier, chiefly about Contraband Control work.
>
> I came to appreciate his tireless energy and the drastic measures he took for the suppression of traffic with the enemy which, however ruthless they might seem, were undoubtedly most necessary in a community so venal and corrupt as Marseilles.
>
> The occasion for Muselier to have been placed on the retirement list would appear to be his refusal to carry out an order from the Ministry of Interior (Justice) instructing him to release M. Jean Baptise Rocca, one of the biggest business men in Marseilles and President of the Seed Crusher's Association,

whom he had arrested on suspicion of trafficking with the enemy via neutral countries.

But the real motive lying behind Muselier's retirement would appear to be his opposition to Admiral Darlan, who is a man of entirely different temperament and whose views on naval strategy were opposed to Muselier's.

Darlan was naturally opposed to his nomination as Director of Contraband Control, which would have necessitated Muselier's presence on the Supreme Marine Council.

Muselier has an intimate knowledge of the working s of the Deuxieme Bureau [French Secret Service], has worked with Clemenceau, and was in charge of anti-espionage work during the two year French Occupation of the Rhineland.

He is in my opinion completely disinterested and in his fanatical opposition to Germany a most valuable addition to our defense. He has the faults of his race, talks too much, and is not careful enough to whom he is talking, but I think his period in the wilderness has sobered him. These faults tend to obscure the real qualities of the man and if handled properly can be of great service to England.

From Marjoribanks account, one could easily draw the conclusion that Darlan condoned selling contraband to Germany and Italy months before his open collaboration with them and long after the Fall of France.

Sir Alexander Cadogan's diary entry for January 3 was:

De Gaulle came to see Eden and me at 1045. He made an impassioned, but quite undocumented defense of Muselier. Of course he doesn't want a scandal. We promised an impartial investigation. I tried to get the Muselier story right. There isn't a case yet. It was that "Baby Dictator" Winston who ordered immediate punishment for Muselier.

Sir Alexander's entry on the 4th was:

Alexander[7] rang me up this morning to say that Muselier's lot should be alleviated. I agreed. I wanted to hand him over to the admiralty. But, when Alexander realized that Churchill had a hand in the affair, he went all wacky and said we should be very careful. I said I was quite prepared to take the responsibility of making Muselier more comfortable.

I discovered later that Alexander had called "Winnie" and asked whether the Admiralty could take over Muselier and he said "No". How frightened of Churchill these people are.

So am I, because he's impulsive and undependable. So when Admiral Dickens came to see me later I said I could do no more. Muselier had been moved from Pentonville to Brixton, which is better, and I rang up Maxwell and told him to do the best Brixton allowed.

Muselier's correlative statement was:

Admiral Dickens and Commander Collett came to see me. They seem to be more upset than I by this sinister affair. They tell me that General de Gaulle is doing everything he can to get me out, and that the Admiralty is also for me. Admiral Dickens insisted he was going to find me a lawyer. I repeat to him that I haven't said or done anything against the British Government. At any rate, I am preaching to a convert who knows very well that my whole efforts has been directed to the outfitting of our ships to contribute to Victory. I show him my cell. He left me with kind words of comfort and friendship.

During our conversation, I went over a list of persons who might profit by my detention. Since, on the day of my arrest, I had read in the press that negotiations had been going on between the British Government and Darlan. I, therefore, had the thought that my detention might have been one of the conditions exacted by Darlan for the collaboration of the two fleets. This idea had sustained me, for I reasoned that my personal sacrifice was a little thing for the result it may achieve.

That same morning, having gone escorted by guards to find some underwear in a suitcase which had been bought to me, but which I could not keep in the cell, I noticed the name of a Doctor de Kerguelon on another suitcase. During the night, some signals in Morse code had reached me from a neighboring cell. I had not answered them, not wishing to be put in the wrong about anything.

I was certain, now, that other Frenchmen had been arrested at the same time as I. Then, I heard some cries and recognized the voices of my orderly, who was at the end of his rope, in a neighboring cell, and already seriously ill prior to his arrest. He was suffering from one of his attacks of epilepsy. At the sight of the suitcase of Doctor de Kerguelon, I immediately thought of Howard, with whom the doctor had some difficulties, and whom I knew to be my personal enemy. I gave his name to Admiral Dickens as the possible author of the plot of which I was the victim.

In the afternoon I learned that by the intervention of Admiral Dickens and the Admiralty with the Foreign Secretary, I was to be transferred to the prison at Brixton. They again made an inventory of my few personal effects and escorted me to Brixton by automobile. All of my valuable possessions remained at Pentonville: watch, insignia of the Cross of Lorraine of the Free French National Forces, cigarette case once presented by the Second Division of Cruisers, and the papers they found on me. I still managed to keep my insignia of the Legion of Honor.

At Brixton, a furnished room much more suitable was available to me. But I was very cold. A broken window pane, no radiator and a severe draft; I became seriously ill during the night. And, in the morning I was forced to clean up myself the results of my repeated illness.

I must add that during those nights the aerial bombing recurred repeatedly and added nothing to cheer the situation. I had reached the point of wishing that a "lucky" bomb would free me from excess of moral and physical suffering.

On Sunday morning, the 5th, of January, I saw the doctor and was sent to the infirmary where I must say that the guards did all they could to improve my lot. The same day, I received the visit of Capitaine de Vaisseau Auboyneau and Lieutenant de Vaisseau Serreulles; accompanied by a Major [Kenneth] Younger,[8] of the Intelligence Service [MI-5, Scotland Yard] and an English civilian.

They informed me of the intention of General de Gaulle to come to see me and that the affair was certainly going to be cleared up. Younger, having learned at the prison that I had no money, lent me a pound note, which enabled me to buy fruit and cigarettes.

On January 5, Free French Navy Capitaine de Vaisseau Auboyneau and Moret (pseudonym for Capitaine de Vaisseau Moullec, Chief of Staff for Muselier) and Capitaine de Frégaté Gayral, Wietzel, and Ortoli, as the instigation of Moullec, signed a memorandum addressed to the British Admiralty supporting Muselier. They presented it as a delegation to Admiral Dickens on the 6th. (Ortoli was not present, however, as he was readying SURCOUF for departure from HMS Dockyard, Devonsport, Plymouth, England, to Holy Loch, Scotland.)

On January 7, Cadogan wrote: "Churchill has authorized removal of Muselier to Greenwich (where Byng was held before being shot). At 3:30 was with the Brazilian whom I graveled about Muselier "affairs".

The Brazilian Connection centered around a beautiful Mlle d'Anjou, who had recently arrived from Indo-China to join the Free French Forces. For a few days she served as a relief secretary to Lieutenant Villers, in the research office, Carlton Gardens. Her permit to enter Carlton Gardens, Muselier wrote, had not been authorized by a Major Howard (pseudonym for a Capitaine de Frégaté Meffre). The latter ordered de Soubeyran to have her excluded from the Free French

Headquarters, but as Mlle d' Anjou protested Soubeyran insulted her. Mlle d'Anjou's finance, a Brazilian diplomat, therefore, provoked Soubeyran into a duel.

Muselier was informed of the incident, opposed the duel, and having received the visit and complaint of the young diplomat and of Villers, severely rebuked Howard for his clumsiness and Soubeyran for his rudeness and otherwise settled the matter. But, Howard, for reasons of his own, became all the more inflamed against the Free French Navy, Muselier, Villers, and Mlle d'Anjou.

In justice to Soubeyran, father of five children, he had joined the Free French in spite of a serious head wound inflicted during the German shelling of Cherbourg. This explained instances of his irrationability, which led Muselier to consider replacing him.

Muselier's collateral statement continues:

> The Admiralty, having succeeded in taking me in charge until the end of the inquiry, transferred me to the School of Greenwich, a dependent institution of the Royal Navy. But first, at the end of the morning, I was taken to Scotland Yard where General de Gaulle was to see me. Before seeing the general, Commander Younger showed me, in the presence of an agent of the Surete, the evidence used as a reason for my arrest.
>
> As soon as I saw the first letter, written on paper with the letterhead of the Consulate of France at London, signed by General Rozoy[9], naming me in all the letters and speaking of the Expedition to Dakar, I said laughingly to Younger that it was a forgery, and that I was astonished that the important British Secret Service had been so easily duped.
>
> "I beg of you, be so good as to consult a specialist in counter espionage from Scotland Yard [MI-5] in my presence".
>
> They bought in a high official and I said to him: First of all, if the facts were true, the correspondent would certainly not have named me. Secondly, he would not have used official paper of the Consulate. Thirdly, the supposed author of the letter, General Rozoy, is too intelligent and too prudent to sign

such a writing, which, in case of being intercepted, ran the risk of having him immediately arrested. In the fourth place, has anyone even verified the signature of Rozoy and characters of the typewriter.

This letter is an obvious forgery! In my career, I have often had in my hands documents of this kind, as Chief of the Information Service, in Germany, particularly, or as Chairman of the Council in France, I assume you that I would not have been fooled by it.

The Scotland Yard Specialist concluded: "The admiral is exactly right".

Younger, who had been only recently attached to the Intelligence Service and who had been overwhelmed by the events, then wished to show me the other papers. I answered him laughing:

"No use if they are all like that one. I have no time to lose. I believe General de Gaulle is waiting for me".

I was taken into an office where I saw him alone. He assured me that my detention would not last very long and that he would do all he could to shorten it. The interview was very short.

My aides de camp had asked for themselves to share my lot but I refused to inflict the fatigue on them. But, the Admiralty let me know that one of my orderly officers could accompany me to Greenwich School where I was to be a guest of the Royal Navy.

What was my surprise upon seeing Lieutenant Villers (an artillery officer), also at Scotland Yard. He told me that he was arrested at the same time as I, and that he had been detailed to serve me as orderly officer during my stay at Greenwich. We were transferred during the day, considered to be under arrest "de rigueur" and guarded by brave marines who must have been under orders to carry out their task with kindliness and tact.

Two police officers slept in the room next to mine. A Royal Navy Officer was attached as a liaison officer and an enlisted orderly was placed at my disposition. I could not speak kindly enough of all the attentions of the Greenwich commander and more generally of the Admiralty; evidently convinced of my innocence, to mitigate my detention. I had a radio set; I could receive the visits of my staff officers; the table and wine were excellent. Needless to say, Villers and I used them only with the greatest discretion. We gained the impression of being treated as honored guests and not as officers subject to trial or arrest.

During the days of my residence I was able with Villers and my staff to reconstruct the events. Included in the arrest of Villers and myself were Doctor de Kerguelon, his fiancée, Mlle Herrinex, Mlle d'Anjou, the fiancée of a Brazilian diplomat, my chauffer (a soldier in the Air Force), and my orderly (a seaman). I addition, a whole group of officers from my staff had been on the verge of arrest, especially Capitaine de Vaisseau Moret and his wife; Capitaine de Frégaté Wietzel; Captain La Porte, an aide de camp; Lieutenant Savary, a naval aide de camp; Captain Michel, an air force aide de camp; a total of 18 arrests had been planned by the British.

All this was the effect of a series of contrivances plotted at Carlton Gardens by a group of suspect individuals headed by Commander Meffre, alias Howard [also a Sergeant Colin, Free French Air Force]. Howard was Chief of Security for General de Gaulle, who later fired him. I had caught him in falsehoods several times, and was disgusted even more by his low police practices. I had noted that my apartment had been searched illegally, and my chauffer had been offered bribes by a deserter from the Free French Air Force, who had attached himself to Howard, to spy on me

On January 9, Cadogan wrote in his diary: "X" (who remains unidentified throughout Cadogan's diary) has confessed that the Muselier documents are forged! So we are releasing everyone and

Churchill apologized to de Gaulle at 5 this afternoon! I gather he did fairly well, though he said to Eden: "When I'm in the wrong" (I didn't know he ever admitted he was), "I'm always very angry"! *(The Lord openeth the eyes of the blind: the Lord raiseth them that are bowed down: the Lord loveth the righteous. Psalms: 116-8 KJV)*

On January 10, Cadogan wrote: "The British Government released Muselier. Churchill apologized to de Gaulle yesterday, but won't have anything to do with Muselier! We have to apologize to him!

Muselier returned to duty as though nothing happened. However, a coolness and breach occurred between Muselier and de Gaulle until their definite break occurred over the St. Pierre and Miquelon Affair, an event that would again deeply involve SURCOUF, please Churchill, frustrate Roosevelt, and cause a lasting breach between Roosevelt and the American Secretary of State, Cordell Hull.

Here is Ortoli's July 21, 1976 and March 13, 1978 subsequent input about *The SURCOUF and Muselier Affair*:

> At no time was Admiral Muselier capable of such an ugly action. He never had the slight idea of turning SURCOUF over to Vichy. His book, which you have read, is quite clear on his point. It had been told that Muselier, intending to turn SURCOUF to Vichy, decided to relieve me of my command of SURCOUF because he wanted to give me the honour of believing me unable to partake in such a dastardly compromise.
>
> Muselier was a man with some weaknesses, but of great honour, and I personally have no feelings towards him but that of the highest respect, gratitude and affection.
>
> I must say that the attitude of the Royal Navy was impeccable and entirely on Admiral Muselier's side during this unfortunate episode. It is regrettable; however, that there were Frenchmen involved who duped the good intentions of that powerful intelligence organization MI-5.

Now follows de Gaulle's input concerning Muselier's arrest, as extracted from his book *The Call to Honor*. He explains that Brazilian Connection, who Rozay was and why he wasn't available for questioning, and how he (de Gaulle) pressed for Muselier's release under the threat of a Free French break with the British Government and that SURCOUF had been one cause of the "affair."

During my absence in Africa, Admiral Muselier had fallen afoul of the other services. Some bitter personal conflicts and office tragic comedies had arisen at Carlton Gardens scandalizing our volunteers and worrying our allies. I found myself up against a startling error on the part up the British Government, itself led astray by insidious Intelligence.

The siege fever with which England was then afflicted made information and security organizations increase and multiply there. Intelligence to the British is a passion quite as much as a direction of Free France. On this, it employed some who were well inspired and others who were not. In short, at the instigation of certain undesirable agents, the British Cabinet was suddenly to inflict upon the Free French a wound which just missed being disastrous.

In the evening of January 1, when I was in Shropshire with my family, Mr. Eden sent me a request to come and see him urgently at the Foreign Office, where he had recently replaced Lord Halifax, now appointed Ambassador to the United States. I went straight there the next morning. As he welcomed me, Eden showed signs of being deeply disturbed. "Something lamentable," he said, "has occurred." We have just had proof that Admiral Muselier is secretly in touch with Vichy, that he attempted to transmit the plan of the Dakar Expedition to Darlan at the moment when it was being prepared, and that he is planning to hand over the SURCOUF to him. The Prime Minister, as soon as he heard, gave the order to arrest the admiral. It has been approved by the Cabinet. Muselier is therefore in prison. We have no illusions about the impression this dreadful affair will make on your people and on ours. But it is impossible for us not to act without delay".

Mr. Eden then showed me the documents on which the accusation was based. They consisted of typed notes on the headed paper and stamp of the French Consulate in London still occupied by a Vichy official and apparently signed by General Rozoy, formerly head of the Air Mission and recently repatriated. These notes gave an account of information allegedly supplied by Admiral Muselier to Rozoy. The latter was supposed to have passed them on to a South American legation in London, from which they were to reach Vichy. But, on their way, according to Mr. Eden, clever Intelligence agents had intercepted the documents. "After a thorough inquiry," he added, "the British authorities were, alas, forced to believe in their authenticity".

Though dumbfounded at first, I immediately had the feeling that "it was laid on a bit too thick" and that it could only be a huge mistake arising from some machination. I said so clearly to Mr. Eden and told him that I was going to see for myself what there might be in it, and that, meanwhile, I would treat this extraordinary affair with every possible reserve.

Not however, at first, going so far as to imagine that the affair could have been staged under cover of the British Secret Service, I attributed it to Vichy. Might not some of Vichy's henchmen have manufactured and left in England this delayed action bomb? After forty-eight hours of inquiry and reflection, I went to see the British Minister and said to him, "The documents are ultrasupect, both in their context and in their supposed source. In any case, they are not proofs.

Nothing justifies the shocking arrest of a French vice admiral. Besides, he has not been heard. I myself am not allowed to see him. All this is unjustifiable. For the moment, at the very least, Admiral Muselier must come out of prison and be treated honorably until this dark business has been cleared up".

Mr. Eden though disconcerted, did not consent to give me satisfaction, alleging the seriousness of the inquiry made by the British Secret Service. In a letter, then a memorandum, I confirmed my protest. I visited Admiral Sir Dudley Pound, First Sea Lord, and invoking the admirals' international code, invited him to intervene in this dishonoring quarrel picked with one of his peers. As the result of the steps I had taken, the attitude of the British authorities showed some hesitation. And so I obtained permission, as I had demanded, to go and see Muselier at Scotland Yard, not in a cell but in an office, without guard and without witnesses in order to demonstrate to everyone, and to tell him, that I rejected the imputation of which he was victim. Finally, certain indications having led me to think that two individuals, who had been incorporated in our own "security service" during my time in Africa, in French uniform but at the insistence of the British, had something to do with the affair. I sent for them and became convinced, at the sight of their terror, that this was decidedly an "Intelligence business".

To General Sir Edward L. Spears, British Army Liaison Officer to my staff, summoned by me on January 8, I formally confirmed my certainty. I told him that I gave the British Government twenty-four hours in which to set the admiral free and make reparation to him, failing which all relations between Free France and Great Britain would be broken off, whatever might be the consequences. That same day Spears came, crest fallen, to tell me that the error was admitted, that the documents were simply fakes, that the men to blame confessed, and that Muselier was coming out of prison. Next day the Attorney General visited me, told me to appoint someone to follow the inquiry and the trial, in the name of Free France, which I did.

That afternoon at 10 Downing Street, Mr. Churchill and Mr. Eden, obviously much put out, expressed to me the British Government's excuses and its promise to repair, in regard to Muselier, the insult which had been done him. I must say this promise was kept. Indeed, the reciprocal change of attitudes on the part of the British and of the admiral was so complete that it soon turned out to be excessive, as will be seen later.

I will not conceal that this lamentable incident, by setting in relief the element of precariousness always present in our situation relative to our Allies, did not fail to influence my philosophy on the question of what should definitely be our relations with the British. However, the immediate consequences of the trouble were not all bad. For the British, no doubt desirous of making up for their error, showed themselves more disposed to discuss with us matters awaiting settlement between us.

So it was that, on January 15, I signed with Mr. Eden a "jurisdiction" agreement concerning the Free French in British territory and especially our own courts, which would operate "in accordance with the national military legislation". At the same time we were able to open negotiations with the British Treasury with a view to a financial, economic, and monetary agreement.

Muselier's troubles became the troubles of all Free French naval officers and men, and the event was not without troubling SURCOUF's crew for Blaison wrote to Theresa:

> The admiral was imprisoned by the British for four days at Pentonville, with ordinary convicts, and poor Ortoli and I just missed ending our days in the Tower of London.
>
> Poor Cabanier[10] was detailed by Muselier and Scotland Yard to unravel the affair. He said to me, "I believe it possible for me to someday end up in the Thames. Come, Blaison, old man, let's have a good dinner. It would perhaps be our last one."

As events turned, it was Blaison, not Cabanier, who ended up on the bottom—not of the Thames—but on the bottom of the Caribbean Sea.

For some unexplained reason, as evidenced by Blaison's letter, the charges against Muselier seemed to have also involved the Free French Navy submarine officers. Perhaps it was a Nazi or Vichy plot to cast suspicion upon them to limit the effectiveness of the minelayer RUBIS (Capitaine de Corvette Georges Etienne Jules Cabanier) and to keep SURCOUF (Capitaine de Frégaté Ortoli) from going on North Atlantic patrol, operating out of Halifax, which she was about to do.

Regrettably, too late to contact him, Squadron Vice Admiral Cabanier passed away during the week of October 24, 1976, during the process of the author's writing about this fascinating episode. Fortunately, however, we do have Ortoli's 1976 input about the Muselier affair, along with brief remarks by Blaison as excerpted from his war time correspondence to Theresa.

On January 11, Muselier received this letter of apology from Anthony Eden:

> Foreign Office SWI
> 11 January 1941
>
> PERSONAL
> Dear Admiral Muselier,
>
> I have been ordered to transmit to you the expression of profound regret from his Majesty's Government for your detention by British authorities on suspicions which are now shown to be without foundation.
>
> His Majesty's Government has been convinced that these documents which, at the outset, seemed to throw suspicion on you, are false.
>
> As soon as these conclusions were reached, instructions were given for you to be released immediately.
>
> His Majesty's Government hopes to continue its collaboration with yourself and with the Free French Naval Forces, under your command, which are rendering such signal services to the allied cause.

I beg of you, at the same time, to be so good as to transmit the regrets of His Majesty's Government to Lieutenant Villers.

And in Mr. Eden's handwriting the following:

In renewing to you the expression of profound regret,

Believe me,

Sincerely yours,
/s/A. Eden

Muselier's input:

Shortly afterward, I was invited to lunch at 10 Downing Street by Prime Minister Churchill and Mrs. Churchill, and later had the honor of an audience with His Majesty the King. I refused to receive the press, anxious to avoid publicity for an incident equally regrettable for the British Government, for General de Gaulle, and for the Free French Navy; whose chief had been infamously treated. It was necessary to win the War and I had no desire to lower the prestige of the Churchill Government which the press could have attacked.

It was agreed between General de Gaulle, the Attorney General (Sir Donald Somervell) and myself that Commander Cabanier, commanding the RUBIS, who had no part in the difficulties arising between Carlton Gardens and the Navy, would follow the direction of the inquiry and that the guilty ones, whoever they were, would be prosecuted.

Cabanier, returning to sea, was replaced, in spite of my protests, by Lieutenant Dechelette of the General War Staff. Dechelette received orders to report directly to General Gaulle or his chief of staff, and not to me. In spite of my insistence to Sir Donald, the instigators of the affair could not be prosecuted. Howard was only called up as a witness, but was finally detained for the duration of the war on orders of the Home Secretary. As for his liar friend, Colin, he was sentenced to 12 months in prison by the jury of Old Bailey. Both were also stricken from the rolls of the Free French Forces, which saved them from the harder authority of a military tribunal.

After receiving the letter of apology and vindication from Mr. Eden and following a conversation with General de Gaulle, I agreed, for the sake of our cause, to retain my office and continue my work of organizing the Free French Navy.

Here are excerpts from what Commander Collett, Liaison Officer of the Royal Navy to the Free French Naval Forces, wrote of the "affaire" when he left office:

These internal plots are most disagreeable for Admiral Muselier, whose only aim is to get on with this war. The climax of this internecine quarrel is too recent to be discussed. But this tragic story has left its mark. All of London, from the most elegant houses to the journalists of Fleet Street, has heard rumors of Admiral Muselier's arrest.

Few people knew why; but it was accepted simply in confirmation of other rumors that had been heard, and of which it was spoken aloud. Few people knew of his liberation, and although Admiral Muselier received an apology from His Majesty's Government, an impression of doubt and of suspicion remains in the minds of those who do not know the whole story.

This does not matter much to those with whom the admiral has no contact, but for those with whom he has direct contact, the importance is very great. His own sailors, for example, had learned to admire him and to consider him their leader and inspiration. Almost all of them had heard the story of his arrest, and a half knowledge of the story can be as dangerous as no knowledge and the discipline of the Free French Forces can suffer severely from it.

In a conspiracy which had amazing similarity with the Dreyfus Affair, a case which bitterly divided France in the 1890's, Muselier became the only flag rank officer, of World War I or II, to be arrested on a charge of treason. And, SURCOUF was one of the stated reasons for his being so charged and imprisoned.

In view of the degrading and horrendous experience encountered by Muselier at the hands of Scotland Yard, the British penal system and the wrath of Churchill a report in Muselier's favor would be timely, so here it is. It was a memorandum (minute) signal by no other than by Rear Admiral John H. "Speed" Godfrey, Royal Navy, Director of Naval Intelligence (1939-42), as an endorsement to Collett's *Pamphlet on Muselier and the Free French Navy:*

MOST SECRET   N.I.D 0651 February 3rd,
                                                    1941
                                M. 01509/41 (Copy)

REPORT BY COMMANDER COLLETT ON
FREE FRENCH NAVY

Even if Admiral Muselier has not reached the standard of perfection attributed to him by Commander Collett, there can be no doubt that he has made a courageous effort in the face of many difficulties to build up the Free French Navy, that he co-operates well with us and is now easy to work with and that his popularity with his personnel has increased. He has a great admiration for our Navy and his gratitude to the Admiralty for their attitude in a recent delicate situation is profound.

He could exercise more influence on his Navy if he visited ships and ports more frequently. A faulty system of control of the Naval Staff by civilian and military authorities inclines him to remain on guard at Headquarters. General de Gaulle like most continental

Generals, cannot think in terms of sea power and subordinates naval operations and requirements to military.

This question of French staff organization is being fought out now and if Admiral Muselier cannot obtain a reasonable decision Admiralty help may be necessary. If Muselier asks for this we can tactfully make certain useful suggestions without hurting anybody's feelings. The Free French Navy is operationally part of our own and we are therefore entitled to express our view if, owing to faulty principles of higher command, that force is handicapped, as it is, in reaching maximum efficiency.

The poor standard of good order in some of the Free French ships is due to the small number of suitable officers available from which Muselier can pic his captains. He has shown his broadmindedness by asking that British senior officers should send for captains of French ships when dissatisfied with their appearance and discipline and tell them off.

/s/ JOHN H. GODFREY
Director of Naval Intelligence

Distribution:
CINC, The North
CINC, Western Approaches
CINC, Home Fleet
CINC, Portsmouth
CINC, China
CINC, America and West Indies
CINC. Mediterranean
CINC. Rosyth
CINC. South Atlantic
CINC. East Indies

FOC, Orkneys and Shetlands
FOC, North Atlantic
FOC, Dover

Evident from Godfrey's minute is his caustic remark about General de Gaulle's limited knowledge of sea power, whose intrusion into naval matters, involving SURCOUF, was to greatly annoy and hamper Muselier and result in the latter's resignation as Commander-in-Chief, Free French Navy. Although the British Admiralty had sympathized with Muselier and had just saved his hide from a black Vichy plot, it would be helpless to save Muselier in his confrontation, with de Gaulle, in March 1942, following the involvement of SURCOUF in the St. Pierre and Miquelon Affair and her loss.

It is also very important to note from Godfrey's minute that:

1. SURCOUF, as an element of the Free French Navy, was operationally a part of the Royal Navy.

2. Senior Royal Navy officers were authorized to express their views and to take corrective action when dissatisfied with the appearance, discipline and performance of Free French captains and then ships.

As will be evident through the Burney liaison reports, the Royal Navy seemed not to exercise this authority or prerogative to the fullest possible measure. Perhaps this was avoided in the interest of preserving harmony between the Free French and Royal Navies, or perhaps the word didn't get around. Or, it is possible that the Royal Navy had enough of SURCOUF, and her ills and involvements in the Atlantic, and was only to glad to be rid of her by releasing her, in January 1942, to American naval command in Pacific.

On February 13, 1941, to offset any possible ill-feeling of the Royal Navy towards the Free French Navy, even though The Free French were not involved in Operation CATAPULT, and no doubt to pacify De

Gaulle and Muselier, the Admiralty issued the following <u>Confidential Admiralty Fleet Order</u> (CAFO):

CAFO 314 Free French Navy; Need for more Cordial Relations with (M. 023894/40)

Their Lordships have received information from various sources that the relations existing between ratings of the British Navy and the Free French Navy are not as satisfactory as they might be and, indeed, that, in a number of cases, grave discourtesy has been shown by British ratings toward ratings in the Free French Navy.

Their Lordships feel that this state of affairs is possibly due to a lack of discrimination between the status of men in the Free French Navy and of those French who adhere to the Vichy Government. Their Lordships desire that British Naval officers in a position to do so will make clear to those under their command the very special position which the Free French personnel occupy in relation to ourselves, and how essential it is that this position should be recognized.

The Frenchmen who have joined the de Gaulle movement comprise a very small minority of their countrymen and, in taking this step they have invited much harsh and hostile criticism from many other Frenchmen. They are, moreover, fully aware that the line of action which they have taken may lead to the victimization of their families in France.

Their Lordships feel that the courageous attitude adopted by these Frenchmen is worthy of the highest praise and encouragement, and that not only are their services of appreciable value in the present difficult manning situation, but that the example given may have a great effect as time goes on in swaying public opinion in France more and more in our favour.

Their Lordships are assured that, having these considerations in mind, the men of the Royal Navy will give every possible support to the policy of showing encouragement, respect and sympathy towards those Frenchmen who are serving in the Free French Navy as well as those who have joined our own Navy.

As this work will testify, CAFO 314 seemed to accomplish very little toward pacifying relations between the ratings of the Royal and Free French Navies, especially as concerned SURCOUF. There were too many remembrances and external disrupting influences impinging upon both groups, such as long historical differences and distrust coupled with the tumultuous SURCOUF Affray of July 3, 1940 and disinformation being spread by Nazism and Vichyism, to bring about this union.

Perhaps, also, this was unfortunate situation was compounded by CAFO 314 having been classified CONFIDENTIAL, which resulted in its limited and controlled circulation that kept it away from the eyes of most British ratings.

It is also probable that the release of CAFO 314 was specifically timed to coincide with SURCOUF's commencing joint operations with the Royal and Royal Canadian Navies on February 18 for on January 11,1941 to escort merchant convoys from Halifax to the Western Approaches to the United Kingdom(Vice Admiral Percy Noble, Royal Navy, Commander-in-Chief, Western Approaches).

On March 7, as if to substantiate CAFO 314 and to provide an example of why the Free French ratings and officers, were frightened about their families' probable "victimization" by Vichy, aside from being mistreated by the Germans in the Occupied Zone of France, Madame Blaison received a letter from the Ministry of Marine, Vichy, demanding return of a 2,000 franc "loan of honor" given to her, in January, 1941, by Contre-Admiral L. M. G. Cayol, Vichy French Navy (Ecole Navale Class of 1900) during her visit to Toulon.

Because of Blaison's continued association with the Free French Navy and SURCOUF and for reason that he was guilty of desertion, she, as a navy wife, was no longer entitled to receive a pay allotment from Vichy. In addition, she was requested to return the "loan of honor" which she did with a strong denunciation of Vichy. Here is what she wrote about this episode on January 9, 1978: "I was left, therefore, without any resources, despite the lies of Admiral Auphan."

Madame Blaison's horrendous experience with the Vichy naval official is what could make Auphan's and Mordal's book otherwise informative book, *The French Navy in World War II*, published in the United States by the U.S. Naval Institute, Annapolis, unpalatable to those who know better. Here is a citation from their work, which runs counter to Madame Blaison's experience with the Vichy French Navy:

> Any anxiety the sailors of the Free French navy might have had for their families back in France was quickly dispelled. These families were of course immediately dropped from the list of naval personel receiving the legally established allotment of the husband's or fathers pay and allowances. But they were just as promptly taken upon on another list, entitled "Assistance D". The "D" was for dissidents. Here they received exactly the same allotments as was prescribed by regulations for families of men in the regular French Navy. Even those in the Occupied Zone received this money. Thus, the wife of a FFNF petty officer living in her small Breton fishing village found herself in the same financial situation as her neighbor who's husband was serving on a cruiser at Toulon.
>
> Later, during the dark hours of 1944, a few extremists at Vichy insisted that these payments be stopped, but the new measures applied solely to the families of a few leaders, and only in theory, at that.
>
> For instance, the family of the Chief of Staff of the Free French Navy, who were living in Algiers, continued to receive regular monthly allotment from secret funds.

French against French. Who to believe? In the light of the dastardly treatment the Blaison woman folk received at the hands of Vichyists, and after having met with Vice Admiral Paul Auphan, in May 1978, in his retreat near Versailles, ironically while the author was accompanied by Mademoiselle Francine Blaison, the weight of his acceptance is on the side of Madame and Mademoiselle Blaison. Kill the enemy, not his family!

So concludes *SURCOUF and the Muselier Affair* with its many hidden and open facets, ramifications and side-affects, a few of which you have just read. What has been told has enormous implication, and sets the pace, for what follows throughout the remainder of this work; the background without which the reader would be exposed to just plain historical account of SURCOUF's assassination.

It's like Robert Mengin suggested in his book, *No Laurels for de Gaulle,* when he gave his version of the Muselier Affair, to which he was a witness:

> Some film director of the future [should realize] that here is a film to make [about de Gaulle vis-à-vis Muselier], against the background of wartime London under bombs, and against Scotland Yard, always reliably sinister in films.

Truly, had Muselier's two works not been suppressed throughout France, and had they been translated for an international audience, it is not likely that de Gaulle would have survived for as long as he did politically.

If the French Navy should ever build a series of warships bearing the names of her famous admirals, it should well be called the Muselier-class.[11] According to *Warship International, No. 1, 1984,* two nuclear aircraft carriers were to be built at Brest by the French Navy, one of which is to be named CHARLES DE GAULLE.

Part III

Blaison's Last Letter to Therese Analyzed

Its been years since I've heard his dear voice, and even yet the ascendency of his spirit is as strong with me as before. I cannot make a decision, hear any judgment, without invoking the reaction he would have effected in a similar situation, and then I act accordingly.

Madame Therese Blaison, Paris, September 25, 1977

'For this reason a man will leave his father and mother and be united to his wife, and the two will become one flesh.

Mark 10:6-9

Show me a hero and I will write you a tragedy.

F. Scott Fitzgerald

If the things a man writes are an expression of his personality (and they cannot be anything else) then what greater influence can his personality and his writings have than that of a woman with whom he has lived with for many years.

Richard Rogers, Musical Stages, An Autobiography

Honour is nobler than Gold.

Gaelic Proverb

The letters we write represent our inner most subconscious thoughts and seldom fail to provide the key to our underlying personality when writing to those we love and trust about what beguiles or vividly concerns us most. A letter written in love or another powerful emotion, because its words remain where we cannot, can provide a life in itself for years after being read. It may provide just what is needed to start, strengthen, or encourage a precious soul on the road to life or save one from devastation.

Blaison's soul revealing letters to Therese, each filled with words of beauty and meaning, provided him a field of escape for his fiercely competitive spirit, a spirit in which his hostility and stress could be expressed or relieved using his mind rather than through combat which seldom came his way after June 1940. Rather, it seemed that his worst enemy was aboard SURCOUF, rather than against that Nazi enemy at sea.

On February 11, 1942, from Bermuda, Blaison wrote the last of his encoded letters to Therese and Francine. This one was loaded with forebodings and secret references.

Understandably, because he named French whom he believed used the Free French movement as a cover for continuing their manipulations for Vichy France, they were sought after during the postwar period. As late as 2006, even after the passing of Blaison's womenfolk, the author had inquiries about them. For years, they were secure in a Paris bank vault to preclude further attempts to steal them from the apartment of Therese and Francine. In a bank vault, they also served as their protection against malicious French interests who occasionally coerced her and Francine until their deaths.

Only the author has been privileged to read most of the *Blaison Dossier of Wartime Letters to Therese* for purposes of appropriate inclusion in narratives about SURCOUF.

One letter because of its strong sense of loyalty and obligation to France, as Blaison knew and loved it and because of its sound patriotic appeal to save her from German tyranny, was exhibited in the Museum of Liberation, Paris. Several non-controversial letters were read before interested religious and veteran groups. A select few, in 1952, appeared in the work *L' Epogee de Surcouf et l' Commandante Louis Blaison,* by Captained de Frégaté Maurice Guierre, French Navy, Retired, but the others have not appeared publically since. *(I charge you by the Lord that this epistle be read unto all the holy brethren. 1 Thessalonians 5-27 KJV)*

Blaison's brilliancy, power of expression, choice of words, as only the French can write them, reveal the fineness and purity of the man and aesthetic quality of his mind, and exemplifies why Therese and Francine were so intrinsically attached to him; beyond anyone and above all else, except SURCOUF. *(Learn the value of a man's words and expressions, and you know him. Lavater.)*

However, Fate was inevitably against him. As a ship's captain Blaison had to pay the price of traditional of command, and if it was within his power to do so—without loss of a soul serving him.

Many years after Blaison's letter, his morally inspiring words continued to have a profound effect upon Francine: "I always feel near to my father. He is very much alive in my heart and mind," she wrote the author in 1978.

Now follows Blaison's last letter to Therese, who he always referred to as his "little girl":

February 11, 1942

My darling little girl,

Once more I have the opportunity to try to get a letter to you by way of America. I hope that those I have sent you by this means have reached you. Alas, I have had no news of you and it is very hard! Must I forever remain in silence? My confidence is immense, but my loneliness is great. I cannot refrain from worrying over you.

At night my heart is especially wrung, but it is a fine solitude as my thoughts are about you.

I have just spent some restful days, but with all the stream of my usual occupations, of course. I am perfectly well and do not suffer any hardship. How much I wish it were the same for you, my adored ones! I would like so much especially, on the so longed-for day of my return, to recreate for each one of you a beautiful life, pure and gay. So many hours of our previous happiness should not be sacrificed in vain. I cannot imagine not having our finest recompense, that of finding each other again.

I reread that letter you wrote me about the "sad song." What an immense weight will be lifted on the day of my return. That will be my new birth to life. For the past two years, almost, I have not known for one second what it is not to have a weight on my heart, not to have transports of sadness that run through each hour, because of you.

It is a difficult test, but we shall pass through it victoriously. Keep your faith and your love for me, as I keep mine for you. Twenty-five years ago others and many still this time, passed through the same torture. We paid for nothing then [Blaison is referring to World War I]. Think of all those who suffer and who are in solitude more than you, and who do not know the value of the slightest gesture of affection, of sympathy or of a least word of encouragement.

I am happy to know that you received the money I sent you. I learned it by an official telegram that Mme D. sent me. It is the only means of communication remaining open to me, about you, and difficult to use.

In any case do not worry about me, I have been and will still be exposed to the minimum of risks of war.

Poor Robert gives me some anxiety, his legs ache following some rude changes in climate and he has a long journey to make to reach his next destination.

It will be difficult for me to go into darkness again without your loving letters. In spite of the fact that I can mail my letters, yours seldom reach me when I am wandering about. I know very well that you are writing to me, but regrettably, your cherished letters are not reaching me. If mine reach you, even though rarely and that thus you are spared this ordeal, I shall not have enough words to thank God. I never ask anything for myself, and the little that I have has been given me. But for you, so many things to ask: to escape privations, discouragement, and especially what I fear above all, those words that wound, and which can make more ill than blows.

Remember well and always that there is not an hour of my life that is not filled with love and tenderness for you and our little Francine. I look forward to the day that I can build castles in Spain for you both and to surround and overwhelm you both, with a life in which there is no longer a shadow of fear and war, and in one that is filled with that kind of tenderness that wants the presence of the other at their side. For me there is nothing more to wish for on earth than this.

How many beautiful hours we had together and didn't know how to appreciate them for their true worth, letting them be obscured by meanness which we should have ignored! I remain more than persuaded that happiness is not purchased by cowardice or by a resignation to weakness. It is he who gets mired in meanness who transforms love into a vague association in order not to pass his life alone. You would want none of that, or I. Do you remember how much you, like myself, was afraid of that practice?

My dearest one, do not permit yourself to accept the idea of blaming me for your troubles. Believe me, these present ones will save us from the more difficult ones. With faith and confidence, others have struggled before us, through worst trials, and have overcome. It will be hard, but we shall overcome also. We will swamp the enemy and it will all be an atrocious memory for us. From these difficult times we will always be able to draw on our self-respect after we have endured and won.

Never forget the message of Christ. Read and reread the *Gospel*, thus only will you avoid the fascination of the accomplished fact. The message of pity and love, never forget it, it is the only one. We will find each other again through it and through it alone.

Embrace well my parents and your Mama and pat Black for me. Tell them I am counting on them to watch over you. As for my little one yonder, it is your hour to go to bed. I say goodnight. Sleep well, calm and serene and surrounded and rocked by the tenderness of my love. Remember that your dream of happiness and tender joy is locked with mine. We are closer to one another than we have ever been. Goodnight my little one. Goodnight my little Francine.

Yours in love and life,
/s/ Louis, Papa

"Robert" was the code name for SURCOUF between the Blaison's and was derived from the name of Baron **Robert** Surcouf of St. Malo, the Napoleonic corsair, after whom SURCOUF was named.

It is not known how Blaison had his mail routed to Madame Blaison in Vichy France via the United States, nor was she aware of how this was done. It is believed, however, that Blaison's mail was forwarded via Madame "D" (Madame Rachel Desseignet) who, at the time, was a minor official of the Free French movement, on the staff of Admiral Muselier, 4 Carlton Gardens, London.

How would we have fared under a similar stress-strain situation during those last days of Blaison and SURCOUF in the Bermuda Triangle had he known, as we do now, of The MOST SECRET (IMPORTANT) and KEEP UNDER LOCK AND KEY naval messages between The British Admiralty and CINC,AWI dealing with the behind the scenes manipulations and intrigue seemingly intended to rid the Atlantic Ocean of SURCOUF. Perhaps it is just as well that Blaison did not know what we know now. Had he known, it may have shattered his faith and respect for his British ally. *(Letters that are warmly sealed are often coldly opened. Jean Paul)*

Using *BIORHYTHM: A Personal Science*, by Bernard Gittelson, as a guide, it is interesting to retrospectively analyze Blaison, from a biorhythmic standpoint, on the day he wrote his last letter to Therese and Francine, February 11, 1942. Then, Blaison's emotional rhythm was on the negative side and sloping downward, after his having just experienced a biorhythmically emotionally critical Day on the 9th.

This could explain why he seemed to be sinking into black despair, feeling emotionally depressed, and why he was apparently trying desperately hard to bolster his own ego as well as trying to reinforce confidence in Therese and Francine by mention of his eventual return to them and France.

For examples: The author refers to these statements by Blaison: "on the longed-for day of my return", (our) "finding each other again", "It is a difficult test, but we shall pass through it victoriously.", "Keep your faith, I shall keep mine for you."

In writing his loving, but powerfully penetrating words to Therese and Francine, did Blaison sense that he was to be his last voyage, "the accomplished fact", with "Robert" and that he would never return to his "little girl" and Francine, except through the word of Christ???

The author believes so from these entries: "Never forget the message of Christ. Read and Reread the *Gospel*, thus only will you avoid the fascination of the accomplished fact. We will find each other through it and through it alone."

It is a "fact", in a Christian sense, that Blaison could now only be reunited with Therese and Francine through Jesus Christ.

Unlike Boyer, Burney, Gough and Warner, Blaison did not seem to share any inner warning that death was upon him and SURCOUF. ("Do not worry about me.")

Perhaps the closest Blaison came to prophesying SURCOUF's death was contained in his phase "he [Robert] has a long journey to reach his next destination. *(I have a rendezvous with Death at some secluded barricade and to my pledged word and true, I shall fail that rendezvous. Alan Seeger)*.

But *The Sad Song (Chanson Triste)* by Jean Lahore, of unbearable beauty and love which reminded Blaison of Therese, was overflowing with portents of ill omen, each with deep personal meaning (a fatal rapture of the deep). First to cite the song and then to analyze its words as concerned the death of Blaison and SURCOUF, a case of fiction, that merciless occult force in action, before fact:

> In thy heart, love, in moon-light slumbers,
> Soft and sweet like summer's clear night.
> And to flee from life's supplication,
> 0 let me die, lost in its light.

> All my grief there will be forgotten,
> When from my sad heart thou lullest restless grief and
>   longing
> In the calm loving care of thine arm.
> Then I will rest my head on Thy bosom

> Ah then shall grief from me depart,
> And thou wilt tell one little story,
> Some lover's story,
> A song of love close to our hearts

> Then from thine eyes, tearful with sorrow,
> In thine eyes, I'll drink from Thy soul

Kisses of love and sweet caresses,
Then my life shall be whole.

Because of the Blaisons' emotional and intellectual affinity for *The Sad Song*—a unity of mind and soul—through their telepathic letters, could it be that Therese had an unconscious premonition that she would never see Louis again???

Indeed, this was Blaison's swan song. He would never return from the depths of the Caribbean Sea to see Therese's "eyes, tearful with sorrow" over his loss or to receive her kiss of life. *(Although swans sing in early life, they do not do so as beautifully as before they die. An ancient Greek proverb.)*

The overwrought, fatigued Blaison did "flee from life's supplication", especially that turmoil incurred during his last days in Bermuda; involving SURCOUF, the British Admiralty, and the Royal Navy. Blaison did die—lost in the night of the Caribbean Sea—and all his "grief [would] be forgotten."

O let me die, lost in its light.
All my grief there will be forgotten,

His "life" could never again "be whole" without receiving kisses of love and sweet caresses" from the woman he loved; a past connection which could never be renewed. "Until death doth we part?"

Vaughan, author of *Incredible Coincidence*, would probably classify the Blaisons' turn of coincidence to destiny as an Encounter of the Fourth Kind, since *The Sad Song* had such deep personal meaning to them; "involving life's mates and lovers."

Blaison was right in that he and "Robert" would be sharing a wanderer's fate during "a long journey" into "darkness" of the Lesser Antilles Deep, beyond the point of no return—likened to the legendary "wandering" of Falkenburg, Captain of the illusive *FLYING DUTCHMAN*, who sought his redemption through womanly love. *(And, the earth was without form, and void; and darkness was upon the face of the deep. Genesis 1:2 KJV)*

But, in a sense, Blaison was wrong, for, as you shall learn in **Part III, SURCOUF's Rendezvous with Death,** it was not "difficult [for him] "to go into [that] darkness" where he would never receive Therese's "loving letters". There, in the darkness of the Caribbean Deep, he would "forever remain in silence" in "fine solitude" with only loving thoughts and concern about "his little girl" and Francine.

To the end, Blaison never lost his resolve that the Allies would ultimately win, and that France would be restored to her former dignity as a free nation. *(Liberté toute entière. M.)*

In a sense, Blaison was wrong again about the outcome of he and "Robert". They were devastatingly exposed to "the risks of war" while in the fringes of the Caribbean sector of the Bermuda Triangle. There, they were victims of not only the Triangle's full wrath and mercilessness but also from wrath of a human kind, beyond expectation.

There is an ancient Oriental proverb that: "*He who fears most, lives longest.*" There is not one shred of evidence to conclude, from Blaison's last letter, that he feared making that "long journey" with "Robert" to Tahiti. But he should, as a commanding officer must be in constant fear that a situation could occur which would be beyond his ability to avoid or rectify. Collision at sea is one such event.

That Blaison overlooked the risk of dying by a means other than being combat connected—seemed to be his fatal error; the "albatross around his neck", the "immense weight" that would only "be lifted on the day of (his) return." That he was preordained to "remain in silence" with that "immense weight" for eternity, with no "new birth to life" was inevitable.

Strange that among Blaison first letters to Therese, specifically that one of his March 18, 1931 from Toulon, and in this, his last letter, he strongly mentioned "a weight" as if he were referring to the lifting of the weight of that dead albatross from the neck of the Ancient Mariner.

In his so doing, from another point of view, it appears evident that the obvious "weight" was his concern for the welfare of Therese and Francine rather than concern for any hardships he would encounter with "Robert" while enroute to, or in, the Pacific.

What Francine has recalled about her father's last letter is that his last written thought was mention of her name.

What is extremely baffling about Blaison's last letter to Therese is that there not the remotest hint that he nor SURCOUF where intending sail to any destination other than to Tahiti via the Panama Canal. Yet, SURCOUF's movement south unleashed rumors that she was determined to liberate Martinique and to obtain that gold required to finance de Gaulle's Free French movement.

Regardless, and above all, you must know now that Blaison did not have an alien thought in his mind and that he and his submarine could never have done anything treacherous against Free France or her Allies; nothing like those despicable rumors that you shall read about in **Part IV: SURCOUF's Rendezvous with Death.**

Part IV

SURCOUF's Rendezvous with Death

I did not accept my sword at the Ecole Navale to bring dishonor to France or myself!!!

> Capitaine de Frigate Georges Louis Blaison
> in a letter to his wife, Theresa, October 1941.

Disaster is unlike anything in human experience. It strikes quickly. It changes the lives of all it touches, and its effects are felt long after the event. And, perhaps more important, its forces are largely outside the control of people whom it most affects.

> Francis Kennett,
> *The Greatest Disasters of the 20th Century.*

It is never one single mistake that causes a disaster. It is always a series of contributory errors, most of them of small consequence, but taken with a little bad luck . . . ."!!!

> *Hungry as the Sea* by Wilbur Smith

If you disbelieve the occult and mystical implications about Blaison and SURCOUF revealed in Part I, you will have to accept that SURCOUF was positively destined to die, one way or another, while reading Part III.

Permit me to reveal why!!! On February 5, 1942, the day after SURCOUF had arrived in Bermuda, the Commander-in-Chief, Americas and West Indies (Vice Admiral Sir Charles Kennedy-Purvis, Royal Navy), after conferring with Burney and after reading copies of his liaison reports to Flag Officer, Submarines (Vice Admiral Sir Max Kennedy Horton, Royal Navy), sent a MOST SECRET message to Horton—paragraph 4 of which is cited as follows:

> SURCOUF departs Bermuda 12th Feb for Tahiti via the Panama Canal unless otherwise ordered. For political reasons it may be considered desirable to keep her in commission, but my view is that she should proceed to the United Kingdom and be paid-off.

To be "paid-off", in Royal Navy parlance meant to be placed on the as good as dead list by the Admiralty or for indefinite lay-up or the breaker's yard for ships no longer serviceable. Or, in other words, the Royal Navy was trying to rid itself of an albatross (SURCOUF) around its neck. *(The Ninja lures the enemy into making false estimates and judgments that result in erroneous military or naval actions. Or, when the enemy was united, the Ninja divided him.)*

From what we know about how SURCOUF pitifully gave herself up to the sea, we can surmise that whichever course she took from Bermuda—whether to England or to Tahiti—she faced crucifixion either by decommissioning or by collision with SS THOMPSON LYKES. SURCOUF had somehow incurred the maximum allowable demerits, and now was about to be eliminated from the surface of the sea for her beauty and infractions against conventionality. SURCOUF was being ordered to leave our world as there was no longer anything she could accomplish for the Royal Navy. Throughout military and naval history, the conventional way of dealing with an awkward situation is to place the matter into harm's way and then eliminate it.

However, Horton seemingly came to SURCOUF'S rescue by a return message on the 6th that was also MOST SECRET:

> I am sure Commander, Free French Forces, Southwest Pacific, can make use of SURCOUF in an active war zone. In defense of their soil, I consider SURCOUF may be of considerable use. SURCOUF occupies a peculiar position in the French mentality and the Free French would hate to pay her off.
>
> In any case, her care and maintenance would be a nuisance in the United Kingdom, therefore, I strongly recommend SURCOUF proceeding as already ordered.

Horton implied that SURCOUF's presence in England would be "a nuisance" or persona non grata—as if she were a lethal enemy—or that she was an albatross around the neck of the Royal Navy. It was an obvious subliminal message that someone never, ever, wanted SURCOUF, *l'enfant terrible,* back in England again.

However, Admiral Horton's intervention was still a prescription for disaster because SURCOUF's survival probability was greatly reduced; such as to invite her total destruction. For one, she was required to depart Bermuda with only one propulsion motor operable. This would have reduced her underwater speed and maneuverability substantially. Second, she was routed by Admiralty orders as to compel her to remain surfaced at night in the heavily trafficked Caribbean Sea approaches to the Panama Canal without running lights. This was a dangerous area in which to die, likened to ordering SURCOUF to enter into a mousetrap. (Panama Canal's wartime requirements were that vessels approaching its entrance at night had to remain 80 nautical miles off either side of the Canal, and, for their own safety against German surface raiders or U-boats, without running lights!!!)

Another woman entered SURCOUF's life story.

The forlorn Muselier, an idealistic individual, the man who missed postwar greatness by a hairsbreadth, could not have come to Bermuda at that time because he was being treated by a woman, in an unconventional way.

For this bit of behind-the-scenes intervention, we refer to her sympathetic husband's unpublished testimony. The following is an excerpt from a postwar interview with Rear Admiral Leonard W. Murray, Royal Canadian Navy, Retired, conducted in Ottawa in May 1970, by a historian of the Canadian Ministry of Defence, for purposes of officially recording oral histories of senior officers who were prominent in the Royal Canadian Navy.

> Well poor old Muselier came back from the St. Pierre and Miquelon operation with a very bad case of bronchitis, and we had him in bed at our home for five days and my wife rubbed his chest with liniment and things like that.

Muselier's trip to Bermuda to say bon voyage and adieu to SURCOUF, Blaison, and her officers and men, was "cancelled"—because he was enticed by the comfort of that woman's hand, which could be likened to a siren diverting Muselier from his objective. *(In his study of human psychology, the dreaded Ninja makes exhaustive investigations of the behavior of his victim while under the influence of a woman. Under such a situation, man exhibits weakness in judgment like no other time in his life.)*

If you are dubious about the Ninja's assertions concerning the powerful, amorous, and often adverse, effect of women upon men, permit the author to provide an unparalleled example by inserting excerpts from Geoffrey Bennett's study, *Nelson, The Commander*:

> Nelson's contemporaries were at a loss to understand how a man of his creative genius and greatness as a naval admiral, and as one who put his trust in God Almighty, could have become the enslaved lover of Lady Emma Hamilton. She could make him believe anything because he could not resist the passion

offered by such a Queen. He was her dupe, and she dominated his thoughts and actions, which explains his consequent mistakes. Theirs was a love that lasted until his death.

As an aside: From a reading of Geoffrey Bennett's study, one could easily be led to believe that the alluring Lady Emma Hamilton was a secret agent for Napoleon, as the Mata Hari of her day, to mislead Lord Nelson.

According to *The Black Art, A Black Magic Book of Terror*, by Rollo Ahmed, in mariner's lore it is told that of all the spell-workers in human form, none is so dreaded as the female brewers of hell-broth, as they live by conjuring contrary winds and wrecked vessels. Because of that directional similarity of motion—circular—could there have been some unearthly connection between the death of SURCOUF and Alain malevolently stirring that pond, in the presence of Francine, and that woman soothingly rubbing Muselier's chest??? Again, we may never know that answer, but from a psychic venue it is an intriguing and legitimate inquiry.

How Muselier's cancellation—a decision postponed, affected SURCOUF is evident, for had he arrived in Bermuda—if only for a matter of hours—the resulting delay in her departure could have averted the worst submarine disaster in history.

May we speculate, therefore, that had that noble woman not comforted Muselier, the SURCOUF-SS THOMPSON LYKES Collision may have been averted: That behind the death of SURCOUF and those 130 souls was a woman??? (Behind every *l'affaire du etat* and event is the touch of a woman!!!)

We may never know, but Muselier knows, wherever the soul of "that man with a heart of gold" hovers today??? This we do know: that man's admiration for woman, a name that conquers man and that never waivers, and that Muselier, with a lock of a women's hair in his wallet, was no exception to this universal rule.

So here it was at last from Muselier: PROCEED ON YOUR MISSION!!! (Die "quickly as possible.") Blaison and SURCOUF were committed. Time would be no longer on their side. Muselier, because of his own problems with General de Gaulle over the St. Pierre and Miquelon Affair, and unaware of SURCOUF's fatal disabilities, had, when he ordered: PROCEED WITH YOUR MISSION!!!, unwittingly committed her, Blaison and his crew, to what was virtually her suicide voyage. It was as if Muselier were re-enacting the role of Pontius Pilate, who had ordered Christ's crucifixion, when he reluctantly committed SURCOUF to her death. *(To die, as if by Japanese Samurai Code, for the cause of an Imperial Edict, which demanded victory or death, and preferred death to dishonor.)*

In the view of the Royal Navy, SURCOUF was to be forgotten, forsaken, unforgiven, and Baron Robert Surcouf's savagery aboard KENT would ultimately be avenged.

According to Yutaka Yokota, in *Kamikaze Submarine*, "one must either fight honorably to victory, or use the short sword to commit seppuku, which the Westerners call 'hara kiri' as atonement for failing." SURCOUF, the greatest, most powerful submarine in the world, even if she had to go beyond the limits of prudence and good reason, would never have to suffer the dishonor of being paid-off and decommissioned during the greatest war in history.

SURCOUF's rendezvous with death was awaiting her. Dying in a black hole of the Caribbean Sea was more honorable than the fate awaiting her in England. Yet, unlike the Samurai, who had seven lives to give to their Emperor, SURCOUF had but one to offer for the liberation of France and the likes of her would never be reborn seven times by the French Navy to serve France.

Blaison was no longer master of his fate, as he was when Fate decreed that he avoid death with PHENIX. Now, Muselier had made a pronouncement of doom on all human beings aboard SURCOUF, French and English alike. His decision led SURCOUF straight to disaster and death, "as quickly as possible."

SURCOUF and Blaison had no escape. They were now irrevocably committed to keeping their rendezvous with the SS THOMPSON LYKES, an uninvited stranger from out of the night who would serve as the deadly instrument for their becoming the world's worst submarine disaster—together!!!

SURCOUF—with Death closing in upon her fast—would be "paid off" by being impaled by SS THOMPSON LYKES—an Allied merchant ship—and Blaison would die with her. Some embodiment of evil would soullessly allow no divine intercession—like a mother's soulful plea for the safety of her son, Blaison, or for SURCOUF that night. It was as if SS THOMPSON LYKES were a hunting dog seeking its prey in the direction that its nose (bow) was pointed.

If mathematicians were to determine the probabilities of the SS THOMPSON LYKES-SURCOUF collision occurring, they would practically have to use infinity as the yardstick of measurement for the odds against it. Yet it happened!!!

As if it were a portent for a disaster beyond a disaster, on February 9, 1942, the 83,423 ton USNT LAFAYETTE (AP 53), the ex-French luxury liner SS NORMANDIE (Captain Joseph Blancart), renown for her high speed and competition for the covered Blue Riband of the Atlantic with the SS QUEEN MARY, caught fire alongside her pier on North River, near the foot of West 49th Street New York City. While the SS NORMANDIE was outlived by her English rivals QUEEN MARY and QUEEN ELIZABETH, this magnificent triumph of the ship builder's art set a standard for luxurious ocean travel that has rarely been rivaled.

Within an hour, she was a raging inferno. By late evening the beautiful ex-NORMANDIE, the finest creation of architectural and marine engineering in the world and equipped with one of the finest fire control and extinguishing systems that could be installed aboard such a ship, as if stricken by a wrathful god and weighed down by tons of fire fighting water, capsized and settled on her side in fifty feet of water. She was dead, and of no further use to any navy, except for sale as 1,000 feet of scrap.

USNT LAFAYETTE, while blacked-out had zig-zagged her way across the Atlantic to escape Nazi U-boats, was being converted from a smart luxury liner, of magnificent arrogance, into a drab troopship for operation by the U. S. Navy.

Thus, during February 1942, Free French morale was dealt a double blow by the American Navy, as the pride of her merchant marine and that of her navy, each the epitome of their kind in the world, became victims of tragedy.

As an aside, Captain William Vincent Astor, USNR, who was serving as Coordinator of Intelligence for the Third Naval District, Boston, but with an office in New York City, was relieved from his position immediately following the USNT LAFAYETTE disaster. The reason given in Hyde's *Room 3603*, was that Astor's cover had been blown by his conspicuous presence while fire fighters fought to extinguish the flames that engulfed ex-NORMANDIE.

As a further aside, during the author's May 1978 visit with Madam Therese Blaison and Mlle Francine Blaison and while meeting their friends at the Free French Club in Paris, our discussions switched from SURCOUF to the loss of the SS NORMANDIE in New York Harbor. One elderly Free French member adamantly charged that the fire was deliberately set by pro-Vichyists within the French Line (Compagnie Générale Transatlantique) who were sympathetic to Nazi Germany. He continued, so the ex-NORMANDIE would not be available for use by the Americans during their war against Germany.

That the gentleman's remark was not far afield as Waverly Root, in his book, *The Secret History of the War,* wrote that during April 1939, four months before the beginning of World War II, Germans agents had tried to destroy the NORMANDIE while she was dry docked at Le Havre, France. The German attempt was frustrated because the French military counter-espionage service had learned about the German plan, and thus had heavy guards placed around the ship. So, the German agents, Root stated, shifted their attention to the nearby liner, SS PARIS, which was undergoing repairs.

About the destruction of the USNT LAYAYETTE (ex-SS NORMANDIE) in New York Harbor, Root wrote:

> The public knew nothing about the German attempt to destroy the NORMANDIE at Le Havre, so the official explanation that the fire and flooding that destroyed her alongside the North River Pier 82, New York, was accepted as an accident. However, authorities knew that the origin of the

fire was not as innocent as all that. They knew that flames had appeared simultaneously at several different locations aboard her, and that they spread with incredible rapidity. A post-mortem study of the fire led to the opinion that inflammable chemicals of the type used by Nazi Germans had provoked it.

The official announcement concerning NORMANDIE's disaster was that it was not sabotage, but an accident. But doubt persisted, not only because it is often the official attitude to disclaim that possibility in such cases so as not to warn the perpetrators of the crime that investigations are continuing, but because of the timing and nature of the blow.

Since the NORMANDIE was being prepared for use as a troop transport, her destruction would have been of direct use to the enemy, and that it occurred on the eve of her sailing likewise seemed suspicious, since that would be the optimum moment for an act of sabotage to be committed—after the expenditure of the time, money, and effort to convert and outfit her, and just before that investment was about to be utilized. The loss of the NORMANDIE must have caused a considerable derangement of military and naval intentions for her deployment.

Regardless of the differences of opinion as to how the NORMANDIE was destroyed in New York Harbor, whether by German or Vichy agents, her pathetic loss was an outstanding example of history repeating itself and of persons who should have known better ignoring it.

Here is why: On April 18, 1939, the SS PARIS caught fire and heeled over in her berth due to over flooding by French fire fighters. This disastrous episode was widely publicized internationally, and the May 8, 1939 edition of the highly popular *Life Magazine* profusely illustrated the casualty. Thus, with the body of evidence that appeared in *Life Magazine*, which widely circulated in New York City and throughout the United States, there should have been no intellectual reason—a no-brainer or exertion of brain-horsepower—why New

York City fire fighters took no precautions from the offset to avoid duplication of the unfortunate and widely publicized circumstance that befell SS PARIS. No excuse what so ever, as once ex-NORMANDIE showed the slightest indication of inclining fighting that fire should have stopped. It would have been the lesser of two evils to do so, rather than expending months of salvage effort and considerable monies to upright her. Thus, it was possible that ex-NORMANDIE could have been rehabilitated for wartime service. Even after she was up righted, her hulk was seriously considered for use as an aircraft carrier.

It is a stark fact that ex-NORMANDIE's senior naval architect and designer, the Russian-American Vladimir Ivanovich Yourkevitch, was on the scene and offered his technical expertise. The suggestion of Yourkevitch, who early in his career was a designer of several Russian submarines passenger liners, was to open ex-NORMANDIE's sea cock's to flood the lower decks so she would settle on the harbor bottom that was only a few feet below her hull. With the ship stabilized, water could be pumped into burning areas without the risk of her capsizing. However, his suggestion was allegedly rejected by the Commander, Eastern Sea Frontier and Commandant, Third Naval District, Rear Admiral Adolphus Andrews, USN, Annapolis Class of 1901.

On the scene, the Mayor of New York City, Fiorello H. *Little Flower* La Guardia, severely chastised Admiral Andrews for ignoring Yourkevitch's sound practical advice. Yet, the mayor, having control over the New York City Fire Department, could have ordered the fire fighters to stop the flooding when the inclination of the ex-NORMANDIE was obviously noticeable. But he did not.

Mayor Foirello H. La Guardia's mind set to not transgress an authority outside of his organizational jurisdiction, even though it involved the fate of the USNS LAYAYETTE (ex-SS NORMANDIE), was an outstanding example of not having the courage to implement the power of his municipal office to effect and support his firm and intellectual conviction during an international and wartime emergency. The SURCOUF Conspiracy is replete with several such climatic and decisive incidents.

Regarding the author's opinion as to who may have sabotaged the ex-NORMANDIE? he believes it was by Vichyists as related to him by that elderly gentleman at the Free French Club, Paris, in the presence of the Blaison women folk. While German agents in the New York City area may have known about the conspiracy, Vichyists in the employ of the French Line would have had unrestricted access to ex-NORMANDIE to facilitate their treachery.

Now back to the main stream of this story: Amid all this fatalism and mysticism, glory and honor, and diplomatic and political intrigue surrounding the fate of SURCOUF, and as much as she attempted to gallantly engage the enemy and to emerge victorious, she is the only submarine of World War II to be unofficially accused of replenishing German U-boats and for sinking Allied shipping. These rumors first surfaced in November 1941, while SURCOUF was training with American submarines out of the American naval submarine base at New London, Connecticut.

"It is rare," said Louis Nizer in *The Implosion Conspiracy*, "that defendants charged with serious crimes have no prior criminal record." SURCOUF had an impeccable past. Yet, here she was—serving gallantly in war and on the threshold of the nuclear age for submarines—being wildly accused of the most heinous charge in the catalog of crimes—treason!!!

But my exhaustive analysis of SURCOUF's wartime chronology disclosed not one shred of evidence to support these vicious lies and conspiratory rumors.

For example, German U-boats did not appear along the East Coast of the United States until January 12, 1942, when at 1940 hours U-123 torpedoed the 10,000 ton British flag passenger ship SS CYCLOPS (Captain Leslie Kerslie) 300 miles west of Cape Cod. This sinking was the beginning of Operation DRUMBEAT, Hitler's undersea campaign to extend the Battle of the Atlantic as close as possible to America's supply lines to her Allies.

By June 1942, U-boats, according to Captain John M. Waters, Jr., USCG, Retired, in *Bloody Winter,* slaughtered 360 Allied merchant ships off the American coastline, due to American Navy unpreparedness and to its ineffective anti-submarine effort, at the cost of only 8 U-boats. It was a "happy time" for German submariners.

On the day CYCLOPS was sunk, SURCOUF had departed the St. Pierre and Miquelon Islands for Halifax, arriving there on the 14th. She lay at Halifax until February 1, readying for her departure to Tahiti. According to her sailing orders, issued by the Commander, Atlantic Coastal Command (Rear Admiral G. C. "Jetty" Jones, Royal Canadian Navy), SURCOUF then departed for Tahiti, via Bermuda, under escort by the corvette HMCS WEYBURN (Lieutenant Commander T. M. Golby, Royal Canadian Navy Reserve), attached to the Newfoundland Escort Force. She arrived at Ireland Dockyard, Somerset, Bermuda, on February 4th. At that time, Vice Admiral Sir Charles Kennedy-Purvis, Royal Navy, was Commander-in-Chief, Americas and West Indies, with headquarters, on board HMS MALABAR, in Hamilton, Bermuda.

Therefore, to accept that SURCOUF replenished German U-boats in January 1942 would be likened to believing that her hulk had been dematerialized and teleported from the Caribbean to the East Coast of the United States by a war magician, or in conformance with Einstein's Unified Field Theory, or in a manner described in *Thin Air,* by George E. Simpson and Neal R. Burger, where-in they describe how the destroyer USS STURMAN was allegedly teleported from Philadelphia Naval Shipyard to Norfolk Naval Base—coupled with accepting that SURCOUF's death was retrogressed-in-time from February to January 1942.[12]

The rumors that SURCOUF sank Allied shipping can be similarly discounted because no war in history has been documented better than that of World War II. Through comparative and comprehensive consultation of Allied and Axis maritime and naval records, it is possible to pin-point, with near 100 percent accuracy, which Allied ship was sunk by which Axis submarine. There is no evidence that SURCOUF attacked or sank any Allied ship, or any ship for that matter. Except for firing her anti-aircraft guns at German bombers over Plymouth, she never fired her guns or torpedoes at any other enemy during the war.

Obviously, it was chronologically and physically impossible for SURCOUF, and inconsistent and out-of-phase with her honorable life and death time cycles, to have been around the East Coast of the United States operating as a treacherous traitor submarine.

Besides, for SURCOUF to have aided and abetted the enemy anywhere would have been as alien to her as it would be for a French waiter to serve California vintage wine during a fine crusine at a Paris restaurant. And, with a British Naval Liaison Officer and his staff continuously aboard SURCOUF, the act would have been impossible to conduct without being reported.

It is a fact that in 1980-1, to thwart further rumor mongering about SURCOUF, during an interview with staff writer, Antar Makansi, of the *Norwich Bulletin,* of Norwich, Connecticut, I first offered $100,000 to anyone who could prove that SURCOUF had betrayed the Allied cause in any manner whatsoever. Earlier a similar offer had been made to the readers of the periodical *Warship International* as at the time its reader column was the avenue for repeated allegations against SURCOUF. So I charged unswervingly to her defense.

Through all these years, no one has come forth to substantiate their rumor, but my offer stands. Subsequently, my wager was increased to $1,000,000!!!

As an interesting aside, by one of those strange coincidences, which only seem to occur as a result of war, in June 1947, the highly successful U-123, which was the only one of its class of 14 captured intact by the Allies at St. Lorient, France, in May 1945, was re-commissioned BLAISON—to honor the memory of the last commanding officer of SURCOUF.

Subsequently, in 1976, the French Navy commissioned a naval training center, at Cherbourg, in honor of Blaison. Then, in 1979, a second warship, a corvette destroyer (F-793), was commissioned in the honor of Blaison. Few, if any, submarine officers of any war have ever been accorded equivalent or continued recognition.

Then, a war memorial to the Free French Naval Forces who fought and died in the Second World War stands on the western brow of Lyle Hill, overlooking Cardwell bay, Greenock, Renfrewshire, Scotland. It is in the form of the Cross of Lorraine, the emblem of the Free French Forces, integrated with an anchor. It is dedicated to the memory of the officers, men, and ships of the Free French Naval Forces who sailed from Greenock in the years 1940-1945 and to those souls who gave their lives during the Battle of the Atlantic for the liberation of France and the success of the Allied cause.

While many other Free French ships were referred to, Blaison and SURCOUF, and his officers and men, were specifically mentioned as follows:

**TO THE MEMORY OF
COMMANDER BLAISON
THE OFFICERS AND MEN
OF THE SUBMARINE SURCOUF
LOST IN THE ATLANTIC
FEBRUARY 1942**

Madam Therese and Mlle Francine Blaison were present at the dedication ceremony.

Blaison that man with a high sense of personal honor and strength of character and whose idol was the Maid—Joan of Arc—did not accept his sword at the Ecole Navale, the French Navy Academy (Class of August 26, 1928), Brest, to bring dishonor to France, the Free French Navy, or to himself as did Fleet Admiral Darlan. *(To thine own self be true, and it must follow, as the night the day, thou canst not then be false to any man. Polonius' advise to his son, Laertes, William Shakespeare, Hamlet, Act I, Scene 3.)*

Blaison lived and died with these noble words of Joan indelibly etched in his heart, mind, and soul: "All the hands of France in a single hand. A hand that is never divided!" When the English shouted at Joan, "Everything is dead." She retorted: "But there is hope, which is stronger." In these words you can also recognize Blaison, the Free French naval officer, who wrote to his beloved Theresa: "The only real meaning of what I am doing with SURCOUF is to be the messenger of hope, to be he who says, 'No, everything is not lost, France will be saved.' And France was saved from an eternity of Nazi tyranny. *(He leadeth me in the paths of righteousness for His name's sake/Yea, though I walk through the valley of the shadow of death I will fear no evil: for thou art with me; thy rod and thy staff they comfort me./Thou preparest a table before me in the presence of mine enemies . . . . Psalms 23:3-5 KJV)*

According to Deborah Fraioli, in *Joan of Arc, Virgin Warrior:*

> The English never feared a captain or chief as much as they feared the Maid.
>
> Not until she was burned at the stake and her ashes gathered, and thrown into the Seine, could the English breathe easily and think about resuming their conquest of France.

How magnanimous then of Burney, an Englishman, to have rendered, in his Dec 26, 1941 liaison report to Flag Officer, Submarines (Vice Admiral Sir Max Kennedy Horton, Royal Navy), only the highest praise for Blaison's loyalty to the Free French Movement and about his intentions for SURCOUF and her officers and men:

> The Captain has the most loyal sentiment possible and is anxious to come completely and irrevocably under British Admiralty control, and to put SURCOUF to the use for which she was designed.

If supremely possible, Blaison encountered, on Judgment Day, that arch demon Lieutenant de Vaisseau with a murderous temper, not as many other men, who threatened to kill him if he joined the Free French Navy, and to do harm to Madam Blaison and young Francine.

Blaison, in an August 2, 1940 letter to Therese, strongly alluded to that monstrous threat, beyond a shadow of a doubt made by the "Skull", that man who, seemed to have an unusual influence throughout France and the Vichy French Navy, and with whom the author had a near deathly encounter in Hiroshima, Japan on August 4, 1978. (For reasons expressed shortly, it was the author who tabbed this unworthy fellow as "The Skull".)

Here is what Blaison wrote to Therese about his encounter with the Skull:

> I am very glad some people are nice to you, but you must be careful. One of the party goers (meaning a Vichyist), with a wild vertigo instinct, threatened me with reprisals against you and Francine, if I remained in England to continue the fight.

The Skull's "wild" threats against Blaison's womenfolk left such a deep impression upon him that he spoke about that sinister man, with an alien mind, during a radio broadcast over WRUL, Boston, on October 28, 1941, which broadcast over Intrepid's propaganda network by shortwave to France and throughout her Empire:

> Lieutenant de Vaisseau "X" (I wish to withhold your name), do you remember that day in England when, with wild-eyed and foaming at the mouth, you screamed at me and to my crew: "I've had enough of ridiculous England. Let the English be finished off quickly."

As an aside: Madame Blaison mentioned to the author that she was the only Free French Navy wife to receive letters from her husband. Most of those letters were stamped with the Nazi swastika such as to indicate that his letters were passed through German censorship. She believed that Blaison's letters were only allowed to pass to her because of the German and Vichy French desire to learn of the activities of Blaison and SURCOUF.)

The author was similarly confronted with a hideous experience in Hiroshima, Japan, on October 1, 1978, during my interview with a retired French Naval officer, who had the facial features of a "Skull".

He had served aboard SURCOUF before World War II as and engineering officer. All progressed smoothly enough until he was asked if he knew Capitaine de Frigate Blaison. At that instance, the "Skull" lost his *sang-froid*, calmness, by exploding with white-faced fury and threats to kill me, in the presence of my son, Julius III. Of course, our conversation concluded immediately.

Although SURCOUF's sudden death in the Caribbean, 90 miles NNE of the Panama Canal, in 8,000 feet of water, was considered circumstantial for several years, evidence accumulated by the United States Maritime Commission, for the purpose of assigning war reparations and payments for owners of American merchant ships damaged or sunk during the war, concluded in 1948 that it was, indeed, SURCOUF which was sunk by the SS THOMPSON LYKES—the uninvited night stalker—that fateful night of February 18, 1942. This evidence did not surface from sequestered archives until about 1982, and then only through the auspices of the Freedom of Information Act.

SURCOUF'S loss with souls on board was the world's worst submarine disaster of its kind, but this became known only after my having casually compared her patrol report for January 1942 with the list of her was dead on the SURCOUF War Memorial at Cherbourg, France.

Missing was the name of Electrician's Mate Paul Raso (aka Paul Rapson), the 130th soul. Paul was a French lad who had enlisted in the Royal Navy in the Suez Canal, before the formation of the Free French Navy, and who, while serving aboard HMS MONTGOMERY (ex-U.S. Navy USS WYCKES), had requested transfer to SURCOUF so he could join his cousin. SURCOUF at the time, January 14 to February 1, 1942, alongside of MONTGOMERY at Halifax. (Note: WYCKES was one of those 50 World War I, four stack, destroyers given to England in September 1940, under the scope of the U. S. Lend Lease Act, in exchange for establishment of United States bases on certain Atlantic and Caribbean crown colony islands, like Bermuda, on 99 year leases.)

My findings, which were made in December 1978, were accepted by the British and French Admiralties and then by the *Guinness Book of World Records* on November 8, 1979. And, at my suggestion, Paul Raso's (aka Rapson) name was finally placed on the Cherbourg Memorial in June 1980.

The submarine previously holding that unenviable record was the USS THRESHER (Lieutenant Commander John Wesley "Wes" Harvey, U.S. Navy,), which was lost on Apr 19, 1963, 220 miles off Cape Cod, with only 129 on board. (As an aside, a reading of *The*

THRESHER Disaster, by John Bentley, revealed that USS THRESHER was not without strong premonitions foretelling her death.)

SURCOUF was the first Atlantic-based submarine of the foreign Allied navies to be ordered to join American naval forces in the Southwest Pacific—with "MacArthur's Navy."

It is disheartening to mention that, according to Edwin C. Hoyt in *Submarines at War*, the American Navy "did not learn the advantages of using deck guns" installed on its submarines until the beginning of 1943." Perhaps if SURCOUF, with its powerful twin 8-inch guns, had made it to the Pacific infernal, may have served as an incentive to American submariners to hasten the use of such weapons against Japanese targets.

SURCOUF was the only Allied submarine to collide with, and be sunk, by and Allied merchant ship.

It is interesting to note that during the war one-fourth of all ship losses were due to collision, foundering, and marine losses not directly attributable to enemy action.

SURCOUF was the first Allied submarine to die in the Caribbean Sea during World War II.

By dying in the Caribbean, SURCOUF had some full circle—for she had begun the war at Fort d' France, Martinique—not too far from where she collided with SS THOMPSON LYKES. In a way, Blaison may have come full circle also, as during his midshipman years at the l'Ecole Navale he served aboard the French training cruiser *Jeanne d Arc* which had transited the Panama Canal and paid a port call at the island of Martinique.

Strange to say, but true, on the moonless night that SS THOMPSON LYKES and SURCOUF locked themselves in an embrace of death, in SURCOUF's third and last encounter with a wartime ally, Blaison and Captain Henry Johnson, the Master of THOMPSON LYKES, were both biorhythmically accident prone.

Despite conclusive evidence, and determinations in her favor, a second category of rumors insists that SURCOUF was deliberately sunk in one of the following ways by Allied forces:

By a British or by an American cruiser.

By bombers of the RAF, RCAF, USAAF, or US Navy.

By the cruiser USS MONTEREY or by either the American submarines USS MARLIN, MACKERAL, by an unnamed American submarine while SURCOUF was allegedly attacking the QUEEN MARY, or by destroyers of the Royal or Royal Canadian Navies.

And that she was sunk in the following areas:

    Off Bermuda by British aircraft,

    Off Newfoundland by RCAF aircraft,

    Off the San Blas Islands, Panama, by American aircraft,

    Off the St. Pierre and Miquelon Islands by Royal Navy,

        Royal Canadian Navy, or by American destroyers, or

    In Long Island Sound or in the Florida Straits.

The author, in an August 16, 1980 telephone conversation with Rear Admiral John Frederick Davidson, USN, Annapolis, Class of 1929 and former Superintendent, U.S. Naval Academy, Annapolis, 1960-62, learned that while he (Davidson) commanded USS MACKERAL, during November 1942, when she was based and operating out of New London, MACKERAL did not shadow or sink SURCOUF, although he had heard such rumors later in the war.

Now, from a completely unexpected source, there will be related that shadowing SURCOUF, even trying to intercept her in the event she fled for Martinique instead of for Cristobal, Canal Zone, as ordered, was not an inconceivable possibility by the Allied warships!!!

Up to now the United States Army and Air Force, Navy, Coast Guard, Merchant Marine, the Panama Canal Authority, the Attorney General's Office, the Federal Bureau of Investigation, the Immigration and Naturalization Service, the State Department and the Treasury Department have entered SURCOUF's story. Now, at a most crucial point, it is time to call in the United States Marines to tell how members of that proud corps—an enlisted man, a junior reserve officer based in Tangiers, Spanish Morocco, and a major's daughter living 3327 O Street, Georgetown, Washington, D. C.—had close connections with the after death of SURCOUF.

What follows, from a more widely divergent source, came through response to the author's appeal in, the June 1980 issue of, *The Veteran's of Foreign Wars Magazine.* He received the startling response, one which could provide an important breakthrough in support of some American, British, Canadian and French opinion, that American and British warships actually may have tried to intercept or shadow SURCOUF while she was in the southern sector of the Bermuda Triangle and while she was entering the Caribbean Sea.

This extraordinary account was provided by Julius B. Williams of Bogalusa, Louisiana, formerly a Private First Class, U.S. Marine Corps while he was an orderly, aboard the 6-inch cruiser USS SAVANNAH (Captain Andrew Carl "Andy" Bennett, USN, Annapolis, Class of 1912).

In his June 11, 21 and 30, 1980 letters, Williams wrote this about SAVANNAH'S ("SAVVY'S") possible near-encounter with SURCOUF in the Caribbean Sea:

> I believe I can tell you of an incident that makes me believe that we were close to SURCOUF on February 18, 1942. At the time we were approaching the Caribbean, after having just completed a South American cruise.
>
> To begin with, I don't remember ever seeing SURCOUF's name in print or ever hearing it. This can be understood because our wartime security was so tight and our activities so secret that we were under threat of court martial if we discussed our operations.
>
> Our purpose in the Atlantic was many times puzzling, especially when we used to leave convoy or escort duty to hurriedly proceed on some unknown assignment with only one destroyer escort.
>
> I served as orderly to Captain Bennett, and naturally was around all the departments' heads. Mostly, however, I served as Communications Orderly. This job kept me in touch with every officer aboard whom at one time or another had a message to receive or acknowledge. In this way, I was in touch with all the radio and signalmen. Besides this, my gun station was No. Two, portside, abeam of the Radio Shack, but below the Signal Bridge.

We received an urgent message ordering us to proceed immediately to Martinique to join a British heavy cruiser in an effort to prevent a French submarine, the world's largest, from leaving a harbor to get back to sea.

While proceeding in that direction a question arose, amongst the crew, as to: 'Why would we be heading into conflict with a country's submarine that was our Ally?' This was answered by word that she was known to be collaborating with the Nazis. After we received the message, I'm sure our speed to intercept the French sub approached 30 knots.

It was dark when we got to the rendezvous area, but we could see offshore lights.

We stayed underway all night in contact with our destroyer escort and a British cruiser. At daybreak we launched all of our seaplanes, which flew in different directions and stayed for what seemed forever. I'd never known them to stay away for that long a time. They returned with no word and we went on our way not knowing for sure what had taken place, but that was not uncommon for the crew.

Later, and all I can say is later, because when you're standing Condition TWO and carrying on regular ship's routine time means nothing, word was passed that the French sub we'd gone to Martinique to "capture" had collided with a ship and disappeared.

William's remarks are too credible, and close-to-home, to be disbelieved especially when his account practically matches, hand-and-glove, with one involving the 6-inch cruiser HMS DIOMEDE, whose crew jubilantly claimed had sunk SURCOUF.

How could Williams have connected distinctly independent, but related, incidents with what really happened to SURCOUF; SAVVY'S attempt, in company with a British cruiser, to intercept or "capture the world's largest" submarine with the report that the "French sub", which had to be SURCOUF, had collided with a ship and disappeared???

Indeed, as revealed in the official diary of SAVANNAH's lifetime of activity, in *American Fighting Ships,* published by the Department of the Navy, SAVANNAH served as the flagship of Cruiser Division EIGHT, and, at the time that Williams was aboard, was assigned, as part of the American Neutrality Patrol, South Atlantic Squadron, to patrol offshore of the Vichy controlled islands of Martinique and Guadeloupe.

Even if there had been another "French sub" attempting to depart Martinique, which there wasn't, William's remarks were specific: "the "French sub was the world's largest."

His exact choice of words leave no doubt that the "French sub" was SURCOUF!!! ONLY SURCOUF WAS THAT BIG!!!

Seemingly, when SURCOUF entered the Caribbean sector of the Bermuda Triangle, something was out there—other than the THOMPSON LYKES—waiting for her—the likes of which some official naval historians either will not admit to or do not suspect ever happened.

Commander John A. "Jaw" Whitacre, USN, Retired, now of Newberry, South Carolina, served aboard "SAVVY" as an Ensign and was one of her Officers-of-the Deck when young Williams was aboard.

In reply to the an author's inquiry in the October 1980 issue of *Shipmate Magazine,* requesting contact with anyone who had served aboard "SAVVY" during January-February 1942, Commander Whitacre subsequently wrote on November 13, 1980:

It is possible that it is a case of mistaken nationality. SAVANNAH was involved in covering or intercepting German and Vichy French forces during that time.

Sometime during January or February 1942 there was a report that the German raiders, GNEISENAU and SCHARNHORST then loose in the Atlantic, were headed for South America. SAVANNAH in company with two other cruisers and possibly the battleship USS MISSISSIPPI, were assigned to chase. The task force ran all the way to the north coast of South America before the report was declared to be a false contact.

During this period, SAVANNAH made at least two runs to Martinique in what was referred to on board as the "French and Indian War." The United States prior to the Fall of France had provided 90 Curtiss SBC-4, Hell Divers, to France. A shipment of 44, aboard the French aircraft carrier BEARN, had gotten as far as Martinique in June of 1940. There was a report that Vichy France would attempt to move them to North Africa.

During the last run I made with the SAVANNAH to Martinique we were within minutes of opening fire with our main battery of 6-inch guns when the State Department in direct contact brought the operation to a halt.

Strange that Commander Whitacre should mention that "SAVVY" was searching the middle Atlantic and Caribbean areas for the German heavy surface units GNEISENAU ("Salmon") and SCHARNHORST ("Gluckstein"). It was publicly known that, after a long period of inactively, both super-warships, along with the cruiser PRINZ EUGEN, had escaped from Brest making an epic dash up the English Channel, on February 11-12, 1942, while under almost continual attack by the Royal Navy and Royal Air Force Bomber, Coastal and Fighter Commands.

Supported by an incredible sequence of failures and misjudgments by the British, the German squadron was able to successfully pass within a few miles of Dover before the British became aware of what occurred. THE GERMAN NAVY'S EXTRAORDINARY FEAT WAS PUBLICIZED WORLD-WIDE AS IT HAPPENED!!!

Commander Whitacre went on to relate that he departed SAVANNAH on March 22, 1942, while she was at Bermuda, following his receipt of orders, logged aboard "SAVVY" on March 8, to report to Submarine School at New London.

What is exciting—and equally pertinent—about Commander Whitacre's input is that, while "SAVVY's" log book is imprecise about this point, she, Commander Whitacre stated, made two voyages to Martinique, one of which was apparently to intercept or attack a target, either on that island or offshore. The author's subsequent correspondence with Commander Whitacre, which included providing him with a copy of "SAVVY's" log book for February 1942, was cutoff when the author's questions apparently became too pointed or tedious.

Specifically asked of Commander Whitacre was what target would "SAVVY" have fired upon, at or near Martinique, before having been deferred by the American State Department. (If SURCOUF had been "SAVVY's" target that night, she, with only 6-inch guns, would have been no match for SURCOUF's powerful twin 8-inch guns, unless SURCOUF was surprised, out-numbered or helpless.

In fairness "SAVVY", her log book showed her to be at anchor in berth S-13-2, Shelly Bay, Bermuda, with COMTASKGROUP 2.7 in USS RANGER, and with USS AUGUSTA and various other units of the American and British Fleets present at the time of the SURCOUF-THOMPSON LYKES Collision (at 2230 on February 18, 1942).

If Commander Whitacre's input is accurate we have a another instance of direct State Department involvement in a naval operation at sea, something which seems to have escaped the history books covering the Battle of the Atlantic during World War II. The first being her involvement in the St. Pierre and Miquelon Affair, which Secretary of State Cordell Hull referred to it as a "tempest in a tea pot."

If the State Department was so involved, it no doubt also concerned Adolf Augustus "Gus" Berle, Jr., one of Roosevelt's Brain Trustee's, "Father's Privy Council", who was Assistant Secretary of State for Latin American Affairs, which included acting as Chief, Intelligence and Research Division, and as a statesman who knew how to guard secrets. Of all that has been written and published about World War II, involving participation by various organizations of the United States Government, Berle's Intelligence and Research Division, State Department, remains conspicuous for having been barely mentioned in its official history about the war. Why???

Regardless, it is important to reveal that Commander Whitacre's report about a possible American hostile involvement in Martinique is not far-fetched. By his own admission Berle, in his book *Navigating the Rapids, 1918-1971*, told of official Free French concern about a possible attack on Martinique by American naval forces—two days before SURCOUF was lost in the Caribbean and while "SAVVY" may have been shadowing her:

> On February 16, 1942, Adrien P. Tixler, representing the Free French movement, wished to serve notice on us on behalf of General de Gaulle that if we took any defense measures with respect to Martinique, General de Gaulle expected to be consulted and to participate.

What had prompted Tixler to pay an official call on Berle about Martinique? Somewhere Tixler may have overheard a chance remark throughout Washington circles, or had received a report from de Gaulle, that the American Government may be encompassing a protective cloak around Martinique—if only to forestall a similar move by de Gaulle.

Obviously, however, de Gaulle had no such intention at that moment—else wise he would not have dispatched his envoy, Tixler, to confront the American Government about the subject—particularly after the "tempest in a teapot" he had recently caused by his and Muselier's and Muselier's seizure of the St. Pierre and Miquelon Islands with SURCOUF.

To eliminate doubt about the serious implications and worth of Williams' report, the author will shortly divulge several divergent, but supportive, statements from persons serving with the British Army and Royal Navy at that time.

That the United States government actually had intentions to militarily seize Martinique is evident from Berle's diary entry for May 7, 13 and 19, 1942.

> A fascinating evening-ridden to a degree, at the close of it, the watch officer [State Department] telephoned. A cable had

come in from Martinique. Admiral Robert [Georges Robert, Governor of Martinique] had agreed to dismantle the warships, and negotiations as to the remaining points were continuing. In other words, we were over the hump. Killing our people in an attack on Frenchmen, or Frenchmen killing Frenchman, seemed to me about the most useless form of activity.

There seems to be no real reason to kill a lot of Frenchmen for the sole purpose of putting a de Gaullist in as Governor of Martinique.

There have to be carefully thought out plans; every instinct should be for diplomatic rather than military action. And, yet you cannot leave a Vichy controlled island inside the American Caribbean defense zone.

These excerpts from Berle's diary give enormous support to William's and Whittaker's remarks.

Could it be that during SURCOUF's passage along her Caribbean route to the Panama Canal she was also shadowed by Vichy warships based in Martinique.

If "SAVVY" had been involved in shadowing SURCOUF she would not have done so without authority from the highest levels within the Roosevelt Administration, from "The Boss" himself.

What would it have meant to Roosevelt—who according to Rear Admiral Alfred Theobold, USN, Annapolis Class of 1907, in his damning book *The Final Secret of Pearl Harbor*, allegedly allowed the Imperial Japanese Navy to deliberately attack Pearl Harbor, resulting in America's greatest naval disaster and also the greatest in American personnel injured or killed, to sacrifice General Charles de Gaulle's SURCOUF in vengeance for her involvement in the St. Pierre and Miquelon Affair; to pacify Vichy France in anticipation of receiving her cooperation during Operation TORCH; or to keep de Gaulle from seizing that gold on Martinique.???

Here is what Admiral Theobold wrote about President Roosevelt's possible permissiveness at Pearl Harbor:

Admiral Stark and General Marshall would have done everything in their power to prevent such an attack. Yet, on the morning of December 7, Washington refused to send one short message to Hawaii in time to cushion the effects of the Japanese attack!

That is the most revealing fact of the entire Pearl Harbor story. There is only one conceivable reason for it—nothing must be done to prejudice the attack, even at the last moment. Japan was about to bring war to the United States, and President Roosevelt had no intention that any American should cause them to change their plans.

Does it seem fantastic to associate a great political leader of World War II with the death of SURCOUF? (Perhaps such secrets are a cover for their other crimes.)

Now, what follows is an excerpt from a CONFIDENTIAL American naval intelligence report, which was extracted from another report originating in the Office of Vice Consul David King (Casablanca), of the American State Department. And the naval intelligence report of June 18, 1942 that was dated five months after SURCOUF died which was forwarded to the Chief of Naval Operations, Intelligence Division, Washington by the Naval Attaché, Tangiers (a second lieutenant in the U.S. Marine Corps) via the Joint Allied Intelligence Committee, Gibraltar, that in-turn forwarded copies to appropriate members of the diplomatic, intelligence and naval communities in London and Washington.

This report remains a classic among the SURCOUF dossier of rumors, and it is significant because of its:

1. Authoritative, official origin.

2. Connecting with Williams' input by introducing another American cruiser (unnamed) into SURCOUF's death.

3. Connecting with Burney's allegation that there may have existed the possibility of disloyalty or munity aboard SURCOUF.

4. Connecting with John Edgar Hoover's official letter to the Director's of U. S. Army and Naval Intelligence stating that SURCOUF had been sunk off St. Pierre on March 12, 1942.

5. Introducing another woman into *The SURCOUF Conspiracy*.

Its greatest significance, however, is that it pinpoints the rumor was probably first circulated by "officers of the Vichy French Navy in Casablanca."

According to Richard Harris Smith, in *OSS, the Secret History of America's First Central Intelligence Agency*, King was working for Colonel (later Major General) William Joseph "Wild Bill" Donavon, USA, Director of the Office of Strategic Services (OSS). King was a man of wide experience who had fought in the French Legion, sold burlap in India, interpreted for a diplomatic mission in Ethiopia and made a small fortune in the business world.

In Algiers, according to Harris, the Special Intelligence Branch, one comparable to King's in Casablanca, Donovan's man was a twenty-nine year-old New York attorney, Henry Hyde. Born in France, where his father resided after embarrassment resulting from United States Government intervention into his business interests. Completely bilingual, jokingly referred to by Americans as a monarchist, Hyde had studied at Cambridge, received his law degree from Harvard, and was "a vigorous opponent of de Gaulle."

According to Harris, "Henry Hyde's Secret Intelligence Branch, Algiers, had become the focal point for French dissidents who could not accept de Gaulle's supremacy as Head of the Free French Movement. The intellectual light of the dissidents was Antoine de Saint-Exupery, an old and close friend of General Donovan's, who consistently condemned

Gaullism as "fascism without doctrine." Curiously, it was while flying from an U.S. Air Force Base in Algiers that Saint-Exupery was killed in his Lockheed P-38 photo-reconnaissance aircraft, possibly, wrote Harris, "a victim of political assassination." Rumors were rife, however, that Saint-Exupery had been shot down by a German Messerschmitt fighter aircraft, over the Mediterranean, while returning from a mission.

And it was in Algiers that Admiral Darlan, one of the godfathers of SURCOUF, was assassinated in his office, on Christmas Eve, 1942; allegedly by a member of the monarchist faction. (David Raynolds writes in his book, *In Command of History*, that Sir Stewart Menzies, the Chief of the British Secret Intelligence Service (MI6)—who rarely left London during the war—was in Algiers in those days.)

It should not be surprising that some French are convinced that the Holcomb-SURCOUF Rumor originated in Algiers, not Casablanca. Here is how Holcomb reported it to higher authorities:

> Madame Drogou called this week and reported that following the loss of SURCOUF, officers of the Vichy French Navy in Casablanca had circulated the rumor that SURCOUF had been deliberately sunk by gunfire from an American cruiser in the North Atlantic because "its crew was not considered loyal and reliable by the Americans."
>
> She stated that a friend of hers had gone to the French Admiralty in Casablanca and there had been shown a paper in which it was stated definitely that the American Navy admitted sinking SURCOUF under these circumstances and had made this admission to Vichy.
>
> This friend was informed that SURCOUF had been resting on the surface when the American cruiser sighted it and fired without warning.
>
> This information had a disturbing effect on Gaullist and pro-American French in Casablanca. They cannot understand why the American Government would have communicated directly with Vichy regarding the loss of a Free French

submarine. The Admiral Commanding the French Fleet in Morocco, Admiral Jean-Bernard-Armand d' Hourcourt, apparently is cognizant of the rumor but has made no attempt to check it.

It is suggested that prompt action be taken to dispel the rumors now being circulated regarding the loss of SURCOUF.

PREPARED AND FORWARDED BY:
/S/ F. P. HOLCOMB
2nd Lt, U. S. Marine Corps
Assistant Naval Attaché

If the American Government had "communicated" with the Vichy French Navy, Casablanca, about the death of SURCOUF, it would have been through their intermediary, Vice Consul King; working under his cover as an OSS agent for Colonel Donavon.

Holcomb's report was upgraded to SECRET by Lordships of the British Admiralty after it had been passed to them by the Joint Allied Intelligence Committee, Gibraltar ("The Rock").

Franklin P. Holcomb, the son of the Lieutenant General Thomas "Tommy" Holcomb, Commandant, U. S. Marine Corps, had not believed the rumor. In his all-American mind, historically imbued with a strong sense of righteousness and fair-play, it was too incredible for him to accept that an American warship would have attacked and sunk an Allied submarine without warning. After what the treacherous Imperial Japanese Navy had just done to the American Navy at Pearl Harbor anything or anyone suspected of disloyalty would have revengefully received that kind of treatment rumored to have been dealt SURCOUF.

If SURCOUF had been used as a pawn of war, and eradicated as rumored, then, logically as an exigency of war, the American Government would have done it to pacify the Vichy French Government to assure the complete success of the proposed invasion of Vichy controlled French North Africa; if only to save thousands of American and French lives during and after the landings.

How better to cultivate a friend in-need than by speaking adversely about a common enemy, SURCOUF. To satisfy the "exigencies of war," what would have the crew of one Free French submarine, "A White Elephant," have mattered to the Allies; particularly if they believed that they had reasonable cause to sink her . . . But, saying and thinking black things about SURCOUF did not really make it so. SURCOUF, nor Blaison, and those who were loyal to him, would never have been treacherous to the Free French or Allied cause. The author will never believe this about them.

Holcomb's report is made more dramatic by the introduction of Madame Drogou, who was the wife of the Commanding Officer of the Free French submarine NARVAL, which submarine the Vichy French Navy (in September of 1941) claimed had been deliberately sunk by the Royal Navy. (It must be mentioned that young Holcomb, at the time, was a junior U.S. Marine Corps officer, supposedly assigned to, and performing primary services for, the State Department in a diplomatic status. But, this was only a cover. Actually, Holcomb worked for Donovan's shop, the Office of the Coordinator of Information (the predecessor organization to the Office of Strategic Services.)

Holcomb went on to relate that Madame Drogou had reported previously that the Vichy French Admiralty in Casablanca, where there was also located a black propaganda specialist of the Morale Operations Branch, OSS, had also fabricated a vicious rumor about the Free French submarine NARVAL, which, when lost, had been commanded by her husband:

> Commandant François Drogou, finding himself to have been mistaken in his ideas of duty and misled, attempted to return to France and was thereupon assassinated, with all his crew, by the British, who sent two vessels after NARVAL and sank her with all hands.

But, Commandant Drogou and NARVAL, at the time of the Franco-German Armistice of June 22, 1940, were in the Sousse Harbor, Tunisia. Without saying a word to his Division Commander, Lieutenant de Vaisseau François Drogou took NARVAL to sea and proceeded to Malta to join forces with the Royal Navy. Drogou reached the pinnacles of immortality for the words he uttered as NARVAL cleared Sousse: "Betrayal all along the line, we are heading for an English port to continue the fight against the Germans!!!"

While the courage of Drogou and his men was long, NARVAL's life, and theirs, was shorter than SURCOUF's during the war. This is how Admiral Simpson sadly, but conclusively, wrote of NARVAL's death, the submarine that would have been under his operating command had she lived:

> On my first day at Malta, as Commander, Tenth Submarine Flotilla, my old friend, Lieutenant Commander Bob Tanner, who was now my Staff Officer (Operations), explained that at present we had only one submarine operating from Malta.
>
> It was the Free French submarine NARVAL, which was on patrol and should have been returning from the Tobruk direction. In fact NARVAL had already been sunk off Derna by the Italian torpedo boat CLIO on January 7. (Commander Marc' Antonio Bragadin, Italian Navy, in *The Italian Navy in World War II* confirmed that "the Free French submarine NARVAL" was sunk by the CLIO.)
>
> It was particularly sad that the only French submarine in the Mediterranean that rallied to the Allied cause was at once lost and it seemed to auger ill that my first report to the Commander-in-Chief, Mediterranean, Admiral Lord Andrew B. Cunningham, should be, 'Regret to report that NARVAL now three days overdue and must be considered lost'—that matter of fact phasing with its load of doom, so often repeated in the two years ahead, which on each occasion seemed to increase in my mind the searching self-criticism which responsibility brings.

In August 1981, Holcomb, now a retired Foreign Service Officer, was finally located in Washington. He would not meet with the author personally, nor provide his photograph for inclusion in this work. Holcomb, who was listed in *The Social List of Washington, 1982,* only vaguely recalled his writing about SURCOUF, and he recalled next to nothing about Madame Drogou, who, from reading between the lines of his report, seemed to have been a frequent visitor to the offices of the OSS in North Africa. "Madame Drogou called this week" 'not a Madame Drogou, but Madame Drogou, such to imply that he had submitted intelligence reports about her before—something beyond just being a mindless matter.

If the Vichy French Navy had not fabricated that rumor, one so disconcertingly similar to the others about SURCOUF, especially the Hoover Rumor (which will follow), where did it originate??? Was it passed to them by an official of the United States Government??? Was it the same source that had passed a mis-leading rumor about SURCOUF to J. Edgar Hoover, Director of the FBI, during March 1942???

A possible clue to this perplexing question emerges from Deacon's *History of the British Secret Service*:

> Most Of the information that came to the American State Department from Vichy France was prejudiced, unobjective and wrong. It relied far too much in early stages of the war on intelligence from Vichyists in France, which was one reason for both its and Roosevelt's antagonism toward de Gaulle.

It is obvious that the French Vichyists were doing much to undercut relations between the Free French and their Allies. Planting of the SURCOUF rumor (or many such foul rumors about her) could have been one such attempt.

According to Harris; "In the spring of 1942, subversive operations in North Africa became the responsibility of the new Donavan, the Coordinator of Information. Harris specifically mentioned Colonel William Eddy, USMC, as being Donavon's chief agent in North Africa, second only to Robert D. Murphy of State. Holcomb was Eddy's deputy based in Tangiers, Spanish Morocco, which was a notorious center of espionage and dirty tricks.

According to Cave, in *The Secret War Report of the OSS,* Donavon directed that all intelligence reports be channeled through Tangiers for appropriate dissemination, instead of being dispatched direct to Washington from the various vice consulates in North Africa, where British services had been excluded by the Vichy French and German-Italian Armistice Commission. This explains how Holcomb came to be involved in the funneling of the Holcomb-SURCOUF Rumor to the Joint Allied Intelligence Committee, Gibraltar.

It is also interesting to note that, at the time of Holcomb's intelligence report about SURCOUF, Harold Adrian Russell "Kim" Philby (the "Third Man", besides Guy Burgess and Donald Maclean, who had defected to the Soviets on January 25, 1960), held a prominent post inside of the British Secret Intelligence Service (SIS), code MI-6, and that he was a close confident of Colonel Charles Howard "Dick" Ellis, British Army, who years later, according to *Wild Bill and Intrepid, The Origin of the CIA, by Thomas F. Troy,* later, admitted to being a double agent for the Nazi Germany, and was documented in *Too Secret, Too Long,* the most powerful, infuriating, heartbreaking book ever published about spies, by Chapman Pincher, as also being a Soviet agent. (Pincher's referral to Ellis; who he was and his malicious betrayals against England, encompasses as least twenty pages of the 639 within his book.

However, Ellis was best known for his World War II service as deputy to Sir William S. Stephenson, "the Man Called Intrepid". In that critical position, Ellis had access to high level secrets of Intrepid's Office of British Security Co-ordination (BSC) in New York, London and Bermuda. (If Ellis concealed that he was a traitor on Intrepid's staff, who wasn't???)

Ellis, whose loyalty was considered beyond reproach, had been a British secret agent in Egypt, India, Persia, Russia, and Afghanistan and had held consular posts in Turkey, the Balkans, Germany and Asia between the wars. According to Hyde, in *Room 3603,* Ellis came from the Foreign Office in London, and could speak fluent Russian. "Dick's" double life was withheld from the Allied public until the appearance of Pincer's book.

(Obtain employment at a temple as a caretaker and work hard to get the high priest's recommendation to be transferred to the enemy lord's compound Once assigned as a caretaker in the enemy lord's area, the Ninja was in an ideal position to carry out intelligence missions or assassinate an enemy.)

After the war, while assigned to MI-6, London, as the third most important official in the Secret Service, "Dick" was assigned to "weed" out secret, sensitive documents considered by an expert, such as Ellis, to be of no further value, or too sensitive to retain, and to consign them to the burn basket. Also, Ellis, on behalf of his former master, Intrepid, was tasked by Hyde to edit *Room 3603*, while in manuscript, and "made suggestions which improved it in many ways." *(An important aspect of the Ninja's work was the quality of his loyalty and utter determination to serve and deceive his master.)*

But who was Intrepid (Sir William "Little Bill" Stephenson)??? Intrepid, who served at the bequest of Winston Churchill, was Director of British Security Coordination (BSC), an integrated, super secret intelligence network, under the public title of being a British Passport Control Office, operating out of the 35th and 36th floors of The International Building, 630 Fifth Avenue, Rockefeller Plaza, New York City, across from St. Patrick's Cathedral.

Interpid's primarily function was to unofficially coordinate between England's Special Operations, Executive (MI-5 and 6 branches); J. Edgar "Big John" Hoover's Federal Bureau of Investigation; and the Department of State's intelligence section headed by Adolf A. "Buck" Berle (an exclusive member of President Roosevelt's brain trust.)

BSC's other purpose was to act as an undercover entity, with authority to act far beyond intelligence and with executive action capability, to protect England's interests within the Western Hemisphere.

By mutual agreement, with the concurrence of Prime Minister Churchill and President Roosevelt, Stephenson and Hoover exchanged intelligence for dissemination throughout their respective governments. Hoover's FBI acted in this capacity, through its wartime role of conducting counter-espionage and secret intelligence, until a great part of the FBI's roles were absorbed, in June 1942, by the Office of

Strategic Services (Referred to by some Washington wags of the time as "Oh So Social" because of the prestige of being a club member of the OSS.)

According to *Spotlight Magazine* of May 17, 1982, referred to Intrepid as a suave jackal and a "Perfidious Albion" who was sent by Prime Minister Churchill to work on intimate, illegal collusion with President Roosevelt, in ultra top secret, to plant false rumors and disinformation in the American press and to eliminate people who were not liked—all with immunity from American law. His primary mission was to conduct all forms of clandestine operations in the Western Hemisphere—covert activities, counterespionage, and intelligence collection from his New York City office at Rockefeller Center under the cover of being a British Passport Control Office. Timothy J. Naftali, in his paper *Interpol's Last Deception: Documenting the Career of Sir William S. Stephenson,* cited Intrepid's British Security Co-ordination (BSC) network as ". . . . the most efficient binational intelligence system ever constructed."

Spotlight further alleged that Intrepid's organization was an intelligence brothel that employed more than 2,000 assorted thieves, assassins, forgers, publicity personnel, illegal mail openers, double agents, prostitutes, and criminals working for him in and out of Rockefeller Center.

Even today, decades after the end of World War II, literature barely scratches beneath the surface about the extent of BSC's operations in the Americas. The full story may never be told to an inquiring public.

Intrepid, as told in *A Man Called Intrepid,* had concocted a plan to deprive the Vichyists from using that vast hoard of gold stored in Martinique without the necessity for Allied seizure of the island. Part of this plan was for his black propaganda specialists to "gossip that the Free French intended to liberate the island." (Recall from-Burney's special, ultra-secret liaison report, made in the presence of Mrs. Le Blanc, that he suspected SURCOUF would flee to Martinique.)

In addition, H. Montgomery Hyde wrote, in *Room 3603,* Intrepid's communications experts were able to intercept and decode the radio signals of enemy submarines, pinpointing their positions so that they could be destroyed by Allied naval action."

And, according to Chapman Pincher, in *Their Trade is Treachery*, "It was not learned, until long after the war, that Philby, who had been a Soviet agent since 1934, had sent many British agents to their deaths behind the Iron Curtain, and that at least twenty agents of the CIA and SIS were never heard from again because of Philby having blown their cover to the Soviet's during Operation CLIMBER; the 1950-1 infiltration of Albania (an attempt to free Albania from Communist influence.) Philby, then, served in Section "D" (for Destruction), War Office, which, according to Andrew Doyle, in *The Fourth Man*, trained propagandists and saboteurs to wreak havoc behind enemy lines.

Circa 1967, Philby was revealed as a member of the Communist spy ring now known as the Cambridge Five, comprising Donald Maclean, Guy Burgess, Anthony Blunt and John Cairncross. Of this Cambridge connection, Philby was believed to have been most successful in providing classified information to the Soviet Union.

Philby, admitted to sabotaging the Anglo-American operation, which began in 1946, to infiltrate agents and guerillas into Albania and Ukraine. Philby's betrayal caused the lives of about 300 anti-communists because he, through devilish link with Moscow, had treacherously blown their cover.

It is of further interest to mention that Philby was Chief of British Intelligence, Iberian Peninsula and Gibraltar Section, at the time of the air crash of Liberator AL 523 off Gibraltar, which, on the night of July 4, 1943, carried General Wladyslaw Sikorski, the Prime Minister and Commander-in-Chief Free Polish Forces-in-exile, to his death.

And, according to Janusz Piekslkiewicz, in *Secret Agents, Spies, and Saboteurs: Famous Undercover Missions of World War II*, it was Philby who betrayed the famous frogman Lieutenant Commander Lionel Kenneth Philip "Buster" Crabbe, Royal Navy Volunteer Reserve, to the Soviets, while Crabbe was carrying out a secret underwater mission. Crabbe disappeared on April 19, 1965, it was learned, while diving beneath the Russian warship ORDZHONIKIDZE to inspect a newly developed propeller, which could run silent. At the time, ORDZHONIKIDZE was moored in Stokes Bay near Portsmouth, England, on the occasion of Premier Khruschev's visit of State.

SURCOUF could have been similarly betrayed by such sources within the British Government. At this time during the war, Burgess and Philby also belonged to Special Operations, Executive (SOE), London. Burgess, serving as a propagandist, was on the staff of the military controlled British Broadcasting Company as an inside linkman between BBC and SOE.

Burgess and Philby, in concert with Ellis, were in an excellent position, as black specialists in that dark world of intelligence, to ruthlessly undermine the proud name of SURCOUF and to destroy the image of de Gaulle's Free French Movement.

In a reply to the author's inquiry about Ellis having the ear of Intrepid, here is what Chapman Pincher, who wrote *Their Trade was Treachery*, remarked:

> I have no evidence to implicate Ellis in the Surcouf Affair, but it is an interesting suggestion. He certainly had great influence over Intrepid and there is no doubt that he confessed to having been a German spy before and in the early part of the war.

With a triad of such "friends" in the "right places", one could conclude that they easily could have conspired to deliberately dispose of SURCOUF "for reasons political," to satisfy French Communists who had their thought fixed on upsetting de Gaulle's intention to become the first president of France after her liberation. It is not unlikely that disinformation spread about SURCOUF, while she was at Halifax and in Bermuda, could have been covertly inspired and disseminated at the direction of "Dick".

Thus, it could have also been Philby, in cooperation with Ellis or others like him, who had planted those false rumors through Vichy about poor SURCOUF. Such black propaganda would serve the purpose of causing dissension between England, Free France and the United States, thereby giving French Communists more of a foothold in the French Resistance and subsequently more political voice, above that of de Gaulle's, after France was liberated.

It is with this foreknowledge of silent conspirators in high places, and of what follows as the Halifax Rumor, that SURCOUF's pathetic story approaches its climax.

Curiously, according to Cave and Harris, American secret agents were dumbfounded by the attitude of British secret agents in the field, practically in North Africa; their reception was a good deal less cordial than that afforded their seniors when they arrived in London. "R. Harris," Cave wrote, "the former CIA research and analysis officer, would record in his unofficial history of the OSS that the MI-6 station chief at Tangiers was a man who would "sell his country, his soul, or his mother for a peseta" and that he was so "violently jealous of the Americans" that "he allegedly plotted to poison his own assistant, a British major, for being 'too straightforward with Donavon's officers."

Thus, the author firmly believes that the Holcomb and Hoover rumors originated from the same source, Vichy. They are both similar and, as you shall soon read, the author believes that the Hoover rumor was passed to the FBI by an informant within the Vichy Embassy, Washington via British Security Cooperation channels.

Should some readers have doubt about the serious implications and worth of Julius B. William's report, then permit the author to include supporting statements from other persons who had served with the British Army and Royal Navy at that time. Again, we are fortunate in having obtained an input from George Burns of Nova Scotia.

With George on this phase of the SURCOUF story it seems certain that another important breakthrough could occur; one, which if true, some Allied diplomats, historians and politicians would not want to have told. It was on April 21, 1980, following his interview on Canadian national radio about Paul Razo that George received a telephone call. (Strange that Razo's story should open more doors than it closed. It seems that what unfolded through Razo is something straight from *The Airmen Who Would Not Die.*):

A man phoned to say that early in 1942 he was stationed at the naval base at Ireland Island, with the Bermuda Regiment. At that time a British cruiser was in readiness, at immediate call, with "steam-up" at Bermuda. He believes the ship's name was either HMS DIOMODE or DUNEDIN. Anyway, they took off one day, "like a bat out of hell." When she returned a few days later, the crew were "Full of it", "cock-a-hoop" about having sunk SURCOUF.

He said he used to go on board the cruiser often to visit a drinking "pal". The boys on the cruiser told him SURCOUF had been sinking Allied ships. All of the crew were talking about the incident. They had caught her on the surface and "blew her out of the water" with gunfire.

When the word got around, the Admiral gave the ship's company a "bloody bawling out", ordering them to "Keep it Quiet". He did not want them talking about their gallant Ally in this manner and, in any case, the story was untrue. He says the Admiral's comments left the crew in hysteria of laughter.

From an entirely different source, a former British soldier once stationed in Bermuda, provided a supporting statement that SURCOUF could have been eliminated by gunfire while surfaced.

The situation is who to believe, the Admiral or the crew of the British cruiser??? The only British Admiral, as we know, aboard Bermuda at that time was Vice Admiral Sir Charles Kennedy-Purvis, Royal Navy.

George Burns subsequently contacted that "man" and documented his anonymous statement. The cruiser HMS DIOMEDE, with 6-inch guns, was allegedly the one involved. Could the HMS DIOMEDE have been that Royal Navy cruiser which Williams said had accompanied USS SAVANNAH that night SURCOUF was reported sunk by collision with a merchantman???

The "man" had several acquaintances among the Chiefs and Petty Officers aboard DIOMEDE, who frequently met for recreation and drinking at the Royal Navy Base, MALABAR, on Ireland Island. This is what George mentioned further in his letter of September 13, 1980:

> There it is! I have written here what the man told me again. I have no reason to believe he "spun me a yarn," neither can I validate it. He in turn believes that the crew of DIOMEDE were speaking of an incident that, to them, was reality!

In a June 5, 1980 letter, Stan F. Warner, "Plum's" uncle, supported George's report that SURCOUF was finished off while surfaced:

> Regarding rumors, the prevailing one was always that SURCOUF was sunk by an American ship, and the implication was that it was deliberate. Your letter referring to the accidental ramming of SURCOUF by the SS THOMPSON LYKES was completely new to my Aunt Lillian, "Molly", and ourselves.
>   I served in submarines from 1946-52, and frequently sought to find the truth, but always came up against a vagueness that was baffling, particularly after the war ended. I did hear one version from colleagues who had been in the West Indies at the time. It was to the effect that SURCOUF was behaving mysteriously, could not be raised on the wireless (presuming she was on the surface), and that she was ordered to be destroyed by Churchill.

Note that Stan's report had a connection with the West Indies, just as did the one told by that British Army soldier; but Stan's rumor was told by a naval "colleague" who had been stationed there.

Both stories were too straight-forward, too strongly interlocked and having a solid ring of authencity, to be discounted as hokum or even as black propaganda.

Then we must consider the sources. They sought no financial gain and had no political axe to grind.

Why should such seemingly authentic accounts of how SURCOUF died continue to surface; even at this late date in the postwar period???

There may be no other explanation than that there exists some World War II types who are determined that the truth about how they believe SURCOUF died be told during their lifetime. One such probable example occurred when Lieutenant Arthur T. Weiss, USN, Retired, Class of 1942, reported to the author, on April 2, 1979, a rumor that dovetailed neatly with that one told subsequently by Julius E. Williams, i.e., specifically that part which told of USS SAVANNAH rarely proceeding without a destroyer escort:

> I was serving aboard the cruiser USS MONTEREY during World War II, and in a conversation with one of my Chief Warrant Officers, I was told that he had been aboard a destroyer in the Atlantic Fleet which had been assigned, with others, to trail SURCOUF, during what he said was SURCOUF's last patrol. His story was that it had been observed that each time SURCOUF went on patrol, Allied sinkings increased.
>
> He stated that SURCOUF had been caught in the act of attacking an Allied ship during that patrol. In return, the American destroyers attacked and sank SURCOUF. To avoid a Free French-United States confrontation, the matter was kept secret, and after a discreet period a release was given out that SURCOUF was overdue on patrol and presumed lost.
>
> The Chief's name escapes me, but his story was so straightforward that I never questioned it.

It should be observed from the Weiss and Williams inputs that they seem to give reality to the superstition of the number eight, related to the death of SURCOUF, that each of their statements are as tightly interlocked as a knot.

Later, you shall read of how a Free French-United States confrontation was neatly avoided, by a shift of the inquiry into SURCOUF's death to an agency within the United States Government other than the one primarily involved, a maneuver which seemed contrived to preclude the presence of a Free French Navy representative at the inquiry.

The author, however, scoffs vehemently about reports that SURCOUF was deliberately sunk by Allied warships. And up to three years ago he would have scoffed at reports that she had been shadowed across the Caribbean, following her departure from Bermuda. But, from the commonality of reports from widely divergent sources, and after probing even deeper into the morass of SURCOUF's story, particularly after receiving word of Burney's report from Mrs. Le Blanc, the author now firmly believes that the American and Royal Navies would have been justified in shadowing SURCOUF.

But there are those who are just as firmly convinced that SURCOUF's real killers were still at large??? If so, what we would have is one of the great unsolved crimes of the century, and, if so, shouldn't an attempt be made to bring them to justice???

With more inputs such as those provided by Weiss, Whitacre, Williams and Burns, it is likely that the truth about SURCOUF's venture into the Bermuda Triangle portion of the Caribbean Sea could be unraveled, but not likely that the truth will be discovered in any government archive.

Perhaps one of the strangest of all the possible ways that SURCOUF was reported to have been sunk was the one told the author in a May 27, 1981 letter from Edward R. Rumpf, a most indefatigable researcher and the author of *Ernst Kals: Knight of the Sea.* Ed was doubtful that the SURCOUF-THOMPSON LYKES Collision occurred.

I will throw you another curve, Julius. I love a mystery, and although SURCOUF is all your work, I can't help being interested in it! Someday, perhaps we will have positive proof that SS THOMPSON LYKES actually rammed and sunk the big submarine, but until that day there are many other possibilities to ponder upon.

During the early part of the U-boat warfare, the German commanders reported their attacks and sinkings with extraordinary accuracy, almost perfectly! It was only later with the acoustic torpedo and the overwhelming presence of Allied antisubmarine forces that they were compelled to guesstamate and overestimate the results of their attacks. Now consider this; During the month of February, every vessel claimed sunk by German submarines in the greater Atlantic area was confirmed after the war, except one.

On February 16th or 17th, U-502 reported sinking a large vessel of about 5,000 tons in the Caribbean. It was never identified. Mistaken identity? In the dark, could a strange shaped vessel like SURCOUF have been mistaken for a tanker?

Concerning the three alleged attacks by American submarines on German U-boats during February, I found one of them to be true. The attack was made on U-582, positively! I discovered this from German War Diaries. The other two attacks were NOT, repeat were NOT, against U-boats.

SURCOUF could not have been attacked and sunk by U-502 (Kapitanleutnant Jurgen von Rosenstiel) as SURCOUF was still alive up to the time of her 1800 GCT position report on the 18th.

Besides, at the time of the SURCOUF-THOMPSON LYKES Collision, U-502, as a part of Admiral Donitz's Operation NEULAND, was on the prowl for enemy shipping in the Gulf of Venezuela.

It is a fact that no other submarine in history has had so many foul inferences, misconceptions and rumors, and otherwise false tales, spread about how she lived and died than poor SURCOUF. Probably, only the rumors told about how Amelia Earhart, the celebrated aviatrix, and Glenn Miller, the popular orchestra leader, disappeared exceed those told about SURCOUF.

Generally, rumors collapse with time, but those about SURCOUF never have. Sissela Bok, in *Lying*, wrote:

> The many experiments on rumors show how information can be distorted, added to, partially lost, when passed from one person to another, until it is almost unrecognizable.

Yet, considering the variety and diverse source of the SURCOUF dossier of rumors, we would have to admit that those spread about her have remained consistently the same since World War II. That such untruths have been carried forth, even by prominent people who were in positions to have known, or to learn the true facts, it is all the more despicable because of the hardship and torment that it has caused those left behind. For example, the Blaison womenfolk.

As for another example, consider the following misconception passed by officialdom by the Director of the Federal Bureau of Investigation, John Edgar Hoover, brother of Dickerson Naylor Hoover, Jr. (Head, Steamboat Inspection Service, Department of Commerce, during the American Government's investigation into the SS MORRO CASTLE Disaster). On March 12, 1942 he wrote to Rear Admiral T. S. Wilkerson, USN, Director, Office of Naval Intelligence, with copy to Brigadier General Raymond E. Lee, USA, Head, U.S. Army Intelligence, a PERSONAL AND CONFIDENTIAL, SPECIAL MESSENGER letter, to the effect that:

> Information has been received from a confidentially high source that the French submarine "Surcouf" was sunk off St. Pierre on March 3, 1942.

This revelation by Mr. Hoover, that forceful fighter of crime and injustice and author of *Masters of Deceit* and *A Study of Communism,* would not seem to speak well for the wartime efficiency of his famed FBI. **For, while he was writing his letter, SURCOUF had been dead for almost a month, and that at the very moment of his writing a Board of Inquiry was being held, in New Orleans, by the Office of the Attorney General, Department of Justice, Washington (the same department which Hoover administered), into how and why SURCOUF had been rammed by SS THOMPSON LYKES in the Caribbean on the night of February 18, 1942!!!**

Who was the "confidentially high source", what was that source's motive in passing such red-hot, but erroneous, intelligence to "the Boss" Hoover???

Why did Hoover give the date as March 3, 1942 and why "off St. Pierre??? And which St. Pierre??? Was the town of St. Pierre on the St. Pierre and Miquelon Islands, or was it the town of St. Pierre on the island of Martinique???

We may never learn the answers to these perplexing questions as information about FBI sources, and its inner sanctum, can often be, and necessarily so, as difficult to obtain or penetrate as it has been for the author to obtain details about SURCOUF from the cloistered French Naval Archives at Vincennes. (Don't Ask (about what we don't want you to know). Don't Tell (the truth about that we want to conceal).

From documents found in the National Archives, Washington, and observed on the Internet, one can conjecture who that "high source" was. The author believes it to have been Minneapolis-born (November 22, 1910 (Sagittarius) Elizabeth Amy "Betty" Thorpe, code-named by Intrepid as "Cynthia", the daughter of a "Devil Dog", Major George Cyrus Thorpe (originally Thaar P.), U.S. Marine Corps, and the former Cora Wells (daughter of Minnesota state senator H. H. Wells).

"Cynthia", with auburn hair and flashing green eyes, and "whose first love was literature and writing fresh and engaging letters, was extremely courageous, exotic," and, according to H. Montgomery Hyde, a former intelligence officer and the author of the sensational bestsellers, *The Quiet Canadian: The Secret Service Story of Sir William Stephenson [Intrepid], Room 3603, The Story of the British Intelligence Center in New York During World War II, Secret Intelligence Agent,* and *Cynthia,* was "A product of British intelligence and the most seductive secret weapon and the war's greatest unsung heroine in the arsenal of Intrepid's." **Hyde had been a Captain, British Army and, during World War II, served as BSC Security Officer, Censorship Station, Bermuda, for "Intrepid".)**

As a matter of further interest, Intrepid, according to Stevenson, in *A Man Called Intrepid,* also had a connection with another feminine spy, with the cover name of "Madeleine"; "a young woman of haunting beauty, and still the center of postwar controversy concerning her death" in Germany.

Noor Inayat Khan was born in the Kremlin on January 1, 1914. "Intrepid", according to Stevenson, supposedly met her in India before the war, but there is no mention of this in a movie starring James Cagney and Annabella in *13 Rue Madeleine or* that comprehensive book *Madeleine, Born for Sacrifice*, by Jean Overton Fuller, who was a close friend of Noor's.

During the Fall of France, Noor fled to England and joined the Woman's Air Auxiliary Force (WAAF). From that service she was recruited into British Intelligence, being the only British Muslim spy princess recruited, and later volunteered to return to France as a radio operator. She was the first female radio operator sent into Nazi held France. While serving in Paris, she was allegedly betrayed by a Frenchman, captured by the Gestapo, held in captivity in Paris, and subsequently tortured and shot in the crematorium at Dachau Camp, Germany on September 12, 1944. Some French adamantly believe her cover was venomously blown by double agent within Intrepid's organization, MI-5, or in the Foreign Office. These same French also believe that they were the same traitors who had conspired against the Free French and SURCOUF in London. An analysis of Note No. 8 provides extremely strong credulence to support their plausible theories.

Postwar German records revealed that during Noor's cruel interrogation by the Gestapo, she was amazed over what they knew about her and her operation, to the extent that she exclaimed **"But you know everything! You must have an agent in London!"** That agent could have also been Colonel Charles Howard "Dick" Ellis, Intrepid's supposedly trusted deputy in New York, who during hostile interrogation, in the mid-1960s, confessed to being a German agent. (Noor was awarded the Croix de Guerre with Gold Star by France and the George Cross by England. She was the only woman to be awarded the George Cross, which was highest award rendered by England for gallantry during war.)

Among the major coups by Cynthia, the alert Irish-Scandinavian beauty, who was in the ranks of British Intelligence in Poland, as early as 1937, as the wife of the British diplomat (commercial counselor) Arthur Pack, was the discovery, in Poland, of the code machine ENIGMA, of which much is written about in *The Code Breakers*, by David Hahn; the alleged seduction of Rear Admiral Alberto Lais, Italian Navy, from whom she reportedly learned that Italian ships were to be scuttled in

American harbors, and from whom she reportedly obtained Italian naval ciphers that contributed to the Royal Navy's resounding defeat of the Italian Fleet at Cape Matapan, and the infiltration of the Vichy French diplomatic corps, in Washington, to obtain political plans and secret naval codes. Immediately, these codes was used by the Allies in preparation for Operation TORCH and to learn the pro-German activities of Vichy French diplomats in Washington.)

By sheer chance, after searching through thousands of pages of documents at the National Archives Center, Suitland, Maryland, the writer discovered a letter having a Federal Bureau of Investigation-French connection with one in the files of his (Grigore) Florida writing sanctuary. This March 12, 1942 document was signed by J. Edgar Hoover, with File 7945, France, in the upper right hand corner, followed by PERSONAL AND CONFIDENTIAL, SPECIAL MESSENGER.

Also found was a unsigned July 14, 1942 letter, File 7115, France, which appears to have also originated within Hoover's FBI. It had SPECIAL MESSENGER below the file number coupled with identical phrasing, such as to indicate that both letters were drafted by the same person within the Federal Bureau of Investigation: "Information has been received from a highly confidential source that . . .".

The July 14, 1942 letter specifically mentioned Capitaine de Vaisseau Charles Le Brousse, who was Press Officer and Naval Attaché at the Vichy French Embassy, Washington. Le Brousse, formerly a naval fighter pilot who had served on the Anglo-French Air Intelligence Board before the surrender of France in June 1940, was the lover and source of much Vichy French Navy intelligence for the alluring "Cynthia", who reported her findings, obtained by great personal sacrifice (there are no secrets in bedrooms), directly to William Stephenson, "Intrepid", Director, British Security Coordination Corporation of New York, London, and Bermuda. (t the time, Cynthia lived at 3327 "O" Street, Washington, D.C., a house that Intrepid allegedly frequented.)

History proved that the "highly confidential source", who the author believes was Capitaine Le Brousse, was unreliable. SURCOUF was sunk in the Caribbean and French warships at Alexandria were never scuttled.

Could it be that Le Brousse had been instructed to deliberately dupe Cynthia, who was fanatically pro-British and one of the war's unsung heroines, with the intention of deceiving Intrepid and the Allies???

What may not have been beyond pale was the creditability of the Cynthia-Le Brousse Connection, who eventually married each other, as reliable intelligence sources during World War II. We may never learn the truth, but such conjecture is interesting, if not enlightening.

What Hoover's letter of March 12, 1942 indicated to the author—supposing that that there had been a plot to eliminate SURCOUF—was that Hoover was not privy to that rumored affair d' accompli, or else why would he have written to the directors of the U.S. Army and Navy intelligence about SURCOUF's death well after that sad event occurred in the Caribbean, and especially while the Board of Inquiry into the SURCOUF-THOMPSON LYKES Collision was in-progress in New Orleans???

From reading many works about Mr. Hoover, and the operations of the FBI, it was learned that he required his personnel to maintain a detailed summary of back-up information in FBI files for drafting, and before his signature and release, of important correspondence. Inquiry, under the Freedom of Information Act, failed to reveal back-up information relative to these two letters, or any knowledge of their existence, such as could reveal who his "highly confidential source" was.

It is unlikely that Mr. Hoover's source was Intrepid, since SURCOUF was operating under the aegis of the British Royal Navy, and she was too important of a naval unit of the Free French for word of her loss in the Caribbean not to have passed quickly through secret channels—including to Intrepid's New York City office.

SURCOUF's loss, therefore, was widely known among the upper echelons, like the State Department (Berle), The Panama Canal, and civil, military, and naval authorities of the United States Government. It is strange that Mr. Hoover was not informed about SURCOUF's loss when it occurred—such as to provide him with a prepared investigative summary—before the drafting and transmittal of his letter to U.S. Army and U.S. Navy directors of intelligence?

It must have been embarrassing for him when he learned that he had informed the military and naval intelligence officials of the United States Government about something they, including the intelligence activity of the State Department (Berle), had known about weeks before receipt of Hoover's March 14 letter.

However, if, even in today's world of extraordinary events, SURCOUF were to be found off St. Pierre, a town on the St. Pierre and Miquelon Islands, or offshore of the town of St. Pierre on the Caribbean island of Martinique, then the naval and political history of World War II would be drastically changed.

In any event, still another woman (Cynthia)—in the role of a superspy—the Mata Hari of World War II—had figured in SURCOUF's fascinating after death life.

Incidentally, about Hyde's writing of *Cynthia*, Christopher Andrew and David Dilks, Editors of *The Missing Dimension, Governments and Intelligence in the Twentieth Century,* cited *Cynthia* as "a more valuable work than its publishers (Ballantine Books, New York) sensational presentation suggests."

What one could be easily led to believe, however, is that the Royal Navy did sink SURCOUF, as Burney apparently feared would happen, and as was reported to George Burns by that "man" associated with the Bermuda Regiment.

Why should so many different, seemingly authentic, accounts of how SURCOUF died continue to surface; even at this late date in the postwar period? There may be no better explanation other than that there are some World War II enthusiastic or veterans who are determined that the truth about how they believe SURCOUF died should be told during their lifetime; not wanting to die with dark secrets on their mind or hidden with their souls.

One such testament, as was related during a telephone conversation between John McGill Reyner, of Halifax, Canada, and an anonymous caller. Their conversation, about a horrifying event aboard SURCOUF, gave birth to the "BNLO Staff Death Rumor," took place on the evening of December 23, 1982, nearly forty-six years to the day after SURCOUF's involvement in the St. Pierre Miquelon Affair:

Last evening I had a very strange phone call. So strange that I felt that I must give it to you right away for your book.

The caller had an educated Canadian accent, but would not reveal his name. He asked if I were the person who has doing research on SURCOUF. He then said he was calling from New Brunswick.

'Early in 1942,' he said, 'he was in the Royal Canadian Navy, stationed at MALABAR [Bermuda].' I gathered that he was a communications rating.

One day, there was a 'big flap' in his office. A signal had came in from an American submarine that had been shadowing SURCOUF at periscope depth, from a great distance.

The sub had seen something odd take place on SURCOUF and shortly after she dived. The American sub cautiously worked her way to where SURCOUF had been and found three floating bodies, each of which had been shot.

It was believed that the bodies were those of the three members of the British Naval Officer Liaison team off SURCOUF.

He said that a cruiser and a destroyer were sent out to get SURCOUF, but he couldn't recall the ships names. 'And other forces were called in too,' there were his words, 'including the Yanks.'

He heard afterwards that "they'd got her". He didn't know who, but a lot of conflicting stories came in making it hard to tell what really happened.

John's narrative also connects with a story reported years earlier by *The New York Times*, Monday, January 29, 1945, "American Ship May Have Sunk Big French Submarine Surcouf," which cited a weekend dispatch by *The Montreal Standard*. Excerpts follow:

The details of the sinking of Surcouf never were officially disclosed because General Charles de Gaulle decided against it through fear that French reaction would jeopardize his efforts to obtain American recognition.

Surcouf was sent to the bottom by Allied naval units after pro-Vichy crew members had seized it and murdered the three members of the British Naval Liaison Officer staff aboard.

The New York Times article went on to state that there was no official confirmation or denial of *The Montreal Standard* dispatch.

Note the remarkable similarity between John's narrative with Oliver Hull's input which follows. Oliver submitted his version of how SURCOUF died in reply to my inquiry in the summer issue of *The King's Pointer Magazine*. Oliver, of Bedford Village, New York, was graduate of the United States Merchant Marine Academy, Kings Point, New York, Class of 1945. (The author was in the Class of 1946.)

Here is what Oliver Hull wrote, in his July 15, 1981 letter, and in his telling we return to New London, Connecticut, SURCOUF's old haunt:

> Your article about SURCOUF and submarine disasters brought me back the days when I was stationed at Fort Trumbull, New London, Connecticut. At the time, I was in the U.S. Coast Guard as a Yeoman 3rd Class, and had been assigned to coding and decoding highly secret "strip code" messages.
>
> While on duty in February 1942, a message came through from an American submarine that it had observed a sinking of an American merchant ship by the Free French submarine SURCOUF. This sighting, as I remember, was off Florida. The next message was a confirmed sinking of SURCOUF by that submarine.
>
> Subsequently, I was accepted as a Cadet-Midshipman, USNR, by the U.S. Merchant Marine Academy, Kings Point, New York, and graduated in 1945. In later years, my endeavors to obtain the details of the SURCOUF sinking have been "stonewalled" by the United States Navy.

Please consider this as a signed affidavit as to the truth regarding the loss of the Free French submarine SURCOUF.

Sincerely,

/s/ Oliver Hull

Note that John's anonymous caller may have been a naval communications type, just as Oliver was, and that both rumors involved SURCOUF being sunk by an American submarine while it was shadowing her! It would be difficult to disprove Oliver Hull's "bombshell" letter, and it would probably be impossible to obtain copies of those messages received from that American submarine, which he, as a Yeoman 3rd Class, had decoded in February 1942.

Oliver, whose bone fides are unquestionable, presented to the author convincing evidence that, for years, he had attempted to query naval intelligence authorities on the subject of SURCOUF's loss, only to be politely rebuffed or indirectly dissuaded from pursuing his endeavor.

In the Foreword to Hyde's book, ROOM 3603 Ian Fleming, who, from 1940 to 1942, was Personal Assistant to Rear Admiral John H. "Speed" Godfrey, Royal Navy (Deputy for Naval Intelligence), wrote:

> 'Little Bill,' from his highly mechanized situation in Rockefeller Center and his quiet apartment in Dorset House, New York City, was able to render innumerable services to the Royal Navy that could not have been asked for, let alone execute, through normal channels.

Some friends of Therese and Francine Blaison, who were of a type that never believed their reflection in a mirror, firmly held the opinion that SURCOUF was not done-in by collision with the SS THOMPSON LYKES. They are of the opinion that SURCOUF was "paid-off" by specialists trained at superspy Intrepid's Camp "X", the secret nerve center for England's war against Nazism and to set Europe ablaze while doing so. It was on the Canadian shore of Lake Ontario where saboteurs were trained to affix magnetic, time-delayed limpet mines to her hull while she lay at Ireland Dockyard, Somerset,

Bermuda—before her departure for Tahiti, on Feb 12, 1942, via the Panama Canal.

After reading the following article that appeared in *Spotlight* on July 31, 1980 entitled: *Did Winston Churchill order the sinking of a friendly submarine,* which, incidentally was the Dutch submarine HM K-17, do not accept that the French opinion is totally beyond belief. Permit the author to reiterate the words of the poem, *Open Your Mind,* that followed the Introduction:

Open Your Mind
That your eyes may see
The vast channels of reality.
Project your components
So the reaches inscribed
Let not the darkness
Cause you to hide.
For to fear the unknown
Or what you might find
Is to fear the truth
In our fabrics design.
Through each of us channel
Ourselves in some way
All the elements still have their say

Now for the *Spotlight* article (verbatim):

The Dutch TV show "TV Prize" often makes sensational exposes. Recently it had an interview with Christopher Creighton from England, protagonist of an English book, *Paladin,* by Brien Garfield. Creighton was Winston Churchill's personal secret agent in World War II. [Creighton, the paladin, was recruited by Winston Churchill during WWII and sent around the world on missions of state—usually violent missions.] During the interview, he stated that in 1941 he was ordered by Churchill to destroy the Dutch submarine "HMS K-17."

He said he succeeded in bringing cyanide gas containers on board K-17. Then, 24 hours later—when he was no longer aboard—the gas containers supposedly exploded; and the dead crew and their vessel sank. Why this crime against an Allied submarine?

Creighton claimed that the sub had discovered the Japanese fleet steaming toward Pearl Harbor. Churchill feared that this information would reach America and that prompt countermeasures would then forestall the hoped for excuse for the United States entering into the war, said Creighton. The Dutch newspaper *"de Telegraaf"* is printing excerpts from the book.

It is well established that the sub disappeared during the war, but the British say that it is not where Creighton says it sank. Creighton answers that the British secret service obviously was careful that such a deed could not be reconstructed and that the Dutch naval archives were during World War II in London so that the falsification was simple.

The *Telegraaf* printed the story with the remark, "Judge for yourself whether the story is true."

Thus, if asked to consider which rumor about how SURCOUF was done-in, the one which had the most validity in my absolute opinion, but without proof, would be the one citing she was disenfranchised by professional assassins—a garbage squad—consisting of experts in the use of limpet mines.

Someone within Intrepid's secret world could have tasked such a team to do this alien thing—one where documentation was not required, with all leads negative, and without possibility of establishing the truth. In such an environment, members could get away scot-free, without detection, while SURCOUF died. (Every conspiracy or secret agent needs a cover.)

Camp "X" would have been the likely place to recruit this garbage squad as it was there that select personnel were schooled in a wide variety of special techniques of espionage, and including fraud, silent killing, sabotage, seduction, demolition, and more extreme methods. The problem with membership in a garbage squad is that after the execution of a clandestine operation something permanent could happen to keep participants forever silent.

From sources like *The Invisible Raiders, The History of the Special Boat Squadron During World War II*, by James D. Ladd, which confirmed that the British were experts in the use of limpet mines, and from *A Matter of Trust* and *Thread of Deceit* both by Nigel West and *Spy Catcher* by Peter Wright, which were critical about the nature of Intrepid's operations, and of the questionable loyalty of some of his operatives—like Colonel Charles Howard "Dick" Ellis, British Army, who was Interpid's deputy, like Anthony Blunt, who was in MI-5, London; Kim Philby, who was in Special Operations, Executive and later in MI-6, London; Donald McLean and Guy burgess, who both worked in the Foreign Office, London;—who long after the war were charged with being the Cambridge Conspirators who, except for Blunt, fled to the Soviet Union—one could have grave doubts about the integrity and security of some of Intrepid's operations during the World War II.

These notorious operatives, just as during the Muselier Affair, were in trusted positions to conspire against the Free French and to blackball SURCOUF and to then dupe their superiors into accepting that SURCOUF should be terminated. By the same token, they were also in position to communicate and conspire with other Communists within the Free French movement, which Chapman Pincer, in *Too Secret Too Long*, published in 1984, said was "riddled with Soviet agents."

Regardless, Pincher proved that there was a continuous link between Ellis and Philby throughout their careers of duplicity within the British Secret Service. To reveal the insidious position that Ellis held while serving as Intrepid's deputy, and one which has a strong similarity the probability that misinformation was passed about SURCOUF from within BSC, New York, we again refer to Pincher:

Ellis's relations with the FBI deserve critical study by historians as he may have been responsible for Hoover's decision [in early 1941] to ignore warnings from Popov about the Japanese attack on Pearl Harbor. Ellis may have given a bad report to Hoover about Popov, who was disinclined to believe him.

(Author's Note: According to *The Dictionary of Espionage*, by Christopher Dobson and Ronald Payne, Dusko Popov was the son of a wealthy Yugoslav and hated Nazis. Although he worked for them as a secret agent, he became an agent, code named "Tricycle," attached to the Double Cross (XX) operation run by Sir John Masterman who specialized in turning German agents to plant false information.)

Even if poor SURCOUF had not been a victim on some operative's hit-list within Interpid's New York organization—she still did not stand a ghost of chance of survival against the deadly impact of SS THOMPSON LYKES, which with unerring instinct and a mysterious sense of direction in the black Caribbean night, did collide with and sink her.

Puzzling, however, as you shall read, is why SURCOUF violently exploded twice—with huge flashes of flame emitting from her hulk—even when she passed under THOMPSON LYKES—as she plummeted into the depths of the Caribbean—faster than she could have crash-dived—forever???

Of course, Intrepid was in the game of covert operations—a sea of devious tricks, half-truths, betrayals, and complex lies—including blackmail to forgery to murder—all apart from official diplomatic and political business.

Intrepid would have had to by-pass normal channels to obtain an unwritten termination order from within the highest levels of the British government—like as high as Churchill—before he could order in "a garbage-disposal squad" to nullify SURCOUF.

Also, he would have had to apply the first rule of assassination, which was that SURCOUF's real cause of death had to go undetected and that she must be seen to have died as a natural course of war. The second rule would be that her assassination would have to be one of the most carefully and skillfully guarded secrets in history.

Any vendetta against SURCOUF would not have been due to someone accomplishing a masterpiece of intelligence, rather it would have been to an appalling permissiveness within the secret service communities—which allowed 'good chaps' like the Cambridge Conspirators—to spy for Russia completely undetected, and to have condoned them when they were suspected.

Such an untoward attempt against SURCOUF would only occur if Intrepid and Churchill had been maliciously duped—by Communist, Nazi, or Vichy moles within Special Operations, Executive; MI-5; MI-6; or BSC—into believing that SURCOUF was a political liability, a menace to, or a source of international conflict for, the Allies.

Room 3603 provides strong precedence and almost incriminating evidence to support the Halifax Rumor, as concerned the use of planting explosives on ships, and which involved the BSC, the American State Department and the American and Royal Navies in Mexican territorial waters of the Gulf of Mexico over a year before America's formal entry into World War II:

> Hoover of the FBI was encouraged on occasion to invoke the help of the service Departments on behalf of the British, even when it ran counter to the State Department's strict policy of neutrality. The following incident, which took place in the autumn of 1940, provided a good example of such intervention.
>
> Stephenson's representative in Mexico reported that he had reason to believe that four German and twelve Italian ships, which were lying in the Gulf ports of Tampico and Vera Cruz, were planning to run the British blockade. It certainly looked as if the Axis vessels might succeed in their intention as the Royal Navy could not patrol Mexican territorial waters.
>
> Stephenson passed this information to Hoover for transmission to ONI (Office of Naval Intelligence). He also informed London, who authorized his action he considered

appropriate provided the British Ambassador in Washington, Lord Philip Henry Kerr, 11th Marques of Lothian, was first informed.

Stephenson then sent his representative in Mexico a quantity of 'limpet' bombs—small explosive charges, which would adhere to the steel plates of a ship's hull. However, no effective steps could be taken without the assistance of the United States Navy.

After discussion with Lord Lothian, Stephenson went to Hoover, asking him to arrange for a naval patrol in the area of the Mexican Gulf ports.

After meeting with considerable difficulties, Hoover won over the State Department which agreed to the plan with the strict understanding that no act should be committed which might be construed as a breach of American neutrality.

Four American destroyers were dispatched to the Gulf of Mexico with orders to lie off Tampico and report by radio *en clair* any movements which the Axis ships might make.

On November 15, 1940, the four German ships steamed into the Gulf of Mexico. American destroyers approached and trained the full battery of their searchlights upon them. This was not a belligerent act, but it made the German captains think that it was the prelude to an all-out attack.

Panic ensued. One of the German ships, the PHRYGIA, either caught fire accidentally or was scuttled. She was abandoned as a total loss. The others steamed back into port.

Intelligence reports revealed that the German captains believed they had encountered some of the old four-stack destroyers which had recently been transferred by the American Navy to Britain; they informed sources in Tampico the next day that they 'had been ordered to surrender by British warships.'

A fortnight later, two of the three remaining German ships put to sea in broad daylight. American destroyers shadowed them and, by transmitting position signals, enabled warships of the Royal Navy to intercept and to take them as prizes of war.

This is how, according to *WWW.Belligerent Acts Prior to US Entry into WW2*, on the Internet, how it ultimately occurred; much of which was in conformance with Hyde's remarks:

> On November 16, 1940, the U. S. Navy destroyer MCCORMACK (DD-223), on neutrality patrol off Tampico, Mexico, radios the attempt of German freighter ORINOCO to make for European waters. Destroyer PLUNKETT (DD-431), by her presence, thwarts the German tanker PHRYGIA'S bid for freedom; AND PHRYGIA'S crew scuttles her. On December 8, 1940, the destroyer STURTEVANT (DD-240) stood by while British light cruiser HMS DIOMEDE intercepts German freighter IDARWALD.
>
> On December 11, 1940, the German freighter RHEIN, having been SHADOWED by the U. S. Navy destroyer SIMPSON (DD-221) and, later, the MACLEISH (DD-220), is intercepted by Dutch destroyer leader VAN KINSBERGEN near the Florida Straits, and is scuttled by her crew to avoid capture.
>
> And on December 11th, the United States extended its s "neutral zone" to 300 miles.

The author's supplements to Hyde's remarks are for the purpose of not only informing the reader with subsequent events concerning the German attempts to break-out of Tampico, Mexico, but to also reveal how American and Royal Navy warships worked in concert, especially the HMS DIOMEDE, even before the war, and reveal that Intrepid, at that time, was quite familiar with the use of limpet mines.

It also had extended its neutrality zone to 200 miles beyond its borders, which included the Caribbean Sea and Pacific sides of the Panama Canal Zone. Moreover, the Caribbean Sea extension should be recalled when reading events concerning SURCOUF's death appearing shortly.

Now back to the main stream of this story: My two attempts to interview Intrepid in Paget, Bermuda, in May 1981, to verify some of my findings, drew a reply through his attractive nurse-housekeeper, Mrs. Marie Baptise, and his chauffer, Simon, that he knew nothing about SURCOUF. Sometimes when people do not want to talk with you it's generally a sign that they may be concealing something. But, it was Intrepid's oath of secrecy and loyalty to the Crown of England never to reveal the truth unless it served a purpose. Those that know the most, reveal the least.

Intrepid's memory could not have been so deficient that day, as *Interpid's Last Case,* published in 1983, revealed many of BSC's overt and covert operations during World War II.

Intrepid had to have known about SURCOUF and her Free French officers and men, particularly while she was undergoing overhaul at Portsmouth Naval Shipyard and during her training period with Commander, Submarine Forces, Atlantic.

The evidence is that Capitaine de Frigate Georges Louis Nicolas Blaison, likely with the concurrence of Intrepid's office and that of the Royal Navy, made a propaganda broadcast, on October 28, 1941, to the French people over the 50,000 watt radio station controlled by Intrepid, WRUL, based in Boston, while SURCOUF was undergoing overhaul at the U. S. Naval shipyard at Portsmouth, New Hampshire. **Thus, Intrepid, and his hierarchy, had to have been personally aware of this occasion.**

And, according to *Room 3603,* by H. Montgomery Hyde, concerning Intrepid's secret intelligence network, he (Intrepid) had to have been thoroughly aware of SURCOUF's involvement, as were Churchill, de Gaulle, Mackenzie King, and Roosevelt, following the liberation of the St. Pierre and Miquelon Islands on December 24, 1941, led by Vice Admiral Muselier, since it caused a "tempest in a teapot"—as U. S. Secretary of State Cordell Hull expressed himself about the affair.

Some in Bermuda, Canada, England, and France believe that the Royal Navy continues to hide a deep truth as to how SURCOUF really died, to cover Intrepid's alleged involvement in her death.

The editors of *The London Sunday Times* are among these advocates. For, in their November 27, 1983 edition there appeared a devastating article by Alison Miller and Antony Terry with the headline: *Did the Allies Sink SURCOUF?* Terry and Miller questioned SURCOUF's loyalty—alluding that her crew had betrayed the Allies and joined the Nazis. They also charged that inquiry into the disappearance of SURCOUF, after 40 years, still was meeting with official obstruction.

There is an amazing revelation, which surfaced in 1982, despite possible official obstruction, which has a close correspondence with SURCOUF's death, and which also involves a citizen of France—Napoleon.

In a startling who-done-it, by Ben Weider and David Hapgood, in *The Murder of Napoleon*, they investigated one of the history's greatest crimes. They provided evidence which, to them, conclusively revealed that Napoleon, while in British custody, had been murdered by frequent dosages of arsenic, something which he, on his deathbed, suspected:

> After my death I want you to open my body. Make a precise report on it. I charge you to overlook nothing in this examination. I bequeath to all the ruling families the horror and shame of my last moments.

For 150 years, Weider and Hapgood wrote, everyone believed that Napoleon had died of stomach cancer. Then a Swedish dentist, Dr. Sten Forshufvud, aided by a Napoleon-buff, Gregory Troubetzkoy, living in New York City, read an account of Napoleon's last days on St. Helena. Forshufvud was stunned—the dying emperor displayed all the symptoms of arsenic poisoning. He proved it, through what remains a classic testament to modern forensic technique!

Must we wait 150 years before we discover what SURCOUF's last days were as she transited from Bermuda to the Panama Canal? We have Boyer's, Burney's, Gough's, Warner's testaments that they feared death was upon them on-board SURCOUF. Must we now wait for the year 2092, 150 years after SURCOUF's death, to discover the cause of their fears, or must we wait until then to learn the truth about the rumor that the cruiser USS SAVANNAH had been shadowing SURCOUF hours before she was rammed by the SS THOMPSON LYKES???

The fact that the someone within the Allied cause seemed to suspect SURCOUF or wanted her demise, coupled with the "highly reliable source" of that rumor—from within the U.S. Marine Corps—lends strong justification for probing to the bottom of SURCOUF's death now!!!

It would have been impossible for Intrepid, in his Rockefeller Center Headquarters, to not know about SURCOUF—the world's largest, most powerful submarine—the one involved in the SURCOUF Affray of July 3, 1940; the St. Pierre and Miquelon Affair; and the collision with THOMPSON LYKES—each being a tempestuous encounter that alienated an ally. Absolutely impossible. If so, then his high-place friends and acquaintances or his wartime secret intelligence service informed him badly or he was living in a world of his own.

Arithmetically speaking, SURCOUF could have died in at least 110 different scenarios. In *The SURCOUF Dossier of Rumors* there are included 42 versions, which were submitted by contributors. No submarine in history has been the victim of so much disinformation and slander than SURCOUF! Why!!! Yet, SURCOUF served the Allied war cause loyally and gallantly—dying honorably.

If we were to rank the frequency of the two categories of rumors spread about SURCOUF, coupled with the number of their variations, the broadness of their area of spread, their popularity, and their ability to sustain intensity, on a scale of 1 to 10, the author would rank those applicable to SURCOUF as a **3**.

In continuation of this analysis, and for reader interest, there follows what the author considers to be the 10 most out standing mysteries or rumors of our time—as orientated to the United States and as observed by an American. They are, as compiled in 1978, the:

Aircraft, ships, and people lost in the Bermuda Triangle.

Assassination of President John F. Kennedy.

SURCOUF category of rumors.

Disappearance of Amelia Earhart, the aviatrix, on July 3, 1937, over the South Pacific.

Hindenburg disaster on May 6, 1937.

Whereabouts and death of Adolph Hitler.

Kidnapping of the Lindbergh baby on March 1, 1932.

Band leader Major Glen Miller, U.S. Army Air Force, who disappeared over the North Sea, on Dec 15, 1944, during World War II.

Disappearance of the collier USS CYCLOPS in the Caribbean during World War I.

Loss of the renown French writer and aviator, Antoine Saint-Exupery over the Mediterranean Sea on July 31, 1941.
Destruction of the SS NORMANDIE in New York Harbor on Feb 8, 1942—during World War II.
Disappearance of Leslie Howard, the British film star, over the Bay of Biscay on June 1943—during World War II.

The three rumors in categories 10 to 12 were given equal status because they have been noted to surface with about equal frequency in either France, England, or the United States.

On variations alone, however, the rumors adrift about SURCOUF could rank her as a strong number two.

Understandably, the above listing of the ten most predominant rumors of our time is based upon the author's personal experience, observation, reading, and exposure to affairs in the United States, Europe, Asia, Latin America, and Canada. His selections are, admittedly, open to broad commentary and interpretation. For example, each nation has its own category of rumors which are most peculiar and prevalent to its history, culture, times and thought. Therefore, this listing could be subject to drastic change—say in the Far East, the Caribbean, throughout Latin America, or in Europe.

Some of these rumors, as the one about USS CYCLOPS, which held the American public's attention throughout the Twenties and Thirties, fade with time through a process of elimination. This occurs when interest and publicity levels about a rumor declines, when truth is discovered about one, or when a rumor is superseded by a more popular or powerful one—such as those associated with the assassination of President Kennedy in 1963, which immediately captured second place that the SURCOUF category of rumors had held in my thought since 1978.

There can be little doubt, however, that the rumors about the Bermuda Triangle and about the assassination of John F. Kennedy hold center stage, worldwide. They should continue to do so for many generations. It is in this light and perspective that the category of rumors told about SURCOUF, after concerted study by the author, was interjected as a **3**.

A strange, but fascinating, thing about rumors is that as they persist, spread, and pass from generation to generation as they evolve into mysteries. Once they are accepted as mysteries, then the salient question always asked is who were the conspirators were behind the dastardly act? The truth seldom surfaces.

Even when rumors are officially denied, or are proved to be misconceptions, much of the public remains disbelieving. Their acceptance usually is in direct proportion to the confidence level they hold relative to the Government which represents them, and as to who stands to gain the most within the group making the official announcement.

The scene now opens as SURCOUF and THOMPSON LYKES, no longer masters of' their fate, but are slaves of circumstances beyond their control, move through the night like hypnotized gladiators—the blind and the intruder—stabbing empty during a moonless night, ship against ship, programmed to duel until death.

But, unlike most duels between submarines and surface ships, SURCOUF would not have her choice of weapons that night.

Before that deadly strike could be made at SURCOUF, through her shields of sea and darkness, the Master of the SS THOMPSON LYKES, as if he were a Pawn of Death, had to make three incredible refinements in course and speed, each at an exact place and time in that vast expanse of the Caribbean, in the black of night, such as to place his ship upon a direct heading to annihilate poor SURCOUF!!! *(If the Ninja chose the right kind of background, no enemy looking in his direction would be able to observe him. Because of his mastery over nature, which included an ability to sense the presence of an enemy on the darkest night, many credited the Ninja as bbeing a magician with supernatural powers.)*

**Quoth she, and whistles thrice.
Swiftly, swiftly flew the ship.
How fast she nears and nears.**

Modern navigation practice dictates that a ship maintain a direct and accurate course, yet it seemed as if Captain Johnson, through some sixth sense, had been compelled to make three fatal changes, when he did, as if he had known SURCOUF's whereabouts. It seems as if Captain Johnson was beckoning the gyroscopic law of precession to come into effect: When a deflecting force is applied to the rim of a spinning gyro, the gyro will move not away from, but *directly towards* that force.

Even the slightest shift in wind, sea condition or direction could have diverted SS THOMPSON LYKES off her heading on SURCOUF. But even in hydro space man is the ultimate enemy!!!

She nears and nears.

This is not to say that the author does not accept that Captain Johnson made these changes in the way that he did, only to say that it was very strange that he made them when and as he did, and for the reasons he gave. It was as if they were made to satisfy something out of this world.

In light of Madame Blaison's extraordinary psychic reaction, as a child, to the horrible loss of L-24, Francine's horrific encounter beside a garden pool, and of Blaison's affinity for submarine disaster, there are Frenchmen, some even hardened skeptics, who believe SURCOUF was the victim of some strange occult happening, as nobody could find any plausible explanation for why and how she died that night. It was as if an event of the distant past, by some unexplainable connection, was recurring in the present.

Was some invisible entity, a master controller out of the dark recesses of that Caribbean night, or in the Canal Zone, deliberately guiding Captain Johnson and THOMPSON LYKES, through an evil eye or radar device, to steer into and destroy SURCOUF??? This is a question to which no logical answer is possible, only to say that ghastly accident seemed destined to happen. But destiny is a fool's excuse for failure. And failures had occurred, with the ultimate one about to take place.

"Take away the divinity of Christ," Coleridge wrote, "and God becomes no more than a power of darkness."

And it is an ancient Japanese superstition that evil spirits travel in straight lines, and only approach their victim from the northeast, the direction from which SURCOUF was approaching THOMPSON LYKES!!!

In my manuscript *Surcouf and the Alien Mind*, it was mentioned that one could be led to believe that Captain Johnson, while effecting his three speed and course changes, had been psychokinetically influenced through an alien mind or a "third eye." This possibility should not be overlooked from this point onward. In fact, after reading the following excerpt from *Operation Mind Control*, by Walter Bowart, such a thought should not seem too incredible to accept:

> During World War 1, a leading psychologist made a startling proposal to the Navy. He offered to take a submarine steered by a captured U-boat captain, placed under his hypnotic control, through enemy mine fields to attack the German fleet.

Bowart's study gains support from the novel *Death in the Mind* by Professor George "Esty" Estabrooks, a consultant to American intelligence and military services on mind control, wherein Estaboorks wrote about a series of seemingly treasonable acts committed by an American submarine captain who was hypnotized by the Germans to torpedo one of his own battleships, and about a beautiful American heroine who was similarly controlled to serve their cause. At that time, in 1945, Dr. Estabrooks was Head, Department of Psychology, and Colgate University, New York.

The cumulative effect of Captain Johnson's three changes, at the time that each was executed, two of which were of his own volition, the other as a result of an alleged message from American naval authorities in the Canal Zone, sealed the fate of SURCOUF and caused the worst submarine disaster in history. Had any one of the three changes been varied even slightly in magnitude—or not made at all—SURCOUF could have sailed on to Tahiti, oblivious of her close encounter with Death. But Death was not on leave that dreadful night.

One of three

These three fatal changes, when each is evaluated from the standpoint of chance and time, place the odds of SURCOUF'S casualty occurring almost beyond the bounds of infinite probability. But it did occur!!! Why???

The SURCOUF-THOMPSON LYKES Collision had "but one chance" of happening in "a century or more", and under conditions which could only be sustained for but a few seconds. But Chance does nothing that has not been prepared beforehand

Does the author seem to exaggerate the odds of the SURCOUF-THOMPSON LYKES Collision having occurred??? If you believe so, read the following excerpt from *Nautical Magazine*, December 1979, published by the National Maritime Institute of Glasgow, Scotland, about the possibilities of collisions occurring with even fixed installations at sea, having known positions:

The National Maritime Institute has studied the possibilities of ships colliding with offshore platforms in the Forties Field (North Sea). Using traffic data collected in a one-month survey, together with collision histories of light vessels in the English Channel, the NMI estimated that the risk of direct collision between a ship and any of the Forties platforms is one every 3,300 years. For any single platform, the risk gets down to one every 12,500 years. For an indirect collision, i.e., a ship drifting after a collision with a previous ship, the risk is only one in 200,000 years.

It, however, only requires two determined mariners, with a violent dislike of statistical calculations, in two different ships, to make nonsense of all that. Or even only one determined mariner. Steady men! Relax men! Restrain all those evil thoughts and temptations!

We know that Blaison and Captain Johnson, aboard two different kinds of ships, were determined men: Blaison was determined to take SURCOUF to Tahiti via the Panama Canal, and Captain Johnson, with his violent dislike of submarines, as you shall read, seemed determined to sink one the very night that SURCOUF died.

No similar collision ever occurred in Panama Canal waters, one of the more heavily trafficked ocean routes of the world. And, according to *A Bloody War*, of the tens of thousands of crossings by merchant ships, while in convoy, at close quarters, with little sea room for maneuvering during the Battle of the Atlantic and involving operations in darkness, fog, ice, snow, storm and smoke and harassment by enemy attack, not a single merchant ship was lost through collision. "Merchant seaman were put to the test time and again; the skill, sea sense, and seamanship of their masters passed belief."

In contrast, it seemed as if Captain Johnson had been guided, by some alien controller, to assume a collision course on SURCOUF, or that he instinctively knew where to find her, so that THOMPSON LYKES could destroy SURCOUF in the dead of night.

Was Captain Johnson an involuntary accomplice to a monstrous evil??? If "SAVVY" had, indeed, been ordered to intercept SURCOUF, why not also an American merchant ship under the command of a merchant marine captain, who was also a naval reserve officer???

No book about the American Merchant Marine—at war—is complete without mention of the SURCOUF-THOMPSON LYKES Collision, which caused the world's worst submarine disaster. But this incident is not mentioned in any such book. (However, the Internet is quite informative about SURCOUF's wartime experience, but much of it is wrong.)

Since our view of the SURCOUF-THOMPSON LYKES Collision is through the words of the joint Department of Justice and Commandant, States Coast Guard *Board of Inquiry Report*, it is essential, at this point, to tell who requested and authorized the convening of the Board, who comprised its membership and how it came to meet at 10:30 A.M., March 11, 1942, as a private hearing., and conclude at 11:05 A.M., March 13, 1942, and to otherwise analyze what would appear to be a simple, straightforward request. *(Put not your trust in princes, nor in the son of man, in whom there is no help. Psalms 146:3 KJV)*

Below follows the letter of authority requesting that Board's convening and stating its composition.

UNITED STATES COAST GUARD
WASHINGTON

THOMPSON LYKES A4
VESSEL "A"
9 March 1942

My dear Mr. Finn:

In accordance with Title 46 U.S. Code 239, as amended, I hereby appoint the following "A" Marine Investigation Board to conduct an investigation into the facts surrounding the recent collision between the THOMPSON LYKES and Vessel "A", in the Gulf of Mexico, resulting in the sinking of Vessel "A" and loss of life:

Mr. Harold B. Finn   Chairman

Assistant Attorney General
Washington, D.C.

Captain J. L. Ahern   Member
United States Coast Guard
New Orleans,. Louisiana

Mr. John F. Oettl;   Member
U. S. Supervising Inspector
New Orleans,. Louisiana

Upon completion of the investigation, the Board
will forward to the Commandant the complete file
together with its findings and recommendations.

/s/Russell R. Waesche
Rear Admiral, U.S. Coast Guard
Commandant

*(Counsel in the heart of man is like deep water; but a man of
understanding will draw it out. Proverbs 20:5)*
    This letter and the convening and conducting of the Board of
Inquiry by the Commandant, United States Coast Guard, who was
then under wartime jurisdiction of the United States Navy, and the
Department of Justice, is very strange and significant for the following
reasons:

    1. There was no representative of the United States Navy present,
or called to testify during the Board of Inquiry, not even from the
Fifteenth Navy District, Canal Zone, or the Panama Canal Company,
under whose jurisdiction the SURCOUF-THOMPSON LYKES
Collision occurred.
    As an aside: The U. S. Coast Guard had no jurisdiction to investigate
marine accidents until February 28, 1942. This occurred, ten days after
the SURCOUF-SS THOMPSON LYKES Collision, when President

Franklin Roosevelt signed Executive Order 9083, which transferred the Bureau of Marine Inspection and Navigation of the Department of Commerce to the custody of the U.S. Coast Guard of the U. S. Treasury Department.

During World War II the quasi-Navy, United States Coast Guard organization, by public law, operated as a part of the United States Navy, under the direction of the Secretary of the Navy.

Regardless, in the opinion of the author, the USCG should not have been chosen to act as an investigating authority for the United States Navy on a marine accident that involved the Panama Canal, the U. S. Navy, Royal Navy and the Free French Navy and SURCOUF (on a matter involving submarines). No member of that Board was qualified to delve into accidents concerning that highly specialized field of naval submarine operations and warfare.

Moreover, the USCG had no authority to investigate marine accidents occurring in Canal Zone waters. When the United States Coast Guard investigated the SURCOUF-THOMPSON LYKES Collision, it did so under the guise of Title 46, United States Code 239. But, this legislation did not authorize that agency to investigate marine accidents that occurred in or near Canal Zone waters. This may be the reason why Rear Admiral Waesche stated that the collision occurred in the Gulf of Mexico instead of where it actually occurred, in the Caribbean Sea, and why the Board of Inquiry conducted its inquiry in New Orleans! In the author's opinion, this deception was a conspiracy for reasons that are still indiscernible.

Since the SURCOUF-THOMPSON LYKES Collision occurred in Caribbean Sea waters under the jurisdiction of the Panama Sea Frontier, a question arises as to why The Panama Canal organization did not convene its own inquiry into the collision in the interests of improving Canal Zone marine traffic control and safety.

The author speaks somewhat as an authority—in a qualified sense—on this subject, having sat on boards of inquiry into marine accidents that occurred in and around Canal Zone waters

At the very least, the board of inquiry should have convened in the Canal Zone, where the collision occurred and not in New Orleans. The author has never known the United States Coast Guard or Department of Justice to be involved as the lead in a board of inquiry concerning a marine accident occurring in or near Canal Zone waters.

In other words, there was no known precedence for the U.S. Coast Guard to have conducted a full Board of Inquiry concerning a collision, or for any kind of marine accident, occurring in Canal Zone waters, especially one involving and chaired by the Department of Justice. It is a fact, based on the experience of the author in the Canal Zone, that the Panama Canal organization guarded its jurisdiction over Canal Zone waters religiously and jealously, especially as concerned possible infringement by the United States Coast Guard, or by any other agency of the United States Government.

Also, there was established in the Canal Zone, at that time, a Department of Justice, Federal Attorney's Office. So why was it necessary to conduct the hearing in New Orleans???

The United States Navy would not likely ever sit on the sidelines, without representation, observing the investigation into the loss if one of its own submarines by a U. S. Coast Guard Board of Inquiry. And, it is a fact that no U. S. Coast Guard representative was present when the Commandant, Fifteenth Naval District (Rear Admiral Frank H. Sadler, USN, Annapolis Class of 1903) conducted a Board of Inquiry into the loss of S-26 in Canal Zone waters on the night of January 24, 1942. (Commander, later Captain, Retired) Girvin B. Wait, Port Director, Fifteenth Naval District, was a member of the Board of Inquiry investigating the loss of S-26. He will enter this commentary shortly.)

A thorough and continuing personal search of Panama Canal Company and Canal Zone Government archives, frequently between 1964 and 1972, when the author was a well placed employee of the Canal Company, and while he was researching for material to write his first article about the loss of SURCOUF for *The Panama Canal Review*, August 1967, revealed not one document that the SURCOUF-THOMPSON LYKES Collision ever occurred in the vicinity of the Canal Zone.

2. Why was a representative of the Royal Navy invited to be present at the Board of Inquiry, and not one from the Free French Navy or from the Free French Delegation, Washington???

The invited representative of the Royal Navy was Commander R. C. S. "Tubby" Garwood (later Captain, Retired), an experienced submariner then serving in Washington on the staff of the British Admiralty Repair Mission, Submarines. His presence could be likened to his having received a formal invitation to a funeral—SURCOUF's!!!

Even though SURCOUF had been serving under the operational control of the British Admiralty, Flag Officer, Submarines (Vice Admiral Sir Max Horton, Royal Navy), she still was under the custody of the Minster of Marine, Free French Navy, London, and for administrative purposes associated with SURCOUF's loss and for increasing submarine safety standards within its Navy, it should have been represented at least by the Office of the Free French Delegation to Washington, Mr. Adrien Tixler, or by the Free French Navy Liaison Officer, Montreal. It seems that deliberately depriving the de Gaulle Government and Free French Navy from participation in the Board of Inquiry was a conspiracy set in motion at the highest levels of the American and British Governments.

A Coast Guard letter of March 7, 1942, signed by a R. S. Field, introducing Commander Garwood of the Royal Navy to Mr. Finn, authorized Garwood "to submit such questions as he may desire to ask incident to the investigation."

This was greatly more than that permitted the Free French Navy, which had many, many questions to ask concerning the death of its beloved SURCOUF and her officers and men—questions which have never been acceptably answered by the American and Royal Navies even to this day!!! Imagine the consternation and depth of inquiry that would have evolved had Vice Admiral Emile Muselier, commander of the Free French Naval Forces and one of the innovators of the submarine SURCOUF, been a member of the Board!!!

Garwood, as another seeming harbinger of death, was well qualified to serve as the apostle of the Royal Navy at SURCOUF's inquest. It was as if he were there to make sure she was dead. As a Lieutenant, he had served aboard HMS submarine K-12 as her Navigating Officer, which submarine was involved in a collision with K-2 after Garwood was relieved after less than two months service aboard her. In 1928, after serving aboard HMS TIGER as Signals Officer, he was returned to submarines as First Lieutenant of HMS L-21, and then H-49. (H-49 was lost during World War II, on October 27, 1940, off the Dutch coast due to German anti-submarine activity.) In August 1932, he successively assumed command of HMS H-48, L-22 (June 1933), HMS REGULUS, June 1934. (REGULUS lost on patrol off Otranto Straits, cause unknown, December 12, 1940.) He was temporarily, assigned as Commanding Officer of HMS OXLEY in 1937 and 1938. (OXLEY was lost on September 9, 1939 when she was mistakenly torpedoed by HMS TRITON off Norway.)

In 1938, after promotion to Commander, Garwood stood by HMS TARPON during her construction from September 1938 to March 1939. Fortunately, for him, he was reappointed before TARPON's commissioning, as she was lost, on April 22, 1940, on her first patrol—presumably she was mined in the North Sea.

Captain Johnson, in his December 6, 1975 letter, remarked about Garwood's presence at the Board of Inquiry: "I don't recollect that he asked any direct questions or suggested any."

In August 1942, as if to deliberately get Garwood far away from inquiring minds, he was promoted to Acting Captain to serve as British Naval Liaison Officer with the Soviet Navy's Black Sea Fleet.

In a May 1976 letter, Garwood had this single "magnanimous" recollection about the American inquiry into SURCOUF'S death:

> As the crew of THOMPSON LYKES had been paid off and had been enjoying the night haunts of New Orleans extracting evidence was somewhat difficult. One chap who had a terrific hang-over was broke and quite incoherent. The U. S. Coast Guard Captain (Ahern) threw a coin on the table and told him to go out and get a drink and return when he felt better. This he did.

In the late, late 1970's, when Garwood realized that the author was beginning to make profound inquiries about SURCOUF and the Royal Navy, he never replied to the author, and at the end of a brief chain of correspondence Garwood returned the author's letters unopened. When Garwood dies, it seems he intends taking with him forever, all that he has never told about SURCOUF and her loss. But if it is supernaturally possible, Blaison may unseal Garwood's lips when they meet in the haunts of "Bobbie" Burns "unknown Bourne."

3. Why did Rear Admiral Waesche specifically state that the SURCOUF-THOMPSON LYKES Collision occurred in the Gulf of Mexico rather than in the Caribbean Sea, where it actually happened???

Discussion: In the author's opinion, this was not an oversight by Admiral Waesche. Experienced "blue water" Coast Guardsmen such as the admiral knew the geographic difference between the Caribbean Sea and the Gulf of Mexico—a war zone into which SURCOUF never came close to entering.

The author believes Admiral Waesche's letter was cleverly contrived so, for some secret reason, the affairs of the United States Navy, especially those of the Fifteenth Naval District, would not be horrendously exposed as to how the collision really occurred; from within that District.

This deception may have been deliberate for reason that the American Navy was in a dilemma recovering from its devastating defeat at Pearl Harbor; its involvement in the Battle of the Atlantic and the Caribbean Sea against U-boats; and because civil, military and naval authorities in the Canal were bracing against another possible surprise attack by Imperial Japanese Navy forces. (12 of 51 ships damaged or sunk during February 1942, worldwide, were lost in the Caribbean Sea.)

Under the cover of wartime secrecy and faced by the specter of possible Allied defeat, who was to learn exactly where the SURCOUF-THOMPSON LYKES occurred, or who much cared about SURCOUF's death, except those among the Free French

Movement and the survivors of SURCOUF's dead, like, for example, Blaison's womenfolk.

How de Gaulle and Muselier were pacified to prevent their representative from attending the New Orleans inquiry remains an enigma, but, undoubtedly, it seems to have been done through a masterpiece of delusion and duplicity for a supreme purpose. The facts of history, like the letters of the alphabet, can be arranged to mean anything.

At the time, American and British allied commands were planning for Operation TORCH, the invasion of Vichy controlled and heavily defended North Africa on November 8, 1942. Thus, it may have been considered that bitter French grudges over Operations CATAPULT and GRASP on July 3, 1940 and SURCOUF's involvement in the seizure of the Vichy held St Pierre and Miquelon Islands would strengthen Vichy French resistance to Anglo-American landings along North Africa.

Perhaps an over display of courtesy to the Free French, at the time of the SURCOUF-SS THOMPSON LYKES hearings, could have been detrimental to TORCH's invasion of North Africa.)

Why the inviolable Panama Canal organization did not conduct its own inquiry into the SURCOUF-THOMPSON LYKES Collision, in the interests of improving marine traffic control and safety in the approaches to the Panama Canal, is also suspect. Since the civilian Governor of the Canal Zone was actually a U. S. Army Corps of Engineers general, on detached duty, it is possible that an investigation was deliberately relegated to the jurisdiction of the U. S. Coast Guard, under the guise that there is a law for every occasion, through the auspices of an American version of the "old boy network", i.e., the military and naval community banding while under outside attack, such as occurred between British Admiralty hierarchy and statesman, after SS LUSITANIA was sunk by U-20 in 1916.

With jurisdiction for investigation of the SURCOUF-THOMPSON LYKES Collision cloaked under the vagueness of civil law, the U. S. Coast Guard, in cooperation with another civil organization, the U.S. Department of Justice, could conduct the Board of Inquiry outside of

Canal Zone jurisdiction and limit the proceedings of inquiry to one of strict merchant marine nature.

It would not have to request witnesses from the American Navy, the Free French or from any other organization, or anybody, it did not choose to invite. The invitation of Garwood is a case in point. To satisfy the British Admiralty he was invited, but the Free French Admiralty, also in London and with a legation in Washington, was not.

Thus the sanctimony of the U. S. Navy was shrouded with the legality that an investigation had been conducted, even though it was not that kind routinely held by the United States Navy when the loss of its own vessels, such as when the submarines USS S-26 was involved.

Moreover, the Panama Canal, for the benefit of the Allied Navies, could still effect improvements to marine navigation and safety in Canal Zone waters, without needless coercion from the outside.

Another point to be considered is that even before the start of World War II the Caribbean Sea and Gulf of Mexico were divided by the U.S. Navy, in conjunction with the U.S. Army Air Force, into the Caribbean, Gulf, and Panama Sea Frontier(s).

Therefore, for a senior officer of the U.S. Coast Guard, which during the war was an adjunct of the U. S. Navy, to have specifically referred to the SURCOUF-THOMPSON LYKES Collision as having occurred in the Gulf Sea Frontier, which comprised only the Gulf of Mexico, when it actually occurred in the Panama Sea Frontier was not only wrong, but was a seeming objective attempt to confuse, for purposes known only to the Coast Guard, the Department of Justice, and the U.S. Navy, where the collision actually occurred. If it was not intended by these parties to deliberately remove the board of inquiry from U.S. Navy and Panama Canal jurisdiction then why wasn't the inquiry held in Panama Canal Zone waters where the collision actually occurred???

When queried about this matter, the Historian, U.S. Coast Guard, Mr. Robert L. Schema, on October 20, 1980, who, as keeper of Coast Guard secrets, also acclaimed himself to be a Latin Americanist, replied:

The U. S. Coast Guard had jurisdiction because and American flag vessel was involved.

There is no way of knowing why Admiral Waesche stated that the SURCOUF-THOMPSON LYKES collision occurred in the Gulf of Mexico and not the Caribbean. As a Latin Americanist, I have heard people use these terms interchangeably. Perhaps Admiral Waesche did on this occasion, but this is speculation on my part.

Agreed, that the U.S. Coast Guard did have jurisdiction to investigate the SURCOUF-THOMPSON LYKES Collision, but why didn't the U.S. Navy hold its own inquiry into the collision, if only as a courtesy to the Free French Navy??? Or, why wasn't a representative in attendance as an observer???

The author, in probing further, learned that at no time in history, particularly that period immediately following the discovery of America by Columbus, was the Gulf of Mexico ever confused with the Caribbean Sea, or vice versa. This is what the Library of Congress wrote in reply to the author's inquiry about this possibility:

In reply to your letter of July 7, 1981, referred to the Library's Geography and Map Division, and your July 25 and 30 telephone conversation with our Mr. Thomas de Claire of our staff, a search of our uncataloged titled collection of separate maps under the geographic description "North America," from Juan de la Cosa map of 1500 through 1680, has not yielded a map on which we have seen the Caribbean Sea referred to as the Gulf of Mexico. This search covered the first three drawers of our titled "North America" collection, encompassing approximately 120 separate maps, about 3/4 of which included all or part of the Caribbean Sea and Gulf of Mexico area.

Most of the maps we examined in this 1500-1680 period named the Gulf of Mexico, while the Caribbean Sea was either unnamed or referred to as the "Mar del Nort," "Mare del Nord," etc., or occasionally "Mer de Lentille," or "Las Amtilhas," etc.

Then Mr. Francisco Ramos of the Library of Congress staff picked up the search and found, from *The Early Spanish Main,* by Carl Ortwin Sauer, that the Caribbean Sea was positively identified as such as early as 1773:

Although the best-known sea of the New World, the Caribbean Sea remained nameless longest. The Gulf of Mexico was well known and well shown on maps. It is known to have been recorded on the Sebastian Cabot map of 1544 as Golfo de la Nueva Espana, then as Golfo de Mexican on the Zaltieri map of 1566 and the famous Mercator map of 1569.

In Velasco's GEOGRAFIA the Gulf of Mexico was previously known as the Golfo de la Nueva Espana y Florida. Velasco tried to find a proper name for it, saying: "de los Canibales llaman el golf grande del mar Oceano desede la Deseade y Dominica por toda la Costa de Tierre Firme, Yucatan, Golfo de Tierra Firme y de las isles del mar del Norte." This compiler in Spain, regarding the maps before him, finally made the distinction we do today between the Caribbean Sea and Gulf of Mexico. Velasco remained in manuscript until the nineteenth century. In the introduction to his West Indies Atlas, 1773, Thomas Jeffery's wrote, two centuries later: "It has been sometimes called the Caribbean Sea, which name it would be better to adopt, than to leave this space quite anonymous," and he did so on his map.

Then we have only to consult *Atlas of the Ocean,* by Robert Barton, to further support our contention that the Caribbean Sea and Gulf of Mexico are still considered two different bodies of water, despite Mr. Scheina's best effort, and that the Atlantic entrance to the Panama Canal has its beginnings in the Caribbean Sea, and not the Gulf of Mexico:

Like the Eastern Seas, the Caribbean Sea is bounded to the west by a land mass and to the east by an arc of islands, subsea ridges and trenches. The Caribbean's southern boundary is formed by the northern coast of the South American countries of Venezuela and Colombia, and by the Isthmus of Panama, with the Panama Canal providing a threadlike link between the Caribbean and the Pacific Ocean. Honduras and the Yucatan form the eastern boundary and the narrow gap between the Yucatan and Cuba, the 137-mile-wide Yucatan Strait, leads into the Gulf of Mexico. Together the Gulf of Mexico and the Caribbean Sea make up the American Mediterranean.

What all this should tell the reader is that there should have been absolutely no way possible for an experienced mariner—of Admiral Waesche's education, caliber, and experience at sea—to have confused one body of water (the Gulf of Mexico) for the other (the Caribbean), especially relative to where the SURCOUF-THOMPSON LYKES Collision occurred off the coast of Panama. It was either a grave mistake or intentional on his part.

Whichever it was, his conclusive error continues to be believed by the uninformed, even to this day. Many gullible historians, as evidenced in the French Navy's pamphlet to the public about the life and death of SURCOUF, perpetuate the Waesche error.

Then, in reply to the author's subsequent letter asking for more specific information about the Coast Guard's involvement in the inquiry into the collision, Mr. Scheina replied on February 28, 1981 as follows:

> Thank you for your 27 January 1981 letter. Our historical files do not contain any information relating to the French submarine SURCOUF. Might I suggest you write the National Archives, 6th and Pennsylvania Avenues, N.W., D.C. 20408.

What Mr. Scheina's comments should also reveal to the reader is that records of the U.S. Coast Guard about the SURCOUF-THOMPSON LYKES Collision, of a kind that the author was searching for, have either been destroyed, misplaced or are not going to be made public at this time; perhaps not in our lifetime. However, the real interplay has been between the Coast Guard and the National Archives as the author has so frequently been referred from one to the other in his quest for information concerning the collision without much tangible result. Someone seems to have the U.S. Coast Guard SURCOUF-THOMPSON LYKES file, but it is not about to be made public.

Strange also is that in Malcolm F. Willoughby's otherwise comprehensive work, *The U. S. Coast Guard in World War II,* no mention was made of any inquiry into the SURCOUF—THOMPSON LYKES Collision, which collision resulted in the loss of soul in the world's worst submarine disaster in American controlled waters, and involving an "American flag vessel."

4. Could SURCOUF have been sunk in the Straits of Florida, or near by, which are considered as a part of the Gulf of Mexico and the Gulf Stream???

Discussion: Yes, if the Hull and Reyner inputs, coupled with the remarks of Rumpf, alleging that SURCOUF, commanded by a mutinous crew, may have been caught in the act of attacking the SS QUEEN MARY and then sunk by American or Royal Navy warships. If true, then, Rear Admiral Waesche could have been correct in his assertion that SURCOUF was sunk in the Gulf of Mexico.

5. Why wasn't the Free French Navy invited to the joint Board of Inquiry held by the U.S. Coast Guard and the Department of Justice???

Discussion: On the basis of Mr. Scheina's remarks we are not likely to learn the official reply to this question. If we do, it is not likely to be acceptable to many readers or to the French. It certainly was not acceptable to Madame Therese and Mlle Francine Blaison.

To be sure, however, there are few, if any, precedents in naval history for the United States Navy having eliminated the Free French Navy from an inquiry into the death of the latter's submarine; especially when the event occurred in the waters of an American zone of operations; the Panama Canal Zone.

Even if SURCOUF's death had occurred in the Gulf of Mexico, which comprises international waters, the Free French should have been invited to SURCOUF's inquest. If American authorities were not certain that the submarine sunk was SURCOUF, because of the evidence surrounding her disappearance being considered circumstantial at the time, why did they invite a representative of the Royal Navy and not one from the Free French Navy???

The purpose of a Board of Inquiry, prodding from evidence to new evidence, is to question all parties associated with, and witnesses to, an accident under investigation, including expert witnesses, to try to bring into focus—as clear as possible—the circumstances. A board of inquiry does not work with preconceived ideas, such as did the Coast Guard and Department of Justice when representatives of those agencies took it upon themselves to exclude the Free French Navy!!!

In fact, without the presence of the Free French Navy, that board of inquiry held by the U.S. Coast Guard and the Department of Justice should, even at this late date, be considered to have been only a partial inquiry into SURCOUF's death.

6. Why was SURCOUF referred to as Vessel "A" by Rear Admiral Waesche???

Discussion: The explanation will become evident later in this Part. Similarly, it will be told why the log of THOMPSON LYKES was classified SECRET following the conclusion of the U. S. Coast Guard Board of Inquiry on March 13, 1942.

It could be a narrow squeak for the American Navy, even today, if the whole truth, and nothing but the truth, behind the Waesche Letter were made known. It is not likely that such evidence lies buried in an archive. (In fact, contact with the Historian, Headquarters, U.S. Coast Guard, Washington, D.C., in early December 1980, revealed that no files referring to the SURCOUF-THOMPSON LYKES Collision could be found.)

More likely that **this** secret gradually has turned to dust as those **within the hierarchy** of the Roosevelt Administration and "the old boy network" have died off.

Perhaps in our lifetime, the true story may emerge as did that leather bound case containing a carbon copy of LUSITANIA's cargo manifest; found in the Naval Manuscript Collection of Franklin Delano Roosevelt by the journalist-investigator Colin Simpson in 1972, fifty-seven years after the event.

Below follows the list of witnesses from the SS THOMPSON LYKES that were required to appear before the Marine Board of Investigation chaired by Mr. Harold B. Finn:

March 11, 1942:

Henry Johnson,
Master

Andrew Thompson,
Junior Third Mate

Arthur Georges Atwell,
Able Seaman

Howard G. Trim,
Able Seaman

March 12, 1942:

A. B. Cumiskey,
Chief Engineer

Henry Johnson,
Master (Recalled)

Herman J.V. Myers,
U.S. Army, 58th Coastal Artillery
Member of Gun Crew

Dohrman Henke,
U.S. Army, 58th Coastal Artillery
Member of Gun Crew

John Lee Brady,
Third Assistant Engineer

Ramon A. Moraga,
Oiler

Joseph Narbutt,
Fireman

March 13,1942

John E. Fitzpatrick
Ordinary Seaman

Not all of the testimony of the witnesses is included here, only that portion which was most applicable. Notice that there were no other witnesses called, from **else**where, only from SS THOMPSON LYKES.

Despite the best efforts of the author, including extensive advertising, except for Captain Johnson (that Ancient Mariner), he has never located any of the witnesses, or other officers or crew members who served aboard SS THOMPSON LYKES at that time. It was as if she were a ship with a phantom crew.

It is important to mention before proceeding that according to a September 4, 1943 letter to Archie B. Stevenson, Assistant General Counsel, War Shipping Administration, from his fellow counsel, Lieutenant Commander Claude E. Wakefield, she "carried no Army personnel in the [operating] crew, nor did any Army Officer, who might have been aboard, have any authority over the Master or officers of THOMPSON LYKES with respect to navigation."

Since we cannot positively attribute the SURCOUF-THOMPSON LYKES Collision to human error—a costly mistake—by Blaison or Johnson—the SURCOUF tragedy, the worst submarine disaster of its kind in history, invokes few, if any, parallels in the history of maritime casualties when analyzed from the standpoint of how it occurred.

Even the probabilities of the ANDREA DORIA-STOCKHOLM Collision occurring, which collision is to be discussed briefly, did not compare with those of the SURCOUF-THOMPSON LYKES Collision. This is primarily because both luxury liners were equipped with radar and because it was shown that ANDREA DORIA could have been sunk by human error.

The way SS LUSITANIA was intercepted and sunk by U-20 can be statistically compared with the SURCOUF-THOMPSON LYKES Collision. Here, according to Simpson, is how LUSITANIA was precisely guided by Captain Turner to enable her to be rammed by U-20's torpedo:

> Ever a cautious man he ordered the officer of the watch to help him establish his precise position before he (Turner) navigated his way into Queenstown without either tugs or pilot, and through the only channel swept daily for mines. The [resultant] course change led him directly into U-20's trap.

Whereas Captain Turner effected only one course change to head his ship toward disaster, Captain Johnson, as if guided by an alien eye, effected three precisely timed speed and course changes to place the SS THOMPSON LYKES on a true heading onto poor SURCOUF. It was as if someone or something with the "unique powers of telepathy" had controlled Captain Johnson's mind such as to deliberately guide the SS THOMPSON LYKES into SURCOUF and kill her.

Statistically, if the sinking of SS LUSITANIA was a million to one possibility, then comparatively the SURCOUF-THOMPSON LYKES Collision was in realms almost beyond calculation by conventional computers.

Now to list the scenarios under which SURCOUF entered the Caribbean Sea:

> Was she shadowed by a American or Royal Navy cruiser of submarine?;
> Did she have a limpet affixed to her hull?;

Was she going to make a dash Martinique to liberate that island, and, equally as important, to gain control of the vast hoard of gold stored in Fort Desaix in the name of General Charles de Gaulle leader of French Committee of National Liberation (or the Free French Movement)?

Now to introduce and analyze those three incredible changes by Captain Henry Johnson. But, **before doing so, and as another segment of the above scenarios, it is very pertinent to mention that friends of Therese and Francine, as told to the author, believe that Captain Henry Johnson, a Lieutenant Commander in the U. S. Naval Reserve, had been brainwashed through hypnosis to react to subliminal content in the three messages he received prior to the collision of SS THOMPSON LYKES with SURCOUF!!!**

The First Change

SS THOMPSON LYKES, like an invisible, uninvited, predator, proceeded on a northeasterly course of 28° by gyro (to make 27° true) at 15 knots, until 6:30 pm, when, 30 minutes before darkness, Captain Johnson reduced speed to 13 knots because of heavy seas. This speed reduction was made 30 minutes after COMINCH TRANSMITTED SURCOUF's 1800Z estimated course, position and speed, in accordance with CINC, A and WI SECRET Sailing Order No. 1602P on the 11th.

It is at this point that some sleuths claim SURCOUF's 1700Z position by radio was determined by a direction finding device so she could be intercepted in the dead of night.

Some other French are curious as to why Captain Johnson ordered SS THOMPSON LYKES to be operated at her full speed for almost two hours immediately after clearing Cristobal.

But why drives on that ship so fast
Without wind or wave?

Usually a ship is shaken down before setting her voyage speed, not at full speed, thus giving the engineers on watch an opportunity to set electrical, mechanical and thermodynamic conditions in-order before tasking the vessel to her maximum. This is especially true after a ship has laid in port as did THOMPSON LYKES in the Canal Zone. Whether this change was justified may forever remain one of the unanswered questions of the disaster.

In accordance with his sailing instructions, Captain Johnson ordered running lights off. Therefore, from about 7:00 pm and until just after the collision, THOMPSON LYKES sailed alone and totally blacked out and into an area where there were no witnesses. *(The Ninja prefers to work alone, and in darkness, when committing the deadly act of assassination. Then he is an unseen and insidious foe since nature contributes to concealing his movements and activities by reducing visibility to naught.)*

The sun's rim dips . . . .
At one stride comes the dark:
The stars were dim, and thick the night . . . .

The Second Change

When SURCOUF was about 32.5 miles distant from THOMPSON LYKES, acting upon what seems to have been impulse, and what seemed to be in anticipation of making his third change, Captain Johnson decided to head directly for Guantanamo Bay instead of passing close by to Navassa Island. He therefore altered course, at 8:00 pm, from 28° to 23° true [by gyro]. (There was an error in the gyro-compass of SS THOMPSON LYKES. On February 9th, at 1000, it was an one degree Easterly error, and at 1600 a .9 Easterly error, prior to her arrival at Cristobal. On the 8th of February, at 1000, it was a one degree Easterly error.)

Scientists report that pigeons are able to hear sounds far below the human threshold, like surf crashing hundreds of miles away. Some French, therefore, after reading of this phenomenon in *Fate*

Magazine, July 1980, opened the question as to whether those aboard THOMPSON LYKES could have been guided unto SURCOUF by sound waves. One could be led to wonder; was there something out there seen or heard by Captain Johnson that most of us would have been unable to sense without an aid??? A message written on the wind.

Perhaps a clue to this perplexing question may be found in a statement from that Defense Intelligence Agency report delving, in part, on telepathic hypnosis:

> The ability to wake people by telepathic impulse from a distance of a few yards to over a thousand miles is the most thoroughly tested and perfected contribution of the Soviets to international parapsychology.
>
> In espionage, one could telepathically hypnotize an individual with the post-hypnotic suggestion to steal classified documents or detonate important military equipment. The mission is accomplished without the individual knowing that he has done anything.
>
> The agent need not be willing to enter into such a condition, and there is no test by which he can be discovered. Most important is the conviction of innocence the man (plant) has after the event; convinced that he has served an honest purpose.

When skillfully questioned, by Mr. Finn, about the second and third course changes, Captain Johnson, who even now at ninety-seven years of age was very precise in his conversation and writing, seemed to give a vague, indirect reply:

> Q. What was the purpose of changing course at 8:00 pm?
> A. I don't remember, but I think I wanted to go between—yes I remember now. I set the course direct for Guantanamo Bay.

Originally, I intended to keep on course to Navassa Island but at 8:00 pm I decided to head direct for Guantanamo Bay which changed our course slightly. This is the reason I did it.

But why???

He cannot choose but hear;
If he may know which way to go

That Captain Johnson elected to incrementally refine the heading of SS THOMPSON LYKES while she was still almost 700 miles, almost two days run, from Navassa Island, and, as a result, place the eastern tip of Jamaica between her and Guantanamo Bay, rather than the open sea, is another one of the perplexing mysteries associated with his three course and speed changes.

Because Captain Johnson was in a wartime stress situation demanding enormous emotional stability, intellectual perceptiveness and physical stamina, his three course and speed changes seem to justify retro analysis biorhythmically to attempt to interpret why he performed as he did.

On February 18, 1942, the date of the collision, Captain Johnson's physical biorhythmic cycle was two days from descending to its lowest point negatively (bad days), and he was intellectually critical. Emotionally, Captain Johnson's biorhythm was positive (good days) and on an ascendency.

Gittelson stated:

> The certainty of trouble on critical days of the intellectual cycle is much greater when the environment contains a situation calling for intellectual acuity. When the [physical] rhythm is changing from positive to negative or vice versa, [then the subject] becomes so erratic and unstable that extra caution is an absolute necessity.

At the time of the collision, Captain Johnson was just two days short of being at such a changeover point, physically.

Thus, on February 18, 1942, if Gittelson is believed, Captain Johnson, because of the wartime "situation" prevalent in the Caribbean coupled with his apparent adverse biorhythmic pattern, seemed highly vulnerable to incurring an accident to himself or with SS THOMPSON LYKES. In fact, by Gittleson's rules for precise interpretation of biorhythms, February 18, 1942 seemed to be an accident prone day for Captain Johnson.

Moreover, from a study for the American Society of Safety Engineers of 1,200 human-error accidents on critical days of subjects, Doctor Russell K. Anderson, *Biorhythm-Man's Timing Mechanism* discovered that 70 percent of the accidents happened on a subject's intellectually critical day, with the incident rate much higher if his physical biorhythm was also negative, as was Captain Johnson's. Anderson also concluded that in those cases, when the subject was intellectually critical on the day of the accident, the subject, when later asked why he had done an uncharacteristic thing was unable to explain. As you have just read, Captain Johnson demonstrated hesitancy in replying positively to Mr. Finn about that second change.

If the reader finds it difficult to accept that that February 18, 1942 was an accident prone day for Captain Johnson, merely because he was critical intellectually, then can the reader explain why the Commanding Officer of USS THRESHER, the submarine which almost tied SURCOUF's record for being the worst submarine disaster in history, was also critical intellectually on, April 10, 1963, the day of the THRESHER's tragedy???

As for Blaison, his biorhythmic cycle revealed that on February 18, 1942 he was negatively depressed for all three of his rhythms, emotionally, intellectually and physically. Not only that, but, on the 18th, his emotional and physical curves had crossed at next to low, low; with his emotional cycle moving from negative to positive, and his physical cycle moving negatively; toward an extreme low on the 20th.

According to Anderson, 'if all three rhythms are in their low phase, we are not likely to perform at our peak of effectiveness", and "the most severe accidents happen on days of contrary, critical rhythms, when the individual appears to be violently pulled in opposite directions—creating a day of acute instability during which there is special danger. Our judgment and skills it seems, are quite fallible when we are pulled in opposite directions by our biorhythms and we are especially vulnerable to that conflict because of the instability associated with critical days." (Blaison had just passed through an intellectually critical day, biorhythmically,, on the 16-17th.)

Doctor Douglas E. Neil and his associates at the Man-Machine Systems Design Laboratory, U.S. Naval Postgraduate School, Monterey, California, considering only the physical rhythm, found that twice as many accidents happened during the negative portion of the physical cycle as during the positive. (Captain Johnson was in such a situation on the day of the collision.)

With biorhythmic complications such as possessed by Blaison and Johnson on February 18, 1942, an accident of some kind or another for either of them would seem to have been difficult to avoid. Because mentally we are still insufficiently equipped, we cannot tell with certainty that their adverse biological predicament was the precise cause of the collision of their ships, except to say that it happened; without forewarning and as if it had been prearranged, more than being just an incredible coincidence. It was as if it were a causal event artfully arranged in the subconscious minds of Blaison and Captain Johnson.

Alan Vaughan, author of *Incredible Coincidence*, would probably identify the SURCOUF-THOMPSON LYKES Collision, as the meeting of two dissimilar birds of passage, as a "close encounter of the third kind", a physic tour de force; one taking us a step or two into that baffling world of synchronicity, which only happens when people need or want something to happen."

But this we can say with certainty, this brief biorhythmic analysis of the two principals involved in the SURCOUF-THOMPSON LYKES Collision, when linked with that of Lieutenant Commander "Wes" Harvey, USN, Commanding Officer of the ill-fated THRESHER, provides ample, startling and provocative evidence for intensifying biorhythmic study when viewed in the light of the world's two worst submarine disasters occurring.

The Third Change

Q. Did you make any further change in course?
A. Yes sir, at 9:45 pm I changed course to 356° true by gyro.

Q. What was the purpose of that change?
A. About 9:30 pa I received a message from naval authorities at the Panama Canal to proceed to Cienfuegos instead of Guantanamo.

Some French claim that it was at this point in time, 9:45 pm, that someone in the Canal Zone began to more precisely guide SS THOMPSON LYKES into the hulk of SURCOUF, which, they also claim, had been previously attacked, and severely damaged, by American or British warships.

(As an aside: At this time, tests with MAD gear (Magnetic Airborne Detector) aboard a PBY *Catalina* from Quonset Point Naval Air Station, Rhode Island, located the submarine USS S-48. The tests were carried out in cooperation with the National Defense Research Committee.

Patrol Squadron 82 received the first of a complement of *Catalinas* at the Norfolk Naval Air Station, Norfolk, Virginia. Assignment of these aircraft were to the Royal Air Force and were painted with its markings. This was the beginning of what became an extensive use of submarine hunter-killer patrol squadrons during the war.

In addition, 122 B-18 U. S. Army bombers were modified with SCR-517 radar in their nose and the Mark IV MAD in their tail sting. In this configuration, they were B-18Bs. A squadron of B-18Bs flew missions from the Canal Zone over the Caribbean Sea. They were credited with detecting and sinking U-654 on August 22, 1942 and U-154 on October 2, 1942.

Actually, according to *Tempest, Fire & Foe,* by Commander Lewis M. Andrews, Jr., USNR, U-154 was sunk by the U. S. Navy Destroyer Escort *Inch* off the coast of Casablanca, North Africa on July 3, 1942.

Captain Johnson was not asked by the Board to produce this message nor, after extensive search by the author and professional searchers, was there any evidence of this message having been sent or received. This is strange, as other messages pertaining to the SURCOUF-THOMPSON LYKES Collision, before and after, were easily found, and referred to, by American naval authorities.

Strange also that this message should cause THOMPSON LYKES to radically change to a more northwesterly heading, in a direction that would take her about 500 miles to the westward of Guantanamo Bay, along the Cuban coast, such as to place her exactly on a collision course with SURCOUF.

A 356° heading placed SS THOMPSON LYKES on a course passing by the shallows of Roncador Bank and unnecessarily heading into the shoals of Serranilla Bank, inward of Alice Shoal, when, if the author were Captain Johnson, a course less radical in departure should have been made between Alice Shoal and Bajo Nueva. The fact that Captain Johnson did not set the latter course casts great suspicion, in the mind of the author, on the reason for his having set SS THOMPSON LYKES on 356° in the first instance.

The occurrence of this second course change is questioned from another standpoint. American Naval authorities in the Canal Zone, specifically those concerned with ship operations and movements at that time in the Fifteenth Naval District, did not seem efficacious enough to maintain a sensible hour-by-hour scheduling and deployment of merchant vessels underway on a twenty-four basis.

The fact that they, as a point of pride and knife-edge professionalism, seemed not to have learned any lessons from the submarine USS S-26 nightmare collision with her escort vessel, PC-460, which had only recently occurred at 2210 hours, in the Gulf of Panama, on January 24, 1942, provides ample justification for the author making this statement. It seems that few, if any, lessons were learned from the S-26 tragedy, involving the loss of forty-two men, such as could be useful for saving other American or Allied submarines from disaster in Canal Zone waters.

The fact that no other serious accidents to submarines occurred in Canal Zone waters, during or after the war, may be indicative that the SURCOUF Disaster provided such lessons, but this is also conjectural. Only sailors who live in ships should attack other ships.

Regardless, like Doctor Faustus, in Marlowe's tragic history of the doctor, SURCOUF now had less than "one bare hour to live" before she sank howling and flaming into the depths of the Caribbean Sea.

Why wasn't the instruction to proceed to Cienfuegos given to Captain Johnson by the American Naval Routing Officer at Cristobal, rather than five hours after he left that port??? When asked about this point, Captain Wait could only reply in his November 8, 1979 letter:

> As regards the diversion of the SS THOMPSON LYKES from Guantanamo Bay to Cienfuegos, Cuba, these diversions were not standard practice but were sometimes necessary due to the availability of cargoes.
>
> The cargo which awaited THOMPSON LYKES at Cienfuegos, about 400 miles westward of Guantanamo Bay, was 8,000 tons of sugar to be delivered to New Orleans.

Why would a cargo of sugar suddenly have made itself available in the dead of that particular night for THOMPSON LYKES??? Particularly, since there never was a cargo of sugar for THOMPSON LYKES at Guantanamo Bay as that location was not a sugar loading port—it was, and still is, an U. S. Naval Operating Base. So why was THOMPSON LYKES heading there in the first place??? This is further evidence that SURCOUF was the unfortunate victim of a sequence of errors, or mischief, the timing and precision of which borders on fantasy or intention.

It is a fact, however, that in August 1980, after over fourteen years of casual conversation and correspondence with Captain Johnson about the SURCOUF-THOMPSON LYKES Collision, he asked the author to discontinue further inquiry. This odd occurrence was preceded by the author's beginning to ask more pointed, serious questions about events surrounding the collision; questions the author did not know enough to ask until he began probing into the matter more deeply for purposes of this book and as a consequence of questions asked by others.

Similarly, when the Free French Navy, which had not been invited to the United States Government Board of Inquiry into the death of SURCOUF, began asking questions of like nature they also were put off or diverted from the issue by officials of the American and Royal Navies in Washington and London.

After reviewing the second and third course changes, one could be easily led to suspect that something was rather unorthodox about their being effected at the place and time they were executed, and that the unsuspecting SURCOUF may have been sailing into a cal de sac—a death trap—without a ghost of a chance of escaping!!!

To this day there are some French, Madame and Mademoiselle Blaison and Rear Admiral Le Nistour among them, who are convinced that SURCOUF was the victim of foul play; "that SURCOUF's death was wanted" and that the accounts of her death have been whitewashed to conceal truth.

Nevertheless, thirty-seven years later, after piecing together the intriguing mosaic of SURCOUF's death, it is clear that she was inevitably and irrevocably doomed to die on the night of February 18, 1942.

Looking back, one could be also led to believe that an ancient curse had been cast upon her, from the archives of evil, by revengeful merchantmen.

The pang, the curse, with which they died
Had never passed away.

Before following the wake of SURCOUF's voyage further into the perilous darkness of the Caribbean, to the time of her collision with THOMPSON LYKES, another item of indefinable sense, which could be construed as being Bermuda Triangle connected, must be introduced. It involved Captain Johnson's night orders to his deck watch officers.

Although the influence of exorcism, as a conscious or subconscious attempt to achieve a desired result, was beyond the scope of the Board of Inquiry to examine, it should be considered now and in light of the points Charles Berlitz raised in *Without a Trace* about mind disorientation and affliction by unidentified forces acting in the Bermuda Triangle.

Mary Baker Eddy, author of *Science and Health, with Key to the Scriptures,* wrote: "Error of thought is reflected into error of action." How often have we held a thought and have seen it occur in reality, especially a negative one???

An apparent offending thought, which Captain Johnson held that dreadful night, as was incorporated into his night orders, became a reality—the worst submarine disaster in history. (The Unspeakable Law: As soon as you mention something good it goes away, if it's bad it happens!)

The bête noir (black beast) of commanding officers and ship masters is collision. Yet most puzzling about Captain Johnson's sensitivity to collision was his seeming aversion to posting a bow lookout, to avoid one, though required by United States Coast Guard regulations. Finn questioned him on this point minutely:

> Q. Don't you think a lookout, if he had been stationed in the bow, could have observed a low-lying better than the lookout you posted in the crow'
>
> A. Possibly.

> Q. If a lookout had seen a low-lying object in the water sooner, do you think the collision could have been avoided?
>
> A. No, sir. I don't believe a bow lookout could have seen ahead more than 150 feet~ as dark as it was~ and at the speed the ship was going it would not have been sufficient time to avoid a collision.

Finn: However, you can't deny, had a lookout been in the bow we could have seen something sooner than a man 200 feet aft.

(Stars are the official guardians of the night, standing watch over us. But that night there were none on guard for SURCOUF and Blaison.)

> Q. If it had been a ship high in the water do you think you could have seen it further on the night of the collision?
> A. Yes,. sir, I think so.

> Q. About how far would you estimate that?
> A. Probably a quarter of a mile.

At times there are segments of our behavior and thinking retained in thought of which we are not aware until some special occasion, or mysterious force, triggers the need for their surfacing. A striking example of this seemed to have occurred in the sub consciousness of Captain Johnson on the night of the catastrophe, through a hint of his foreboding of disaster by collision and its timing which appeared in his night orders.

This suggestion of impending danger emerged during the questioning of Captain Johnson, under oath, by Mr. Harold B. Finn, Special Attorney, Office of the Attorney General, Department of Justice, Washington, and Chairman of the Board of Inquiry:

> Q. When you temporarily left the bridge you were proceeding on a course 356° true at a speed of 13 knots?
> A. That's right. I went into my office just aft the bridge.

> Q. Did you leave any special night orders when you left the bridge at 10:20 pm?
> (This was about eight minutes before the collision.)
> A. Yes, sir.

Q. Had you left the bridge for the night?
A. No sir, but I issued night orders.

Q. What were your night orders Captain Johnson?
A. To keep the present course that we were steering, to
   keep a good lookout, to turn on the running lights in
   an emergency, and to make frequent inspections of the
   ship to see that the blackout was complete.

Captain Johnson's night orders, as written in the log of SS
THOMPSON LYKES at 9:50 pm, about thirty-eight minutes before
his ship's encounter with SURCOUF are repeated below. They agree
essentially with the reply he gave Finn. The weirdness, however, begins
at that paragraph starting with: "Keep a sharp lookout . . . ." From this
part on, Captain Johnson's night orders seem to reveal an unusually deep,
inner concern over the "danger" of his ship encountering "collision".
(The power of observation lies with the mind, and not with the eye.)

Keep the present course until further orders. Have the ship inspected
at least every two hours to see that the blackout is complete.

Make certain that blackout curtains in the alleyways are completely
drawn and secured in place and that the outside doors are closed.

Keep a sharp lookout and let me know if anything of a suspicious
character is sighted.

The running lights should never be turned on except in dire
emergency to avoid collision.

If danger of immediate collision confronts you do not hesitate to
take instant action to avoid it, but call me as soon as possible.

In what seems to be an extraordinary act of prescience, as evidenced
from the last paragraph of his night orders, Captain Johnson's inner
mind seemingly foresaw, even though his conscious mind did not, that
SS THOMPSON LYKES would encounter an "immediate collision"
and that his Deck Officer, Junior Third Mate Andrew Thompson,
would have to "take instant action to avoid it"; but Thompson's attempt
would fail miserably.

Apparently, Captain Johnson's psychic radar system, at that moment, was not tuned finely enough for him to avoid any impending disaster.

After a reading of Vaughan's *Incredible Coincidence*, one could be led to believe that Captain Johnson's conscience triggered the SURCOUF-THOMPSON LYKES Collision, as though desperately willing such an accident to occur that night. One could also hypothesize that he was a Manchurian Candidate case, hypnotized to carry out an assassination plan of another organization.

Unfortunately, as Vaughan explains, "there is no viable way of reckoning the odds against the chance of such synchronicities happening. So it must be left to the reader" [to discern for himself].

In the case of Captain Johnson's night orders, do you think he subconsciously invited a collision to occur that night—as if he were beckoning for a demon event to happen in the dark recesses of the Caribbean??? If the SURCOUF-THOMPSON LYKES Collision had happened in any other way, that, also would have been an incredible coincidence!!!

He holds him with his glittering eye
The Ancient Mariner hath his will.

Questioning Captain Johnson from another tack, Finn was startled to learn that the Captain had an intense dislike for submarines.

> Q. Have you any suggestions how similar accidents could be avoided under wartime circumstances?
> A. I would not try to avoid an accident like that. Had I seen it, I would have done the same thing.

Captain Johnson again seemingly evaded making a direct reply to Finn's question:

> Q. You think it just happened?

A. I would have done it deliberately. My idea is that if you see a submarine close to you the best thing is to sink it before it sinks you!

Thus, killing the submarine SURCOUF was a Righteous Kill for Captain Henry Johnson. But, there can be no worst evil than that which is masqueraded in the trappings of righteousness.

Permit the author, at this crucial point in the story, to introduce a startling, all-important piece of evidence from Burney's February 10, 1942 report, which beyond a doubt identifies that "light" which you are about to read about. The following is an extract from what is believed to have been Burney's last liaison report to Horton before SURCOUF departed Bermuda:

> On the way from Halifax to Bermuda, as indeed at all times, the Officer of the Watch would use a small hand flashing lamp, quite unshaded, to read bearings on the bearing indicators.

From this tidbit of information, referring to that "small flashing hand lamp", we obtain that raw body of evidence needed to conclusively prove that the submarine SS THOMPSON LYKES rammed and sank that night was indeed SURCOUF, and no other.

When you read the testimony given by Junior Third Mate Thompson and Atwell, the helmsman, given before the Board of Inquiry, with regard to their having seen that small wavering "light", you instantly realize that it had to have been SURCOUF, for there was no way for those aboard SS THOMPSON LYKES, an American cargo ship, to have known what had been written by Burney in his last report to Vice Admiral Sir Max Horton, Royal Navy.

Strange how this small tidbit of evidence was connected with the Board of Inquiry report, from two widely divergent sources, each of which had remained buried in different national archives, American, British and Canadian, for over thirty-five years before being analyzed. Cruel, that Burney, the producer of that crucial proof, should have died because of it—as if it had been deliberately intended to produce his death through the means of that "light"—likened to a final precaution which would be of no life saving value to poor SURCOUF and the 130 helpless souls aboard her.

Even so, not all discrepancies concerning the horror of the SURCOUF-THOMPSON LYKES Collision have been sorted out since there is still a legacy of unsolved blunders associated with that disaster.

Now let us shift to the bridge of SS THOMPSON LYKES so "you are there", as a mute witness to a forbidden picture, when that ghostly enchantress of the sea gives SURCOUF the *coup de grace*—crushing her into the depths of the Caribbean with all hands—forever beyond hope of rescue.

For this traumatic episode of savagery at sea—the grinding, shrieking and tearing of metal in the agony of collision—and a bird's-eye view of history in the making—a tragic page of it—imagine yourself with Junior Third Mate Thompson, on his watch of death and destruction, through the terse question and answer exchange of Finn and Thompson.

Watchman tell us of that night.

Your eyes strain to see into the night, but there is only the approaching darkness of death in your face. *(Darkness is the Ninja's best friend as he works best in pitch blackness, and the treacherous Ninja warrior is trained to attack his victim with such stealth that he is invisible until he strikes.)* Suddenly and unexpectedly, breaking through the blackness, there is a flick of light!!!

This tormenting spectacle, enough to satisfy a pyromaniac's dream and a phenomenon not likely to be duplicated in our time, unfolds as Finn deftly asked Junior Third Mate Thompson:

> Q. Shortly before the collision, at 10:15 P.M., was the THOMPSON LYKES showing any lights?
> A. No sir, no lights

Q. Up to 10:15 P.M. did you observe the lights of any other ship?
A. No sir.

Q. Did you hear any whistle up to that time?
A. No sir.

> **Alone on a wide wide sea**
> **So lonely t'was, that God himself**
> **Scarce seemed there to be.**

Q. After 10:15 P.M. what was the first thing you saw or heard off your own ship?
A. The first thing I saw was about 10:28 P.M. I saw a light on the starboard bow.

> **That signal made but now**

Q. Will you describe the light to us
A. It could have been a spotlight or some powerful flashlight or searchlight. It was not a regular navigation light and it was blinking or someone was waving it up and down.

Atwell, the helmsman for the second trick of the watch, in response to that same question said, "It was too low for a mast light. I say it was a flashlight because it wavered a bit. I mean not steady, just a little motion."

Q. How did the light bear from you?
A. She was about one point off the starboard bow.

SS THOMPSON TYKES was on a northerly heading, therefore the light Junior Third Mate Thompson saw was from a northeasterly direction, the one direction which the Japanese dread as being unlucky, and to which they refer to as "Kimon" or the "Devil's Gate". Strange how SURCOUF, even in her final moments, conformed to things Japanese!

> Q. Was the light directed toward you?
> A. Yes sir.
>
> Q. What color was the light?
> A. White.
>
> Q. Did anyone report the light before you saw it?
> A. Not before I saw it. The lookout in the crow's nest saw it at the same time, and the soldier on the deck atop the wheel house reported it immediately also.

Atwell, whose visual acuity seemed keener than Thompson's, said, "I saw this light and at the same instant saw a little object on the starboard bow and I heard the lookout and the soldier on the upper deck and the Mate all hollering at the same time, "There's a light!"

At first it seemed a little speck,
It moved and moved, and took at last
A certain shape,

If Blaison was on the bridge of SURCOUF that dreadful night he must have immediately recognized his situation as being the one sailors dread most: Collision!!!

If there was a moment in Blaison's life that transcended all others this was it, but it was an experience that could not be measured in time. At that moment, Blaison would have liked to have turned merciless darkness into a divine light!!!

There was not a *bonne chance* in Heaven or Hell for SURCOUF to avoid that "certain shape" which would instantly answer that age old question of antiquity: Where does death come from??? It comes from out of the darkness!

While a silver cross was effective in resisting the fiendish Count Dracula, son of the Devil and the "Impaler" of the undead, not even that flag bearing the Cross of Lorraine, designed by Vice Admiral Emile Muselier, "that man with a heart of gold", could have saved SURCOUF from the horror of being impaled by SS THOMPSON LYKES that dark night.

Questioning of Third Mate Thompson continued by Finn:

Q. Where was it the next time you saw it?
A. Just about right ahead.

Q. What did you do when you first sighted this white light?
A. I immediately ordered the helm hard left.

Q. Did your vessel swing to the left?
A. Before she began to swing I saw the light changed on-the-bow, and I immediately ordered hard right.

Q. Did your vessel change heading under the hard right rudder?
A. Before it had a chance we struck it.

When that strange shape drove suddenly Betwixt us . . .

Q. What was your estimate as to the interval of the time in seconds or minutes from the time you first sighted the white light and the time you collided?
A. About 20 seconds.

Q. Did you have any impression as to what you hit?
A. I was almost certain it was a submarine!

Deep in the bowels of SURCOUF her officers and men, some asleep, some on duty, some at leisure, were oblivious that instant Death was upon them; each were deprived of that privilege of time to be afraid or to ask God to forgive their trespasses. "Mon Dieu"!!!

Without interrupting continuity, Atwell's testimony, before Finn, is now introduced because of his sensitive remarks about what he witnessed.

> Q. What happened after the collision so far as the other vessel is concerned. What did you see or hear?
>
> A. As soon as we hit there was an explosion and a big sheet of red flame shot over the bow of our ship which immediately extinguished.

Was a flash of flame.

It smelled like a heavy oil smoke, and a dark cloud of smoke went up. It seemed to follow the shape of the bow just about 6 feet aft on the starboard side and break across the forecastle head on the port. (As THOMPSON LYKES was on a northerly heading, her port side would have been facing westerly.)

The western wave was all aflame.
The thick black cloud was cleft . . . .

Then all of a sudden there was a second explosion which appeared abreast and to the port of No. 1 hatch. I saw phosphorous underneath the water, along both sides of the object, mostly on the port side of our ship, and just a little on the starboard.

Also, I saw a little bit of the object to the starboard. The second explosion gave us quite a jolt. It was worse than the collision itself.

As SURCOUF bucked and twisted under the hull of SS THOMPSON LYKES, it was as if she were alive. Atwell's senses had been sharpened by the roar of stereophonic noises from Hell and the smell of death as he told about that evil scene. Those flashes of flame, were they SURCOUF's agonizing death spasm as the blanket of the sea was pulled over those helpless souls aboard her.

Now, SURCOUF was no more than a hulk of broken, twisted steel sinking to the bottom of the Caribbean with 130 souls dying as if all were one soul. All for one, and one for all!!!

Whatever force could do this to SURCOUF was not likely to leave survivors or evidence that she ever existed!!!

Note Atwell's referral to the phosphorescence effect of a tropical sea. If this effect had been generated by SURCOUF while she was underway, then those on watch aboard SS THOMPSON LYKES may have sighted it in time to avoid the collision. The absence of such a sighting was indicative that SURCOUF may have heaved to, awaiting dawn; before she made a daylight run for Cristobal Harbor (the Caribbean entrance to the Panama Canal).

The first and second explosions, in such quick order, aroused the suspicions of some members of the Free French Club in Paris. They believed that Intrepid's garbage men had indeed planted mines on SURCOUF's hull, as was rumored in Bermuda, and that the mines had been caused to explode by the force of the collision. Concerning the French opinion, it is at this point that seems appropriate to enter the following paragraphs. The italicized portion serves as an introduction.

The Secret Service had no qualms about handing over a captive to a third party intent on killing him.

On the evening of February 25, 1983, during a telephone conversation with a "highly confidential source" residing in Halifax, the author was told that Intrepid reached the conclusion that SURCOUF had turned Vichyist.

After reporting his findings to Churchill, Intrepid, it was said, was ordered to dispose of SURCOUF.

The method chosen was to plant magnetic explosives with delayed fuses on the hull of SURCOUF, while she lay alongside her berth at Ireland Dockyard, Bermuda.

The odious task to eliminate SURCOUF, it was said, was supposedly attempted by two Royal Navy frogmen: a Murray Wakefield (deceased) and a Standish Randall (not their real names).

The source also alleged that Wakefield and Randall were members of the British Secret Service, probably the wartime Special Operations Executive (SOE), an activity with which "Intrepid Bermuda" was closely associated and which was engaged in worldwide overt operations: execution, sabotage, and subversion.

If the Halifax Rumor is believed, it is conceivable that Randall and Wakefield (or whoever they were), also secretly affixed an antenna somewhere on SURCOUF'S hull to enable overhead aircraft to explode the planted charges by a radio signal from aloft.

As an aside: *The X-Craft Raid,* by Thomas Gallagher, is the incredibly true story of the Royal Navy's nearly impossible mission to sink the German battleship TRIPITZ by air, while she was along her berth at Hammerfest, Norway. The ultimate method for destroying TRIPITZ was for Royal Navy divers, volunteers, to plant underwater explosive charges, with timing devices, against her hull!!! They were successful.

Intrepid, had he been privy to Burney's liaison reports to Admiral Max Horton and to Burney's his verbal remarks to Admirals "Jetty" Jones and Kennedy-Purvis, especially Burney's report that SURCOUF was making for Martinique, would have had good reason to suggest to Churchill that the Atlantic be rid of SURCOUF.

Intrepid knew that if SURCOUF reached Martinique her presence there could have inspired the populace to revolt against the Vichyists in power—under the governorship of a Darlanist, Rear Admiral Georges Roberts, Vichy French Navy—in an attempt to seize the island and the Bank of France gold stored there for the Government of France-in-exile.

And then Hyde subsequently remarked:

Whenever Special Operations Executive in London was anxious that something drastic should be done, Stephenson was instructed accordingly.

It is to be noted that the rumor was specific in stating that Randall and Wakefield were Royal Navy divers (not a part of Intrepid's New York secret organization, the BSC). *In Spy-Counterspy, The Autobiography of Dusko Popov*, Popov ("Tricycle" to the British, "Ivan" to the Germans), who was a double agent for Intrepid and who reputedly was the model for Ian Fleming's James Bond, was specific in stating:

> When someone was to be eliminated—as did happen at times—Intelligence never used one of its own agents to do the job. The killing was always done by specialists, a garbage-disposal squad, called in from the outside.

Popov's remark, set in the scenario that the Atlantic should be rid of SURCOUF coupled with the above rumor implicating Royal Navy divers, if such evidence constituted proof, could be incriminating.

Some French firmly believe that one of the "innumerable services" rendered to the Royal Navy by Intrepid, upon instruction from SOE, was to bypass "normal channels," similarly as told by Admiral Robert B. Carney in *A Well-kept Secret,* to arrange, in ultra-secret, silent ways, with the highest level of the American Government for the elimination of SURCOUF. That Royal Navy divers, outside "specialists," could have been ordered to assist in eliminating SURCOUF conforms with Popov's remarks, and adds credulence to the Halifax Rumor.

If the Halifax Rumor were true, who within the American government would have condoned that "odious task"!!! It would have been the same conspirators who were accused by Rear Admiral Robert A. Theobold, USN, Retired, Annapolis Class of 1906, in *The Final Secret of Pearl Harbor, The Washington Contribution to the Attack,* of having deliberately allowed the Imperial Japanese Navy to attack American naval installations at Pearl Harbor on December 7, 1941, with the consequent total of 3,684 personnel killed and wounded.

Here is Admiral Theobold wrote:

> Both Admiral Stark and General Marshall would have done everything in their power to prevent such an attack. And, yet, on the morning of December 7, Washington refused to send one short message to Hawaii in time to cushion the effects f the Japanese attack!
>
> That is the most revealing fact of the entire Pearl Harbor disaster. There is only one conceivable reason for it—nothing must be done to prejudice the chances of the attack, even at the last moment. Japan was about to bring war to the United States, and President Roosevelt did not intend that any American should cause them to change their plans at the last minute.

Obviously, if such personages were determined to stop SURCOUF!!! they would STOP SURCOUF BY ANY MEANS!!!

The French also speculated, because of the conciseness of the hour and date of her arrival at Cristobal, as stipulated in her sailing orders, that the timers on the detonators could have been deliberately set to explode the mines while SURCOUF was transiting the Panama Canal so as to block it!!!

A conspiracy can be planned or committed without any formal meeting or agreements. Only a tacit understanding among the conspirators to achieve an unlawful act is necessary.

Intrepid would **never** have condoned blocking the Panama Canal as that would have been mutually destructive to God and Country, King and Queen, Churchill, and the Allied cause, which he so devotedly, faithfully, honorably, and religiously served. But with an undercover German agent on his staff as was his senior deputy, Colonel Charles H. "Dick" Ellis, who would have been knowledgeable about any intent to eliminate SURCOUF, a garbage squad member could have been easily usurped to time-set the detonator of any limpet mine on SURCOUF and to also actuate it in the Panama Canal. *Too often in war you never know who are your real enemies are until their foul deed is done!!!*

Now, back to the main stream of *The SURCOUF CONSPIRACY:*

"It shook the ship violently," Captain Johnson told Finn, "I thought we had been torpedoed by a second submarine." (This was a resounding response by Captain Johnson. Was it his subconscious admission that there had been a "first" submarine that SS THOMPSON LYKES had collided with???)

> **Stunned by that loud and dreadful sound.**
> **About, about, in a reel and rout,**
> **The death-fires danced at night;**
> **The watery like a witch's oils,**
> **Burnt green, and blue, and white."** . . . .
> **Mighty armies of the dead**
> **Dance like death-fires, round her tomb!**

Questioned by Finn, Narbutt the Fireman on watch testified:

Q. Did you have any knowledge of what was going on?
A. I thought we went aground. The ship seemed to raise and then we got the next contact and it was worse than the first. She began shaking. She shook up and down.

> **With a short uneasy motion,**
> **Backwards and forewards half her length**
> **Then like a pawing horse let go,**
> **She made a sudden bound,—**

Brady, the Third Engineer on watch, was questioned next by Finn:

Q. What shock did you feel or hear?
A. It felt as though the explosion occurred between No. 4 and 5 hatches. The stern of the THOMPSON LYKES came up and the blade came out of the water and the turbine raced.

Still maintaining the sequence of the collision's events, Finn questioned Henke, a member of the U. S. Army gun crew, who had been atop the wheel house on watch:

> Q. After observation of that object alongside your ship what happened next?
>
> A. It went under the THOMPSON LYKES and exploded.
>
> Q. About how far off the port side of the ship do you think you saw the object?
>
> A. About 10 feet, just opposite No. 2 hatch.

> **The naked hull alongside came,**
> **Where the ship's huge shadow lay.**
> **The charmed water burnt away**
> **A still and awful red.**
> **The ship went down like lead.**
> **Under the water it rumbled on,**
> **Still more louder and more dread.**
> **Under the keel.**

Captain Johnson was recalled for questioning by Finn:

> Q. After you rushed onto the bridge did you see any light or vessel
>
> A. Of course, coming out from the bright lights I was sort of blinded but I walked over to the port side of the bridge and saw some dark object, about 50 feet off the port beam, then it sank immediately.

> **I turned my eyes upon the deck,—**
> **O Christ what I saw there!**
> **Dear Lord! it bath a fiendish look,**

At this point, another aspect of human interest must be injected, one of behavioral control, related to Captain Johnson's immediate reaction to the collision, as it was occurring.

Under the calamitous circumstance of his ship having just endured an enormous collision with an unidentified underwater object, in the black of night, it would seem that Captain Johnson, as master of the ship involved, would have been psychologically shaken. But, no, notice that in response to Finn's question "after you rushed unto the bridge" Captain Johnson replied instead, almost methodically, or almost nonchalantly, "I walked over to the port side of the bridge."

Personally, under an identical situation, the author would have "rushed" unto the bridge, if only to immediately satisfy his curiosity as to what occurred or to avert further consequences. But not Captain Johnson, he had "walked over", apparently with great calm, beyond reach, like a victim of mind control who had stepped out of another dimension.

Queried about his obvious calm at that traumatic episode, Captain Johnson pointedly wrote, on January 24, 1979:

> In answering your latest question, it seems to me that you would rather have me running than walking to the wing of the bridge. I think the method of "locomotion" employed to get out on the bridge from the pilothouse is rather immaterial. You take your choice. For practical reasons, running aboard a ship at sea ends up in nasty falls, and is not recommended. A vessel is not a steady platform when it is rolling and pitching. The more rolling, the more attention to balancing is required. I should explain that my cabin was located on the boat deck below the bridge. The door to the cabin was a step or two aft of the bridge ladder. I took the ladder figuratively, if not literally, in a couple of flying leaps. After that I was too busy to get excited. Over the years of command, I had mentally conditioned myself to be in control of myself under whatever circumstances of emergency occurred.

> With kindest regards,
> /s/Henry Johnson
> "Ye Olde Mariner"

For whatever it is worth, for readers inclined to play the role of a Sherlock Holmes—after reading Captain Johnson's reply—one could detect a trivial flaw in Captain Johnson's testimony.

Recall that Captain Johnson had replied to Finn that he had "walked". To the author, he wrote that he "took the ladder in a couple of flying leaps".

But more important, as concerns the Blaison-Johnson Albatross Connection, notice that Captain Johnson no longer referred to himself as "The Ancient Mariner", but as "Ye Olde Mariner".

For some inexplicable reason, because of Captain Johnson's cool and concise reply, and obvious "control" of himself, over that tumultuous moment in naval history, one could be led to conclude that Captain Johnson had been an unwitting victim of the sinister black science of mind control, something beyond science fiction; satanically programmed by an "alien mind" to "detect and destroy" poor SURCOUF, the submarine no navy wanted, on cue.

"I can hypnotize a man—without his even knowing it—into committing treason against the United States. We do not need the subject's consent when we wish to hypnotize him for we use 'disguised' technique," boosted Dr. George Easterbrooks, a skilled mind controller, in early 1940's. "And without any possibility of the controller being detected, and without any memory of having performed the act."

And in the declassified Defense Intelligence Agency document, Controlled Offensive Behavior—USSR, published in July 1972, it is stated: "There are disguised techniques available for hypnotizing an unsuspecting or unwilling subject "without his consent". Telepathy may be one such method."

It is a curious and strange thing, a coincidence perhaps, but in that previously SECRET DIA record there appeared a contemporary submarine connection between the American and French Navies, through the nuclear powered USS NAUTILUS (named after Jules Verne's infamous undersea monster), following the same theme presented here:

French journalists splashed the now rather infamous NAUTILUS story in headlines "US Navy Uses ESP on Atomic Sub!" Ship to shore telepathy, according to the French, blipped along nicely even when NAUTILUS was far underwater. "Is telepathy a new secret weapon?" Will ESP be a deciding factor in future warfare?" The speculating French sensationalized, "Has the American military learned the secret of mind power?"

Soviet efforts," the DIA document continued, "in the field of psi [telepathy] research, might enable them to disable, at a distance, US military equipment of all types including space craft.

There are other French who are convinced that such destructive power—the power of thought—was applied by the American and Royal Navies, as a secret weapon of war, against SURCOUF on the night of February 18, 1942!!!

The Finn-Captain Johnson dialogue now ends:

Q. When you saw the object how did it bear from your vessel?

A. Right off the port beam, about abreast of No. 3 hatch, before it disappeared completely. However, Thompson told me he definitely saw what looked like the bow stand up vertically in the water and sink about 100 feet off the port bow.

And I had done a hellish thing,

It was done!!! SURCOUF the largest and most powerful undersea creation ever built, *an enfant terrible*, was finally reduced to a state of non-existence—destroyed!!! Her death was by a friend, not an enemy simply because she happened to be at the wrong place at the wrong time. (. . . . *but time and chance happeneth to them all. Ecclesiastes 9-11 KJV)*

In addition, the three of the Royal Navy had satisfied the terms of the ransom with their lives for they were expendable. Moreover, the monastic Blaison, who had once wanted to enter the priesthood, finally had his "little adventure" when he, SURCOUF, and all the other souls aboard her vanished forever—into that deep sleep from which they could never be awakened. *(My God, my God, why hast thou forsaken me? Matthew 27:47 KJV.)*

C'est la guerre. **Adieu SURCOUF. Adieu.**

SURCOUF's death by the steel bow of the SS THOMPSON LYKES could be likened to when the young Sheppard boy, David, with slingshot and stone, slew Goliath, the powerful nephal.

It was as if SURCOUF could no longer endure further indignity as she sank, without time for pandemonium or for a Chaplain, which regrettably she did not have, to pray for the poor souls aboard her who were unable to pray for themselves. *(Yea, though I walk through the valley of the shadow of death, I will fear no evil; for thou are with me; thy rod and thy staff, they comfort me. Psalm 23:4. KJV)*

SURCOUF, as a flaming crematorium, plunged into the depths of the Caribbean faster than she could "crash dive." It was a setting reminiscent of when the English had burned Joan of Arc at the stake. Yet, was it not better that SURCOUF should die by collision at sea rather than ending her tormented life being "paid-off" and unceremoniously destined to a scrap heap??? *(I have glorified thee on earth: I have finished the work thou gavest me to do. John 17-5. KJV)*

Eeriness swept over SURCOUF's watery grave, covered by waves of sadness. All was dark and silent as before, as SURCOUF kept her rendezvous with Death in an abyss of perpetual night; that inverted world far below the undulating surface of the Caribbean Sea.

The game is done! I've won! I've won! I've won!
And there the dead men lay.
Upon the whirl where sank the ship
All was still

> **Living men,**
> **And I heard nor sigh nor groan!**
> **With heavy thump, a lifeless lump,**
> **And every soul it passed me by,**
> **I blessed them unaware**
> **And yet I could not die.**

True, SURCOUF and her officers and men were expendable. But why were they all destined to die just then??? Those who respect, and know of, the oddities of the sea, and know of death and ships, cannot overlook such ominous occurrences, but we are powerless to sense and to avoid them. Yet:

> **The Devil knows**
> **And it was he**
> **That made the ship go.**

Often the answer lies in the weakness of the victim. It is a fact, however, that the Master of SS THOMPSON LYKES did guide his ship in such a way as to consign SURCOUF and her crew to an instant watery grave. BUT WHY CAPTAIN JOHNSON??? The Specter of Death works in evil and mysterious ways, sometimes making mortal men or objects its means to effect for others "that fatal voyage to the unknown Bourne, whence there is no return."

> **God save thee, ancient mariner**
> **From the fiends that plague thee thus!**

As if he "could not die", Captain Henry Johnson, the "Ancient Mariner" lived for what seemed an eternity!!! But he was condemned to live with the thought on his mind that he and his ship had caused the world's worst submarine disaster. If you kill, you are a murderer, even if you are a hundred and thirty times justified. God forgive thee Ancient Mariner.

Concluding Remarks

Blaison and SURCOUF died as one soul, just as his god son, Alain, had conjured into Francine's unprotected thought, while alongside that garden pool.

Blaison and SURCOUF simply did not have much luck defending themselves against abusive attacks. They were everyone else's scapegoat—two souls as ONE locked in a psychic embrace against humiliating diplomatic, naval, political, and public ill-founded charges. SURCOUF, particularly, was falsely condemned by vicious conspiratorial rumors that have not subsided. *(A false witness that speaketh lies, and he that soweth discord among brethren. Proverbs 6:19 KJV.)*

An English Francophobic of a metaphysical inclination remarked that through the death of SURCOUF the submarine, the Royal Navy had finally obtained its ultimate revenge against Baron Robert Surcouf for viciously ravaging the British East Indiaman KENT in the Bay of Bengal during 1800.

That English Francophobic would have been justified in making this belated charge, for that brutal action aboard KENT by Baron Surcouf's band of corsairs remains almost unparalleled among famous sea fights. Surcouf's inhuman rape of KENT caused to the British Government to offer a £250,000 reward for his arrest—preferably dead!!! *([SURCOUF] will be enticed [into the Caribbean Sea fringes of the Bermuda Triangle] and there we shall prevail against her to take our revenge on her. (Paraphrase of Jeremiah 20:10 KJV).* In other words, the Englishman pointedly alluded that SURCOUF had been diabolically lured into a death trap to satisfy an ancient grudge.

Strangers are fated to meet when they are directed by that all-consuming attraction—LOVE. However, would the dire consequences revealed here have occurred to Blaison and SURCOUF had he not met and married Therese??? There seems to have been a hidden reason, unknown to themselves, for their strange extrasensory, inexorable union.

The author is almost on the verge of being able to tell you why, but for some inexplicable reason he cannot. There is no human way to describe their seemingly unearthly match; a strange alliance, which only God, or devil forces, professes to know. If you believe, no further explanation is necessary. If you don't believe, then no explanation is possible. No one here is forcing you to choose between believing and not believing.

Vaughan might suggest that their lives became enmeshed when Therese suffered her trauma over the loss of HMS L-24. However, this we can conjecture: "Would Therese have done well to have heeded her mother's sage advice—not to marry a submariner??? If she had obeyed, would the history of Blaison and SURCOUF been written differently???

In the final analysis, Blaison died just as his mother-in-law, as sort of her wish fulfillment, foretold would happen if Therese married a submariner.

Moreover, SURCOUF died just as Bywater, in 1925, had prophesized that a submarine of her size and kind would—by collision!!!

And, Blaison and SURCOUF died, together, just as his god son Alain had conjured into Francine's unprotected mind, while she observed helplessly alongside that drowning pool.

And, Burney, Gough and Warner, too, died just as they prophesized would happen, as would have Boyer, had he remained aboard SURCOUF!!!

SURCOUF's death ride was over "without a trace", but not without serious repercussions and prolonged inquiry into what turned out to be the worst submarine tragedy of its kind in maritime history; a dreadful monument to error. However, Death was not to be Blaison's and SURCOUF's last enemy.

There was no scapegoat connected with the SURCOUF-THOMPSON LYKES Collision, but there still remains a tense shroud of guilt over SURCOUF's tragic loss. The Free French made vain attempts to blame the United States Navy, but they were futile for lack of concise and positive information as appears in *The SURCOUF Conspiracy.*

SURCOUF's annihilation was serious to the Free French Navy, but not crippling. Unlike the Maginot Line, however, she was not a symbol to French defeatism. Important was that her loss did not signal the end of an era.

Thinking outside of main stream thought about SURCOUF during her World War II role, it is unfortunate that SURCOUF did not survive to transfer from Royal Navy to American Navy command. Had she entered the Panama Canal Zone, and transited to Balboa, where there was the huge Balboa Shipyard complex, the best and largest below the continental United States, her inoperable main propulsion armature could have been repaired and the BNLO staff would have been replaced with one from the American Navy. While she was undergoing repairs, she would have been equipped with RADAR for her protection and for search and gunnery purposes.

Definitely, the American Navy would not have allowed SURCOUF, for her own safety, to sail to the Southwest Pacific Theater of War in her disabled condition. Also, crippled as she was, SURCOUF would have been an extreme burden on limited war zone repair facilities and it is doubtful that her propulsion armature could have been repaired there.

The author speaks with authority about his commentary above because he worked and lived in the Panama Canal Zone as Superintendent of the Cristobal and Balboa Shops, which were Atlantic and Pacific-side shipyard complexes. He also can speak with authority concerning the naval relevance mentioned below since he had served in the Canal Zone as a Captain, U. S. Navy, in the Fifteenth Naval District.

The author would have suggested to more senior Army and Navy officers charged with the defense of the Panama Canal, which included its Caribbean Sea and Pacific frontiers, at that time, to deploy SURCOUF, once repaired, to search the Caribbean Sea for German U-boats or to patrol the Pacific Areas beyond the range of aircraft to guard against a Japanese attack on the Panama Canal from the sea, which at that time was of deep concern of officialdom.

This last statement has relevance because at that time the Imperial Japanese Navy was secretly constructing seven submarines of the I-400 class, much larger than SURCOUF, that were capable of carrying and launching three aircraft bombers. The long-range I-400 class submarines were intended to destroy the Panama Canal locks and de-moralize the populace by bombing Washington and New York. *(There were giants in the earth in those days; and also after that . . . . Genesis 6:4 KJV)*

Later in the war, during August 1945, the Imperial Japanese Navy had ordered an attack on the Panama Canal by two of its newly introduced huge I-400 class submarines, but the dropping of the American atomic bomb on Hiroshima and Nagasaki brought about the surrender of the Japanese.

Had SURCOUF survived and been permitted to proceed to the Southwest Pacific Theater of War, she would have served under the operational command of Captain (later Vice Admiral) Ralph Waldo Christie, USN, Annapolis Class of 1915, who was Commander, Task Force 71, Submarines, Southwest Pacific, operating out of Brisbane, Australia, as a part of General Douglas MacArthur's Navy.

Obviously, because of Japan's involvement with the huge I-400 class submarines, the Japanese Navy would have more likely than not appreciated the presence of the powerful SURCOUF in the Southwest Pacific Theater of War, such as cause them to cautiously re-consider taking action in her vicinity.

An awesome example of SURCOUF's capability and devastating firepower against the Japanese appears in fiction—in that international best seller *Strike From the Sea* by Douglas Reeman. *Strike*, published in 1978, is about the world's largest and most dangerous submarine—the French SOUFRIERE (Commander Robert Ainslie, Royal Navy).

Ironically, Reeman fictionalizes the capture by the Royal Navy of a SURCOUF-type submarine (SOUFRIERE) from the Far East command of the Vichy French Navy, based at Saigon, Indochina, and of her role, under Royal Navy command, against the Imperial Japanese Navy in the defense of British colonial Singapore.

Reeman places SOUFRIERE, surfaced, in an artillery attack upon a Japanese amphibious landing force off the coast of Malaysia:

'Open fire!'

'Right gun shoot!' Ainslie heard Farrant's (Gunnery Officer) voice through the turret speaker, and then ducked as the bang exploded across the bow.

Ainslie saw a brilliant flash as the shell hit the side of the Japanese vessel, a violent explosion amidships as the second shell burst dead on target.

A machine gunner yelled, 'Second ship, sir! Starboard beam!' As SOUFRIERE swept from the inlet's last protection, Ainslie saw the other ship, her warning flash of her guns, as two shells screamed overhead and exploded in the shallows.

Then both of Farrant's guns fired. A mushroom of fierce flame burst upwards from the vessel's after part, wreckage splashing amongst the released landing craft like missiles.

He saw the first warship settling by the bows, her deck slightly towards him as she began to capsize. About the size of a corvette, she was no match for Farrant's two 8-inch shells.

Farrant continued fire on the major warship, until with tremendous explosion she spewed flames and dense smoke from everywhere on her bridge. The warship had ceased firing, and was surrounded by blazing fuel, amongst which soldiers and sailors were silenced forever.

'Cease firing.' Control room, this is the Captain. Resume course and check all departments for damage.

Minutes later the sea was unruffled once more, with nothing to show that SOUFRIERE had ever been there.

There is every reason to believe that had SURCOUF reached the Southwest Pacific Theater of War in 1942 she could have been similarly deployed by the American Navy against the powerful Japanese advance bases on Truk Island in the Carolina group, on Rabaul, New Britain, and especially against various Japanese occupied bases along the coast of New Guinea from Milne Bay to Hollandia.

Set in Reeman's scenario: imagine what devastation SURCOUF, with her immense firepower, could have effected upon the Japanese stronghold at Truk, as exemplified in *The Great Pacific War* by Hector C. Bywater, the man who invented the American-Japanese War of the Pacific, 1941-1945.

So, SURCOUF's loss, although it would never be admitted by the American Army and Navy hierarchy, proved detrimental to shortening the American-Japanese War of the Pacific. Really, it is not hard to envision that her presence and proper deployment could have influenced the conduct of the American-Japanese War of the Pacific even more favorably for American forces.

Had SURCOUF been successfully deployed during the Southwest Pacific Theater of War, as she was designed and built to do, imagine the enormous prestige General de Gaulle's Free French movement would have diplomatically, psychologically (morale-wise), and politically attained during that war and France's postwar period.

SURCOUF had died on the threshold of the introduction of bigger, more powerful, seaplane carrying submarines, of the 1-400 class, this time built by the Imperial Japanese Navy.

At the time of her death, also, there occurred the metamorphosis of a bomb, built under the auspices of the Manhattan Project (General Leslie R. Groves, U.S. Army, Corps of Engineers), which was to serve as the genesis of power for propelling atomic, missile-carrying, submarines of the American Navy's TRIDENT-class. TRIDENT's,, twice SURCOUF's length, over six times her tonnage and having tens of millions of times more destructive power than SURCOUF's twin 8-inch guns, were built to serve as that best deterrent weapon system against the start of World War III.

SURCOUF was more than a French tri-color submarine. She had served alongside the American, Bermudian, Canadian, French, Free French and Royal Navies; had flown the flags of the Third Republic of France, England and Free France; had frequently berthed under the flags of the Commonwealth of Canada, of the Crown Colony of Bermuda and of the United States of America, and she died, in the world's worst submarine disaster, under the shadow of the Seal of the American Panama Canal Zone, which area is now the sovereignty of the proud Republic of Panama.

The Caribbean Sea now owns SURCOUF. She and Blaison did not die valiantly in battle, but in her war grave, forever at the bottom of the Caribbean, SURCOUF is a lasting shrine to her Free French Navy officers and men, along with three of the Royal Navy, who fought and died to liberate France from the brutal tyranny of Hitler's Third Reich. SURCOUF's history cannot be written without each Navy, including that of the American Navy, sharing in her death and glory. A *beau geste!!!*

> **The dead men stood together on the deck.**
> **Farewell! farewell! but this I tell To thee . . .**
> **He prayeth well who liveth well**
> **All things both great and small;**
> **For the dear God who loveth us,**
> **He made and loveth all.**

Although the French and Royal Navies have had their historic affrays and discords, it is reassuring to know that they can fight and die as one for a common cause. *Morts Pour La France*!!!

The memory of SURCOUF remains as a striking testimony of their solidarity, as during the Anglo-French involvement in the Suez Crisis of 1956.

Regrettably, over SURCOUF's grave no English roses bloom, nor French flags wave or lilies grow, nor is there a sea of crosses, for she lies far beyond where even explorers of the deep would have difficulty finding her.

Hopefully, some day, a floral wreath will be cast and a prayer spoken over her sea grave by an Allied Navy to commemorate and respect her and the 130 souls lost on the tragic night. And the submariners of the German Navy seemed to have a similar view:

> **There are no flowers on a sailor's grave**
> **No lilies on the ocean waves**
> **The only tribute is the seabird's sweeps**
> **And teardrops that a loved one weeps**
> **So far away.**
>
> **German Submariner's Poem**

Nobody lives forever, but death with SURCOUF, in the vicinity of Longitude 10° 28.5' North, Latitude 79° 21' West, at a depth of about 8,000 feet, was perhaps a dark victory for Blaison and his men. Only there in the hostile deep of the Caribbean Sea, not too far from Martinique where SURCOUF began the war, in September 1939, could they, in the strictest sense, find courage, honor and chivalry among men.

Blaison and SURCOUF, and others aboard her, died as one, in a perfect communion of souls, one for all and all for one. Life or death were the same, today or tomorrow would never exist for them again at the bottom most of Hell.

If Joan of Arc had survived the stake, how would she have lived the balance of her life amongst English on French soil, after the Burundians', the French allies of the English and the Church, had denied her???

Similarly, if Blaison and SURCOUF had survived the war how would they have lived, to be dubiously employed, the rest of their lives in a postwar environment which still reeked of Darlanism, remnants of the Vichyism, and amongst those in Allied Navies who had disdained her???

Both Blaison and SURCOUF, as was Lord Nelson, were fortunate from the point of view of fame. Each died when fame was secure. Had Blaison and SURCOUF lived, their careers may have been tarnished for them by the slander of surviving Vichyists, just as SURCOUF's reputation continues to be tarnished by persistent, unfounded rumors, throughout the Allied world, concerning her loyalty to the Free French Movement.

As for Captain Henry Johnson, he, along with the maritime and naval world, did not know, until the author told him in 1976, that the ghastly SURCOUF-THOMPSON LYKES Collision had resulted in the worst submarine disaster in history.

Captain Thompson and THOMPSON LYKES, as a mortal and an object working for others, had accomplished in a few seconds what the American, Italian, Japanese, and Royal Navies had not been able to do at the London Naval Conference of 1930, beyond eliminating a super class of French submarines, i.e., to destroy SURCOUF. SURCOUF had finally joined in the monumental death of those five others of her class killed at that Conference.

It absolutely boggles the author's mind, beyond his ability to emulate, as to how Hector C. Bywater, in 1925, so accurately and openly prophesized the creation of a submarine of SURCOUF's type in 1929, of how SURCOUF should have been deployed during World War II, and her death by collision in 1942???

Bywater, whose name and realistic writings became highly regarded and respected within the Imperial Japanese Navy, also foresaw, in fiction, how a submarine of SURCOUF's distinctive characteristics and awesome firepower should be deployed in combat—by placing NAGOYA, a HAKODATE-class submarine, in a wartime scenario whereby surface ships of the American Navy at Truk, a powerful naval base in the Southwest Pacific, were devastated.

Ironically, as calamitous events occurred, Truk was a powerful Japanese naval base during World War II, from which elements of that navy devastated the American fleet during the bloody battle for Guadalcanal. SURCOUF, in 1942, was enroute to participate in the American-Japanese War of the Pacific when the SS THOMPSON LYKES collided with her in the Caribbean. *(Blessed is he that readth, and they that hear the words of this prophecy, and keep those things which are written therein, for the time is at hand. Revelations 1:3 KJV.)*

Citing again from Bywater's *tour de force, The Great Pacific War:*

> Suffering constantly from machinery troubles, which materially reduced her cruising speed of seventeen knots, she became more of a hindrance than a help, finally ending her career by surfacing a few yards ahead of the battleship YAMASDHIRO, whose bow crushed her like an egg-shell.

As with HADOKATE, SURCOUF was a brute submarine, was the first of what the French Navy intended to be six of a class; SURCOUF achieved no victories at sea; she sailed in convoy with HMS RAMILLIES of the Royal Navy's Third Battle Fleet (Pear Admiral S.S Bonham-Carter, Royal Navy); she suffered constantly from machinery and other troubles; she was a drain on Allied repair facilities; and she was enroute to the Southwest Pacific Theater of war when she was crushed and sunk by the bow of that veritable death ship, SS THOMPSON LYKES, which was safe behind the cloak of a façade of darkness.

You may consider Bywater's eerie account of his psychic connection with SURCOUF's death as pure fantasy, something too incredible to be true???. If so, how can you explain the uncanny fact that in 1898 Morgan Robertson's *Wreck of the Titan* fictionalized with similar accuracy a maritime disaster which was to parallel the death of the unsinkable SS TITANIC in 1912?

TITANIC's sinking resulted in the greatest loss of life in the history of the sea—1,494 souls—fourteen years after Robertson's prediction! Allan Vaughan in *Incredible Coincidence*, cities the Robertson-TITAN-TITANIC Connection as "one of the most celebrated fictional cases of thought by parapsychologists to demonstrate unconscious foreknowledge." But, comparatively, the Robertson-TITAN-TITANIC's Connection with HADOKATE-SURCOUF is but a meager pittance of a coincidence when contrasted with the fruits of Bywater's long years of encyclopedic military and naval knowledge conjoined with his amazing ability to extract tidbits of information from the most unlikely sources and expand them into astounding revelations and then present his findings into reasoned writings for international consumption.

It is pertinent to mention that on August 16, 1940, Hector Charles Bywater, the greatest living authority on Japanese geopolitical, naval, and strategic affairs and sensing that his life was in danger, died under mysterious circumstances. Some believe that he was murdered by a Japanese agent acting upon the instructions of Admiral of the Fleet, Isoroku Yamamoto, Commander-in-Chief, Imperial Japanese Navy, for concern that Japan's bold war plan for conducting Operation Hawaii would be reported by the ever alert naval analyst and Japanese-like thinker, Hector C. Bywater.

Yamamoto would have not wanted even an inkling of evidence that he had copied or been influenced by Bywater's elaborate and singularly bold strategic and tactical plan for Japan's control of the Pacific. But,

Yamamoto did not anticipate that his navy would be engaged in the greatest naval battles ever fought and lost unconditionally. *(For what shall it profit a man, if he gain the whole world, and lose his own soul? Mark 8:36 KJV.)*

Fresh in Yamamoto's memory was that it was Bywater who, in 1936, exposed that the Japanese delegation would deliberately and prematurely withdraw from the London Naval Conference of 1936, and that it was the astute Bywater who, after study of Japan's naval budget for 1937, correctly and internationally revealed that Japan was secretly building two monstrous (72,000 tons), big gun (18 inch) battleships.

To add credence to the Yamamoto-Bywater murder conjecture, at the time of Bywater's death, his naval journalist associate, Melville Cox, the Reuters based correspondent based in Tokyo, who was Bywater's principle informant in Japan, was brutally beaten and allegedly thrown out of a hotel window. Cox's widow was determined Japanese agents committed that foul deed.

Thus, if Yamamoto was to successfully effect Bywater's plan about how to conduct Japan's Pacific war against the United States, it could happen that Bywater and Cox might prematurely detect his master plan, Operation HAWAII, which included a surprise attack on Pearl Harbor. Therefore, Yamamoto would have had an unholy reason to eliminate Bywater and Cox. Bywater sensed that his life was in danger, to the point of his carrying a pistol for self-defense. It is difficult to find any other explanation for the near coincidental deaths of Bywater and Cox.

At the time of Bywater's death, which was slightly more than a year before the Imperial Japanese Navy's surprise attack on Pearl Harbor, President Franklin D. Roosevelt, who had vehemently opposed Bywater's incredibly realistic views about Japan's aggressive intentions against the United States, was President of the United States.

Had Bywater lived to commandingly revive and expound upon his debates with FDR about the Pacific War, i.e., the crushing and violent Japanese attack on Pearl Harbor [Remember Pearl Harbor] and the subsequent fall of the Philippines [Remember the Bataan Death

March] and Guam, President Roosevelt's political star could have dimmed and fallen appreciably. Strange to remark, when referring to the American-Japanese War of the Pacific, is that, as confirmed by Honan in his highly informative and deeply profound *Visions of Infamy*, there seems to be only minimal credits and references to Bywater in articles or books about the dire forewarnings he expressed in *The Great Pacific War*. Regardless, although Bywater was eternally resting in peace, the fulfillment of his prophecies continued until the Japanese signed unconditional surrender documents on September 2, 1945, on board the battleship USS MISSOURI in Tokyo Bay, to officially end the American-Japanese War of the Pacific.

This is as good a place as anywhere in *The SURCOUF Conspiracy* to mention, that, at the explicit direction of President Roosevelt, Yamamoto met his Waterloo from the guns of U. S. Army Air Corps, straight shooting, Lockheed "Lightening" P-38 fighter pilots while his aircraft, a Mitsubishi G4M "Betty" bomber, was approaching Bougainville Island, in the Solomon's Group, on April 18, 1943. *(The wages of sin is death Romans 6:23 KJV)*

The tip-off to "Get Yamamoto," and to his precise whereabouts, was determined by Americans based in Hawaii, who had broken Japanese naval codes. Ironic, that the very war Yamamoto planned and executed, in accordance with the plan of British naval journalist Hector C. Bywater, also resulted in his untimely death. Before that deed of deadly retribution and revenge for the dastardly Imperial Japanese Navy attack upon Pearl Harbor was executed, permission from the highest authority of the land, President Franklin Delano Roosevelt, was obtained. It was a sweet revenge, especially for the American Navy. *(. . . . he will be enticed, and we shall prevail against him, and we shall take our revenge on him. Jeremiah 20:10.KJV.)*

Yamamoto's death was a major blow to Japanese civil military morale, but a tremendously uplifting one for all American military and naval personnel, and including the civilian population, during World War II.

The above commentary about Bywater reiterated his intrinsic ability to visualize and foreordain events, but only vaguely bordered upon how they were genetically conceived by him. Humankind, regrettably, has evolved few of his equal.

If efforts ever were to replicate and decode Hector C. Bywater's brain from a DNA specimen that feat would have to be tasked to neuro genetic scientists to coordinate with computer and software engineers in developing a bio-computer so awesomely powerful that it would artificially create a model of a biological system to mimic and arrange the neural networks of the human mind. It would be one with a capability far beyond existing computers which currently only can provide the physical depiction of subjects from their DNA.

Required would be a super-ultra computer that could marry our past with the treasures of the future—one with a near infinite database and wisdom that chillingly would know more about us, than we knew about ourselves. But, alas, would the consequence of such an unholy alliance make our Lord virtually redundant. Such a super gene machine would have to be restricted to doing good for humanity without tempting evil. Regardless, we do vitally require a second coming of a Hector C. Bywater in our troubled world to protect us from the dire consequences to be suffered because of not having him. When you need a miracle, you have to go what the action is.

Again, back to the main stream of *The SURCOUF Conspiracy*: It was not until April 12, 1942 that Madame Blaison learned of her loss of Blaison and SURCOUF. At the time, she was secretly involved with the French Resistance movement, the C. O. S. O. R., against Nazi Germans occupying France. Here is what she woefully wrote the author about her pitiful loss:

> I received the worst blow that a human being can endure and immediately lost all joy in living; suffering the most intense despair that one can imagine, I reminded myself of the words of Louis: "God doesn't give us a burden that a human being of good breeding cannot bear!"
>
> I had entrusted my husband to God and to the Holy Virgin, they could not be without any pity for me and for the sacrifice that Louis and I had agreed upon.

But, I was going insane with grief as I desperately clung to the idea that Louis was a prisoner.

I (the author) have her written diary of the April 1944 interval that Madame Blaison and young Francine spent in Vichy Occupied France, and the privations they suffered for being her widow of a so-called "deserter" for Blaison having joined the Free French cause. Here is an explicit account of how she refused the help of Vichy naval hierarchy:

> In April 1944, I was requested to appear at the Vichy Minister of Marine, and there I found myself in front of a very pleasant and courteous senior naval officer [Vice Admiral Gabriel Paul Auphan, Chief of Cabinet of Admiral Darlan under Vichy France and later Secrétaire d'État à la Marine of Vichy].
>
> This was something I was not accustomed to. He referred to Louis as being a very courageous fellow-countryman, and wanted to inquire about my means of existence. I told him that being the wife and then widow of a so-called deserter from the Vichy French Navy that I had nothing and was living on a bare existence.
>
> He then offered me a blank check on which I was to put the sum that I judged necessary for the amends of four years of my deprivation. I tore up the check, answering him that I did not accept, at the end of four years of my misery, money offered by those who had condemned Louis to twenty years of forced labor and loss of pay and privileges for his fighting to free France from Nazi German and SS terrorism.
>
> It was apparent that his proposal revealed that the winds of war were changing against the German occupation of France! We coldly took leave of one another.

As an aside: Madam Blaison's assertion that the winds of war were changing were changing within France may have been influenced by Admiral Robert's return to France via Puerto Rico and Lisbon, and when Free French sympathizers took control of the gold at Fort Desaix and remnants of the the French fleet based there.

It is also noteworthy to mention that years previous to Madam Blaison's meeting with Admiral Auphan, in continuation of the above commentary, that on July 29, 1940, *The Official Newspaper of the French Republic Under the Government of Vichy*, directed the Vichy Ministry of Marine, First National Tribunal, Toulon,

> Every Frenchman who delivers arms, ammunition or war materials for foreign countries, including Frenchman who does service to a foreign army or navy, dails under the jurisdiction of the fourth paragraph of Article 75 of the penal code, and from this deed is declared guilty of treason and is punishable by death.

This edict condemned then Lieutenant de Vaissau Georges Louis Nicolas Blaison to twenty years imprisonment and sequestration of his world goods, including all pay and allowances, on the charge of his being guilty of desertion from the Vichy French Navy in time of war.

The tribunal's condemnation also included Madame Blaison as it deprived her of any allotment she would have received from Blaison's pay and allowance as a Vichy French Navy officer, but not as a Free Frenchman. Thus, she was practically penniless for the duration of hostilities.

This edict, which took aim at every Free Frenchman, wrote the Editor, *French Libre Review*, January-February-March 1978 issue, was signed by Marshall Henri Petain, Chief of State; by Raphael Alibert, Director of the Seal of France; and by General Maxine Weygand, Minister of Defense. "It was a surprising death sentence on the part of a Marshall of France, and counter to the soldiers who to continued the struggle to defend their country. From that moment, all bridges were burned between Free French man and the Vichy French."

One of those "bridges" would have included the death penalty for SURCOUF, and as you shall read, according to the rumors, she, figuratively speaking, must have died a thousand deaths from Vichy insinuations and falsehoods about how she lived and really died.

There was another apparent attack on the Blaison's by Vichy. Blaison wrote about it in his May 2, 1941 letter to Therese:

> Did you sent me a telegram telling me that a desperate family situation required my return to France. I doubted it. You'll also be told about my mistresses. You will not be the first to be told such lies, through a casual, delicate remark from supposed friends. Like the kind of person who came to London saying he would join the Free French Navy if he was sure of making more money. I have met so many French enacting Machiavelli: "Let's hurry to sell our honor while it is worth money." Perhaps I am a happy fool living in the past, but I never swore to be faithful to this sort of honor upon receiving my sword from l'Ecole Navales.

Input received from Commander L. C. Audette, Royal Canadian Navy, Retired, OCQC, of Ottawa, Canada, dated September 4, 1980, remarked about Blaison's concern about the welfare of his wife and daughter. Audette had served briefly aboard SURCOUF during December 1941 as Royal Canadian Naval Liaison Officer to Admiral Muselier:

> I can remember Blaison being very bitter about Vichy misleading him about the health of his daughter in France. Either by forged letter or other communication, they tried to lead Blaison to believe that his daughter had tuberculosis and was in bad shape in the hospital.

Now, back to the main stream of our story:

For those who doubt that the SURCOUF-THOMPSON LYKES Collision ever occurred, and who believe that SURCOUF was sunk by warships of the American or Royal Navies, it should be reported that, on February 22, 1942, according to Stanley E. Hilton, in *Hitler's Secret*

War in South America, 1939-1945, "two badly damaged" destroyers, belonging to the American Neutrality Patrol, South Atlantic Force (Rear Admiral Jonas Howard "Howy" Ingram, USN, Annapolis, Class of 1907), arrived in Recife, Brazil for repairs. His force had consisted of four light cruisers and five destroyers to patrol, as Task Force Three, the triangle between Trinidad, Cape Sao Roque and Cape Verde Islands.

The author's inquiry about this incident, involving the two damaged destroyers, received this reply (15 July 1983) from Dr. Dean C. Allard, Head, Operational Archives Branch, Historical Center, Washington Navy Yard, Washington, D.C.:

> We are mystified regarding the German agent's report of two damaged destroyers in Rio or another Brazilian port during February 1942. As you know, U.S. ships were operating in the South Atlantic at the time.
>
> However, there is no indication in our file that any suffered operational or combat damage early in 1942. In this regard, as in many others, the German intelligence network in the Western Hemisphere seems to have been flawed.

Strange, who to believe??? Hilton's book spent months on the American best-seller list there and generated a national furor as former spies and collaborationists were exposed. There was ample time to denounce any of Hilton's facts. Conversely, If two American destroyers were really damaged and that fact was being concealed, then there was a conspiracy to hide the truth.

As if SURCOUF still lived, or as if she had a double image, surveillance around the island of Martinique and around the coasts and rivers of French Guiana were stepped-up by the American Navy, for about ten days following SURCOUF's loss; under the pretext of searching for enemy submarine bases.

According to U. S. Consul General Marcel E. Malige, Martinique, these searches were conducted by the Navy under the express authority of the American State Department. (According to Consul General Malige, Martinique, File of Confidential Reports to the State

Department, February 19, 26 and 28 and early March 1942, Source: National Archives. The Vichy High Commissioner (Admiral Georges Roberts) protested against American warplanes yesterday nose diving twice at the aircraft carrier BEARNE and twice over the cruiser EMIL BERTIN (Telegram No. 48, February 26.) and the search of French Guiana rivers and coasts for enemy submarine bases by United States planes. (Telegram No. 49, February 28, 1942.)

The Vichyists on Martinique were concerned also as Admiral Georges Roberts, the High Commissioner, departed Fort de France, aboard the auxiliary cruiser BARFLEUR on February 19, and early in March the EMIL BERTIN also made two sorties around Martinique waters, to determine for themselves that SURCOUF was not concealing itself in Vichy French waters.

SURCOUF and her Free French crew vainly sought the enemy to fight for glory and to restore the honor of France. But for those who were about to die, they found their worst enemy to be the vindictive sea and the malicious and ugly rumors spread about them and their submarine in every enemy and Allied port. Fighting the foe would have been preferable to being pathetically killed by a friend, but that is how SURCOUF took her last dive—from the bow of a friendly American ship.

One such persistent rumor was published in the January 1967 issue of *Argosy Magazine* entitled: *Found: One Supersub* by Roy Bongartz. According to Bongartz, a retired Navy chief, Lee Prettyman of Hartford, Connecticut, claimed that his salvage firm had found SURCOUF laying at a depth of 140 feet of Long Island Sound—at a site visible from Connecticut, Rhode Island, and New York.

Prettyman specifically told Abongartz that he had salvaged SURCOUF's two "copper" propellers and had sold such evidence to a scrap dealer. This immediately quickly revealed to this author, who was a shipyard manager by profession, that Prettyman's claim was unfounded. Whatever the composition of SURCOUF's propellers, and they certainly were not copper, it would have taken Prettyman weeks to remove and lift them from SURCOUF; a task that his salvage firm was ill equipped to accomplish. It is difficult enough to remove a propeller while a ship is dry-docked, but while she is underwater that job becomes Herculean. Besides, had he actually retrieved SURCOUF's propellers they would have been far more valuable to the French Navy than what a scrap dealer offered him.

According to another vicious rumor, SURCOUF was torpedoed in above the northern end of Long Island Sound by the submarine USS MACKERAL while SURCOUF was caught refueling a German submarine.

But, the erroneous Prettyman rumor, particularly, frequently appeared in the American press, i.e., until the author (Grigore) challenged Prettyman to accept my $1,000,000 wager. Even though Prettyman discontinued spreading his false claim, that foul rumor, as well as the MACKERAL one, continue to be repeated by those too indignant and laggard to probe for truth.

Despite my best efforts, I have not been able to convince any of SURCOUF's allied navies, even the French Navy, to dive upon her grave site—into holy waters—to locate and photograph her hulk—as was done for the SS TITANIC by a private group of Frenchmen and the Woods Hole group of Americans.

SURCOUF deserves this recognition. It should be done—once and for all time—to set to rest those vicious rumors about her. Why this was not done long ago may be her punishment for her transcending the dictates of naval conventionality.

But, there is valid reason why a portion of SURCOUF's hulk, perhaps her anchor, should be salvaged and permanently displayed—ideally in a space in the vicinity of the Louvre, Paris. Imagine the throngs that would be drawn to render honors and say prayers over an artifact of SURCOUF, particularly by: the citizens of France, the naval community of active and veteran personnel from all Nations, relatives of the souls lost with her, those interested in her historical significance, and promotion of the French Navy and France's naval heritage through educational outreach. Also, a physical artifact of SURCOUF would serve as a recollection of how the world's worst submarine disaster occurred and of how it should have been avoided

The Memorial to the war dead of the USS ARIZONA in Pearl Harbor, Hawaii and the ancient, but active, ships USS CONSITUTION (Old Ironsides), Boston Harbor, and Vice Admiral Lord Horatio Nelson's HMS VICTORY, Portsmouth Historic Dockyard, England, are prime examples of such attractions. (The USS ARIZONA Memorial attracts over 1,000,000 people annually.)

If perchance SURCOUF is not in the death zone where navigational studies indicate she should be, then an official board of inquiry should be immediately opened by the United Nations to excise the truth as to where her hulk really lies and who, indeed, was responsibility for her loss and final disposition.

During the post World War II period SURCOUF was awarded the following medals by the French Government: Cité à 'l' Ordre du Corps d' Armée le 04 Août 1945; Décoré de la Médaille de la Résistance avec Rosette le 29 novembre 1946 ; and the Cité à l'ordre de l'Armée de Mer le 08 janvier 1947.

Regardless, generally, when a victim dies, he or she, or even it, is not only mourned but eulogized during a religious ceremony after they leave our earthly world. Unfortunately, for poor SURCOUF, except for the erection of monuments and awarding of medals and plaques, she has never been rendered the customary maritime and naval honors of war over her grave site. This courtesy and respect is due her in accordance with the highest traditions of the sea. The L-24 and SURCOUF disasters had commonalities: Both were unavoidably sunk by collision with the bow of an approaching ship, and both sank instantly with all hands.

Unlike SURCOUF, however, the dead of HMS L-24 were honored by a naval flotilla of twelve submarines and other naval vessels which held a memorial service over where she sank. According to the *New York Times* of January 19, 1924:

> The crews of the vessels stood bareheaded while a naval cortege moved slowly forward to a tossing flag marking the watery grave of the forty-three officers and men who perished in L-24.

Every engine was stopped as salutes to the dead were fired. A naval chaplain read the burial service, a great wreath of flowers was dropped from the stern of the flagship and buglers sounded the "Last Post."

It is firmly believed that, even at this late date, a formal religious service should be conducted by the Allied navies over SURCOUF's hulk—including the casting of the customary floral wreath—to venerate SURCOUF and the 130 souls lost with her.

If the author had the resources, this would be the least that he would do for SURCOUF, for the sanctification of her soul and for the souls of her gallant Free French officers and men—including the three of the Royal Navy.

From a March 1, 1945 exchange of letters between Lykes Brothers Steamship Company and the Contracts Division of the War shipping Administration, it seems that continued hire of the SS THOMPSONJ LYKES would only be granted on a 50% reduced hire because of her having been involved in three marine accidents between February 18 and December 5, 1942, namely: the SURCOUF-SS THOMPSON LYKES Collision; a collision with a destroyer in Boston Harbor; and a grounding near Lewes, Delaware on December 5, 1942, while Captain Henry Johnson was still her captain.

On October 15, 1945, in a letter to the Acting Assistant General Counsel for the War Shipping Administration, the Judge Advocate General of the Navy, based upon the evidence of the U. S. Coast Guard's Board of Inquiry into the SURCOUF-SS THOMPSON LYKES Collision decided that there was sufficient evidence to conclude "that the SS THOMPSON LYKES in fact did strike the Free French submarine SURCOUF."

In the *Paris Match Magazine* of October 1951, there appeared an article about the Memorial dedicated to SURCOUF and her war dead. In that article, its editor referred to Capitaine de Frigate Blaison as "The St. Exupery of the Sea" which was a correlation to France's famous aviator and author Antoine St. Exupery. The same editor also referred to Francine Blaison as "The Orphan of Surcouf."

During July 1955, in an act of contrition or a request for forgiveness of the sin for sinking poor SURCOUF, on the occasion of a routine cargo visit to Cherbourg, France, and unbeknownst to French naval authorities or to the Blaison womenfolk, the Master (name unknown) and officers and crew of the SS THOMPSON LYKES, in a silent, unsolicited ceremony, laid a wreath, inscribed "SS THOMPSON LYKES" at the base of the Surcouf War Memorial to pay tribute to SURCOUF and her dead.

In another act of contrition, nearly forty years after SURCOUF-SS THOMPSON LYKES Collision, Captain Henry Johnson, "the Ancient Mariner" was forgiven by someone **"from far off countree."** This is how Madame Blaison and Mlle Francine expressed themselves following receipt of Captain Johnson's photograph from the author:

> About Captain Johnson, we wish to say that we are not hateful towards him for the loss of our beloved Louis and our cherished SURCOUF. He obeyed his orders, but the remembrance of the death of those 130 souls, in what has proved to be the world's worst submarine disaster, along with the distress caused their families, must certainly remain for him terrible regret.
>
> We were also truly moved when we learned from you that the officers and men of the SS THOPMPSON LYKES, when they were in Cherbourg, had placed a wreath of flowers before the monument erected in memory of SURCOUF, her officers and my husband, their commanding officer.

But strangely, the forgiveness expressed by Blaison's womenfolk was not reciprocated with a thank you or expression of sympathy or respect by Captain Johnson. During May 1980 when Therese and Francine were visiting the author's home, he attempted to arrange for them to visit Captain Johnson in New Orleans. Captain Johnson begged off stating that he "did not want to become further involved with the affairs of SURCOUF."

Admiral of the Fleet and Commander of the Combined Fleet, Isoroku Yamamoto, Imperial Japanese Navy, who, during the London Naval Conference of 1930, advised the Chief Japanese Delegate to vote to kill the French Navy's SURCOUF class aircraft carrying submarine, when he knew that his navy was secretly involved.

Yamamoto was the planner for Operation HAWAII, the IJN's treacherous surprise attack on Pearl Harbor on December 7, 1941, during which 3,600 American civilians and military and naval personnel were killed and wounded, six battleships sunk, plus extensive devastation to other ships and shore facilities. However, in total, accounting to sources on the Internet, over 231,000 American fighting personnel were killed before the American-Japanese War of the Pacific, 1941-1945 ended.

American armed forces and the American public were elated when, at the explicit direction of President Roosevelt, Yamamoto met his Waterloo from the guns of U. S. Army Air Corps, straight shooting, Lockheed "Lightening" P-38 fighter pilots while his aircraft, a Mitsubishi G4M

"Betty" bomber, was approaching Bougainville Island, in the Solomon's Group, on April 18, 1943.

During the latter days of World War II, Japan introduced the long range I-400 class submarines, which were much larger and more powerful than SURCOUF, and carried three seaplane bombers. They were intended to disable the locks of the Panama Canal and to attack New York and Washington. The I-401 submarine was so deployed when Japan unconditionally surrendered following the dropping of atomic bombs by the American B-29 bombers upon Hiroshima and Nagasaki.

Credit: *Wikipedia* and *Time Magazine*, December 11, 1941.

Ancient postcard view of Joan of Arc about to be burnt at the stake.

Joan of Arc was Capitaine de Frégaté Louis Georges Nickolas's cherished role model.

Blaison lived and died with these noble words of Joan indelibly etched in his heart, mind, and soul: "All the hands of France in a single hand. A hand that is never divided!" When the English shouted at Joan, "Everything is dead." She retorted: "But there is hope, which is stronger." In these words you can recognize Blaison, the sailor, who wrote to his beloved Theresa: "The only real meaning of what I am doing with SURCOUF is to be messenger of hope, to be he who says, 'No, everything is not lost, France will be saved.' And, France was saved from an eternity of Nazi tyranny.

When Capitaine de Frégaté Blaison went down with *Surcouf* she was enveloped in a sheet of flames.

Postcard credit: La Panthéon, Jean d' Arc sur le Bûcher (Lenepveu) and Serv. Commercial Monuments Historiques Gd Palais, Av. Alexandre III, Pie G., Paris, circa 1915.

Capitaine de Frégate Louis Georges Nickolas Blaison attendance at a banquet sponsored by the French Club of Norwich, Connecticut.

Capitaine de Frégate Blaison is at the head table, third from the left. All other persons were not identified.

Three *Surcouf* crew members of this group were placed in the brig at the U. S. Naval Shipyard, Portsmouth, New Hampshire, for attempting to flee to Canada.

Credit: Courtesy of Wilford Gionet (deceased), Norwich, Connecticut, 1981,

From left to right, Capitaine de Frégate Louis Blaison, Lieutenant de Vaisseau Jean-Yves Leoquest, Gunnery Officer, Capitaine de Corvette Georges Alphonse Rossignol, Executive Officer, Lieutenant de Vaisseau Francis Alexis Jaffery, Electrical Officer, Bishop Marshall, British War Correspondent, and Ira Wolfert, Author and Journalist for North American Newspaper Alliance.

The occasion was *Surcouf's* involvement in the liberation of the St. Pierre and Miquelon Islands on December 25, 1941 about which Ira Wolfert, journalist for the North American Newspaper Alliance reported: "The liberation of the St. Pierre and Miquelon Islands was the best Christmas present that could be given to peoples desiring to be free. It was what the war was all about, and it was the first occasion during which people were liberated from the political oppression of Vichy France."

Noteworthy about this photograph is the small size of *Surcouf's* wardroom in which the Surcouf Affray of July 3, 1940 occurred and in which four of the Royal Navy were killed or wounded, and one French officer was killed.

Credit: With the permission of Service Historique de la Marine, Vincennes, 1983.

310

At the left is Lieutenant de Vaisseau Pierre Bouillant (later Vice Admiral), French Navy, the Gunnery Officer who fired the first shots at members of the British Royal Navy boarding party that seized *Surcouf* during Operation GRASP.

Commander Denis V. Sprague, Royal Navy, was mortally wounded during this affray, but not without first wounding Bouillant.

Credit: With the permission of Vice Admiral Pierre Bouillant, French Navy, Toulon, France, 1979.

Lieutenant Frank Boyer, Royal Navy, the third British Naval Liaison Officer aboard the Free French submarine *Surcouf,* celebrating his marriage to Josephine Meyers. He is second from the right, whereas Capitaine de Frégate Louis Georges Nicolas Blaison, Free French Navy, and Commander of *Surcouf,* is to the right of Boyer.

Lieutenant Boyer, who slept with a pistol under his pillow, was detached from *Surcouf* after complaining to an admiral that he and his two enlistees of the British Naval Liaison staff would die if they remained aboard *Surcouf.*

The locale is the Officers Club, U. S. Naval Submarine Base, New London, Connecticut.

Credit: With the permission of Mrs. Josephine Boyer (nee Meyers), later Mrs. Josephine Vairnen of Corpus Christi, Texas, 1982.

The casino at St. Malo, France, which was the birthplace and homeport of the French corsair (later Baron) Robert Surcouf.

It was at this casino, in 1930, that Lieutenant de Vasseau Louis Georges Nickolas Blaison was introduced to a *tres chic* Parisian, Mademoiselle Theresa Marie Franchcelli, by a British Royal Navy officer.

Credit: St. Malo, France picture postcard of the 1920s era.

Prime Minister Winston Churchill with his two other World War II Allied leaders, General Sikorski, leader of the Free Polish Forces and General de Gaulle, leader of the Free French forces.

It is still rumored that Churchill had conspired to assassinate both Sikorski and de Gaulle for political reasons. The Internet is alive with such allegations.

Churchill inspecting *Surcouf's* officers and men at Devonsport Dockyard, Plymouth, England.

Credit: With the permission of the Muzeum Wojska Polskiego, Warsaw, 1984 and the Imperial War Museum, London, England.

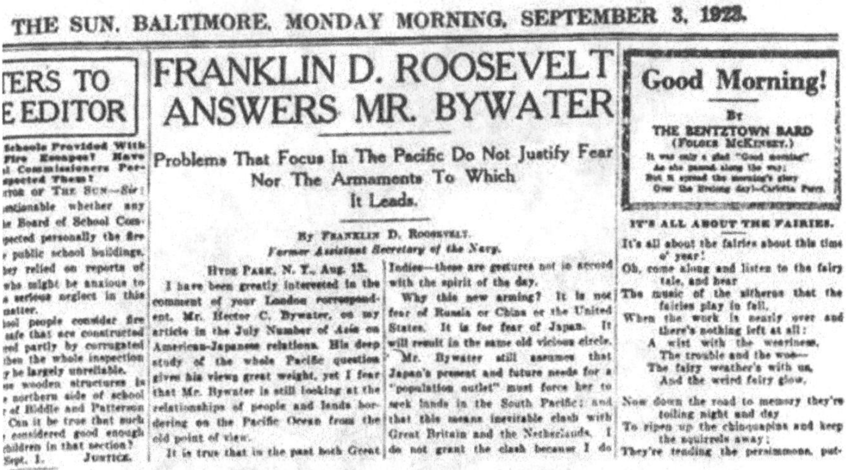

THE SUN, BALTIMORE, MONDAY MORNING, SEPTEMBER 3, 1928.

TERS TO
E EDITOR

Schools Provided With Fire Escapes? Have l Commissioners Personally Inspected Them?

TOR OF THE SUN—Sir: uestionable whether any he Board of School Comspected personally the fire public school buildings. hey relied on reports of who might be anxious to a serious neglect in this matter.

ool people consider fire safe that are constructed ed partly by corrugated then the whole inspection y be largely unreliable.

se wooden structures in northern side of school of Biddle and Patterson Can it be true that such considered good enough children in that section?

Sept. 1. JUSTICE.

FRANKLIN D. ROOSEVELT ANSWERS MR. BYWATER

Problems That Focus In The Pacific Do Not Justify Fear Nor The Armaments To Which It Leads.

By FRANKLIN D. ROOSEVELT.
Former Assistant Secretary of the Navy.

HYDE PARK, N. Y., Aug. 13.

I have been greatly interested in the comment of your London correspondent, Mr. Hector C. Bywater, on my article in the July Number of *Asia* on American-Japanese relations. His deep study of the whole Pacific question gives his views great weight, yet I fear that Mr. Bywater is still looking at the relationships of people and lands bordering on the Pacific Ocean from the old point of view.

It is true that in the past both Great … Indies—these are gestures not in accord with the spirit of the day.

Why this new arming? It is not fear of Russia or China or the United States. It is for fear of Japan. It will result in the same old vicious circle.

Mr. Bywater still assumes that Japan's present and future needs for a "population outlet" must force her to seek lands in the South Pacific; and that this means inevitable clash with Great Britain and the Netherlands. I do not grant the clash because I do

Good Morning!

By
THE BENTZTOWN BARD
(FOLGER MCKINSEY.)

IT'S ALL ABOUT THE FAIRIES.

It's all about the fairies about this time o' year!
Oh, come along and listen to the fairy tale, and hear
The music of the zitheras that the fairies play in fall,
When the work is nearly over and there's nothing left at all:
A wist with the weariness,
The trouble and the woe—
The fairy weather's with us,
And the weird fairy glow.

Now down the road to memory they're toiling night and day
To ripen up the chinquapins and keep the squirrels away;
They're tending the persimmons, put-

Yamamoto during his tenure as naval attaché in Washington, with Navy Secretary Curtis Wilbur (*U.S. Navy Historical Center photo*). Below, the "debate" in the Baltimore *Sun* (Reprinted from the Baltimore *Sun* © 1923, The Baltimore Sun Co.).

During the 1920s and 30s, Franklin D. Roosevelt, as Assistant Secretary of the Navy, who had vehemently opposed Bywater's meticulously realistic views about Japan's aggressive intentions against the United States, was President of the United States when the Imperial Japanese Navy treacherously attacked Pearl Harbor on December 7, 1941.

Had Bywater lived to revive and expound further his debates with FDR about the Pacific War, i.e., the Japanese surprise attack on Pearl Harbor and the fall of the Philippines and Guam, President Roosevelt's political star could have dimmed and fallen appreciably.

Credit: *Baltimore Sun* Archives.

Commander Denis Vaughan "Lofty" Sprague, Royal Navy, and Commander of the submarine *HMS Thames*, who was mortally wounded while leading a boarding party to seize the French submarine *Surcouf* during Operation GRASP.

At Commander Sprague's right is Lieutenant Patrick Griffiths, Royal Navy, who along with Sprague was mortally wounded during the shoot-out between Royal Navy and French Navy officers aboard *Surcouf*. Griffiths was Sprague's Executive Officer aboard *HMS Thames*.

Credit: With the permission of Mrs. Rosemary Sprague, wife, 1978.

Commander (later Captain) Girvin B. Wait, Port Director, Fifteenth
Naval District, at the time *SS Thompson Lykes* collided with *Surcouf.*
Commander Wait is shown in front of his home in Bellingham,
Washington, alongside his son Ralph and their dog *Skipper.*

Credit: With the permission of Captain Girvin B. Wait, U. S. Navy Reserve,
Retired, Bellingham, Washington, 1987.

The Minneapolis-born (November 22, 1910 (Sagittarius) Elizabeth Amy "Betty" Thorpe, who was recruited by the British Intelligence Service in 1938 and code-named *Cynthia* by William S. Stephenson (Intrepid). The alluringly beautiful *Cynthia* was the most seductive secret weapon, and one of the war's greatest unsung heroines, in the arsenal of Intrepid's spies—a modern day Mata Hari.

The center photograph is the house that Cynthia lived in on 3227 "O" street, Georgetown, ?Washington, D C. where Intrepid frequented.

Also shown is Capitaine Charles La Brousse, Cynthia, and their great Dane "Gus" following their marriage and residence in La Brousse's Chateau de Castellnou, East Pyrénées, France.

Credits: National Archives, Washington, D. C. and
Library of Congress, Washington, 1988.

Admiral of the Fleet Jean Louis Xavier Francois Darlan, French Navy, who, as a fierce Anglophobic, refused to allow his fleet of war ships to support England during World War II. Instead they flew the Vichy French flag.

Only a few naval vessels of France fled to England, one of which was *Surcouf*, which fought under the battle ensign of the British Royal **Navy.**

Credit: Wikipedia, the free encyclopedia

It was through Mrs. Eunice *Eunie* Richard, a staff writer for the *Panama Canal Review*, published by the Panama Canal Company, a United States Government Agency, that the author became inescapably involved in his tempestuous affair with SURCOUF, which began in 1967.

Credit: With the permission of Mrs. Eunice Richard (now deceased), 1978.

Extensive article about *Surcouf* and the author (Grigore) which appeared on the front page of the *Royal Gazette*, Hamilton, Bermuda, on June 6, 1980. It was during this period that the author attempted to interview Intrepid, but his nurse said that he was too ill.

Subsequently, after the appearance of this article and by telephone, she remarked that Intrepid knew nothing about *Surcouf.*

Mlle Francine Blaison at the dedication of the monument to *Surcouf* and to her heroic war dead on September 19, 1951. During the ceremony, General Charles de Gaulle, as the President of France, placed a wreath at the monument to glorify the occasion. Dignitaries from the Allied wartime nations were present.

Thereafter, publicity about the occasion resulted in Francine being referred to as "L' Orpheline du Surcouf" throughout France. However, Francine was mostly known throughout France as l'panthère because of her resolute determination to learn the truth about how her father really died with *Surcouf.*

Francine's cat was named "Robert" after Baron Robert Surcouf, and which was the World War II code name for *Surcouf* in letters from her father.

Credit: With the permission of Service archives historique de la défense, Paris, and Madam Therese and Mlle Francine Blaison, 1982, both deceased.

French stamp issued on June 2, 1951 to commemorate the 150th
Anniversary of Baron Robert Surcouf's death.

The stamp portrays Surcouf as a corsair when he viciously attacked the
British East India Company merchant ships plying the Indian Ocean

The statue of Robert Surcouf appears at the harbor entrance to St.
Malo, France, his birthplace and homeport.

Credit: Courtesy of the Service Philatélique de La Poste, Fontenay-aux-Roses,
France, 1983, and the author's photograph collection of things Surcouf.

Captain R. G. S. Garwood, Royal Navy, Retired, who was the only member of the Free French or Royal Navies requested to appear at *Surcouf's* inquest in New Orleans, Louisiana, on March 12, 1942.

About Garwood's presence at the Board of Inquiry it was learned that ". . . he did not ask any direct questions or suggest any."

Credit: Permission of Captain R. G. S. Garwood, Royal Navy, Retired, 1981.

General Charles de Gaulle, President of France, disembarking from *Surcouf* on September 15, 1940 on the day that she was commissioned as a Free French man o'war. Vice Admiral Emil Henri Muselier, Commander-in-Chief, Free French Navy is following.

General de Gaulle laying a wreath at the monument dedicated to *Surcouf*'s 129 heroic war dead. The ceremony was held on September 19, 1951. Years later, through the investigations of the author, it was determined that a 130th man went down with *Surcouf,* and his name was added to the plaque. This discovery confirmed that *Surcouf* was the world's worst submarine disaster, and not the *USS Thresher* which0 went down with only 129 persons.

The monument is located at the entrance to the harbor of Cherbourg, France.

Credit: With the permission of Service archives historique de la défense, Paris, 1980.

Leading Signalman Harold Frank "Plum" Warner, Royal Navy Fleet Reserve, and Telegraphist Bernard "Bernie" Warner, Royal Navy Fleet Reserve, shown in a St. Pierre and Miquelon Islands hotel lobby during January 1942.

"Bernie" is observing "Plum" while he is sketching a preliminary design of *Surcouf* for a stamp to commemorate the liberation of the St. Pierre and Miquelon Islands from Vichy control on December 25, 1941.8

Surcouf would be the only Allied submarine that participated in World War II to be portrayed on a stamp. And, its design was drawn by a Royal Navy sailor at the request of Vice Admiral Emile Henri Muselier, Commander in Chief of the Free French Navy.

Gough and Warner were two of the three Royal Navy enlisted personel who died along the decks of the *Surcouf*. The third was Able Seaman Webb, Royal Navy, when, on July 3, 1940, a Royal Navy boarding party, attempting to seize *Surcouf* during Operation GRASP, encountered fierce French Navy resistance.

It was a bloody sequel to the numerous engagements between the English and the French since the days of Joan de Arc, the Middle Ages, the Battle of Trafalgar, and their bitter diplomatic and political rivalry across the tables of various naval arms limitation conferences.

Hector C. Bywater, European naval correspondent for the *New York Herald*, the *Baltimore Sun*, and the *New York Times*, who, in his book *The Great Pacific War*, published in 1925, anticipated the evolution of SURCOUF in 1929, the American-Japanese War of the Pacific in 1941, and SURCOUF's death by collision at sea in 1942.

Credit: Various sources on the Internet.

The Royal Navy mine laying submarine HMS L-24 (Lieutenant Commander Paul Leatherly Eddis, Royal Navy). On January 10, 1924, while operating off Portland Bill, England, during a mock attack on the Home Fleet battleships HMS RESOLUTION and HMS Revenge, broke surface under the bow of RESOLUTION and was instantly sunk with 43 officers and men. It was the third worst submarine disaster in history.

By some mysterious occult reason, bordering upon precognition and the supernatural, the L-24 disaster had a severe psychological effect upon the *tres chic* Parisian, Mademoiselle Therese Franchcelli (the bride-to-be of then Lieutenant de Vaissau Louis Georges Nicholas Blaison, French Navy).

The marriage of Louis and Therese, beyond any doubt in the author's mind, had a direct connection with Blaison's and SURCOUF's tragic deaths in what is documented in *The Guinness Book of Records* as the world's worst submarine disaster.

Credit: With the permission of the Imperial War Museum, London, 1984.

HMS X-1 was the twin gun abortion that the French Navy avoided copying when it designed and constructed its super powerful, air craft carrying, submarine SURCOUF.

William S. Stephenson, "The Quiet Canadian", also known during World War II by the code-name of "Intrepid." Based in New York City, Intrepid was director of Prime Minister Winston Churchill's intelligence and covert operations in the Western Hemisphere.

His secondary headquarters was at Camp "X," a training center in Canada for secret agents and saboteurs, and in Bermuda where the Free French submarine *Surcouf* was based.

Some French, even to this day, strongly suspect that he played a leading role in the sinking of *Surcouf* in the Caribbean Sea on the night of February 18, 1942.

Credit: With the permission of *Mid—Ocean News*. Hamilton,
Bermuda, May 3-4, 1980

John E. Hoover, Director of the Federal Bureau of Investigation, 1924-1972

Mr. Hoover learned from an undisclosed source that *Surcouf* was sunk off St. Pierre, but his letter to the Directors of Army and Navy intelligence about her loss did not specify whether St. Pierre was a town on the St. Pierre and Miquelon Islands in the North Atlantic or on the Caribbean island of Martinique. Today, if *Surcouf* was found to be at either site, the course of World War II naval history would be drastically changed.

Credit: With the permission National Archives, Washington, 1985.

INSTITUT OCÉANOGRAPHIQUE

FONDATION ALBERT Ier. PRINCE DE MONACO

RECONNU D'UTILITE PUBLIQUE

Monaco, the 8th of January 1980

Mr. Julius GRIGORE, Jr.
International Trade and Technical Consultant
425 Harbor Drive

SOUTH VENICE, Florida 33595

JYC/PR

Dear Captain,

     I should have answered much earlier to you about the Surcouf. The documentation you sent to me was extremely interesting and, as a Navy man, the tragedy of this extraordinary submarine is still felt by all of us.

     Very unfortunately, my little Calypso would be of no help to find or examine the historical wreck of the Surcouf, in spite of the fact that Calypso will be in the Caribbean for several months in 1980 : the depth is at least 1000 fathoms, way beyond the reach of my diving saucer.

     The only hope is to get the French Navy or CNEXO interested. Both have the means for such a search.

Very sincerely Yours,

J. Y. COUSTEAU

Capitaine Jacques Y. Cousteau letter to the author stating that his submersible *Calypso* is incapable of reaching the depth where Surcouf's hulk lays.

However, today's submersible's are entirely capable, as exemplified by having reached the *SS Titanic* at depths of 10,000 feet.

Credit: The Wren Grigore Surcouf memorabilia Collection, Venice, Florida.

When France's leading daily newspaper *Le Figuro* announced the loss of the French submarine *Phenix* in its early June 23, 1939 edition the photograph shown was not that of *Phenix* but of *Surcouf*. Later editions were corrected.

Phenix is shown immediately above this caption.

Rear Admiral Robert Le Nistour, Medical Corps, French Navy, Retired, who, as a Lieutenant de Vasseau, was the doctor aboard *Surcouf* when a Royal Navy boarding party seized *Surcouf* during Operation GRASP on July 3, 1940.

The Royal Navy party, led by Commander Denis V. Sprague, Royal Navy, met extreme opposition when the Lieutenant Le Nistour resisted by killing three of the party, which included Commander Sprague, and seriously wounding another.

When the author interviewed Admiral Le Nistour in 1982, he was met at pistol point, as the Admiral believed I was there on a mission of revenge.

Credit: with the permission of Rear Admiral Robert Le Nistour, Medical Corps, French Navy, Retired, Marseilles, France, 1982.

Leading Electrician's Mate Paul Razo, the Free French seaman, whose death with *Surcouf*, as the 130th man, remained unknown for thirty-six years (from 1942 to 1978). Razo, "The Unknown Sailor of the Free French Navy," boarded Surcouf at Halifax on January 19, 1942.

Razo had been transferred from the Royal Navy to *Surcouf* so he could join his cousin who was already aboard *Surcouf*. This finding was according the Capitaine de Frégate Blaison's January 1942 Patrol Report, which he sent to Vice Admiral Max Kennedy Horton, Flag Officer, Submarines, Northways, London, from HMS Ireland Dockyard, Bermuda, on February 5, 1942.

Because of the adversities or contingencies of war, Paul's name never surfaced during the post-war period so French naval authorities could include his name on the Surcouf Memorial, Cherbourg, France.

It was the author's discovery and subsequent efforts, on behalf of Paul, in 1978, that led to his parents to finally being notified about the whereabouts of Paul, to his name being included on the *Surcouf* Memorial, and to *Surcouf* displacing *USS Thresher* in the *Guinness Book of Records* as the world's worst submarine disaster.

Credit: With the permission of the family survivors of Paul Razo, 1979.

Madam Therese Blaison, right, with Capitaine de Frigate George's Louis Nichols Blaison's mother, Annette, at the dedication of the Surcouf War Memorial, Cherbourg, France.

Credit: With the permission of Service archives historique de la défense, Paris, and Madams Annette and Therese Blaison and Mlle Francine Blaison, 1982, each deceased.

Madame Therese Blaison, and her *Child of the Sea*, Francine, at age near 3. Their photograph dates back to 1934 and was taken off Bizerte, Tunisia.

In later years they were relentless during their quest for the truth about how Capitaine de Frégate Louis Georges Nichols perished with SURCOUF in the world's worst submarine disaster.

During this period, Francine became known throughout France as l'Orphane *de Surcouf.*

Credit: With the permission of Madame Therese and Francine Blaison, Paris, 1981.

Scale model of *Surcouf* showing her exterior amidships section: aircraft, tubular hanger, conning tower, range finder, and twin 8-inch battery. Noteworthy also is her streamlined configuration.

Credit: Credit: With the permission of Service Historique de la Marine, Vincennes, 1983.

Not since Lady Emma Hamilton, Lord Horatio Nelson's mistress, have women appeared as forcefully in naval history as they did throughout Surcouf's embroiled life and after her frightful death.

Lord Nelson is renown in naval history for his devastating defeat of the French Fleet off Cape Trafalgar during the Napoleonic War of 1805.

Credits: George Romney (1734-1802), Artist., *Wikipedia*, the free encyclopedia., and the Imperial War Museum, London, 1989.

On April 18, 1939, the SS PARIS caught fire and heeled over in her berth due to over flooding by French fire fighters. This disastrous episode was widely publicized internationally, and the May 8, 1939 edition of the highly popular *Life Magazine* profusely illustrated the casualty. Thus, with the body of evidence that appeared in *Life Magazine,* which was at the time widely circulated in New York City and throughout the United States, there should have been no intellectual reason why New York City fire fighters did not take precautions from the offset to avoid duplication of the unfortunate circumstance that befell SS PARIS. No excuse what so ever.

In the background, the SS NORMANDIE is shown in dry dock on the on the right is SS NORMANDIE on her side.

Credit: *Life Magazine*, May 8, 1939, *Fire Aboard* by Frank Rushbrook, M I. Fire E., and *Wikipedia.*

Sous-Marin "Surcouf"

Picture postcard of the French submarine *Surcouf* underway circa 1934. During her day, 1929-1942, she was the largest, most powerful submarine in the world.

Her twin 8-inch guns were powerful enough to blow a destroyer out of the water. And, she was the only Allied submarine to carry, launch, and retrieve a seaplane, which was secured in an after watertight hanger.

Postcard maker, Collection Vielle de Marine, Cherbourg, France, 1934

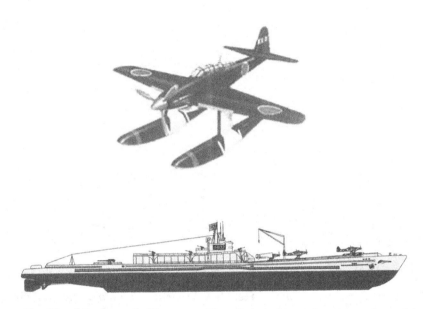

Profile of the Imperial Japanese Navy I-400 class submarine. Operable in 1944, it exceeded the Free French submarine *Surcouf* in size, power, and number of air craft carried. Its Serian seaplane is also shown.

Credit: With the permission of Rear Admiral Zenji Orita, Public Information Officer, Japnese Defense Force, 1978.

Man's admiration for woman, a name that conquers man, never falters. In the mariner's lore, it is told that of all the spellbinders in human form, none is so dreaded as the *fem fatales* or brewers of hell-broth as they conjure contrary seas and winds and wreck ships to abduct sailor's souls.

Some femmes are alluring and compassionate, whereas others were diabolically evil—even great distance was not enough to keep SURCOUF and her Commanding Officer, Blaison, safe from their deadly ways and wiles. Commandante Blaison's mother-in-law was prominently among them.

Credit: *Sea Nymphs on Tile* from the Collection of the Wren Grigore Trust.

The savage cruelty of Surcouf's men during the seizure of KENT, the pride of British East India Company, while she was plying the Indian Ocean, remains almost unparalleled among famous sea fights. Surcouf's victory over KENT, but mainly because of his bitter cruelty, caused the British Government to offer a £250,000 reward for his capture—preferably dead!!!

Credit: *The Seafarers, Time-Life Books,* to commemorate the history of maritime *adventure.*

Some women, like the forthright Mrs. Rosemary Sprague, vehemently detested SURCOUF, as if she were 'a loathsome beast.

Mrs. Sprague was the wife of Commander, Denis Vaughan "Lofty" Sprague, Royal Navy, who was shot and killed by Lieutenant de Vaisseau. Robert Nistour, Medical Officer, French Navy, *during* the *Surcouf Affray of July 3, 1940.*

Credit: Courtesy of Mrs. Rosemary Sprague. 1982.

SS Savannah, the U. S. Navy light cruiser that allegedly shadowed *Surcouf* from her entrance into the Caribbean Sea and to the approaches of the Panama Canal Zone or to offshore of the island of Martinique.

Credit: With the permission of the National Archives, Washington, 1978

Stern quarter, starboard, view of *Surcouf* undergoing overhaul at the U. S. Naval Shipyard, Portsmouth, New Hampshire, between July and December 1941. Her immense size is evident, and it is difficult to accept why she could not have survived her collision with the SS THOMPSON LYKES?

The only probable explanation is that all her watertight doors, between compartments, were open and that she flooded instantly when her hull was penetrated by the bow of the THOMPSON LYKES.

Unexplained is why did two quick, flaming, explosions occurred within her hull as she sank??? Some French believe that saboteurs in Bermuda had planted limpet mines to her hull that were set to detonate as she was transiting the Panama Canal.

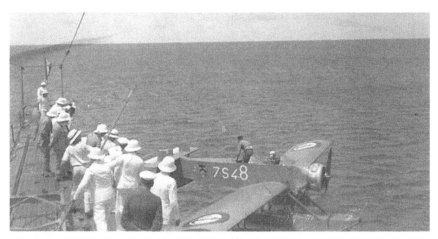

Observers viewing *Surcouf's Bresson MB-411* seaplane which is alongside.

The scene is offshore of the Caribbean Sea island of Martinique, a possession of the Republic of France in 1939.

Ironically, during February 1942, *Surcouf*, flying the Free French flag, *was of* serious concern to the World War II governments of Prime Minister Winston Churchill and President Franklin Roosevelt

Both suspected that *Surcouf*, which had been ordered to sail for the Pacific island of Tahiti via the Panama Canal, would attempt to liberate Martinique from the Vichy French and then seize $250 million of Bank of France gold stored on the island for the Free French government of General Charles de Gaulle.

The beautiful war memorial to the Free French Naval Forces who fought and died in the Second World War stands on the western brow of Lyle Hill, overlooking Cardwell bay, Greenock, Renfrewshire, Scotland.

`````` In the form of the Cross of Lorraine, the emblem of the Free French Navy, integrated with an anchor, it is dedicated to the memory of the officers, men, and ships of the Free French Naval Forces who sailed from Greenock in the years 1940-1945 and who lost their souls during the Battle of the Atlantic for the liberation of France and the success of the Allied cause.

While the names of other officers, men, and ships were referred to, Blaison and SURCOUF were specifically mentioned as follows:

<div align="center">

TO THE MEMORY OF
COMMANDER BLAISON
THE OFFICERS AND MEN
OF THE SUBMARINE SURCOUF
LOST IN THE ATLANTIC

</div>
``````

The author (Grigore) and Mlle Francine Blaison interviewing Vice Admiral Paul Auphan, French Navy, Retired, about the loss of *Surcouf*, which the admiral, in his book, *The French Navy in World War II*, stated had disappeared under mysterious circumstances.

The scene is Admiral Auphan's apartment near Versailles, France, on May 22, 1978. Unusual about our interview is that, in 1943, Admiral Auphan, while serving as the Minister of Marine for the Vichy French Navy, had offered Francine's mother, Madame Therese Blaison, financial retribution for the loss of pay and sentencing to imprisonment *in absentia* of her husband, Capitaine de Frégate Louis Georges Blaison, Free French Navy, because he had refused to serve in the Vichy French Navy.

Madame Blaison, who was secretly serving in the French Resistance Movement at that time, adamantly refused Auphan's offer.

Credit: The Wren Grigore Surcouf Memorabilia Collection,
Venice, Florida, 2003.

The author (Grigore) in the Paris apartment of the Blaison womenfolk during an interview session on May 21, 1978.

Mlle Francine Blaison, the daughter, is on my right. Her mother, Therese Marie, is reading a copy of the last *Surcouf* patrol report to Vice Admiral Max Kennedy Horton, Royal Navy, Flag Officer, Submarines, Northways, London, submitted on February 5, 1942 by her husband, Capitaine de Frégate Louis Georges Blaison, Free French Navy, commander of *Surcouf,*

Credit: The Wren Grigore Surcouf Memorabilia Collection, Venice, Florida, 2001, and with the permission of the Blaison womenfolk, 1978.

The Royal Navy submarine M-2 was an early experiment as an aircraft carrier, which concept was bought to operational proficiency by the French Navy with its mammoth SURCOUF, that also incorporated twin 8-inch guns, and which concept was successfully deployed during World War II by the Imperial Japanese Navy.

Credit: *Submarines, Admirals, and Navies* by Colin Meyers, 1940.

The author, in the foreground, interviewing a former French Naval officer, on the left, who prior to World War II served as *Surcouf's* engineering officer. The author nick-named this officer as "The Skull" because of his facial features.

This interview occurred in Hiroshima, Japan, in 1978. When the author asked the Skull if he served during World War II as Vichy Frenchman he erupted violently and threatened to shoot me.

Later it was learned that it was The Skull had similarly threatened Capitaine de Frégate Louis Georges Blaison, during July 1940, because he had decided to serve aboard *Surcouf* as Free French naval officer.

The gentleman in the center, name not recalled, was a friend of the Francine Blaison, and it was he that arranged the interview.

Credit: Permission of the Wren Grigore *Surcouf* memorabilia Collection.

The Ancient Mariner holds the Wedding Guest with a glittering eye and the Wedding Guest "cannot chuse but hear."

Credit: *The Annotated Rime of the Ancient Mariner*,
Bramhall House, New York, 1995

Vice Admiral Georges Robert, Vichy French Navy, third from the left, with his staff Port de Prince, Martinique.

Until mid-1943, Martinique was officially pro-Vichy, with the U. S. and Great Britain seeking to limit impact of that position on their war with Germany, especially during the Battle of the Atlantic. The U. S. and Great Britain intended to invade the island, but plans came to naught when Admiral Robert agreed to immobilize the French naval vessels if the Allies did invade Martinique.

In June 1940, the French cruiser *Émile Bertin* arrived in Martinique with 286 tons of gold from the Bank of France. The original intent was that Bank's gold reserves go to Canada for safekeeping, and a first shipment went there. When France signed an armistice with Nazi Germany, the second shipment was stored at Fort Desaix, Martinique.

From July 1940 to November 1942, British cruisers *HMS Trinidad* and *HMS Dunedin* maintained a patrol around Martinique to preclude the French aircraft carrier *Béarn* and the other French naval vessels from fleeing to aid Vichy France.

Martinique declared for General Charles de Gaulle and his Free French forces in mid-1943 when Free French sympathizers took control of the gold at Fort Desaix.

Credit: *Wikipedia.*

Vice Admiral Sir Max Kennedy Horton, Royal Navy, KCB, DSC, who, during *Surcouf's* service with the Royal Navy, was Flag Officer, Submarines, Northway, London.

It was Admiral Horton who gave the formal order for *Surcouf* to proceed on her fatal voyage.

Vice Admiral Emile Henri Muselier, Commander-in-Chief, Free French Naval Forces (*Forces navales françaises libres*, or FNFL) during World War II. He distinguished the Free French Fleet from that of the Vichy France Navy by adopting the Cross-of Lorraine as the emblem of the Free French Armed Forces.

Prime Minister Winston Churchill threatened to have Vice Admiral Muselier, "the man with a heart of gold," hanged for treason during World War II, and imprisoned him under the harshest circumstances until it was proven that he was the victim of a Vichy French conspiracy to discredit him, and embarrass the Free French cause.

The Government of St. Pierre and Miquelon Islands honored Admiral Muselier on a stamp for his role in peacefully liberating the islands from the grip of German influenced Vichy France on December 25, 1941. This was the first time since the War of 1812 that any military action had occurred on the North American continent.

The presence of powerful submarine *Surcouf* was a dominant and influencing factor in securing the peaceful political transition of St. Pierre and Miquelon Islands to the Free French cause, and she was likewise honored. No other submarine of World War II is known to have been so distinguished on a national postage stamp. It was Leading Signalman Harold Frank "Plum" Warner, Royal Navy Fleet Reserve, who, at the request of Muselier, drew the preliminary design for the St. Pierre and Miquelon Islands stamp depicting *Surcouf*.

Credit: With the permission of Service Historique de la Marine, Vincennes, and the St. Pierre and Miquelon Islands Philatelic, 1983. Bureau.

It was to Vice Admiral Wilfred Franklin "Pooh" French, Royal Navy, KCB, CMG, whom Lieutenant Francis Boyer, Royal Navy, the British Naval Liaison Officer aboard *Surcouf*, pleaded to remove himself and his staff from *Surcouf* for they would die if they remained aboard her.

Instead of further investigating Boyer's concern, Admiral French reportedly chastised Boyer and had him unceremoniously detached from *Surcouf*.

Boyer's replacement was Sub Lieutenant Roger John Gilbert "Rog" Burney, Royal Navy Volunteer Reserve. Three months later Burney and his two Royal Navy ratings, Leading Signalman Harold Frank "Plum" Warner, Royal Navy Fleet Reserve, and Telegraphist Bernard "Bernie" Warner, Royal Navy Fleet Reserve, died with *Surcouf* in what was the world's worst submarine disaster.

Credit: Mrs. Marianne Nova French, widow of Vice Admiral Wilfred Franklin French, Royal Navy, KCB and CMG and CMG

Vice Admiral Emile Henri Muselier, Commanding Free French Naval forces and Commodore Commanding, New Foundland Force, Rear Admiral L. W Murray, Royal Canadian Navy, immediately following the liberation of the St. Pierre and Miquelon Islands by Muselier; an operation involving SURCOUF.

The liberation of the St. Pierre and Miquelon Islands was the best Christmas present that could be given to peoples desiring to be free. It was what the war all about, and it was one of the first occasions during which people were liberated from the political oppression of Vichy France.

It was also a violation of the Monroe Doctrine and the first military incursion into North America since the War of 1812.

Credit: Courtesy Public Archives, Canada, 1974.

Vice Admiral Gabriel Paul Auphan, Vichy French Navy, after the Fall of France became Secrétaire d'État à la marine of Vichy France.

Although a disciple of Admiral of the Fleet, Francois Darlan, Auphan was vehemently anti-German and made valiant attempts to keep the French Fleet from falling into German hands.

This photograph of Auphan was dedicated to the author during an interview with him at his home in Versailles, France in 1978

Credit: with the permission of Vice Admiral Paul Auphan, Versailles, France, 1978.

Vice Admiral Sir Charles Kennedy-Purvis, Royal Navy, Commander-in-Chief, Americas and West Indies, Bermuda.

Had Admiral Kennedy-Purvis's advice been accepted, *Surcouf* would have been deployed to England for de-commissioning. Thus, 130 lives would have been saved instead of being lost on a dark night in the Caribbean Sea.

Credit: With the permission of the Imperial War Museum, London, 1981.

Vice Admiral Russell R. Waesche, Commandant, U. S. Coast Guard, who appointed the members of the board who investigated the SS Thompson Lykes-Surcouf Collision. He insisted that the collision occurred in the Gulf of Mexico rather than off the Caribbean Sea approach to the Panama Canal.

Credit: With the permission of the National Archives, Washington, in 1982.

Vice Admiral Emile Henri Muselier, Commander-in-Chief, Free French Navy, and others, alongside Cardinal Arthur Hensley, Westminster Cathedral, London, May 11, 1941, after a ceremony honoring Joan of Arc.

And, like it or not, SURCOUF is an intricate part of the history of the Royal Navy, the oldest navy in the world, which can never be erased—just as Joan of Arc is forever woven into England's colorful past. If the powerful choose to forget something in the past, or change it, they can. However, you can't argue with evidence.

Credit: Source unknown.

Blaison's and SURCOUF's death were foretold during a frightful ceremony in a garden pond. It was a demonstration beyond explanation or of being just a subtle influence.

The performer was Blaison's godson, Alain, who seemed to have a psychic power that, through ancestral memory or through some complex mutation of genes, created him as a biological mutant. If so, he was of a kind that required many generations of breeding to produce???

Was Alain capable of looking into another's mind to confuse or twist their thought??? Was he a diabolic mind-scanner???

It was as if Alain were playing out the role of the three witches stirring their black caldron in that famous scene from Shakespeare's *Macbeth* wherein they are conjuring to bring about the downfall of the king.

Credit: *Google Free Images.*

Part V

SURCOUF After Death

The pang, the curse, with which they died, hath never passed away. Like one that hath seven days drowned, my body lay alone on the wide, wide sea.

The Rhyme of the Ancient Mariner
by Samuel Taylor Coleridge

Would the fate of Blaison and SURCOUF been altered had there been a Chaplain aboard to pray for their well-being and for those souls serving her??? So present, his prayers may have referred to that passage from Matthew 24:45: *". . . and ye shall hear of wars . . . but the end is not yet.* Then, from Luke 10:31: *And by chance, there came down the highway a certain priest [SS THOMPSON LYKES] and when he saw him passed by on the other side.* Regrettably, because of the intense darkness of that dreadful night, the Chaplain's prayers would have been for naught since neither SURCOUF nor SS THOMPSON LYKES were outfitted with RADAR to designate the correct side to either for safe passage.

However, there was a hint of reincarnation concerned with SURCOUF's death—as if she were a veritable Phoenix—the legend of a derelict soul returned.

Rumors persisted in the Canal Zone and in Panama that SURCOUF reappeared after she was rammed and sunk by the SS THOMPSON LYKES—as if she had materialized and been teleported like the destroyer USS STURMAN during World War II,12or moved by some war magician, or made an appearance in conformance with Einstein's Unified Field Theory, or that she was resurrected by those dead aboard her—like that ghostly ship in Coleridge's *The Rime of the Ancient Mariner*:

> **Four times fifty living men**
> **They dropped down one by one**
> **And the dead men were at my feet**
> **We were a ghastly crew.**
> **The mariners all 'gan work the ropes,**
> **Yet never a breeze up-blew**
> **They raised their limbs like lifeless tools**
> **The helmsman steered, the ship moved on.**

Not until June 1, 1983, while the author was chatting casually, during Happy Hour at the luxurious Hotel Marriot, Republic of Panama, with John Mann, Cuna Indian authority, and Ted James, Editor of *El Boletin*, a Panama maritime periodical, did he learn what could have ultimately happened to SURCOUF or her hulk after her collision with SS THOMPSON LYKES—such as to give concrete foundation to, and provide a connection with, the many rumors about how she was lost.

During our conversation, the subject of my writing a book about SURCOUF arose. I had asked John Mann if, while he was an employee of the Panama Canal Company, he had read the author's article about SURCOUF's loss off Cristobal, which had appeared in the August 1967 issue of *The Panama Canal Review?* "No," replied John, "but I know where she was finally sunk!"

Of course, I was devastated, and all ears—waiting to hear John's story. But, in no way, during my many investigations, conversations, contemplations, and rationalizations about SURCOUF, or by any stretch of my imagination, was I prepared for what John was about to tell me.

Here is what John, who is a fine writer and illustrator in his own right, subsequently confirmed to me by letter on June 3, 1983:

> You seemed surprised that I knew all about SURCOUF.
> Where I had heard of her, and how I knew so much about her
> loss. The answer: Charles Quarles Peters.[13]

John has written, illustrated, and published two delightful works about the Cuna Indians, who inhabit Panama's San Blas Islands: *Siabibi's of the San Blast Island* and *Siabibi's Little Bird*.

John, a former welder-diver, had worked with the author, from 1964-67, while the author was Assistant Chief of the Industrial Division (the shipyard complex of the Panama Canal Company), Mt. Hope, Canal Zone. The author had not seen John since 1967, although he had often heard of John's activities living among the Cuna Indians after his having resigned from the Division. Subsequently, John became a guest lecturer aboard various cruise ships visiting Panama and the San Blas Islands.

But about John's account about SURCOUF's after death:

> One stormy night in the island of Cheecheemay, in 1956,
> off San Blas Point, Charley and I, while sitting on the veranda
> of my hut, were entertaining each other about things we knew
> or thought we knew, and about our experiences and aspirations,
> when he remarked: 'Did you ever notice, John, how lightning
> (implying that something was out there to attract it) seems to
> always pound the sea in that same place off the Point?" Sensing
> that he may be baiting me, I hesitatingly replied, "No."
> Then Charley, who had been a "Sea Bee"[14] diver for the
> United States Navy, stationed at the U.S. Naval Base at Coco

Solo, Canal Zone during the war, unraveled a strange, almost seemingly absurd, story about how a huge French submarine had been bombed and sunk by an American bomber, off San Blas Point, early in the war. In his telling, I had a strong suspicion that Charley had been there when the bombing of SURCOUF occurred, for he told his story too well. Never once did I suspect a punch line, since he could not tell a story without first introducing elements of mystery and surprise.

He gave the approximate coordinates of the bombing, which would have placed the incident off San Blas Point, and the time it took for SURCOUF's hulk to go down. He included in his story the cemetery—a "Potter's Field" on San Blass Point—as if there were bodies of SURCOUF's unfortunate crew buried there, along with other seamen washed ashore on the Point during the war.

But, there really was a punch line for Charley. Near the end of his intriguing story, he said, 'Well, she was a derelict—a couple of days after the collision what had remained of SURCOUF was observed afloat off San Blas Point, where there was a radar station operated by the U.S. Army.

Asked how SURCOUF could have drifted so far and fast from where she collided with THOMPSON LYKES, John told of an ocean current phenomenon along the Caribbean coast of Panama running almost parallel to the San Blas Islands chain, which the Spanish Conquisitores called a remolinos. These are pools of stagnated water in which flotsam is often driven eastward by sea and wind unto San Blas Point.

SURCOUF's hulk would have been a menace to navigation, along with being a nuisance to coastwise radar stations and minefields protecting the Panama Canal, so it had to be rid of by being sunk.

Did bodies come ashore? I didn't ask. During the war many reportedly did at various times, but to specifically say that some were French off SURCOUF is impossible for me say. Charley, I am sure would have known the answer. It was a real war, and there were many ships sunk off the coast of Panama. Conceivably, some of SURCOUF's crew could have been buried in the quaca[15] cemetery on San Blass Point. It is now covered with shrubs and trees, but burial mounds are recognizable.

One thing for sure, Charley strongly implied that the sinking of SURCOUF was the official action of the United States. There are few secrets in the military personnel across the Canal Zone about the loss of SURCOUF.

Until my talking with you, after not having seen you for several years, I had completely dismissed from my mind the story of the French submarine, which Charley had said was the world's largest, and into which he mixed the story of Vichy French and a mutiny on board. He also mixed in a story of some gold that the Allies didn't want France to have, as well as other political intrigues that only Charley Peters would be interested in.

In concluding his remarks about SURCOUF, John, who has no reputation for fantasizing, emphasized that Charles Quarles Peters "positively knew that SURCOUF was sunk off San Blas Point."

An eerie thing happened while John was talking. Ted—as if he were compelled by some ghostly, telecommunicative event and as if it were someone beckoning from on-board the hulk of SURCOUF somewhere, nearby, in the Caribbean—casually turned to a page of the May 30, 1983 issue of *El Boletin* on which the name of the third SS THOMPSON LYKES appeared!!!

A curious thing about John's story is his suspicion that Charley Peter's had been aboard SURCOUF's hulk after it had presumably been discovered and before it was allegedly sunk by an American bomber. John's suspicion has great validity. John, who was a qualified Panama Canal Company salvage diver, and the author who has worked with divers, knew that divers, if available, are often among the first to board to investigate a derelict or damaged vessel to find and temporarily repair underwater damage to preclude its sinking.

If Charley or one of his diving team members had boarded SURCOUF's hulk, then, it is possible they may have recovered her log or might even have spoken to survivors of the collision. Regardless, how else could Charley have learned of the possibility of French gold on board her—other than through a supernatural force???

There unexpectedly evolved a connecting link with the reports of Charley Peters and John Mann—as concerned the possibility of SURCOUF having penetrated a minefield around the Atlantic entrance to the Panama Canal.

On November 14, 1983, Oliver Hull and the author had a long telephone conversation about l'affairs du SURCOUF—during which the author casually mentioned: "You know, Oliver, with so many rumors adrift about SURCOUF, we're not likely to know where the next one could turn-up. Likely, if you write to the National Archives (which Oliver had never done), asking whatever happened to that Free French submarine named SURCOUF, you might receive an unexpected reply."

Oliver, being the gentleman and scholar that he is, replied: "I'll do that—and we might strike the right person who may find a document that hasn't turned up before." And that is what happened!!!

On December 10, the author was stunned by the reply that Oliver received from the National Archives:

> In reply to your letter of November 17, the Navy's records in our custody do not establish how SURCOUF was sunk. The submarine sank off Colon, Canal Zone, and the prevailing analysis of the time was that SURCOUF entered a defensive mine field and was destroyed by a mine.
>
> /s/ Richard A von Doenhoff
> Navy and Old Army Branch
> Military Archives Division

Although John Mann's input varies with that of Mr. von Doenhoff's letter, as to how SURCOUF may have been finally sunk, both have a defensive minefield commonality.

John's version was that SURCOUF's hulk was bombed to prevent it from entering a minefield, whereas Mr. Doenhoff's letter implies to her hulk had possibly entered the field and was destroyed. However, the possibility that her hulk was bombed to the bottom of the Caribbean should not be discounted—as its possible contact with a mine, if that occurred, may not have been enough to sink her.

The fact that the SS THOMPSON LYKES-SURCOUF collision occurred is uncontroversial. However, because of the ballast, buoyancy, and flooding peculiarities of submarines, coupled with their compartmentation and tank arrangements, it is possible that a section or all of SURCOUF's hulk could have re-surfaced sometime after the collision and that it drifted with the Caribbean current toward a mine field or later to a position off San Blass Point as John said.

Regardless, the author, on February 4, 1984, wrote Mr. von Doenhoff asking him to provide a copy of what turned out to be another elusive SURCOUF document. Mr. von Doenhoff replied:

> The first and only time I saw this document was nearly a year ago when I was searching through the Secretary of the Navy and Chief of Naval Operations records on an entirely unrelated subject. As I recall, it was a one-page communication which merely speculated that SURCOUF had hit a mine off the Canal. Should I encounter it again, I will certainly forward it to you.

And so it goes, when the rumors or misconceptions ever will end about how SURCOUF died—nobody knows. Although SURCOUF disappeared as if she had never been, her story remains open for further investigation. (Author's Note: Mr. von Doenhoff never forwarded the letter.)

The End

The Moving Finger writes and, having writ,
Moves on. not all thy Piety nor Wit
Shall lure it back to cancel half a Line,
Nor all thy Tears wash out a Word of it.
Rubaiyat

Afterword

Now you have the opportunity to play the role of a detective or conspiracy investigator to discover more evidence than the author, with his limited resources, has been able to suggest. Or, you can act as jury to evaluate and pass judgment on the truth of the facts presented. In either case, but in no particular order, determine:

Was there a conspiracy to eliminate SURCOUF???

Did Burney, Gough, and Warner know that their lives were being ransomed (sacrificed) so that the British Government could keep secret that they knew General de Gaulle might order SURCOUF to liberate Martinique for that gold stored at Fort Desaix.

Was SURCOUF "Done-in" to Keep Her From Liberating Martinique????

Why did the Commandant, U. S. Coast Guard insist that the SURCOUF-SS THOMPSON LYKES Collision occurred in the Gulf of Mexico rather than in the Caribbean Sea where it actually happened???

Did SURCOUF have an engagement with three U. S. Navy destroyers which ships, then, had to undergo repairs at Recife, Brazil???

Whether SURCOUF was sunk off St. Pierre, St Pierre and Miquelon Islands or St. Pierre, Martinique as indicated in J. Edgar Hoover's letter of March 12, 1942.

If she is found in either location, then the report that SURCOUF was rammed and sunk by the SS THOMPSON LYKES is a deliberate cover-up. If so, why???

Attempt to locate SURCOUF's hulk at or near Longitude 10° 28.5' North, Latitude 79° 21' West, at a depth of about 8,000 feet.

The outcome of this operation would lend credibility to, or disprove, the content of J. Edgar Hoover's letter of March 12, 1942.

Beforehand, a search should be made to determine if SURCOUF's hulk resurfaced off San Blas Point, Panama, as alleged by Peters.

How did Quarles know that SURCOUF may have made an attempt to secure the gold on Martinique for de Gaulle???

Did a double agent (mole) on Intrepid's staff direct a garbage squad to secure limpet mines unto SURCOUF to destroy her and concurrently block the Panama Canal!

You have been provided with ample clues and facts, now you have the opportunity to investigate further and decide.

However, the author believes that:

SURCOUF was shadowed by American or Royal Navy warships from the time she left Bermuda and until she was sunk by the SS THOMPSON LYKES.

The SURCOUF-SSTHOMPSON LYKES Collision really occurred, but he is undecided as to whether the collision was contrived or was foretold in accordance with the dialogue in Part I.

But, what the author does not know, or can fathom, why or how Eunice Richard's husband, who was a British secret agent based in Panama City, Panama, immediately knew that it was SURCOUF which was sunk on the night of February 18, 1942.

Perhaps the use of powerful artificial intelligence computer programming may be applied as current knowledge-based programs are capable of perceiving, reasoning, and drawing conclusions from incomplete or inexact evidence, or of making a connection between two or more seemingly unrelated thoughts, even though they seem preposterous, to derive an acceptable finding.

Your determinations could lead you to be awarded that $1,000,000 offer by the author if it can be conclusively and officially proven that SURCOUF was not sunk by the SS THOMPSON LYKES on the night of February 18, 1942, or that her loss by collision was deliberately contrived, or that she disappeared in a way not officially reported.

Sub Lieutenant Roger John Gilbert "Rog" Burney, Royal Navy Volunteer Reserve, who, replaced Lieutenant Francis Boyer, was the last of four British Naval Liaison Officers who served aboard *Surcouf.*

Burney, who also slept with a pistol under his pillow, knew that he would die with *Surcouf* for his parting remarks to a Royal Canadian Naval officer at Halifax, New Brunswick, were: "You are shaking hands with a dead man, if I remain aboard *Surcouf.*" And, he did.

Burney was the only submariner of World War II to be honored by a requiem. It was *A War Requiem* which expressed an eloquent plea for peace and denouncing the brutality of war. Sir Benjamin Britten, renown composer, conductor, and pianist, and Burney's close friend at Cambridge University, was the composer.

Burney appears above at age 5, in front of the Royal Navy flag under which he died at age 23 in the world's worst submarine disaster that was of the Free French Navy. Life has its unforeseen twists, and a memory.

Credit: With the permission of Joan Adams (nee Burney, Burney's sister (now deceased), Barn Close, Hayden Hill, England, 1981 and the Britten-Pears Foundation.

Annotated Bibliography

Peacetime Submarine Losses and Major Accidents (1851-1968), complied by the U.S. Navy Safety Center, Norfolk, VA, was referred to with respect to the exact date of each submarine loss. Also referred to was the book *United States Submarine Losses, World War II*, published by the U.S. Naval History Division, Office of Chief of Naval Operations, Washington, 1963. The latter work also contained an excellent Appendix of Axis Submarine Losses for the German, Italian and Japanese Navies during World War II.

Also reviewed were documents about submarine disasters available from the United States Navy Submarine Force Library and Museum, U.S. Naval Base, New London, Connecticut, **and the Investigation of Dirigible Disasters and Marine Disasters by the Seventy-third Congress of the United States, First Session, May 22 to June 6, 1933, which included Submarine Disasters from 1864 to 1933.**

I-Boat Captain, "How Japan's Submarines Almost Defeated the U.S. Navy in the Pacific," Zenji Orita with Joseph D. Harrington, Major Books, Canoga Park, California, 1976; Sunk, "What Happened to Japan's Submarines in World War II," Commander Mochitsura Hashimoto, IJN, Avon Publications, Inc., New York, 1954, and Japanese Destroyer Captain, Captain Tameichi Hara, IJN, Ballantine Books, New York, 1961 were relied upon for accuracy of lost data concerning Japanese submarines during World War II; for information about the I-400 class submarine; about submarine seaplane carriers in general; and for some details relative to Japan's involvement in, and decisions stemming from, the London Naval Conference of 1930.

Remarks on the loss of the submarine USS O-5 were extracted from the author's work *The O-5 is Down,* U.S. Naval Institute Proceedings, February 1972, Annapolis, Maryland.

Information about the world's worst submarine disasters can found in work by the author entitled: *Submarine Disasters: SURCOUF Now Recognized as Worst of All, Shipmate Magazine,* July-August 1980, a publication of the U.S. Naval Academy Alumni Association, Annapolis, Maryland. This article was also reprinted in the Summer 1981 issue of Kings Pointer Magazine, a publication of the U.S. Merchant Marine Academy, Kings Point, New York.

The French Navy in World War II, by Rear Admiral Paul Auphan, Vichy French Navy, and Jacques Mordal, U.S. Naval Institute Press, Annapolis, was referred to for details concerning that dates and incidents concerned with the disposition or losses of the French submarines: AGOSTA, MARSQUIN, PHENIX, REQUIN, AND LA SIBYLLE.

The Director, French Naval Archives (at the time Rear Admiral A. L. C. P. Duval, French Navy), Fort Vincennes, Paris, and his staff members, Monsieur's J. Audouy, Chief, Civilian Assistant, and Pierre Le Maire, Historian, were kind enough to provide a resume detailing Blaison's assignments to various French submarines.

Information about the superstition of threes was obtained from *Encyclopedia of Superstitions,* by E. and M.A. Radford, The Philosophical Library, New York, 1949; from Periscope View, *"A Professional Biography,"* by Rear Admiral G.W.G. Simpson, MacMillian London, Ltd, London and Besingstoke, 1972; and from *Disaster at Sea, "The Last Voyage of the Empress of Ireland,"* by James Croall, Day Books, New York, 1981.

Details concerning the SURCOUF-SS THOMPSON LYKES Collision were extracted from *The Board of Inquiry Report Concerning the Loss of Vessel "A",* an inquiry conducted jointly by the Department of Treasury (Commandant, U.S. Coast Guard), and the Department of justice, Washington, D.C., at New Orleans, Louisiana, on March 10-11, 1942. The report was purchased through the auspices of the U.S. Naval Historical Center, Operational Records Division, Washington Navy Yard, Washington.

Details about the loss of HMS THETIS were found in *Sub Sunk, "The Story of Submarine Escape,"* by Captain W. O. Shelford, Royal Navy, Popular Library, New York, 1962.

Details about the loss of USS THRESHER were obtained from the work of John Bentley, *The THRESHER Disaster*, Doubleday & Company, Inc., Garden City, New York, 1975, and from Joseph William Stierman, Jr., Public Relations Aspects of a Major Disaster: *"A Case Study of the Loss of USS THRESHER,"* prepared for the Office of Public Information, U.S. Navy, Washington, both publications were made available through the auspices of Nimitz Library, U.S. Naval Academy, Annapolis, Maryland.

Details about the Imperial Japanese Navy submarine HADOKATE and prophecies about the start and continuance of the American-Japanese war of the Pacific, 1941-45 were extracted from Hector C. Bywater's book *The Great Pacific War, A Historical Prophecy Now Being Fulfilled,* with an introduction by Hanson W. Baldwin, *New York Times* Military Analyst, and published in 1925 by Houghton Mifflin Company, Boston. Bywater wrote it not as a novel, but as a history of future events.

Hector Charles Bywater was a British journalist and military writer. At age 19, he started part time job writing naval articles for the *New York Herald* and later was sent as foreign correspondent to London. It was there that he became a naval spy for Britain. Naturally gifted with languages, he was proficient to the point that he could pass for a native German. In 1915, he returned to America to investigate suspicious activity on New York's docks and averted a WWI German bombing attempt in New York. Years later, he returned to London to analyze naval data and documents for the Admiralty.

In his 1921 book *Sea-power in the Pacific, A Study of the American-Japanese Naval Problem*, he predicted naval conflict between Imperial Japan and the United States and expanded the topic further in

The Great Pacific War. Here Bywater correctly predicted many actions taken by both the Japanese and the Americans.

The Great Pacific War was published while Isoroku Yamamoto, the admiral who masterminded the Japanese naval strategy in World War II, was an attaché with the Japanese embassy in Washington, D.C.

Bywater died just before WWII broke out in the Pacific with the Japanese surprise attack on Pearl Harbor. He died of "undetermined causes" on the hospital coroner's report, but no autopsy was performed and his body was hastily cremated. Conspiracy theorists believe that the Imperial Japanese Navy had him assassinated to deny the Allied Powers with a potentially important military adviser and strategist during WWII.

Details about offensive behavior, mind control, and mysteries of the mind were obtained from *Espionage, "Mind Spies,"* by William Doxley, Leisure Books, 1979, New York; an article, *Mind Tripping*, by Judith Hooper, which appeared in the October 1982 issue of *Omni Magazine*, Omni International, Ltd, New York; and from and unclassified document of the Defense Intelligence Agency, Directorate for Scientific and Technical Intelligence, Washington, entitled: *Controlled Offensive Behavior—USSR (U)*, prepared by the Office of the Surgeon General, Medical Intelligence Office, Department of the Army, and authored by Captain (now Lieutenant Colonel) John D. LaMotte, Medical Corps, USA, July 1972.

Details about coincidence, parapsychology, and prophecy were extracted from two works by Allen Vaughan: *Patterns of Prophecy*, Hawthorn Press, New York, 1973, and Incredible *Coincidence, "The Baffling World of Synchronicity,"* New American Library, New York 1980; *The ESP Papers, "Scientists Speak Out From Behind the Iron Curtain,"* by Shelia Ostrander and Lynn Schroeder, Bantam Books, New York, 1976; from Robert Tralins work, *Clairvoyant Strangers*, Popular Library, New York 1968.

Details about biorhythm cycles were obtained from Bernard Bittelson's work, *Biorhythm, A Personal Science*, 1980-81-82 Edition, Warner Books, New York, 1980.

Details about the evil eye were obtained from the work of Clarence Mahoney, editor, *The Evil Eye,* Columbia University Press, New York, 1976.

Details about psychokinetics were obtained through the courtesy of John M. Hutchinson (deceased) who provided a rare copy of *The Psychokinetic Laws of Images and Some Significant Postulates* by Robert J. Cassidy, EE, PE (deceased), unpublished, 1966, Troy, Michigan.

Details about the SS THOMPSON LYKES and about Captain Henry Johnson were obtained from the U.S. Maritime Commission, through the Freedom of Information, and through a long sequence of correspondence with the captain, that Ancient Mariner, beginning in about 1975.

Details about the Blaison's were obtained from the Blaison woman folk, from Blaison's wartime letters to his wife, and through personal correspondence with them, beginning in 1975, and personal interviews in Paris and Venice, Florida through 1992.

Details about Vice Admiral Max Kennedy Horton, Royal Navy, came from: *Submarines, Admirals, and Navies,* by Lieutenant Commander Collin Mayers, Royal Navy, Retired, Associated Publications, Los Angeles, California, 1940; *Life Magazine, Admiral Max Horton,* Time Inc., August 2, 1943; *Max Horton and the Western Approaches,* by Rear Admiral W.S. Chalmers, Royal Navy, Retired, Hodder and Stoughton, 1954.

Details about the anthropomorphizing of artificial intelligence were obtained from: *The Brain Changers, "Scientists and the New Mind Control,"* by Maya Pines, New American Library, New York, 1973; *The Immortality Factor, "Man's Search for Eternal Life,"* by Osborn Segerberg, Jr., Bantam Books, New York, 1974; *Engines of the Mind, "From Abacus to Apple—The Men and Women who Created the Computer,"* by Joel Shurkin, Washington Square Press, 1984; and *Artificial Intelligence for Executives,* by Major Richard Allen and Dr. Joseph Poslks, and *Navy Applications for Artificial Intelligence,* by Leslie E. Gutzmann and Sharon M. Hogge, Army Research, Development, and Acquisition Magazine, Department of the Army, Washington, November-December, 1985.

Details about Intrepid and his operations and operatives were obtained from: *A Man Called Intrepid*, William Stevenson, Ballantine Books, New York, 1979 edition; *Interpid's Last Case*, William Stevenson, Villard Books, New York, 1983; *Spy Catcher*, Peter Wright, Viking and Penguin, Inc., New York, 1965; *Room 3603,* H. Montgomery Hyde, Ballantine Books, New York, 1964; *True Intrepid,* by Bill MacDonald, Raincoast Books, Vancouver, Canada, 2001;*Secret Intelligence Agent*, H. Montgomery Hyde, St Martin's Press, New York, 1982; *Cynthia,* H. Montgomery Hyde, Farrer, Straus and Giroux, New York, 1965; *The Super Spies*, Andrew Tully, Pocket Books, New York, 1970; *The Last Hero,* Anthony Cave Brown, First Vintage Books, New York, 1984; *Inside Camp "X"*, by Lynn-Philip Hodgson, Blake Books, Port Perry, Ontario, 2000, Camp "X", by David Stafford, Dodd Mead & Company, New York, 1986, *Will Bill and Intrepid*, Yale University Press, New Haven, CT, 1996, *Donovan of the OSS,* by Corey Ford, Little, Brown and Company, Boston, 1979; *OSS,* by Richard Harris Smith, University of California Press, Berkeley, 1972, *Sabotage and Subversion,* by Ian Dear, Cassell Military Paperbacks, Reading, Berks, England, 1996, and my attempts to personally interview him in Bermuda during May 1982.

Details about the Cambridge Conspirators were obtained from *The Great Betrayal,* by Douglas Sutherland, Penquin Books, London, 1980; *My Silent War,* by Kim Philby, Grove Press, 1968; *The KGB,* by Don Lawson, Simon & Schuster, New York, 1984; *Too Secret Too Long,* by Chapman Pincher, St Martin's Press, New York, 1984; *Their Trade is Treachery,* by Chapman Pincer, St. Martin's Press, New York, 1982; and from many of the publications mentioned in the proceeding paragraphs.

Details about the St Pierre Miquelon Affair were obtained from *The St Pierre and Miquelon Affair* of 1941, Douglas G. Anglin, University of Toronto Press, Toronto, 1966; *Divided Island*, William A. Christian Jr., Harvard University Press, Cambridge, 1969; *Seeds of Discord*, Dorothy Shipley White, Syracuse University Press, 1964; and from many publications in the next paragraph.

Details about the Free French and Vichy French Movements and the Muselier Affair were obtained from the above mentioned works, and from *The French Navy in World War II,* by Rear (later Vice Admiral) Admiral Paul Auphan, FN, Retired, and Jacques Mordal, United States Naval Institute, Annapolis, 1959; *Vichy France,* Robert O. Paxton, Alfred A. Knopf, Inc., New York 1972; *The Role of General Weygand,* J. Weygand, Eyre & Spottiswoode, London, 1948; *The Unpublished Diary of Pierre Laval,* Josee Laval, Falcon Press, Ltd, London 1948; *No Laurels for De Gaulle,* Robert Mengin, Farrer, Straus and Giroux, New York, 1965; *De Gaulle,* Francois Mauriac, Doubleday & Company, Inc., Garden City, New York, 1966; *De Gaulle Contre Le Gaullisme,* Vice Admiral Emile Henri Muselier, FNFL, Retired, Editions du Chene, Paris, 1946; *The Enigma of Admiral Darlan,* Alec de Montmorency, E.P. Dutton & Co., Inc., New York, 1943; *The French Against the French,* J.B. Lippincott Company, Philadelphia and New York, 1974; *Wartime Writings, 1939-1944,* Antoine de Saint-Exupery, Harcourt Brace Jovanovich, Publishers, New York, 1982; and *Vichy France and the Jews,* Michael R. Marrus and Robert O. Paxton, Basic Books, Inc., Publishers, New York, 1981, *The Secret History of the War,* Vol. I and II, by Waverly Root, Charles Scribner's Sons, New York, 1945, and my interview with Vice Admiral Auphan in May 1978.

Details about the analysis of rumors and of lies were obtained from *Telling Lies,* Paul Ekman, W.W. Norton & Company, New York, 1985; *The Politics of Lying,* David Wise, Random House, New York, 1973; *Words Win Wars,* John Hargrave, Wels Gardner, Darton & Co., Ltd., London 1940; *Introduction to Logic,* Irving M. Copi, McMillan Publishing Company, New York, 1986; and *A Concise Logic,* William H. Halverson, Random House, New York, 1984.

Details about the ex-NORMANDIE's burning and her senior naval architect and designer, the Russian-American Vladimir Ivanovich Yourkevitch, were found on various Internet sites.

Details about Hector C. Bywater were obtained from *Vision of Infamy, The Untold Story of How Journalist Hector C. Bywater Devised the Plans that Led to Pearl Harbor,* by William H. Honan, St. Martin's Press, New York, 1991.

Details about the deception by Japanese delegates to the London Naval Conference of 1930, of which Captain (later Admiral of the Fleet) Isoroku Yamamoto, Imperial Japanese Navy, was the Technical Advisor, were found by the author (Grigore) during his visit to Japan in 1978. They appeared in a 1960 brochure entitled *Warships Built by Kawasaki Dockyard*, wherein Kawasaki Dockyard remarked that it had delivered the first aircraft carrying submarine in the world, the I-5, 2,135 tons, on October 31, 1932, the keel for which was laid down January 15, 1930. This was a few days before the London Naval Conference of 1930 convened, and was not bought to the attention of the other Allied delegates present (England, France, Italy, and the United States at the time, during March 1930, when all delegates voted that France should cancel the construction of six other SURCOUF type (aircraft carrying) submarines.

And, Norris McWhirter, editor and compiler, Guinness Superlatives Limited, Middlesex, England, confirmed the author's (Grigore's) submittal that SURCOUF was the world's worst submarine disaster, which was finally published in the *Guinness Book of Records*, Edition 26, in 1982, which record continues to be reported in subsequent editions.

Correlative passages were obtained from the *King James Version* of the Bible; the meticulously detailed, historically accurate compilation of prophetically inspired writings.

Citations about demons, Satan, sirens, and applicable interpretations of and references from the Bible were obtained from *Devils and Demons and the Return of the Nephilim* by Rabbi John Klein and Rabbi Adam Spears, scholars of the Bible's ancient past.

Correlative entries pertaining to Ninjas were obtained from *Ninjutsu, The Art of Invisibility* by Donn Draeger as published by Lotus press, Tokyo, Japan, 1977.

Details about Noor Inayat Klan were found on the Internet: She was born on January 2, 1914 in the Kremlin; a strange place indeed, for an Indian Princess and direct descendant of Tipu Sultan, the last Muslim sovereign of South India. Apparently, the Tsar Nicholas II, his country troubled by internal unrest and impending war, was seeking spiritual solutions to the problems facing his regime. Consequently, the influential Gregory Rasputin, invited the father of Noor, Hazrat Inayat Khan, to visit Russia in order to share with the Emperor's family and court his Sufi teachings of peace and love.

After a time, however, prompted by a concern for the safety of their family, Hazrat Inayat Khan and his American wife, the Begum Sharada Ameena (formerly `Ora-Ray Baker` of Albuquerque, N.M., a niece of Mary Baker Eddy, the founder of Christian Science, decided to depart Moscow during the events leading up to the Bolshevik Revolution of 1917.

Following many adventures, they arrived in Paris, where Noor enrolled in the Ecole Normale de Musique, eventually gaining employment as a writer of children's stories for Paris Radio. The arrival of World War II, however, again caused this peaceful family to flee their adoptive country.

Settling in London, Noor, wanting to do her part in the overthrow of Totalitarianism, became an Assistant Section Officer in the Women's Auxiliary Air Force, seconded to the Women's Transport Service. Her familiarity with France and fluency in the language were qualities very much in demand by the British War Office at that time. The continent had been occupied by 'Axis' forces and the future held in store several more precarious years for the beleaguered occupants of Hitler's 'Fortress Europe'.

After undergoing extensive training in the Special Operations Executive, Inayat Khan, under the code name "Madeline", was the first woman operator to be infiltrated into enemy occupied France, on 16 June 1943. During the weeks immediately following her arrival, the Gestapo made mass arrests in the Paris Resistance Groups to which she was asigned, but although given the opportunity to return to England, she refused to abandon what had become the principal and most dangerous clandestine position in France.

She was a 'wireless' operator and did not wish to leave her French comrades without communications and she hoped also to rebuild her group. The Gestapo did their utmost to catch her and so break the last remaining link with London. After three and a half months, she was betrayed, taken to Gestapo Headquarters in the Avenue Foch and asked to co-operate. She refused to give them information of any kind and was imprisoned in the Gestapo HQ, remaining there for several weeks, and making two unsuccessful attempts to escape during that time.

She was asked to sign a declaration that she would make no further attempts but refused, so was sent to Germany for 'safe custody' (the first agent sent to Germany). She was imprisoned at Karlsruhe in November 1943 and later at Pforzheim, where her cell was apart from the main prison as she was considered a particularly dangerous and uncooperative prisoner. She still refused to give any information either as to her work or her comrades. On 12 September 1944 she was taken to Dachau Concentration Camp and shot on the following day.

Noor Inayat Khan's George Cross was published in the *London Gazette* on 5 April 1949. She is also honored on the Runnymede Memorial in Surrey, for those RAF personnel with no known grave.

Acknowledgements

A work of this magnitude, supported by many contributions and intense investigations, and the power of truth and its implications, was not engendered solely by the author.

Because research for *The SURCOUF Conspiracy* and my other works about SURCOUF was conducted in Bermuda, Bahamas, Bolivia, Canada, Panama Canal Zone, England, France, Germany, Italy, Japan, Monte Carlo, New Zealand, Norway, Panama, Poland, Peru, Russia, South Africa, Spain, St. Pierre and Miquelon Islands, and the United States, most dealing with first-hand experiences, the author incurred an obligation that is widely international in flavor and in depth and scope.

Many kind, knowledgeable and unforgettable people contributed to *The SURCOUF Conspiracy* with their memories, their research and most of all with their interest and time. Then, there were those individuals who responded, unsolicited, to enrich the author's files with information and material about SURCOUF, which they had collected for years—hoping someone would eventually have a use for their memorabilia.

Those who gave their testimonies, in amplification of official records, did so freely and willingly, and some who did, but not willingly or threatening, are acknowledged below or mentioned in the text. Some, as did Intrepid and a former Director, Central Intelligence Agency, claimed failing memory to probably escape their involvements for official reasons. In fairness to Intrepid, his memory was later confirmed to be failing when the author attempted to interview him during May 1982. (You must never, never admit to anything afterwards. You must resolutely go to your grave denying that these things ever happened.)

None of the people who contributed to *The SURCOUF Conspiracy* were required to contribute or had anything much to gain except, perhaps, to want to tell what they believed to be truth, or to perpetuate the memory of loved ones involved or lost with SURCOUF, or to correct what they believed to be a misconception.

By necessity, the author has drawn extensively on the works of many other investigative writers to support his position, many not necessarily SURCOUF connected. He is pleased to acknowledge his gratitude to them here.

The author made many new friends as a result of his concerted, prolonged search, but what touched him most was the confidence and trust given by those who did not know him and who had only his word that he would use their material and testimony properly.

Special mention must be given to three people, who during my early investigations on SURCOUF, took me into their confidence and steered me to the right people and along the right routes to obtain information throughout England, France and Canada. They are:

Rear Admiral Ben Bryant, Royal Navy, Retired, of Glasgow, Scotland and author of *Submarine Commander*, Ballantine Books, New York. (Also Admiral Bryant's book appeared in the United Kingdom under the title: *One Man Band, The Memoirs of a Submarine C.O.*, William Kimber and Co., London).

During the war as a submarine commander, Commander Bryant earned "imperishable fame" for his submarine's effective use of its deck guns against enemy targets.

Captain Robin Gambier, Royal Navy, Retired (now deceased) of Lee-on-the-Solent, England, who, among his many extraordinary duties during World War II, was British Naval Liaison Officer aboard the French submarine RUBIS, April 1940 to May 1941.

Mrs. Rosemary Sprague, widow of Commander Denis Vaughan Sprague, Royal Navy, Commanding Officer, Submarine HMS THAMES, who was fatally wounded during the SURCOUF Affray of July 3, 1940.

Friends and associates, and enemies too, of SURCOUF were eager to talk about her as a great and powerful submarine, but some were extremely cautious, some non-committal, and some were openly hostile and threatening about discussing her personal anguish and the diplomatic, naval and maritime, and political intrigue coupled with vicious rumors which plagued her. For this reason, and because of the sensitive nature of some of their evidence, several English and French contributors requested anonymity. They are persons above reproach, but who if identified would deny the information they have supplied the author. They know who they are and that the contribution they made toward advancing naval history will be greatly appreciated by historians, students of World War II, and the general reading audience. To each of them, my sincerest thank you and deepest appreciation for their cooperation and contribution.

The next equally important reference source was the Inter-Library Loan System, made available through the Venice Public Library, Venice, Florida. At least 53 naval history and various other titles related to *The SURCOUF Conspiracy* were available from world-wide sources through the professional efforts of Pamela Burch, Inter-Library Loan Supervisor and her assistants Sally Downey and Marianne Zann and Reference Librarians: Lisa Bacher, Ann Hall, Ann Lieberman, Melanie Odom, and Lynn Thierry. Without their cooperation, and that of the State Library of Florida, and its tie with the Inter-Library Loan System throughout the United States and the world, this book would have been more difficult and extremely more expensive and prolonged to finish.

Information about SURCOUF that was not available from the Library of Congress and the National Archives was found on the World-Wide Internet, including the OCLC and World Cat databases. At least 250 web sites and blurbs were studied to ferret information about SURCOUF.

Those not mentioned above or below are cited throughout this work. The author, however, wishes to specifically express his appreciation and to say thank you to those other organizations and persons who contributed to *The SURCOUF Conspiracy*. They are:

Mrs. Jane "Jo" Adams, Barn Close, Hayden Hill, near Cheltenham, Gloucestershire, England, sister of the deceased Sub-Lieutenant Roger John Gilbert Burney, who was the last British Naval Liaison Officer aboard SURCOUF and who was lost with her.

Vice Admiral Paul Auphan, French Navy and Vichy French Navy, for his early recollections of SURCOUF and his references to her in *The French Navy in World War II* written in cooperation with Monsieur Jacques Mordal (a pseudonym for Capitaine de Vausseau Herve Cras, Director, French Historical Museum, Paris). Publisher: U.S. Naval Institute, 1947, Annapolis, Maryland.

In company with Mille Francine Blaison, the author interviewed Vice Admiral Auphan in May 1978 at Versailles, France; Vice Admiral Pierre Andre Robert Bouillaut, French Navy, Retired, residing in Toulon, France, who was a Lieutenant de Vaissau SURCOUF's serving as her Gunnery Officer; and Rear Admiral Robert "Bobbie" Le Nistour, Medical Corps, French Navy, Retired, residing in Marseilles, France, who was also a Lieutenant de Vaissau aboard SURCOUF.

Both Bouillaut and Le Nistour were personally involved in The SURCOUF Affray, shoot-out and killings, when she was seized by the British Royal Navy during Operation GRASP on July 3, 1940. Their willing recollections about their determined role during GRASP to uphold the honor of the French Navy coupled with bringing to life the ancient fighting tradition of the corsair Baron Robert Surcouf. who ravaged ships of British East India Company, and about SURCOUF's officers and men before she was turned over to the Free French Navy on September 15, 1940, were invaluable.

Lieutenant Commander Francis L. Boyer, Royal Navy, Retired, Dublin, Ireland, who was British Naval Liaison Officer aboard SURCOUF, April to November 1941, and who provided essential information about his life in SURCOUF, and about the state of affairs aboard her.

Vice Admiral Ralph Waldo Christie, USN, Annapolis, Class of 1915, who provided valuable input about the conduct of surface and submarine operations between New London, Connecticut and the Panama Canal for the months of January and February 1942—the months that SURCOUF was present in the North Atlantic and Caribbean.

Had SURCOUF survived and reached the Southwest Pacific it is very likely she would have come under the operational command of then Captain Christie, who was Commander, Task Force 71, Submarines, Southwest Pacific, operating out of Brisbane, Australia.

Mrs. Lillian Elizabeth "Lil" Gough Cook (nee Persons), wife of Bernard Gough, who was lost with SURCOUF, for photographs of "Bernie" Gough and for recollections of their lives together, especially during his service as Leading Telegraphist, Royal Navy.

Captain Jacques Cousteau, French Navy, Retired, who wrote, in Jan 1980, that the tragedy of "SURCOUF is still felt by all of us," but regrettably CALYPSO's diving saucer would not have been capable of reaching the depth of 8,000 feet to search for SURCOUF.

Vice Admiral Harry De Wolf, Royal Canadian Navy, Retired, of Somerset, Bermuda, for his input regards SURCOUF at Halifax.

Monsieur Andre H. Duchemin of La Chapelle, St. Luc, France, once a Chief Electrician's Mate aboard SURCOUF, for his research efforts in the Southwest of France and his prewar insight about crew life aboard SURCOUF.

Monsieur Albert Duborg of Blanc Mesnil, France, who was one of the few to escape SURCOUF's last voyage and live to tell the author about wartime life aboard SURCOUF.

Captain R. G. S. Garwood, Royal Navy, Retired, who replied to many of the author's questions concerning SURCOUF and her personnel during their stay at Halifax and at Portsmouth Naval Shipyard, New Hampshire and who sat in on the Board of Inquiry into SURCOUF's death in March 1942, New Orleans, LA.

Capitaine de Frigate Alain Le Gouic, French Navy, Retired, whose father, Capitaine de Frigate Eugene Louis Francois Le Gouic, was the third Commanding Officer of SURCOUF (October 1937-Nov 1939) during Convoy KJ-2, Sep-Oct 1939.

Vice Admiral Roscoe H. Hillenkoetter, USN, of Weehawken, New Jersey, who was U.S. Naval Attaché, Paris, during the Fall of France in June 1940, and during the early Petain and Darlan Vichy French regimes, and later Director, Central Intelligence Agency, Washington, 1947-50. (Died on June 18, 1982.)

Mrs. Jules James, widow of Rear Admiral Jules James, USN, for her recollections about life and times in Bermuda during SURCOUF's visits there—while her husband was Commanding Officer, U.S. Naval Base, Bermuda.

Mr. Ted James, Editor, *El Boletin*, Republic of Panama, for his investigations and published articles about the loss of SURCOUF in Panama waters.

Mrs. Barbara Jenkins of the Naval Secretary's Staff, British Admiralty, Whitehall, London, for locating the British contributors to this work.

Monsieur Roger Journee, President, Department des Medailles Militaries des Hauts de Seine et la 558° Section, for his contribution of references to the Free French Navy and for his remarks about Capitaine de Frigate Blaison and Vice Admiral Muselier.

Ms. Ritsuko Kuroji, Mihara, Japan, Hiroshima Prefecture, for her superb translation of Imperial Japanese Navy documents and periodicals pertaining to the monster I-13 and I-400 class submarines, Japanese regards connotations and correspondences appearing in *SURCOUF and the Bermuda Triangle and The SURCOUF Conspiracy.*

Ms. Julia Cousins, retired manuscript editor, *Reader's Digest*, for her editing of Surcouf manuscripts on our premises, especially to confirm and verify sources mentioned and used.

Mr. Antar Makansi, Feature Writer for *The Norwich Bulletin*, who wrote extensively about the SURCOUF Disaster and to the author in the March 3, 1981 issue of the Bulletin.

John Mann, specializing in San Blas Island, Republic of Panama, tourism, for his cogent remarks about how SURCOUF's hulk may have been bombed by an American bomber and sunk around San Blas

Point, Republic of Panama and that some of her dead may have been washed ashore and buried at that location.

Capitaine de Vaisseau Paul Marie Hippolyte Martin, French Navy, Retired, Commanding Officer of SURCOUF when she was seized by the Royal Navy on July 3, 1940, for his insight into life aboard SURCOUF and her operations and his otherwise astute remarks.

Commander Thomas L. Miller, USN, Retired, for his recollections of SURCOUF, and her officers and men, at the U. S. Naval Submarine Base, New London, Connecticut, in November 1941.

Vice Admiral Paul Ange Pierre Ortoli, Free French Navy (later National Navy of France) and first Free French Commanding Officer of SURCOUF; especially for his generous recollections of Blaison and SURCOUF. Deceased.

Capitaine de Vaisseau Louis Jacques Henri Pichevin, French Navy, Retired, Executive Officer at the time the Royal Nave seized SURCOUF, on July 3, 1940, for his keen insight into life aboard SURCOUF and into the Vichy French Navy.

Mrs. Josephine Boyer Vairinen, Corpus Christie, Texas for providing the first clue that something strange was happening aboard SURCOUF while that submarine was operating in the Bermuda Triangle.

Mrs. Lillian Francis Warner, of Hastings, Sussex, England, widow of Leading Signalman Harold Frank "Plum" Warner, Royal Navy, Fleet Reserve, for her insight concerning the loss of SURCOUF, as concerns how she was affected, for providing a profile of Harold, and for numerous photographs of "Plum" and Bernard "Bernie" Gough: Shipmates entombed forever aboard SURCOUF at the bottom of the Caribbean.

Mr. and Mrs. Stanley Warner of Wendover, Rucks, England, nephew of Leading Signalman Harold Frank Warner, Royal Fleet Reserve, who was lost with SURCOUF on February 18, 1942 for their remarks about the widow of Harold's shipmate, Leading Telegraphist Bernard Gough, Royal Fleet Reserve.

Mr. William Zuill, local historian, Hamilton, Bermuda, for his input concerning SURCOUF's presence in Bermuda and information concerning the Bermuda Triangle.

The British Admiralty, Office of the Naval Secretary, Ms. V. M. Dempsey, and the Naval Historical Branch, Earl's Court, London—especially to Mr. J. D. Brown, Esquire, and his helpful Historians: Mr. David Hackings, Miss Muriel Thirkettle, Mr. R. M. Coppock and Lieutenant Commander M. R. Wilson, Royal Navy, Retired, the Foreign Office, and the Public Records Office, Kew Gardens, London.

Mrs. Elaine Gaboney, a hired, professional researcher of East Sheen, London, who placed the author in touch with the above organizations and persons, and who in addition thoroughly searched the records of the The Public Records Office, Kew Gardens, London, for him.

U.S. Naval Academy Alumni Association, Director of Publications and Editor, *Shipmate Magazine* (then editor, Captain Roy C. Smith, III, USN, Retired, Class of 1934), for assistance in finding the several U.S. Naval officers associated with SURCOUF's wartime career and for publishing *Submarine Disasters* in the July-August 1980 and *Needed: Lethal Big Gun Submarines*, in the July-August, 1983 issue of *Shipmate*.

The U.S. Naval Institute Library, Annapolis; especially to Mrs. Patty Maddox who searched for and found rare photographs of SURCOUF while at the U.S. Navy Yard, Portsmouth, New Hampshire.

The Director, U.S. Naval Submarine Base, Submarine Museum, New London, Connecticut for photographs of SURCOUF while she was at that base.

Canadian National Defence Headquarters, especially to the Director, Directorate of History, Mr. W. A. B. Douglas.

The French Naval Historical Museum, Paris; especially to Capitain Vaisseau Herve Cras, French Navy, Retired and Director-Curator, for drawings, photographs, and brochures about SURCOUF.

The Charles de Gaulle Institute, Paris, for input pertaining to the Free French Navy.

The Japanese Ministry of Self-Defense, Maritime Staff College, Ichigaya, Shinuku-ku, Tokyo, especially to Mr. Takami Takeshita, for definitive replies about the development of the I-400 Class seaplane carrying, submarines and things Japanese.

Guinness Superlatives Limited, Enfield, Middlesex, England; especially to Mr. Colin Smith, Correspondence Editor, *Guinness Book of Records*, for including in the records that SURCOUF was the worst submarine disaster in history and not USS THRESHER.

International Graphics Corporation, Bennington, Vermont and Publishers of *The Military Journal*; especially to Mr. Ray Merriam, Editor and Publisher.

International Naval Research Organization, Inc., Publishers of *Warship International*; especially to Mr. Allan C. Harris, Managing Editor.

Institut Oceanograpihique, Fondation Albert Ier, Prince de Monaco, Monaco; especially to Captain Jacques Cousteau and to editors of:

American Legion Magazine, Indianapolis, Indiana
Argosy Magazine, New York, New York
The Bucks Herald, Wendover, Sussex, England
Canadian Legion Magazine, Kingston, Canada
El Boletin, Panama, Republic of Panama
Halifax-Herald, Halifax, Nova Scotia, Canada
Mid-Ocean News, Hamilton, Bermuda
Midweek News, Hastings, Sussex, England
Montreal Gazette, Montreal, Canada
Naval Proceedings, U.S. Naval Institute, Annapolis, Md.
Navy Times, Washington, D.C.
New London Day, New London, Connecticut
Norwich Bulletin, Norwich, Connecticut
Our Navy, Washington, D.C., (1922-1940 issues)
Polaris Magazine, U.S. Submarine Veterans of World War II
Portsmouth Herald, Portsmouth, New Hampshire
Royal Navy News, HMS NELSON, Portsmouth, England
Royal Gazette, Hamilton, Bermuda
Sentinel, Magazine of the Canadian Armed Forces
Shipmate Magazine, Annapolis, Maryland
The Bermudian, Hamilton, Bermuda
The Bridgeport Bulletin, Bridgewater, Nova Scotia, Canada
The Christian Science Monitor, Boston, Massachusetts

The Chronicle-Herald, Halifax, Nova Scotia, Canada
The Kings Pointer Magazine, Kings Point, New York
The Canadian Press, Halifax, Nova Scotia, Canada
The London Sunday Times, London, England
The Mail Star, Halifax Canada
The New York Times, New York City
The Panama Canal Preview, Panama Canal Zone
The Progress Enterprise, Lununborg, Nova Scotia, Canada
The Sun, Westerly, Rhode Island
Veterans of Foreign Wars Magazine

Transcripts of Crown-copyright records in the Public Record Office, London, and the Public Archives, Ottawa appear by permission of the Controller of His Majesty's Stationery Office and the Keeper of Dominion-copyright record of the Public Archives of Ottawa.

Copyright material provided by the National Archives, Washington, appear with the permission of the Director of that establishment.

The views expressed in this work are not necessarily shared by the persons and organizations whose contributions are acknowledged here. Furthermore, the views expressed here are the personal opinions of the author and do not represent the opinions or views of the Department of Defense, the Department of the Navy, or any other agency of the United States Government. Any mistakes, interpretations, or omissions of fact are solely the responsibility of the author.

In concluding, *The SURCOUF Conspiracy* would have been profoundly more difficult to investigate and write had it not been for the encouragement received from my lovely wife, Doris Jean, our son Julius III, and daughter Wren, during the pursue of my avocation and destiny. Then, there was the presence of our faithful friends, *Punk* and *Sushi, Ajax, Atlas, Boy, Tom, Blackie, and Hercules* (our dog and 7 cats around the yard) whose presence nearby was comforting and never a distraction.

Julius Grigore, Jr.
Captain, USN, Retired

Venice, Florida
Oct 15, 1988 (June 20, 2011)

Appendix "A"

The Allegorical Interpretation of Symbols on the Front and Back Covers

Each image on the front and back covers has symbolic significance to *The SURCOUF Conspiracy*; expressing philosophical, psychological, religious, spiritual, supernatural, and superstitious inferences, intentions, meanings. They lend credulence to SURCOUF's bizarre and occult story, relative to how she became the world's worst submarine disaster.

For those who shunt symbolism it is fitting to remark that according to the Hebrew biblical scholars John Klein and Adam Spears, who wrote *Devils and Demons and the Return of the Nephilim*: "God, the Ultimate Symbologist, wove many threads of such implications throughout the Bible's tapestry of Truth to reinforce what He wanted us to know."

The skeleton on the front cover signifies that death was stalking SURCOUF beginning when five others of her class were killed by the majority vote of Allied conferees at the London Naval Conference of 1930. *(I am Death, and have been alongside you for a long time.)*

Skulls have been one of the most powerful objects of symbology in human history, all over the world. **The skull** of the skeleton symbolizes the facial features of the French Naval officer who threatened to shoot

Capitaine de Frégaté Louis Georges Nicholas Blaison, Commanding Officer of the SURCOUF, because he joined the Free French movement instead of resisting Hitler's Nazi forces that occupied Vichy France during World War II.

It was the "Skull" who, in blind fury, also threatened to kill the author of this tale during an interview in Hiroshima, Japan, when Commandant Blaison's name was mentioned.

The protruding left eye of the skeleton signifies the Evil Eye that was enviously focused upon SURCOUF during her existence as the largest and most powerful submarine in the world.

And, one could believe it was an invisible entity, a master controller out of the dark recesses of that Caribbean night, or from the Panama Canal Zone, that deliberately guided Captain Henry Johnson and SS THOMPSON LYKES, through an evil eye or radar device, to maneuver into and destroy SURCOUF??? This is a question to which no logical answer is possible, only to say that ghastly accident seemed destined to happen. Destiny is a fool's excuse for failure. And, the ultimate one caused SURCOUF's death with 130 souls in what remains as the worst submarine disaster in history.

The bright light in the skeleton's bony right eye, surrounded by darkness, is indicative of the small bright light observed from the bridge of the SS THOMSON LYKES at the instant she destroyed SURCOUF on a moonless Caribbean night.

The murky brown color of the skeleton's bones, signify the absence of purity, or that of sin and death.

"666" in Scriptures represents the ultimate in demonic human power and throughout *The SURCOUF Conspiracy* **"666"** is indicative of the malicious persons and devilish influences that affected SURCOUF's tumultuous life before her controversial conception, during her grueling wartime service with the French, Free French, and Royal Navies, and continuing long after her violent and sudden death. *(Let him that hath understanding count the number of the beast: for it is the number of a man; and his number is Six hundred three score and six. Book of Revelation 13:18. KJV)*

The number "3" reflects that this superstitious number surfaces maliciously throughout *The SURCOUF Conspiracy.* The ultimate set of "threes" were Captain Johnson's three course and speed changes, and at the times each were executed; two of which were of his own volition, the other was an alleged message from American naval authorities in the Panama Canal Zone Their cumulative effect hopelessly sealed the fate of SURCOUF and caused the worst submarine disaster in history. Had any one of the three been avoided or minimized it would never have occurred.

> **Quoth she, and whistles thrice.**[*]
> **Swiftly, swiftly flew the ship.**
> **How fast she nears and nears.**

The dreaded Bermuda Triangle is bordered by the names of the three worst submarine disasters in naval history: HMS THETIS, with 99 lost; USS THRESHER, with 129 lost; and FFN SURCOUF, with 130 lost. (Ireland Dockyard, Bermuda was the port from which SURCOUF departed to make her fatal voyage.)

That the Caribbean Sea, just off the southern edge of the Bermuda Triangle, served as the hellish cauldron for Blaison and Johnson to consign poor SURCOUF to the "perdition" of a watery grave makes for reading extraordinaire about one of the most dreadful and penetrating epics of the sea ever told. Beyond being "colorful".

SURCOUF spent a considerable portion of her wartime patrols operating in the Bermuda Triangle, from February to March 1941 and from June 1941 to February 1942, but while enroute to Tahiti via the Panama Canal she emerged from that dreaded graveyard and died along its Caribbean fringes.

Something is very strange about that baffling zone of our inner space as it has earned a most disturbing and almost unbelievable reputation in the world's catalog of the unexplainable occurrences. There, since about 1600, hundreds of aircraft and ships have disappeared, and thousands of lives lost, without a clue. How some strange intelligence, human or otherwise, affected SURCOUF in the sinister Bermuda Triangle will be told.

The Albatross with an arrow piercing its body is indicative of the strong connection between Commandante Blaison and Captain Johnson, Master of the SS THOMPSON LYKES, as both had a strange affinity with Coleridge's *The Rhyme of the Ancient Mariner* that seemed connected to SURCOUF'S death, i.e., she was albatross and SS THOMPSON LYKES was the arrow.

Bill Wisner wrote in *Vanished*: "Mariner's superstitions should be included among mysteries of the sea if for no other reason than their origins are mostly unknown. Besides they form colorful threads in the tapestry of maritime history." Then, Wisner remarked about Coleridge's "Albatross," with its connotations of ill omen, which enters SURCOUF's story insidiously:

> Of all the kinds of sea birds that figure in seafarers' superstitions, historically the most prominent is the albatross, immortalized by Samuel Taylor Coleridge's epic poem *The Rhyme of the Ancient Mariner*. Somewhere, way back, there was born a strong superstition that to harm or kill an albatross brought a sure-fire ticket to perdition. The Ancient Mariner learns this: **"With my cross-bow I shot the Albatross," he confesses. And thereafter his vessel's luck is all the worst kind.**

It is strange facet of this story that Blaison began and ended his submarine career having a strong association with the "Albatross" of Coleridge's *The Rhyme of the Ancient Mariner*, and that Captain Henry Johnson, who had signed off in a September 1, 1967 letter to the author as *The Ancient Mariner*, and who had a harrowing experience with an albatross, was destined to be the man who effected Blaison's death aboard SURCOUF, through the instrument of SS THOMPSON LYKES.

With my cross-bow I shot the Albatross

With his cross-bow (SS THOMPSON LYKES), the Ancient Mariner (Captain Henry Johnson) did kill the Albatross (SURCOUF and Blaison)!!! Why??? To this perplexing question we can only reply, for now, that there seems to be no earthly connection. But, this we can say: In its deepest dimension of existence and meaning, the conjunction of these two men, and of how and why they meet, is one of the great mysteries of the human spirit; that kind of mystery which remains unsolved through the ages of human evolution.

Captain Johnson was an avid reader of 19th century literature and enjoyed Conrad, Poe, Stevenson and the Harvard Classics. One could, therefore, assume that his affinity with *The Rhyme of the Ancient Mariner,* one of Coleridge's three great mystery poems, had been self-induced by first reading that weird epic of the sea. Strange to tell, however, it happened with a more horrible, chilling reality. In his January 2, 1976 letter, this is how he related that grizzly episode, following the slaying of an albatross aboard the sailing ship GLEWARD:

> The belief that killing an albatross brings bad luck to a ship came up on a voyage aboard the Finnish full rigged ship GLEWARD, 3,000 tons, on which I sailed as an Able Bodied Seaman in 1911. She was bound to Melbourne from Sweden with a load of lumber.
>
> On that voyage the carpenter caught and killed an albatross. Not wantonly, but to make a cane for the Captain. The topic of killing the albatross was argued for some length amongst the crew, and it was on that voyage that I heard for the first time:

> **Water,water,everywhere**
> **Nor any drop to drink.**

Captain Johnson's yarn vividly provides hard evidence that *The Rhyme of the Ancient Mariner*, a fable of crime and punishment, was inevitably tied tight as a sailor's knot into his mind, and at an early age.

But more occurred on that long voyage than the slaying of that poor albatross: "Indelibly etched on my mind and memory" is how the ship owner tried to dissuade his determined son from going aloft with on icy rigging "that tempestuous night"!!!

Not until I read *The Rhyme of the Ancient Mariner* in 1928, did I know from where these lines were derived. Since then I have read the poem from time to time, before and after my encounter with SURCOUF.

Besides, as apparent in *The SURCOUF Conspiracy*, SURCOUF continually was an Albatross around the neck of the Royal Navy.

If you accept the connection of Coleridge's *The Rhyme of the Ancient Mariner* with SURCOUF's death, you must accept that it was the *une femme fatal* that killed the beast.

That woman
Death, that woman's mate.

Otherwise, how else could Captain Henry Johnson have been enticed to order three incremental changes in course and speed such as to head his ship directly into SURCOUF, unless **That woman**, a temptress in the guise of a **Nightmare Life-in Death**, had not been preying him subconsciously???

There are many other facets of SURCOUF's story, which amazed me as each unfolded. But one which relentlessly came to thought was the **predominant role that women**—the enchantresses of history—played in SURCOUF's wartime saga on and beneath a souless sea.

Not since Lady Hamilton, Lord Horatio Nelson's mistress, have women appeared as beguiling and forceful in naval history, in the forefront and behind the scenes, as they did throughout SURCOUF's embroiled life and after her frightful death.

Man's admiration for woman, a name that conquers man, never falters. In the mariner's lore, it is told that of all the spellbinders in human form, none is so dreaded as the *fem fatales* or brewers of hell-broth as they conjure contrary seas and winds and wreck ships to abduct sailor's souls.

Some femmes are alluring and compassionate, whereas others were diabolically evil—even great distance was not enough to keep SURCOUF and her Commanding Officer, Blaison, safe from their deadly ways and wiles. Commandante Blaison's mother-in-law was prominently among them.

The alluring pictorial of Francine Blaison, daughter of Capitaine de Frégaté Louis Georges Blaison, Commanding Officer of SURCOUF, and her cat, Robert, was selected to support the accompanying caption because of her intense determination to learn what really happened to her father and SURCOUF and why, and to adamantly refute foul rumors and untruths about poor SURCOUF that persist to this day.

No one should have been deceived by Francine's beauty and charm as they were not in a safe haven if the beguiling and forceful Francine encountered anyone who was even indirectly critical of her father or SURCOUF. Even an adverse comment about the ferocity of Baron Robert Surcouf of St. Malo could unravel the equanimity and graciousness of Francine or her mother, Therese, especially if that unfortunate was an Anglophile.

Robert, that cat in Francine's arms, was appropriately included because of the feline's stealth ability to move deceptively, in silence, and then annihilate its victim such as did that undetectable predator, SS THOMPSON LYKES, when she violently collided with and sank SURCOUF with all hands on that intensely black Caribbean night.

Robert was also appropriate because **"Robert"** was the code name used by Commandante Blaison in his letters to his wife, Therese, when referring to SURCOUF as Baron **Robert** Surcouf, the fierce, Anglophobic, French corsair, was her namesake. *('Poor Robert gives me some anxiety, his legs ache following some rude changes in climate and he has a long journey to make to reach his next destination." Excerpt from Blaison's last letter to Therese before he and SURCOUF departed for the Pacific theater of war.)*

The missing bony right arm of the skeleton represents that SURCOUF was ordered to depart Bermuda for Tahiti with only one of its two main propulsion motors operable. It is reflective of how desirous the Royal Navy was to be rid of its albatross, poor SURCOUF.

It was further indicative that it wanted the American Navy to assume the maintenance and repair responsibility for SURCOUF while she was operating under that command during the American-Japanese War of the Pacific, 1941-45.

Had SURCOUF survived and been permitted to proceed to the Southwest Pacific Theater of War, she would have served under the operational command of Captain (later Vice Admiral) Ralph Waldo Christie, USN, Annapolis Class of 1915, who was Commander, Task Force 71, Submarines, Southwest Pacific, operating out of Brisbane, Australia, as a part of General Douglas MacArthur's Navy.

During my interview with Vice Admiral Christie, he stated that SURCOUF would have never been allowed to get underway during wartime with only one propulsion motor operable unless it was an emergency.

Color, according to Klein and Spears, is another symbol that is part of God's Grand Scheme. So it is apropos for the author to symbolize the intensity of black throughout the front cover to represent that moonless night hovering over the Caribbean Sea when the SURCOUF-SS THOMPSON LYKES Collision occurred. There was not a *bonne chance* in Heaven or Hell for SURCOUF to avoid that "certain shape" which would instantly answer that age old question of antiquity: Where does death come from??? It comes from out of the blackest darkness!!!

"Take away the divinity of Christ," Coleridge wrote, "and God becomes no more than a power of darkness."

> **The sun's rim dips . . .**
> **At one stride comes the dark:**
> **The stars were dim, and thick the night . . . .**

Joan of Arc is shown on the back cover being burnt at the stake. Metaphorically, SURCOUF was a flaming coffin as she sank into the depths of the Caribbean after the SS THOMPSON LYKES rammed her.

And, according to Deborah Fraioli, in *Joan of Arc, Virgin Warrior*:

> The English never feared a captain or chief as much as they feared the Maid.
>
> Not until she was burned at the stake and her ashes gathered, and thrown into the Seine, could the English breathe easily and think about resuming their conquest of France.

Also, Blaison that man with a high sense of personal honor and strength of character and whose idol was the Maid—Joan of Arc—did not accept his sword at the Ecole Navale, the French Navy Academy, Brest, to bring dishonor to France, the French Navy, or to himself.

Blaison lived and died with these noble words of Joan indelibly etched in his heart, mind, and soul: "All the hands of France in a single hand. A hand that is never divided!" When the English shouted at Joan, "Everything is dead." She retorted: "But there is hope, which is stronger." In these words you can recognize Blaison, the sailor, who wrote to his beloved Theresa: "The only real meaning of what I am doing with SURCOUF is to be the messenger of hope, to be he who says, 'No, everything is not lost, France will be saved.'" And France was saved from an eternity of Nazi tyranny.

Joan of Arc also represented the extraordinary affection that only exists between fathers and daughters. With adoring awe, Commandant Blaison would have recognized an aura of nobility about his daughter Francine; her quality of divine fearlessness, such as a modern day Joan of Arc would possess in the face of bureaucratic force or against any undue criticism of him and SURCOUF. With Francine, it was like one of Frances' greatest poets, Pierre Corneille, wrote in *The Wolf's Death*, "To he who seeks to revenge his father's death nothing is impossible."

Baron Robert Surcouf fiercely defied anything English, especially ships of British East India Company and France's traditional enemy, the Royal Navy, whose battle flag, the White Ensign, the submarine SURCOUF, through a twist of fate, which only wars can conceive, would one day sail and fight under its colors.

During Napoleon's war with England, between 1803-1814, **Robert Surcouf** incurred fame, fortune, and title while viciously pirating British East Indiamen in the Indian Ocean. At the time, the British East India Company, established during the reign of Elizabeth I, became the greatest monopoly in history—producing more revenue for the Crown than its homeland. So, pirating the Company's ships was likened to directly attacking the Crown of England and belittling the Royal Navy.

The savage cruelty of Surcouf's men during the seizure of merchantman KENT, the pride of British East India Company, while she was plying the Indian Ocean trade routes, remains almost unparalleled among famous sea fights. This particular Surcouf conquest was colorfully recollected by *Time-Life Books* in *The Seafarers: The East Indiamen,* to commemorate the history of maritime adventure.

Thus, the Royal Navy, and the English, had reason for detesting, the name of Surcouf—a revered name throughout France—even up to the beginning of World War II; when the officers and men of the French and Royal Navies, in their ruthless encounter against each other, spilled their blood along her decks during Operation GRASP, on July 3, 1940. Thereafter, in a war of contrasts, the Free French and Royal Navies formed a blood covenant to defeat Hitler's forces at sea.

SURCOUF, the submarine, was named after **Baron Robert Surcouf,** in anticipation that she, as if she were a clone of the Baron, but as a powerful cruiser submarine with twin 8-inch guns, would seek out and kill enemy shipping as ruthlessly as did her namesake.

For reasons expressed above, and for her service with the Royal Navy during World War II, like it or not, SURCOUF remains an intricate part of the history of the Royal Navy, the oldest navy in the world, which can never be erased—just as Joan of Arc is forever woven into England's colorful past tapestry.

If the powerful choose to forget the past, or change it, they can. But you can't argue with evidence. History is like faith; it is dependent upon what you believe. However, unlike faith, the body of evidence positively supports the thesis that Baron Robert Surcouf and SURCOUF are forever integrally woven into the maritime and naval history of England and the Royal Navy.

Postage stamps are composite works of exquisite art that represent past life in miniature through the events, people, places, and subjects they commemorate. Unlike most other types of art, a stamp reflects an official or semi-official acknowledgement that its subject matter is highly respected as it becomes one of the most distributed works of art in the world.

Stamps enable the artist to insert layers of aesthetically meaningful, natural, pleasing, and stimulating elements. Each one of which expresses transcendent ideas that can be illuminated by adding symbols, words, numbers, letters, images and places to provide the ambiance of allusion of space and time to vividly recall memories and the romance of an era.

Why two particular stamps were selected for the front and back covers follows:

Baron Robert Surcouf, as a fierce looking corsair, but favored son of France, is dramatically portrayed on the French stamp appearing on the lower left corner of the front cover, beside his namesake the Free French submarine SURCOUF.

The Government of the St. Pierre and Miquelon Islands also dedicated three stamps to commemorate the Free French Navy's role in the liberation of these islands from Nazi dominated Vichy France Government on December 25, 1941. One was exclusively dedicated to SURCOUF; the second was to Commandante Blaison and to SURCOUF; and the third to Vice Admiral Henri Emile Muselier, Commander-in-Chief, Free French Naval Forces, who led the expedition to liberate the St. Pierre and Miquelon Islands from Vichy France.

These stamps appear conspicuously among the notable illustrations supporting the text of *The SURCOUF Conspiracy*, and that one, portraying Commandante Louis Georges Blaison and SURCOUF, appears in the lower left corner of the back cover that portrays Joan of Arc, Blaison's idol, being burned at the stake.

The various national flags on the back cover: National flags are a powerful symbol of sovereignty and are proudly flown on many occasions, on land as well as on sea; especially by merchantmen and warships of the nations they represent. Even ancient pirates used flags decorated with the feared skull and crossbones emblem.

National flags are valued much more than just pieces of cloth as they not only illustrate national symbols, culture, and songs of the country of origin. They arouse a passionate emotion of pride and respect in the minds of people whenever they see their flag. Through the centuries, men, women, and children have died to protect the honor of their national flag.

SURCOUF was the only Allied submarine to do service with six Allied navies during World War II:

Between Sep 1939 to Feb 1942 she flew three different flags:

French Navy:	Sep 39 to Jul 40
Royal Navy White Ensign:	Jul 40 to Sep 40
Free French Navy:	Sep 40 to Feb 42

Between Sep 1939 to Feb 1942 she served with the French Navy, Royal Navy, Free French Navy, Royal Canadian Navy, Royal Crown Colony of Bermuda Navy, underwent an extensive overhaul in the shipyard of the American Navy, and died in Caribbean Sea waters controlled by the American Panama Canal Zone Government.

Not all the symbolic inferences peculiar to SURCOUF's story appear on the front cover. Others become undeniably apparent throughout *The SURCOUF Conspiracy.*

*The inserts in **bold** are applicable passages from *The Rhyme of the Ancient Mariner* by Samuel Taylor Coleridge, who was the literary leader of the British Romantic period. Note: the author prefers the spelling of *Rhyme* instead of *Rhime*.

The design, selection, and arrangement for the symbols and illustrations on the front and back covers were the ideas of the author, but the artwork and computer wizardry was done by Mrs. Yuliya Pustovit (nee Shchavlinskiy) of Northport, Florida.

Appendix "B"

The Evolution of SURCOUF

England boldly proved to France the practicality of constructing mastodonic, fast submarines equipped with big guns. Before and during World War I, the Royal Navy leaped into the future with the innovative battleship HHS DREADNAUGHT, introduced in 1906, first flush deck aircraft carrier HMS ARGUS in 1918, by building not one, but seventeen high speed K-class submarines, they were 340 feet long and displacing 1,780-tons surfaced and 2,450-tons submerged, and in 1921 launching its monster HMS X-1 submarine abortion that sported twin, open, turrets, each with a pair of 5.2 inch guns. The result was a technological blunder that gave the naval world, particularly the French Navy, a hint as what to avoid while conducting its own submarine experiments.

However, for purposes of *The SURCOUF Conspiracy*, it is interesting and necessary to relate why the massive K-class evolved by referring to *The K-Boats*, by Don Everett:

> Admiral Sir John Jellico, the man responsible for the safety of British lines of communication against Germany, considered that his Fleet, although superior in gun power, could be

jeopardized during an engagement. Jellico, therefore, requested the Admiralty of 1915 to quickly provide him with a number of high-speed submarines which could operate with the battle fleet in the North Sea, and close behind the enemy to cut off his retreat. As diesel engines of that day could not provide the high speed required by Jellico's Fleet it was necessary to power the submarines by Parsons and Brown steam turbines, even though that kind of propulsion presented serious drawbacks for submarines of that era.

Quite likely, however, the Royal Navy was influenced to use steam driven turbines by the French Navy submarine ARCHIMEDE, which had done an experimental cruise with the Royal Navy submarines E10, 11 and 15.

As evidenced in **Part I: Prelude to SUROUF's Death** and as confirmed by Joseph D. Harrington and Captain (later Rear Admiral) Zenji Oritia in their book *I-Boat Captain*, the Imperial Japanese Navy, was the only navy to effectively deploy submarine based and launched floatplanes during World War II. The Royal Navy could have attained and maintained leadership in this realm of naval warfare had she not elected in 1923 to scrap development of its M-2 class aircraft carrying submarine for reasons beyond the scope of this story to reiterate.

Because, as recounted in Part I, the Imperial Japanese Navy was so successful in the deployment and use of its aircraft carrying submarines, during wartime and because during World War II the IJN elaborated upon the concept of SURCOUF by building three even larger and more capable aircraft carrying submarines (14 were planned), it is essential to briefly delve upon how and why the Japanese were so astute and adaptive in this realm of undersea warfare.

It is known that IJN's motivation for carrying and launching aircraft from submarines, beginning in 1922, was derived from the British Royal Navy's development and operation of its M-2. At that time, the Japanese Navy patterned itself after the Royal Navy, so much so that Eta Jima, their Naval Academy, was a copy of Dartmouth, with bricks imported from England, and with a lock of Nelson's hair enshrined in its memorial hall.

According to Vice Admiral Sir Arthur Hezlet, Royal Navy, Retired, KBE, CB, DSO, DSC, RN, in his absorbing book *The Submarine and Seapower*, the Japanese concept of submarines up to the start of World War II had its origins in the British fleet submarines of the K-class.

Hezlet continued: "The idea of the IJN submarine seaplane carrier for reconnaissance was copied from the British M-2." It was an idea which was to paid handsome dividends to the Imperial Japanese Navy, much to the distress, as was told in Part I, of the American public and embarrassment of the American Navy during World War II.

At any rate, according to Orita and Harrington, Japan began to also work on the concept of marrying the floatplane to a submarine. In 1923, for example, the Imperial Navy had purchased a Heinkel U-1from Germany for their experiments. Two years later the Japanese had a floatplane of their own tailored from the German one, with improvements. It was successfully test-flown, using the mine-laying submarine I-121 as its platform. The floatplane, a biplane without struts, was called YOKO, Type 1. YOKO could make 70 knots with its 80 hp engine and its endurance was about two hours. Orita goes on:

> From this plane was later developed the Type 91 small seaplane. It was the one flown from I-5 in 1936 during Fleet maneuvers, though no catapult was used. The plane was lowered into the water for takeoff. In that same year the Type 96 float plane was accepted by the Naval ministry, after testing by Lieutenant Kunihiro, who later became a general officer in Japan' Self-Defense Force. From that year on, it was the only type aircraft flown from our submarines. It was called GETA because its floats so resembled Japanese footwear.
>
> For storage purposes, the Type 96, submarine scout plane could be disassembled into 12 separate parts: wings, fuselage, tails, floats, etc., and quickly reassembled. It was stored in two hangers in I-7 Class boats and in a single hanger on I-9 and I-15 classes. I (Orita) was attached to I-7 as Communications

Officer during her construction and witnessed many takeoffs and recoveries of this type plane.

Evidence that the American Navy at that line was developing an airplane for use on submarines was found in the National Archives, Washington with date of December 16, 1921:

From: Chief of Bureau of Aeronautics
To: Chief of Bureau of Construction and Repair
Subject: Storage of Airplane on Submarines

1. An airplane is being developed for use on submarines. The preliminary designs have progressed to a point where it is known such airplanes can be stored in a cylinder **22'9"** in length with a diameter of 5'9".

2. It is requested that a study be made of the submarines now under design with the idea of placing a tank of this size in the superstructure for storage of an airplane.

3. It is further requested that this Bureau be informed of the practicability of installing such storage tanks on all submarines of the S-class and later designs

/S/ W. A. MOFFETT

How much the French Navy was influenced by American Navy developments in submarine-borne observation and scouting aircraft is conjectural. But, the *Dictionary Capital of American Naval Capital Fighting Ships,* provided a brief history of American endeavors using submarine USS S-1 (SS-105) as the experimental platform.

For a brief period, in 1923, Lieutenant (later Vice Admiral) Ralph Waldo "Christy" Christie, USN was Commanding Officer of S-1. He reappears in **Part V, SURCOUF's Rendezvous with Death**, as Captain Christie, Commander, Submarine Squadron FIVE, Southwest

Pacific Theater of War, to lend the benefit of his submarine experience concerning the circumstances of SURCOUF's death. Had SURCOUF reached the Pacific, she would have served under his command.

As an aside: S-1 was decommissioned in October 20, 1937 at the Philadelphia Navy Yard. On October 16, 1940, she was recommissioned and made several cruises to Bermuda, training new submariners. She was returned to Philadelphia Navy Yard for transferred to the Royal Navy and served as HMS P-552. It is likely that S-1, while operating in and out of Bermuda, crossed paths with SURCOUF; the grandfather of all submarine aircraft carriers.

What really doomed the American Navy's effort to continue development its submarine of aircraft carrier was the dominant powers of the battleship oriented admirals, and, as Ladislas Farago stated it in *The Game of the Foxes: The Untold Story of German Espionage in the United States and Great Britain During World War II*, "the big bang of the "Gun-Club" (as the powerful clique in the Bureau of Naval Ordnance was referred to) could never work up any real interest in the submarine."

Still another factor defeating submarine development in the American Navy, according to Farago was that: "Between the two world wars, the submarine service strived in vain to gain recognition in the United States Navy. However, it was up against formidable odds as British propaganda against the use of submarines during war was especially effective." It would be black propaganda of another kind that contributed to breaking SURCOUF's will to survive in February 1942.

Farago continued: "unlike the various other new weapons, especially unlike the airplane, the submarine somehow never succeeded in producing a spectacular advocate in the United States. No General Billy Mitchell appeared anywhere to ram against traditions, conventions and prejudices." And, "recurrent disasters with submarines tended to advertise the apparent vulnerability of this precarious weapon."

According to Vice Admiral Christie, who expressed himself on the subject in April 1979, was that the project was discontinued because of the low capability of the small seaplane intended for use aboard submarines. What a self-defeating attitude on the part of the American Navy hierarchy when viewed in the view of what was accomplished by Imperial Japanese Navy seaplane carrying submarines in World War II.

In France, however, there was no lack of advocates for the submarine, and at the time of SURCOUF's conception there were men like Darlan, Muselier, Drujon and Roquebert who rammed headlong into campaigns to make France superior on the sea and under the sea in their determination to spite the Royal Navy.

The French naval mind was seldom one to lag behind the realities of peace or war except at naval conferences when, for example, it allowed itself to be duped at the London Naval Conference of 1930 into accepting that future submarines of the SURCOUF-class be killed. This unexpected adversity was mostly wrought by the insistence of French diplomats and politicians because of the severe financial crisis affecting the world at that time.

But, Capitaine de Vaisseau (later Rear Admiral) Charles Jerome Alexander *l'Croix* Drujon, French Navy, the Rickover of his day, was not alone in this quest to finesse the Royal Navy. The eminent civilian naval engineer Jean Jacques Leon *Camemfort*[16] Roquebert (1880-1963) amply and capably supported him. Roquebert at the time was the civilian Chief, Submarine Section, Bureau of Naval Construction, in Paris, where he was renowned as "Ingenieur eminent en questions de sous-marins", and likened to the Eiffel of his day. Drujon and Roquebert were aggressive, imaginative men. They were highly motivated by their conviction that France required long range, attack submarines to protect her vast colonial empire.

The French Navy had for many years been known to favor the strategy of *guerre de course* and, indeed, some of naval historians claimed that a submarine campaign against ocean commerce had been a French innovation dating back to when SURCOUF's namesake, Robert Surcouf, ravaged British East Indiamen plying between England and India. This line of reasoning and the increase in the size of the French Submarine Fleet, coupled with her small battle fleet and France's refusal to ratify that part of the Washington Naval Treaty of 1922 restricting submarines as commerce raiders, was regarded by Great Britain with deep apprehension and profound suspicion.

But both Drujon and Roquebert, in formulating their theories, were strongly influenced by British and German submarine achievements during World War I. Particularly, both were impressed by the success of Germany's notorious surface raider, the 3,000-ton, light cruiser, EMDEN. Drujon conjectured that if EMDEN could have submerged, with her ten 4.1-inch guns, "What greater destruction might not she have caused." The value of sea-power, was never more clearly illustrated than by EMDEN. (The well documented story of the EMDEN is one of the finest chapters in the history of the German Navy; remaining one of the great epics of the sea. But, it will not be retold here.)

Conversely, should a SURCOUF-type submarine, with its twin 8-inch guns, encounter a surface raider, she would be a formidable foe, capable of out gunning it with her more powerful, quick-firing guns, and then diving to menace the raider with her torpedo armament.

At no time within the French Navy was there serious opposition to Drujon's concept for the submarine cruiser. Actually, between October 1922 and January 1927, France undaunted by movements for world peace and arms limitations, doggedly pursued development and construction of 28 submarines (displacing a total of 41,500 tons); most of which were designed by Roquebert. This pace continued vigorously through the thirties and by the start of World War II, whereby France's submarine fleet was the largest, most modern, and the best in the world.

With men like Drujon and Roquebert at the fore, the evolution of France's submarine cruiser of the future was only a matter of time; mainly devoted to studying the characteristics and performance of Britain's X-1, K, and M-class submarines, and then determining the best features to embody in their own goliath.

It is appropriate here to break the mainstream of *The SURCOUF Conspiracy* to tell more about Roquebert and why it had been difficult to obtain much background information concerning this intriguing Frenchman. Much will become evident through the following portions of an unprecedented January 25, 1978 letter received from his son, Captain

Michel Roquebert, French Navy, Retired. Also, from its privileged content we will obtain an insight into early careers of Vice Admirals Darlan and Muselier as they related to Roquebert and SURCOUF.

Rear Admiral Jean Leon Roquebert, French Navy, who designed the submarine SURCOUF, which was introduced to the naval world in 1929, and which died in 1942 in what remains as the worst submarine disaster in history.

During her life span, SURCOUF was not only the world's largest and most powerful submarine, but she was also an aircraft carrier.

Credit: With the permission of the Roquebert family, 1978.

Dear Captain Grigore,

    I have to very much apologize because, first, I am so late in answering your letter. Second, my English is rather poor. Third, I am afraid that I will not be able to answer all your questions.

My father had many children, eight in all, among them 3 sons. My brothers spent many years in the Army (World War II, Vietnam, Algeria). As for myself, I was born in 1915 and was rather young in years when SURCOUF was designed, constructed and launched.

Nevertheless, I shall try to answer some of your questions.

First, I must say that it was with great emotion that I learned from Francine Blaison that you were writing SURCOUF AND THE ROYAL NAVY and that you were interested in everything concerning my father.

My father was quiet out of the ordinary, extremely clever, imbued with Duty, Honor, Devotion to France, without any moral weakness or compromise, but keenly aware of human and social foibles and problems. He was extremely modest and hated to speak of himself and of his many accomplishments, or how he felt personally. On the other hand, he was always ready to listen to you and to give advice if you asked for it.

All of his children were deeply devoted to him. He never was actually in the French Navy as you believed he was. In 1899 he entered Ecole Polytechnique and when his two years in this great school were completed he chose to enter the Corps of Ingenieur du Genie Maritime, that is to say he became a Naval Engineer.

At that time, young naval technical school engineers-in-training, before entering, were required to train for that profession aboard the same training cruiser as did midshipmen of the French Naval Academy. The name of this cruiser was DUGUAY—TROUIN operating out of Brest, and he spent nine months on her, from October 1901 to July 1902. It was at that time that he met on board DUGUAY-TROUIN, Darlan and Muselier as well as many other midshipmen who became famous in the French Navy. However he was not particularly friendly with either one. (I may add that many years later, 1925-1942; relations between Darlan, Muselier, and my father were rather difficult, but not for moral reasons.)

After two years at the Genie Maritime, Cherbourg, my father was appointed, in 1906, a naval engineer at the Navy Shipyard, Cherbourg. His early years there he was assigned to destroyer construction and maintenance. It was about 1911 that he shifted to submarine construction at Cherbourg. In 1918 he was transferred to Paris to work in the Service Technique des Construction Navales, which is comparable to your navy's Naval Ships Systems Command in Washington, where he was the civilian in charge of submarine design.

Then, in 1933, he was appointed to work in the department of naval construction at Brest in an understudy capacity. My father remained in this position until 1935. During this time he fathered the design of most of France's submarine fleet: 9 of the 1,100 ton, REQUIN-class, 33 of the, 1,500-ton, REDOUBTABLE-class, 6 of the 900-ton, RUBIS-class, 9 of the 600 ton, MINERVE-class, and, of course, the 2,880-ton SURCOUF. It was on November 20, 1934 that the French Navy awarded my father the Officer de l'Ordre de Leopold in recognition for his conception of SUROUF.

In 1935, he was made Director of Naval Construction at Lorient and in 1937 he was transferred back to Brest as Director of Naval Construction at that yard, where many new cruisers and battleships where dry docked and overhauled; more than 70 ships of the French Atlantic Fleet were berthed and maintained at Brest. It was while he was at Brest that received the Commandeur de la Legion d'Honor on December 31, 1935 in recognition for his design of most of the submarines of the French Fleet.

At Brest, is where I found my father during the sad days of defeat for France in June 1940. Many repairs were done under his authority to ready ships for war at sea in his department, among them being SURCOUF. I do not know his particular feelings about SURCOUF during those awful hectic days for France. At that time, I was on board a destroyer fighting the Italians.

Relating to the professional activities of my father as a civilian submarine designer, I have to confess that I somewhat unaware of all his activities in this area. But on the naval staff side, the officer corresponding to my father's position was Capitaine de Vaisseau Charles Jerome Alexander Drujon, who was Chief, Bureau of Submarines. Also, my father spent even more time with a Chief, Bureau of Submarines other than with Drujon. The latter chief's name was Rear Admiral Paul Auphan, who is still living at the age of 83, and I believe it will be to your benefit to write to him regarding some of your inquiries about SURCOUF's evolution. [Subsequently, the author, in the company of Francine Blaison, met with Vice Admiral Auphan in his home outside of Versailles, France.]

Darlan, who was Chief of Staff to the Minister of the French Navy, the same as being the Chief of Naval Operations in your Navy, during SURCOUF's early conception, had much to do with defining the needs of the French Navy and then having them presented to Parliament by the Minister of Marine to obtain authorization of funds for construction. You know that the naval construction programs are defined by the naval staff and then by naval engineers such as my father, who interprets their requirements after much consulting back and forth, into realistic design and construction plans and specifications.

My father told me that the program for SURCOUF, because of her being a submarine cruiser with heavy artillery and capable of carrying an aircraft, was not only very difficult to have approved by the ministry but by the parliamentarians as well. Then, he mentioned the many arduous technical problems that were required to be solved during the three or four years that preceded her construction. Because of her uniqueness, he had to imagine a number of new and different solutions to the problems that his design effort presented. *(And here is the mind which hath wisdom. Revelations 17:9 KJV)*

Profile of *Surcouf* showing her interior arrangement and compartmentation.

Credit: With the permission of Service Historique de la Marine, Vincennes, 1983.

SURCOUF's Principle Capabilities, Characteristics, and Performance Data

LE SURCOUF, CONCEPTION AND DESIGN

In Accordance with the Terms and Conditions of the London Naval Conference of 1930
Admiralty Building, London, 1930

Each of the High Contracting Parties may, however, retain, build or acquire a maximum number of three submarines of a standard displacement not exceeding 2,800 tons (2,845 metric tons); these submarines may carry guns not above 6.1" (155 mm.) caliber. Within this number, France may retain one unit, already launched of 2,880 tons (2,926 metric tons), with twin guns of the caliber of which is 8" (203 mm.).

Thus, permission was granted by the major naval powers of the world for the newly launched *Surcouf* to remain alive. It was not through just kindness that this great submarine was to remain in service as it was closely watched by all nations during its trials to determine even the utter feasibility of copying its design. The idea for such a submarine was conceived in the minds of only a few progressive French mariners who had learned well the harsh lessons taught by the German submarines in World War I. Their realization of the submarine's usefulness and its utilization to fulfill France's future needs of colonial protection was to developed into the world's largest submarine.

When the war ended and the world believed that the last war had been fought, the French naval chiefs were profoundly aware of the huge losses inflicted upon the Allied merchant fleets by the German U-boats. In their approach to the study of the submarine as a future naval combatant weapon, they regarded the boat as a fist on the extended naval arm, capable of striking a damaging surprise blow at long ranges. Many questions concerning design, construction, tactics and strategy were reviewed by naval commissions of investigation throughout the decade beginning in 1920.

Most of these commissions met and adjourned without any real constructive achievements except for several various vital questions that were raised which, when later brought together and answered by the proper persons, were to profoundly influence the design of the *Surcouf.*

These are the principle characteristics and features of SURCOUF as she was built and commissioned:

Cruising range (miles)	12,000 at 10 knots
Endurance:	90 days
Complement:	125 (including a doctor and aircraft pilot, with hospital and space for 40 prisoners.)
Length:	110 meters (361,7 feet)
Beam:	9 meters (29,5 feet)
Displacement (tons):	Submerged: 3,250, Surfaced: 4,300
Bridge deck height above Load waterline:	8 meters (26,24 feet)
Armament:	
Torpedo tubes:	12 (6 forward, 6 aft).
Torpedoes carried:	22 of 21,7-inch diameter.
Guns:	203mm, twin, (8-inch), with 300 projectiles per gun. 27 mm (twin) anti-aircraft. 30 cal. machine gun, four.
Engines:	2-Sulzer diesels@7,600 shp.
Propellers:	2
Rudders:	1
Speed (Surfaced/Submerged) knots:	18/10.
Motors, electric:	3,400 @shp
Diving depth (feet):	420
Submerged endurance (hours):	60@5 knots.
Submergence rate:	1 minute, 10 seconds, with bridge underwater and 2 minutes, 15 seconds submerged to 18 meters.
Aircraft carried:	1-Besson, MB 411, floatplane.
Motor launch:	1

Notes

According to Don McCombs and Fred L. Worth, in *World War II Super Facts*, Vichy was the unoccupied but pro-Nazi portion of France, during World War II, after the surrender of France in June 1940—with Marshal Petain as head of state.

Petain (1856-1951) was put on trial for collaborating with the Germans and was sentenced to death, but this was commuted to life imprisonment.

Jean Francois Darlan (1881-1942), a legend of his time and within his own mind, was the French Admiral of the Fleet and Commander-in-Chief of the French Navy, but fiercely anti-British, at the time of the surrender of France. Instead of surrendering the French Fleet to the British, which may have turned the war against Hitler, Darlan was persuaded by Petainists, and by his own ambition, to switch allegiance from the Allies fighting Germans to one of also collaborating with the Germans, Italians and Japanese, the Axis Powers. In doing so, he joined the Petain Government as Minister of Marine and Commerce.

About Darlan's action, Robert Murphy, in *Diplomats Among Warriors*, wrote:

He made the French Fleet more powerful than any time in history while he was Commander-in-Chief of the Navy.

His influence was so great that he could have taken the fleet aboard if he had chosen to repudiate the Armistice, as de Gaulle and Vice Admiral Emile Muselier did. However, Darlan believed Britain was defeated and that France must negotiate independently with triumphant Germany.

The attraction of the Darlan mystic and forcefulness of his leadership was evidenced by the fact that of the 18,000 French sailors in England, at the time of de Gaulle's radio appeal to them from London, on June 18, 1940, only about 200 remained to join him in his fight against Hitler. And of the 500 officers, only about 50 broke ranks with Darlan. About 29 sailors, but no officers, at that time joined the Free French Navy from off SURCOUF.

Ironically, Darlan, although never overly armored by the British Admiralty, held several British decorations, including the Knight Grand Cross of the Victoria Order.

Darlan, referred to as the "turn-coat admiral", again changed allegiance upon the Allied invasion of North Africa (Operation TORCH) on November 8, 1942, but proved an embarrassment to General Dwight D. Eisenhower, U.S. Army, Supreme Allied Commander (1890-1969). The problem was solved when, on Christmas Eve of 1942, Darlan was assassinated in Algiers by Ferdinan Bonnie de la Chappille, a young Frenchman who had been in training to become a British agent.

According to George Mikes, in *Darlan, A Study*:

Throughout the two years (following the Fall of France to his assassination) Darlan remained faithful to his guiding principle: not to be faithful to anyone. He betrayed the Germans, he betrayed Petain, and he betrayed France.

To Mr. Mike's comment, the author adds that Darlan, the manipulator striving for omnipotence and omnipower, also betrayed the French Navy, the Royal Navy, and the Allied Free World.

With this rundown on Darlan, it is understandable that those who followed him, especially during World War II, were called Darlanists.

Darlanists of the time were not all located in Vichy. They were scattered throughout the world, including the United States and Canada, and represented anyone who believed in Vichyism and those who, among the French Navy of the Third Republic of France, remained loyal to him before and long after the surrender of France—even to this day.

Under the regime of Marshal Petain two admirals, Darlan and Platon, were ministers; another, Rear Admiral Decoux, was Governor of Indochina; Admiral Michelier was Resident General of Tunisia; another (Robert) was High Commissioner of the French Antilles (Martinique) and Guiana; still another was Perfect of Police in Paris; an admiral was Director of Ecole Nationale de Police; and many more were prefects throughout Unoccupied (Vichy) France.

[2]   Sir Alexander was a lineal descendent of William, Earl of Cadogan, Quartermaster-General and Chief of Tactical Combat Intelligence during the late years of the war of the Spanish Succession, 1701-1708.

It is also noteworthy to mention that, according to H. Montgomery Hyde, in *Secret Intelligence Agent*, Sir "Alec", in his position as Permanent Undersecretary of Foreign Affairs, was nominally-in-charge of MI-6 ("Six"), as the Foreign Secretary did not usually interest himself very much in the matter of secret intelligence.

This fact was also confirmed by Anthony Cave Brown, in *The Last Hero, Wild Bill Donovan*: "MI-6 was responsible to the Permanent Secretary at the Foreign Office, the SIS had many branches and functions, but its general labors were divided into acquisition of secret intelligence by all means throughout the world, and counterespionage outside the British Isles."

It is pertinent to note that, according to *The Secret Betrayal, 1944-47,* by Nikolai Tolstoy, Sir Alexander was in the Foreign Office, when the Churchill and Eden Governments condemned nearly 6,000,000 Russians, in territories overrun by the Allies during World War II, to be sent to the Soviet Union without choice. It meant certain death and torture for most, many whom were slave laborers and prisoners of war under the Nazis, civilians, anti-Communist fighters, and women and children. "The Under-Secretary, Sir Alexander Cadogan, wrote that the whole awkward business had 'been cleared up by a most satisfactory assurance [from] Stalin."

3   MI-5 ("Five"), responsible for counter-espionage, counter-sabotage, and counter-subversion in all British territory, usually hands their cases over to Special Branch, Scotland Yard, for arrest as it does not have any formal powers to make arrests or to seek prosecutions in Defense of the Realm.

Nigel West (nom de plume for Rupert Aliason), a military historian and writer specializing in intelligence matters, expressed a conviction in *A Matter of Trust,_1945-71,* that MI-5 "was penetrated during the war by the Russians". This becomes an important consideration when the subject of Communist penetration of Intrepid's British Security Coordination, New York, is discussed in depth.

West's book was published in the United States as *The Circus, MI5 Operations 1945-1972.* A copy of his manuscript for *Circus* was stolen by a senior MI-5 officer in an attempt to stop its being published. On October 12, 1982, the High Court of Justice of Great Britain (Mr. Justice Russell) issued an injunction against publication of this book or any part of it. But, the American publisher had already hand-carried a copy of the manuscript from London to New York a month earlier.

West, in his book MI-5, *British Security Service Operations 1909-1945*, wrote:

> There is good reason for the dearth of information about what is arguably Britain's most secret government department. Its staff are prohibited from publishing their memoirs and there are virtually no papers stored at the Public Records Office.

⁴ Rear Admiral Sir Gerald Dickens, Royal Navy, grandson of the author Charles Dickens, was Director, Naval Intelligence (1931-34) during which period he vainly attempted to warn his superiors about the menace from Japan and the significance of her aircraft carrier building.

Very likely that Admiral Dickens, who according to Gardiner was a friend and collaborator of [Admiral] Richmond's, also may have had a hand in getting young Burney into the Royal Navy, and in obtaining for him his liaison assignment aboard SURCOUF.

⁵ That medical doctor was not quite right. There was another admiral jailed in Pentonville. He was full Admiral Sir Barry Domville, KBE, CB, GMG, Royal Navy, Retired, former Deputy for Naval Intelligence, Admiralty, 1927-39, President of the Royal Naval War College, Greenwich, 1932-34, and honored by King George V by creating him a Knight Commander of the Most Excellent Order of the British Empire. Despite his impressive credentials, he was an accused infiltrating the Establishment with fascist ideas and being a Nazi-sympathizer and an avowed enemy of Churchill's.

Admiral Domville survived his imprisonment to write about his harrowing ordeal in *From Admiral to Cabin Boy*; *Cabin* in the title of his work referred to his dismal cell, 18B in Wing "F", at Brixton Prison, where Muselier was also imprisoned.

Admiral Domville was an outspoken critic against the England's Labor Party and of her participation in, and her naval disarmament resulting from, the Washington Naval Conference of 1922 and the London Naval Conferences of 1930 and 1936.

He referred to the Right Honorable A.V. Alexander, the First Lord of the Admiralty, during the London Naval Conference of 1930 and during World War II, as being nothing more than "a grocer at sea."

Admiral Domville's description of his horrendous life at Brixton Prison, just a sample of what Muselier experienced, is incredible reading.

One of the guards wished to force me to remove the buttons of the coat. It required, after my refusal, the intervention of the director of the prison for me to keep these buttons on my overcoat.

The director instead wanted to make me remove my rosette as Commander of the Legion of Honor. I refused point blank, at the risk of being obliged to defend myself. I must confess that he didn't insist. I obtained permission to write Dickens, the guard returned me to my cell furious at not having gained anything at my expense. He made me a sign that indicated without any doubt that I would be hanged.

6   Also known as the Free French Deuxieme Bureau. BCRA was under the direction of a Colonel "Passy", the nom de guerre for an artillery officer, Colonel Andre Dewavrin, Free French Army, and graduate of and military professor at St. Cyr, the West Point of the French Army.

Richard Harris Smith, in OSS, *The Secret History of America's First Central Intelligence Agency*, wrote of the BCRA: "Passy's BCRA [which was on friendly terms with the British MI-6] was depicted by some critics as a Gestapo-in-miniature which kidnapped and even murdered Frenchmen in London who refused to swear allegiance to General de Gaulle."

Again according to Smith: "In 1947, on the demand of his leftist enemies in the French Government, Dewavrin was arrested and imprisoned on the charge of misappropriating funds of the French intelligence service."

7   Mr. A. V. Alexander (later Viscount Alexander of Hillsborough, KG, PC, and CH), First Lord of the Admiralty ("Alexander's Ragtime Band"), who, along with Italian, Japanese, and United States Delegates at the London Naval Conference of 1930, was responsible for killing the SURCOUF-class submarine for the French navy.

Leslie Gardiner described Alexander, in *The British Admiralty*, as "a nebulous, slightly menacing figure at the Admiralty, and who during his tenures as First Lord, 1929-33 and 1940-45, "was at the centre of betrayals, compromises, heroisms, intrigues, surrenders of the 'battle of Whitehall', and [other] mysterious events which remain, and probably always will remain only partially explained."

8   On the basis of what was just told, and from a reading of content within the Notes, one could easily conclude that Younger probably gained his transfer from MI-5 to the Foreign Office through the influence of Maclean, who was already deeply burrowed there as a subversive Communist mole while serving as a Second Secretary.

In October 1962, Younger, as a former Labour MP from Grimsby, was one of three senior civil servants, with previous intelligence experience, selected by Prime Minister Harold MacMillian to serve on the Radcliffe Tribunal (Lord Radcliffe) to inquire into the Vassall Affair. William John Christopher Vassall, as a clerk to the Naval Attaché, had served in the British Embassy in Moscow and admitted to spying for the Russians for seven years under threat of blackmail. With companions such as Blunt-Burgess-Maclean-Philby, it is likely that Younger should have been the last person in England to have been selected to investigate the guilt of a Soviet spy.

In 1940, journalist and Soviet agent Kim Philby applied for a vacancy in Section D of SIS (Secret Intelligence Service), and was vetted by his friend and fellow Soviet agent Guy Burgess. When Section D was absorbed by Special Operations Executive (SOE) in summer of 1940, Philby was appointed as an instructor in the arts of "black propaganda" at the SOE's training establishment in Beaulieu, Hampshire.

Another bit of information reported about Blunt that has a possible connection with this story, is what Sutherland also remarked: "There seems to have been the question of Allied governments-in-exile in London. Blunt seems to have had access to MI-5 information about them." The Free French government, as well as the Free Polish governments, were Allied governments-in-exile. The leaders of both these governments-in-exile, General de Gaulle and General Sikorski, had attempts made on their lives while they were under British protection. The story of the attempt upon General de Gaulle's life, and of how General Sikorski was killed (in the crash of Liberator AL 523 at Gibraltar) while flying in a British aircraft, will be related in this story.

From the foregoing, one could also conclude that the arrest of Muselier on the basis of forged documents, in which Younger play a leading role, could have been a covert conspiracy which also involved Blunt, a known Communist, in connivance with Vichy agents. In a later footnote you shall read of how a Bolivian diplomat was implicated by documents forged under the watchful eyes of H. Montgomery Hyde, a member of Intrepid's British Coordination Security, New York, and who emerges as a leading character in this work.

Younger, in what could be another probable Communist connection with this story, was further identified, through the work of Nigel West, MI-5, and *A Matter of Trust, MI5, 1945-72*, as a scion of an Scottish brewing family and the wartime director of "E" Division, the MI-5 department responsible for supervision of aliens: neutral, friendly, and otherwise.

It is a curious thing, but having discovered who Younger was through *Wikipedia* and the work of West, his name also appeared conspicuously in *The Great Betrayal, The Definitive Story of the Most Sensational Spy Case of the Century,* by Douglas Sutherland, and in *The Fourth Man, The*

Definitive Account of Kim Philby, Guy Burgess, Anthony Blunt, and Donald Maclean and Who Recruited Them to Spy for Russia, by Andrew Boyle.

Each of the persons named in the sub-title for Boyle's work have been officially identified by the British Government as being the Cambridge Communist Conspirators.

Captain Anthony Blunt, British Royal Army, Intelligence Corps, following his escape from the beaches of Dunkirk, in June 1940, was recruited into MI-5, Section B1(b), a hybrid counter-espionage activity devoted to the art of assessment of the enemy, but within the same organization as Younger. Ordinarily this could be considered as a coincidence, but in the author's opinion, it was not. Blunt, promoted to Major in 1945, remained with MI-5 until 1946.

In 1982, after Blunt's cover as a Communist KGB agent and a double agent within the British Secret Service since 1935 was exposed, and during his interrogation, he was asked how he managed to get accepted by MI-5. He replied that it was on the recommendation of a friend who was already a member. "He has refused to divulge the name of his sponsor," wrote Sutherland.

The works of Boyle and Sutherland give strong evidence that the sponsoring friend may have been Major Kenneth Younger, Director, "E" Division, MI-5! The author supports his contention by quoting citation from Boyle's and Sutherland's works:

Boyle's Version

In 1950, the night before leaving London for Washington, to be being posted to the British Embassy, Burgess gave a party for his friends in his flat. There was Hector McNeil, then Secretary for Scotland; McNeil's successor at the Foreign Office, Kenneth Younger; Putlitz, the former German spy; Professor Anthony Blunt; two young men who had obviously been picked up off the streets either that very evening or not long before; a couple of strange women; two men from MI-5 and one from MI-6; and Sir Harold Nicolson.

Sutherland's Version

Goronwy Rees and David Footman attended the typically mixed and rowdy farewell party at the flat in Lower Bond Street the evening before Burgess departed for Washington; so did Hector McNeil, now in the Cabinet as Secretary of State for Scotland, as well as his successor at the Foreign Office, Kenneth Younger. Apart from Footman, Rees noted among the guests two other senior members of the security service, as well as Anthony Blunt and a distinguished homosexual writer of impeccable origins [Nicolson].

There was a member of the German Embassy, also a homosexual, who before the war had actively plotted against Hitler and now lives in the German Democratic Republic [East Germany]. There were two women there who seemed to be even more out of place than anyone else was.

There were also two very tough looking working-class young men who had very obviously been picked up off the street. The drink flowed fast. One of the young men hit the other over the head with a bottle, and left with the distinguished writer.

9   General Rozoy was Chief of the French Air Mission to England before the Fall of France, in June 1940, but he was repatriated to France late during the summer of 1940. The letters were typed upon the stationary of the French Consulate, London, where a representative of the Vichy Government was still-at-large.

According to Leonard Mosely, in *Backs to the Wall, The Heroic Story of the People of London During World War II*, the alleged Rozy papers were on their way to Vichy in the diplomatic pouch of a South American courier [presumably Brazilian] when they were intercepted by British Intelligence.

10   Cabanier was a classmate of Blaison's, l'Ecole Navale, Brest, Class
     of 1925. Prior to commanding RUBIS, Cabanier served aboard
     SURCOUF, 1937-39, as her Electrical Engineering Officer.

     RUBIS, the submarine commanded by Cabanier under Royal Navy aegis,
     became one of the more celebrated submarines of the war. According to
     Warships in Profile, by Anthony Preston, she laid 630 mines from which:
     14 supply ships of 14,410 grt were sunk, one 1,683 grt supply ship was
     damaged, 7 submarine chasers and minesweepers were sunk, along with
     damaging a U-boat. She also torpedoed and sank a 4,360 grt supply
     ship.

11   French naval plans called for two aircraft carriers, but the French only have
     one, the CHARLES DE GAULLE. The order for the second carrier, based
     on the design of the British Queen Elizabeth class aircraft carrier (under
     construction as of 2009), was delayed several times for budgetary reasons.
     The decision on whether to build the second carrier was setback until 2012.

12   The authors of *Thin Air*, George E, Simpson and Neal R. Berger,
     claim that U.S. Navy had artificially tampered with gravitational and
     magnetic forces to render a USS STURMAN and her crew invisible
     and capable of being teleported, in 1945, from Philadelphia to the area
     of Newport News, Virginia.

13   Charles Quarles Peters, formerly of Vera Cruz, Republic of Panama,
     a town site just off the premises of the United States Howard Air
     Force Base, Republic of Panama, died in September 1982. "Charley",
     while residing on San Blas Point, had served as radio operator for Pan
     American Airways after the war. Eventually he worked for the Dredging
     Division of the Panama Canal Company, from which organization he
     retired. He was the last American buried in the United States Military
     Cemetery, Corozal, Republic of Panama. (Corozal, Howard AFB and
     Vera Cruz, before the Panama Canal Treaties were ratified by the U.S.
     Senate in 1979, were formerly in the American Canal Zone.)

"Charley's" knowledge of Panama, the flora, the fauna, the people, and the politics, was immense. There was hardly any place, person, or historical event he didn't know. Some people are like that, you know. Charley was brought to Panama from Kentucky, at age four, and never returned to the United States.

Charley was hyper-political, but not fanatical. He was scholarly without having had a formal education and scientific without a recognized method. He was considered a little "kooky", very opinionated, a bit loud, good-humored and articulate, but he was very honest and nearly always right in his predictions. In all the years I knew and respected Charley, I never had reason to question his integrity or sources of information.

[14]   "Sea Bee" is an acronym for Construction Battalion—a fighting outfit of the American Navy's Bureau of Yards and Docks, created during World War II to build advance bases, sometimes under fire.

[15]   "Quaca" is the San Blass Indian name for a foreigner in the islands.

[16]   Captaine de Frégaté Alain Le Guoic, French Navy, Retired, in a February 27, 1978 letter to the author provided this interesting tidbit about Roquebert. He wrote:

About Roquebert, all the prewar French submarine officers knew and respected him as being the designer of most of our navy's submarine types built in the thirties. Nicknames are in great favor in the French Navy, as I am sure they are in your navy. So, for Roquebert, we somewhat, and among us only, referred to him as CAMENFORT.

This was a ploy on the two types of cheeses famous in France: Roquefort and Camembert! By reversing the halves of these two names, and by a sleight of imagination, some bright individual derived CAMEMFORT. Of course the reference struck cords of witticism and Roquebert became humorously and respectfully referred to as CAMEMFORT from then on throughout the French Navy.

434

Index

Naval History:

American Navy   xi, xxxiv, 2, 29, 34, 43, 56, 68, 86-7, 90, 93-4, 195-6, 286, 288-90, 411-14, 434-5

Americas and West Indies   168, 178, 361, 435

Annapolis   93, 115-16, 154, 176, 185-6, 192, 239, 275, 287, 300, 378-9, 383, 390-1, 394-5, 404, 435

Bermuda Navy   94, 408, 435

BNLO   68, 75, 108, 216, 286, 435

Brest   xviii, 23, 40, 66, 95, 102, 155, 180, 189, 405, 417-19, 433, 435, 437

British Royal Navy   215, 311, 313, 319, 390, 410, 435

Commander-in-Chief   68, 79, 88, 91, 106, 117, 126, 151, 153, 168, 178, 198, 203, 293, 325, 423-4

Cross of Lorraine   92, 105, 128, 136, 179, 271, 349, 435

Ecole Navale   26, 40, 66, 105, 128, 133, 153, 167, 180, 184, 299, 405, 433, 435

Flag Officer   xix, 30, 58, 60, 68, 76, 168, 181, 240, 335, 351, 356, 435

Flags   30, 92-3, 271, 289-90, 407-8, 435

Free French Navy   xi-xii, 2, 44-5, 75, 91-3, 104-5, 128, 131-2, 137-8, 146-54, 180-3, 240, 248-9, 349-51, 392-4, 407-8

French Navy   2-5, 7, 44-5, 91-3, 95-8, 127-8, 131-3, 146-55, 179-83, 240, 247-9, 349-52, 390-4, 407-10, 414-19, 434-5

Kings Point   218, 378, 396, 435, 445-6

Limpet Mines   x, 219, 221-2, 226, 347, 374, 435, 437

Merchant Marine   x, xxiii, 19, 91, 106, 173, 185, 218, 235-6, 244, 378, 435, 445-6

Northways   xix, 30, 60, 68, 76, 83, 335, 351, 356, 436

Royal Canadian Navy   2, 82-4, 93, 100, 170, 178, 185, 217, 299, 359, 391, 408, 436

Submarines   3-4, 32-5, 43-6, 67-9, 89-90, 106, 109-11, 113-18, 183-5, 238-41, 287, 377-8, 391-4, 409-15, 421, 439-40

U. S. Coast Guard   viii, 64, 237, 239, 241, 243, 245, 248-9, 304, 362, 373, 436

Sea and Ocean Areas:

Bermuda Triangle   ix, xi-xii, xix-xx, xxii, xxiv, xxviii, 2, 16, 18, 63-5, 69, 162, 165, 262-3, 392-3, 399-400

Caribbean Sea   xi, 11, 16, 18-19, 26, 74, 90, 164, 186, 226, 238, 242, 244-7, 286, 290-1, 361-2

Florida Straits   185, 226, 248, 436

Guantanamo Bay   254-6, 260-1, 436

Gulf of Mexico   viii, 224-5, 236, 238, 242, 244-8, 362, 373, 436

Gulf of Panama   260, 436

Gulf of St. Lawrence   99, 436

Long Island Sound   185, 301-2, 436

Panama Canal   ii-iii, x-xi, 61-4, 86-7, 168-9, 184-5, 235, 237-9, 243-4, 246-8, 276, 286-7, 346-8, 366-70, 398-9, 442-6

Events:

American-Japanese War of the Pacific   xxxv, 4, 12, 40, 89, 289, 292, 295, 306, 327, 379, 404, 436

Battle of the Atlantic   63, 94, 99-101, 177, 180, 190, 235, 242, 349, 355, 436

Convoy ONS 154   70, 436

GRASP   xv, xxxi-xxxii, 6, 46, 59, 73, 94-7, 117, 243, 311, 316, 326, 334, 390, 406, 436

HAWAII   40, 193, 276, 293-5, 303, 306, 436

Mers-el-Kébir   xxxii, 436

Operations CATAPULT   46, 73, 243, 436

Pearl Harbor   40-1, 46, 87, 90, 192-3, 196, 221, 223, 242, 275-6, 294-5, 303, 306, 315, 380, 383

Slow Convoy KJ-2   89, 436

Subjects:

Aggressive Mental Suggestion   37, 53, 123, 436

Albatross   xxv, 12, 15-20, 24-9, 75, 115, 165, 168-9, 280, 400-2, 404, 436

Animal Magnetism   52, 436

Battle of the Atlantic   63, 94, 99-101, 177, 180, 190, 235, 242, 349, 355, 436

Beyond Coincidence   114, 436

Christ 31, 38, 161-3, 172, 233, 278, 404, 436

Devil 38, 47, 49-50, 53, 63-4, 120, 212, 270-1, 283, 285, 384, 397, 436

Disasters 15, 33, 36, 38, 59, 115-16, 167, 218, 258, 303, 377-8, 394, 399, 413, 436, 443-4

Dreams xxviii, 15, 17, 47, 108, 161, 437

Enchantress 268, 437

Evil Eye 14, 53, 70, 123, 233, 381, 398, 437

God xxi, xxiv, xxx, 8, 14, 28, 31, 37, 47, 67, 71, 114, 282-5, 296, 404, 437-8

Hope xxix, 35, 52, 61, 158, 180, 268, 308, 367, 405, 437

Hypno-sensorium 47, 437

Imagination xxiv, xxxii, xxxv, 5, 14, 17, 47, 52-3, 82, 367, 434, 437

Limpet Mines x, 219, 221-2, 226, 347, 374, 435, 437

Nightmares 21, 49, 76, 437

Paranormal 18, 116, 437

Parapsychology 121, 255, 380, 437

Precognition 15, 21, 40, 328, 437

Premonition 40, 54-6, 58-9, 98, 108, 112, 164, 437

Psychokinetics 120-1, 381, 437

Relevance 21, 286-7, 437

Space and Time 23, 51, 407, 437

Subliminal Means 121, 437

Places:

Algiers 34-5, 75, 127, 154, 194-5, 424, 437

Balboa xxvi, 286, 437

Bermuda ix-xii, xix-xx, xxiv, 63-5, 68-70, 84-6, 168-71, 178, 188-90, 206, 226-9, 273-4, 391-3, 395, 399-400, 435-7

Boston 56, 174, 182, 227, 303-4, 379, 382, 395, 437

Brest xviii, 23, 40, 66, 95, 102, 155, 180, 189, 405, 417-19, 433, 435, 437

Colon 370, 437

Cristobal ii, 21, 61, 185, 253-4, 261, 273, 276, 286, 366, 437

Devonsport Dockyard xix, 314, 437

England xvii-xix, xxvi, xxx-xxxii, 5, 44-6, 67-9, 79-80, 94-5, 97, 125-8, 168-9, 182-3, 200-1, 213, 395-6, 406-7

Fort Vincennes 378, 437

French Embassy xxvii, 93, 214, 437

Gibraltar 92, 193, 196, 200, 203, 430, 437

Halifax xix, 82-5, 91, 100, 106, 142, 146, 153, 178, 183, 204-5, 216, 224, 273-5, 391, 395-6

Hotel Marriot 366, 437

Ireland Dockyard x, xix, 178, 219, 274, 335, 399, 437

New Hampshire xix, 35, 56, 58,
76, 93, 107, 114, 227, 309,
347, 391, 394-5, 437
New Orleans 19, 211, 215, 237-9,
241, 243, 261, 305, 324, 379,
391, 437
New York City xix, 86, 103,
173-7, 201-2, 215, 219, 228,
330, 340, 396, 437
Panama 61-4, 168-9, 184-5,
237-9, 243-4, 246-8, 276,
286-7, 346-8, 366-70, 374,
391-3, 395-6, 433-4, 436-7,
442-6
Panama Canal Zone xi, xix, xxix,
21, 61, 226, 244, 248, 286,
289, 346, 387, 396, 398-9,
408, 437
Paris xii, xvi, xxviii, 19, 23, 29,
31-2, 39, 156-8, 174-7, 213,
336-7, 340, 385, 394, 447
Plymouth xviii-xix, 69, 95, 117,
137, 178, 314, 437
Rockefeller Center 202, 219,
229, 438
San Blas Point xiv, 367-9, 374,
433, 438
Somerset 178, 219, 391, 438
Spanish Morocco xix, 185, 199, 438
St Pierre and Miquelon Islands 72,
90, 100-1, 104, 243, 374, 438
State xix-xx, xxxiii, 10, 27, 33, 39,
50, 75, 100, 103, 189-91, 199,
215-16, 224-5, 300, 389-90

Tangiers xix, 185, 193, 199-200,
205, 438
Vermont 395, 438
Washington, D. C. 58, 86, 185, 324

People:

Admiral Russell R. Waesche viii,
362, 438
Ancient Mariner x, xxv, 15-19,
25-6, 61, 165, 251, 266, 280,
283, 305, 354, 365-6, 381,
400-2, 408
Antoine de Saint-Exupery 194,
383, 438
Burgess 200, 203-4, 222, 429,
431-2, 438
Captain Jacques Cousteau 391, 395
Charles Quarles Peters xiv, 367,
369, 433, 438
Coleridge xxv, 15-19, 24-6, 28, 61,
233, 365-6, 400-2, 404, 408, 438
Cordell Hull 100, 141, 190, 227, 438
Cuna Indians 366-7, 438
Denis Vaughan 96, 110-12, 316,
345, 389
Fleet Admiral Darlan 105, 180, 438
Franklin D. Roosevelt 41, 294,
315, 438
Francine xi-xii, 29-32, 36-40,
46-7, 49-51, 53-4, 97-8, 120-1,
123-4, 157-8, 160-3, 165-6,
180-2, 322, 336-7, 403
Garbage Squad 221-2, 276,
374, 438-9

General Charles de Gaulle xvii,
100-1, 192, 217, 253, 322,
325, 348, 355, 438
God xxi, xxiv, xxx, 8, 14, 28, 31,
37, 47, 67, 71, 114, 282-5,
296, 404, 437-8
Harold B. Finn 236, 250, 264, 438
Hector C. Bywater xxxv, 40, 289,
292-3, 295-6, 327, 379, 383
Henry Johnson x, xxv, xxxiv, 8, 11,
17-19, 25-6, 61, 184, 250, 253,
267, 279, 283, 304-5, 400-2
J. Edgar Hoover xxix, 199, 214,
374, 438
John Mann xiv, 366, 370-1, 392, 438
Josephine "Jo" Boyer Vairinen
107, 393
King George V 427, 438
King Phillip II 94, 438
Lord Louis Mountbatten 438
MacLean 200, 203, 429, 431
Madeline 385, 438
Marshal Petain xvii, 423, 425
Napoleon xxx, 16, 71, 171, 228,
406, 438
Noor 14, 212-13, 384-6, 438
Oliver Hull 218-19, 370, 438
Philby 200, 203-4, 222, 382, 429,
431, 438
Rear Admiral Zenji Orita 342
Rosemary Sprague 63, 109-10,
316, 345, 389
Theresa Blaison xxviii, 63
USCG 99, 177, 238, 438

Vice Admiral Emile Henri Muselier
326, 357, 359, 363, 383
Vice Admiral Gabriel Paul Auphan
297, 360, 438
Vice Admiral Paul Ange Pierre
Ortoli 393
Vice Admiral Ralph Waldo Christie
391, 438, 448
William Stephenson 103, 212, 214
Winston Churchill xxxi, 94-5,
126, 201, 220, 314, 330, 348,
357, 438

Immoral and Moral Intelligence:

Alien xxii-xxiii, xxxiv, 1, 4, 9,
12-13, 15, 24, 29, 32, 36, 39,
54, 59-60, 120-1, 233
CIA 71, 200, 203, 205, 439
Conspiratory 177, 439
Demons 38, 49, 51, 384, 397, 439
Dirty Tricks 199, 439
Disasters 15, 33, 36, 38, 59,
115-16, 167, 218, 258, 303,
377-8, 394, 399, 413,
436, 443-4
Double Cross (XX) 223, 439
Duplicity 46, 222, 243, 439
FBI 199, 201, 205, 211-12,
214-15, 223-4, 439
Garbage Squad 221-2, 276,
374, 438-9
Intrepid xix, 73-4, 85-6, 103, 182,
200-2, 204, 212-15, 221-4,

226-7, 273-6, 318, 321, 330, 382, 388

Lying 62, 134, 210, 224, 263, 383, 439

MI-5 129, 137-8, 201, 213, 222, 224, 426, 429-32, 439

MI-5 and 6 201

MI-6 201, 222, 224, 425, 432, 439

OSS 71, 194, 196-7, 199-200, 202, 205, 382, 428, 439

Rumors xxxiii-xxxv, 7-8, 68-9, 126, 148, 166, 177-9, 184-5, 193-6, 199, 204-5, 207-8, 210, 228-31, 275, 301-2

SIS 200, 203, 425, 429, 439

SOE 204, 274-5, 429-30, 439

Suspicion 134, 146, 148, 260, 273, 368-9, 415, 439

Tricycle 223, 275, 439

Witches 49, 52, 364, 439

Politics:

British xxviii-xxxi, 74-6, 80-5, 91-6, 101-3, 105-7, 129-33, 140-7, 149-53, 183-7, 199-207, 212-15, 221-6, 310-13, 408-11, 426-33

Diplomacy 42, 73, 439

Free France 65, 72, 128, 142, 144, 166, 204, 289, 297, 439

Gestapo 81, 125, 213, 385-6, 428, 439

Vichy France vi, xvii, 44, 46, 48, 70-1, 94, 100, 103, 105, 157, 161, 357, 359-60, 383, 407

Ships, Submarines, Airships, and Seaplanes

Ships General (Merchant and Naval):

ALYSEE 101

BISMARCK 98-9, 439

HMS FIDELITY 70, 439

HMS GLASCOW 89, 439

HMS MONTGOMERY 183, 439

HMS REVENGE 20, 95-6, 328, 439

MINOSA 101

PC-460 260, 439

PRINZ EUGEN 99, 189, 439

SS NORMANDIE 173-4, 176, 230, 340, 439

SS THOMPSON LYKES xxiv-xxv, xxviii-xxix, 10-12, 42-3, 54, 120, 171-3, 183-4, 250-4, 259-61, 267-8, 304-5, 365-6, 373-5, 400-1, 403-5

SS TITANIC 42, 293, 302, 332, 440

USNT LAFAYETTE 173-4, 440

USS CYCLOPS 230-1, 440

USS MONTEREY 185, 208, 440

USS SARATOGA 88, 440

USS SAVANNAH 186, 206, 208, 228, 440

USS STURMAN 178, 366, 433, 440

United States Submarines:

ARGONAUT 86, 440
MACKERAL 185, 302, 440
MARLIN 185, 440
NAUTILUS 86, 121-3, 280-1, 440
S-26 239, 244, 260, 440
THRESHER xxii-xxiv, xxix, 11,
    54-8, 115, 183, 257-8, 325,
    335, 379, 395, 399, 440

Free French Submarines:

AGOSTA 33-4, 114, 378, 440
LA SIBYLLE 33-7, 109, 114,
    378, 440
MARSQUIN 33-4, 114-15,
    378, 440
NARVAL 197-8, 440
PHENIX 12, 21, 29, 32-40, 47,
    50, 114-15, 172, 333, 378, 440
REQUIN 33, 114, 378, 418, 440
SURCOUF i-xii, xiv-33, 35-47,
    57-91, 93-101, 103-17, 123-9,
    161-219, 221-45, 257-77,
    279-93, 295-314, 319-39,
    341-53, 361-71, 387-42

French Navy Submarine:

Blaison 15-17, 19-27, 29-33,
    36-40, 60, 67, 114-17, 120,
    145-6, 156-9, 161-6, 172-3,
    180-1, 257-8, 297-9, 399-401

Imperial Japanese Navy Submarines:

I-7 88, 411, 440
I-25 87-8, 440
I-26 87-8, 440
I-400 4, 46, 86-7, 287, 307, 342,
    378, 392, 394, 440

Royal Navy Submarines:

HMS THAMES 96, 98, 111-12,
    316, 389, 440
HMS THETIS 21, 33-6, 379,
    399, 440
L-24 12, 20-2, 29, 35-6, 40, 50,
    233, 285, 303, 328, 440

Seaplanes: Imperial Japanese Navy:

GLEN 87, 230, 440
SERIAN 87, 342, 440

By the Same Author

OUT TO SEA ON RAILS

THE GREAT WHITE FLEET

THE JUMBO TRUCK

AMPHIBIANS AGAINST THE FIFTH ELEMENT: MUD

AMPHIBIANS SAVE TIME AND MONEY

NEEDED: THE RETURN OF THE ROUGH RIDERS

PERMIT WIDER TRANSPORTS ON INTERSTATE DEFENSE HIGHWAYS

FIRST CATAMARAN SURVEYBOAT ON THE GREAT LAKES

HELICOPTERS VS AMPHIBIANS

LET'S BE WINDCHILL INTELLIGENT

THE DRAGON

THE METAMORPHOSIS OF THE DRAKE

THE CROWNS OF PANAMA

THE BOQUETE NAVAL ORANGE OF PANAMA

AMPHIBIOUS VEHICLE SUPPORT OF WATER BASED AIRCRAFT

THE CULTIVATED MAN

PEARY AND THE SS ROOSEVELT

THE SURFCOUF CONSPIRACY

THE SURFCOUF CHRONOLOGY

SURFOUF AND THE ROYAL NAVY*

SURFCOUF AND THE ALIEN MIND

THE SURFCOUF DOSSIER OF RUMORS

SURFCOUF AND THE BERMUDA TRIANGLE

SURCOUF AND THE LONDON NAVAL CONFERENCE OF 1930

THE LOSS OF THE FRENCH SUBMARINE SURFCOUF

THE INFLUENCE OF THE U.S. NAVY UPON THE PANAMA CANAL,

THE INFLUENCE OF THE UNITED STATES NAVY UPON THE PANAMA RAILROAD

THE PRESIDENTS OF THE PANAMA RAILROAD COMPANY

THE FINANCIAL HISTORY OF THE PANAMA RAILROAD COMPANY

THE STOCKS AND BOOKS ISSUED BY THE COMPAGNIE INTERCOCEANIQUE DU CANAL DE PANAMA AND THE COMPAGNIE NOUVELLE DU CANAL DE PANAMA

TRIPLE CRASH COVERS OF THE NEW YORK RIO BUENOS AIRES AIR LINE AND THEIR POSTAL MARKINGS

TRIPLE CRASH COVERS OF THE FIRST PAN AMERICAN GOOD WILL FLIGHT

NINE SUBMARINE DISASTERS ANALYZED RELATIVE TO THE SUPERSITITION THREE

THE INFLUENCE OF MAHAN UPON THE PANAMA CANAL

COINCIDENCE OR REINCARNATION

LINDBERGH AUTOGRAPH FORGERIES

NYRBA AIRMAIL COVERS RAREST OF ALL

NUMBERS AND SYMBOLS IN NAVAL HISTORY

IN DEFENSE OF LINDBERGH

THE GREAT LAKES FOR ALL SEASONS

THE COINS AND CURRENCY OF PANAMA

THE BLACK SWAN AND THE RAPE OF AN AIRLINE

THE MEDALS ISSUED BY THE PANAMA CANAL

SAN BLAS INDIAN NUMISMATICA

THE SUBMARINE 0-5 IS DOWN

DEBUNKING FOUL RUMORS ABOU THE FREE FRENCH SUBMARINE SURCOUF

COINCIDENCE OR REINCARNATION

NEEDED: LETHAL BIG GUN SUBMARINES

NUMBERS AND SYMBOLS IN NAVAL HISTORY

HOW TO IMPROVE YOUR GOLF IN THE TROPICS

A BIORHYTMIC ANALYSIS OF TWO SUBMARINE DISASTERS

PEARY'S CONQUEST OF THE NORTH POLE AND THE SS ROOSEVLT

About the Author

Captain Julius Grigore, Jr., USN, Retired, is a graduate of Kings Point, the U.S. Merchant Marine Academy (BS); the University of Detroit (BME and PME); and the Harvard Business School, Advance Management Program (AMP).

He was born in Detroit, Michigan, but resides in Venice, Florida following his service with the Panama Canal Company, and the U.S.

Navy at Fort Amador, Canal Zone as Senior Technical Advisor to the Latin American Navies.

He is a veteran of World War II, the Korean War, and the Vietnam Crisis—which is an enviable, unique record of service for a naval reserve officer.

Captain Grigore received and Outstanding Business Achievement Award from Kings Point in 1961 and was nominated by Rear admiral Gordon S. McClintock, Superintendent, U. S. Merchant Marine Academy, for a Gold Medal Award from the American Society of Naval Architects in 1969 and for the Benjamin Franklin Silver Medal Award, Royal Academy of Arts, London 1980.

However, he is best recognized as an authority on the extraordinary life and controversial death of the Free French submarine SURCOUF and for his numerous books and monographs about the Panama Canal, The Panama Railroad Company, the Air Mail History of the Canal Zone and Panama, and numerous monographs about aerophilately.

His knowledge about SURCOUF is based upon over twenty five years of intense investigations and study of her evolution and death. Few details, no matter how miniscule, come to his attention about SURCOUF that have not been probed. He is relentless in his quest to prove or disprove the enormous dossier of rumors surrounding her wartime operations and death—mainly refuting false and vicious rumors claiming that she was a renegade submarine servicing German U-boats and sinking Allied merchant vessels or that she was deliberately sunk by the American Navy and Royal Navy.

He was accumulated many priceless relics and memorabilia associated with SURCOUF, and his study bulges with hundreds of books about World War II, countless photographs; and thousands of notes he has complied; and hundreds of letters he received, about SURCOUF from world-wide contributors. His holdings about SURCOUF, like a central depository, probably exceed the combined archives of the French Navy or the Royal Navy (under whose aegis SURCOUF served during World War II).

Capitaine de Fregate (later Vice Admiral) Paul Ange "O" Ortoli, Free French Navy, was the first Commanding Officer of SURCOUF when she was commissioned as a Free French Navy submarine on September 15, 1940. Ortoli is at SURCOUF's periscope.

The adjoining photograph is of Vice Admiral Ortoli and the author in May 1978, Paris.

In 1978, Admiral Ortoli casually remarked to the author that SURCOUF with her powerful twin 8-inch guns could have easily knocked out the gates of the Normandie Drydock, St. Nazaire, France, during World War II, rather than the British deploying a flotilla of 21 Royal Navy vessels, consisting of the destroyer HMS CAMPBELTOWN, 70 Wellington bombers, and a force of 611 Commandos. (The bombers proved ineffectual due to cloud cover.)

The obsolete American-built destroyer HMS CAMPBELTOWN (ex-USS BUCHANAN) was used as a ram-ship loaded with explosives. While she and the commandos succeeded in destroying the gates and machinery of the drydock, 162 raiders were killed, 215 were captured, and the CAMPBELTOWN was needlessly expended.

Instead, according to Admiral Ortoli, SURCOUF could have approached the drydock from a safe distance submerged, surface to fire salvos from her big guns, and then depart submerged. (A salvo from SURCOUF's twin guns was capable of sinking a destroyer.)

Credits: Photograph of Ortoli at the periscope is from his personal collection, Paris, 1978. The photo of Ortoli and the author is from the author's collection, 1978.

Captain (later Vice Admiral) Ralph Waldo Christie, USN, Annapolis, Class of 1915, provided valuable input about the conduct of surface and submarine operations between New London, Connecticut and the Panama Canal during the months of January and February 1942.

During my correspondence with Vice Admiral Christie, he discounted, as being ridiculous, rumors that SURCOUF had been involved in sinking Allied merchant ships or that she ever refueled or supplied German U-boats. He also adamantly stated that SURCOUF should have never been allowed to depart Bermuda, for the Southwest Pacific Theater of War, with only one propulsion motor operable unless it was an extreme emergency.

Had SURCOUF survived and been permitted to proceed to the Southwest Pacific Theater of War, she would have served under the operational command of Captain Christie. At that time, he was Commander, Task Force 71, Submarines, Southwest Pacific, operating out of Brisbane, Australia, as a part of General Douglas MacArthur's Navy.

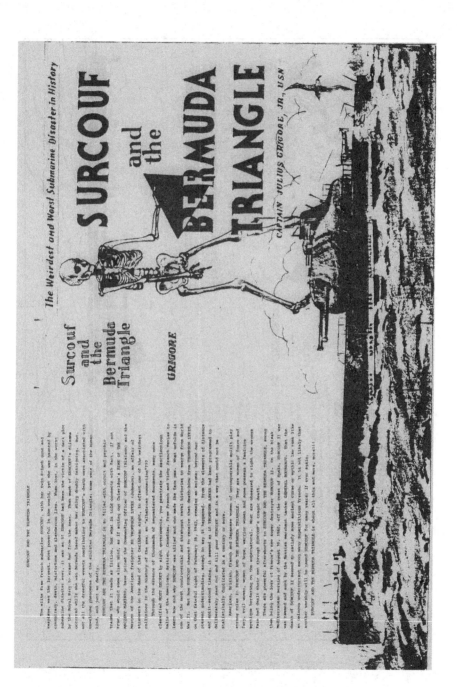

Surcouf and the Royal Navy

Surcouf and the Royal Navy

GRIGORE

The Greatest Submarine Disaster in Naval History

CAPTAIN JULIUS GRIGORE, JR., USNR

DEATH CAME IN THREES FOR *SURCOUF*, pride of France, the world's largest, most powerful submarine — and all three were her own. Not once, however, did she die valiantly in battle. Each time her allies were in on her kill under the ominous shadow of the Royal Navy. Twice the American Navy was involved; twice Darlan, Pope of the French Fleet, could have saved her but did not.

DEATH occurred at the London Naval Conference of 1930 when the French were duped into scrapping the *Surcouf*-class submarine, with her 8-inch guns, a shameful blunder in the history of naval warfare. Warships of her kind, improved and duplicated in great numbers, could have deterred World War II.

DEATH again stalked her decks when French and English fought in bloody violence — their first hand to hand encounter afloat since the Battle of Trafalgar.

DEATH finally came to *Surcouf* from the bow of an American freighter, climaxing a chain of bizarre, almost supernatural events, circumstances and coincidences which seemed determined to destroy her from the outset.

Left behind were the women — pathetic reapers of the chaff of war — obsessed to right the wrongs Fate had dealt their own. Through *Surcouf*'s inglorious death, Time has not erased their scars.

Why did Roosevelt threaten to use the battleship *USS Arkansas* to oust *Surcouf* from the North Atlantic? Why would a Canadian official say, fifteen years after her pathetic loss: "There still may be a distinct reluctance to talk about *Surcouf*"? How did Hitler's lies cause *Surcouf* to flee France? What fascination bound Churchill, Petain, de Gaulle, Mueller and Blaison, *Surcouf*'s last commander, to Joan of Arc? After *Surcouf* had sunk in flames, why would an English admiral write to an American admiral—"I trust this is the last we shall hear of *Surcouf*"?

SURCOUF and the ROYAL NAVY, using reams of unpublished information, answers these perplexing questions and many more!